COLONIZATION AND CHRISTIANITY.

COLONIZATION AND CHRISTIANITY:

A

POPULAR HISTORY

OF THE

TREATMENT OF THE NATIVES

BY THE EUROPEANS

IN ALL THEIR COLONIES.

BY

WILLIAM HOWITT.

Have we not all one father? — hath not one God created us?
Why do we deal treacherously every man against his brother?

Malachi ii. 10.

NEGRO UNIVERSITIES PRESS
NEW YORK

Originally published in 1838
by Longman, Orme, Brown, Greene, & Longmans, London

Reprinted 1969 by
Negro Universities Press
A DIVISION OF GREENWOOD PUBLISHING CORP.
NEW YORK

SBN 8371-1162-5

PRINTED IN UNITED STATES OF AMERICA

THE object of this volume is to lay open to the public the most extensive and extraordinary system of crime which the world ever witnessed. It is a system which has been in full operation for more than three hundred years, and continues yet in unabating activity of evil. The apathy which has hitherto existed in England upon this subject has proceeded in a great measure from want of knowledge. National injustice towards particular tribes, or particular individuals, has excited the most lively feeling, and the most energetic exertions for its redress,—but the whole wide field of unchristian operations in which this country, more than any other, is engaged, has never yet been laid in a clear and comprehensive view before the public mind. It is no part of the present volume to suggest particular plans of remedy. The first business is to make known the nature and the extent of the evil,—that once perceived, in this great country there will not want either heads to plan or hands to accomplish all that is due to the rights of others, or the honour and interest of England.

West End Cottage, Esher,
  June 8th, 1838.

CONTENTS.

COLONIZATION AND CHRISTIANITY.

CHAPTER I.

These are they, O Lord!
Who in thy plain and simple gospel see
All mysteries, but who find no peace enjoined,
No brotherhood, no wrath denounced on them
Who shed their brethren's blood! Blind at noon-day
As owls; lynx-eyed in darkness.—*Southey*.

CHRISTIANITY has now been in the world upwards of
ONE THOUSAND EIGHT HUNDRED YEARS. For
more than a thousand years the European nations
have arrogated to themselves the title of CHRISTIAN!
some of their monarchs, those of MOST SACRED and
MOST CHRISTIAN KINGS! We have long laid to our
souls the flattering unction that we are a civilized
and a Christian people. We talk of all other nations
in all other quarters of the world, as savages, barbarians, uncivilized. We talk of the ravages of the
Huns, the irruptions of the Goths; of the terrible
desolations of Timour, or Zenghis Khan. We talk of
Alaric and Attila, the sweeping carnage of Mahomet,
or the cool cruelties of more modern Tippoos and
Alies. We shudder at the war-cries of naked Indians,
and the ghastly feasts of Cannibals; and bless our

souls that we are redeemed from all these things, and made models of beneficence, and lights of God in the earth !

It is high time that we looked a little more rigidly into our pretences. It is high time that we examined, on the evidence of facts, whether we are quite so refined, quite so civilized, quite so Christian as we have assumed to be. It is high time that we look boldly into the real state of the question, and learn actually, whether the mighty distance between our goodness and the moral depravity of other people really exists. WHETHER, IN FACT, WE ARE CHRISTIAN AT ALL !

Have bloodshed and cruelty then ceased in Europe ? After a thousand years of acquaintance with the most merciful and the most heavenly of religions, do the national characters of the Europeans reflect the beauty and holiness of that religion ? Are we distinguished by our peace, as the followers of the Prince of Peace ? Are we renowned for our eagerness to seek and save, as the followers of the universal Saviour ? Are our annals redolent of the delightful love and fellowship which one would naturally think must, after a thousand years, distinguish those who pride themselves on being the peculiar and adopted children of Him who said, " By this shall all men know that ye are my disciples, if ye have love one to another?" These are very natural, but nevertheless, very awkward questions. If ever there was a quarter of the globe distinguished by its quarrels, its jealousies, its everlasting wars and bloodshed, it is Europe. Since these *soi-disant* Christian nations have risen into any degree of strength, what single evidence of Christian-

ity have they, as nations, exhibited? Eternal warfare!
—is that Christianity? Yet that is the history of
Christian Europe. The most subtle or absurd pretences to seize upon each other's possessions,—the
contempt of all faith in treaties,—the basest policy,—
the most scandalous profligacy of public morals,—the
most abominable international laws!—are they Christianity? And yet they are the history of Europe.
Nations of men selling themselves to do murder, that
ruthless kings might ravish each other's crowns—nations of men, standing with jealous eyes on the perpetual watch against each other, with arms in their hands,
oaths in their mouths, and curses in their hearts;—are
those Christian? Yet there is not a man acquainted
with the history of Europe that will even attempt to
deny that *that* is the history of Europe. For what are
all our international boundaries; our lines of demarcation; our frontier fortresses and sentinels; our mar-
tello towers, and guard-ships; our walled and gated
cities; our bastions and batteries; and our jealous
passports? These are all barefaced and glaring testi-
monies that our pretence of Christianity is a mere
assumption; that after upwards of a thousand years of
the boasted possession of Christianity, Europe has not
yet learned to govern itself by its plainest precepts;
and that her children have no claim to, or reliance in
that spirit of "love which casteth out all fear." It is
very well to vaunt the title of Christian one to another
—every nation knows in its own soul, it is a hollow
pretence. While it boasts of the Christian name,
it dare not for a moment throw itself upon a Christian
faith in its neighbour. No! centuries of the most
unremitted hatred,—blood poured over every plain of

Europe, and sprinkled on its very mountain tops, cry
out too dreadfully, that it is a dismal cheat.   Wars,
the most savage and unprovoked; oppressions, the
most desperate ; tyrannies, the most ruthless; massacres, the most horrible ; death-fires, and tortures the
most exquisite, perpetuated one on another for the
faith, and in the very name of God; dungeons and
inquisitions; the blood of the Vaudois, and the flaming
homes of the Covenanters are all in their memories,
and give the lie to their professions. No ! Poland rent
in sunder; the iron heel of Austria on the prostrate
neck of Italy; and invasions and aggressions without
end, make Christian nations laugh with a hollow
mockery in their hearts, in the very midst of their
solemn professions of the Christian virtue and faith.

But I may be told that this character applies rather
to past Europe than to the present.   What ! are all
these things at an end ?   For what then are all these
standing armies ?   What all these marching armies ?
What these men-of-war on the ocean ?   What these
atrocities going on from year to year in Spain ?   Has
any age or nation seen such battles waged as we have
witnessed in our time ?   How many WATERLOOS
can the annals of the earth reckon ?   What Timour,
or Zenghis Khan, can be compared to the Napoleon
of modern Europe ?   the greatest scourge of nations
that ever arose on this planet; the most tremendous
meteor that ever burnt along its surface !   Have the
multitude of those who deem themselves the philosophical and refined, as well as the Christian of Europe,
ceased to admire this modern Moloch, and to forget
in *his* individual and retributory sufferings at St.
Helena, the countless agonies and the measureless

ruin that he inflicted on innocent and even distant
nations?   While we retain a blind admiration of
martial genius, wilfully shutting our senses and our
minds to the crimes and the pangs that constitute its
shadow, it is laughable to say that we have progressed
beyond our fathers in Christian knowledge.   At this
moment all Europe stands armed to the teeth.   The
peace of every individual nation is preserved, not by
the moral probity and the mutual faith which are the
natural growth of Christian knowledge, but by the
jealous watch of armed bands, and the coarse and
undisguised force of brute strength.   To this moment
not the slightest advance is made towards a regular
system of settling national disputes by the head instead of the hand.   To this moment the stupid practice of settling individual disputes between those who
pride themselves on their superior education and
knowledge, by putting bullets instead of sound reasons
into each other's heads, is as common as ever.   If we
really are a civilized people, why do we not abandon
barbarian practices?   If we really are philosophical,
why do we not shew it?   It is a poor compliment to
our learning, our moral and political philosophy, and
above all, to our religion, that at this time of day if
a dispute arise between us as nations or as men, we
fall to blows, instead of to rational inquiry and adjust-
ment.   Is Christianity then so abstruse?   No! " He
that runneth may read, and the way-faring man,
though a fool, cannot err therein."   Then why, in the
name of common sense, have we not learned it, seeing that it so closely concerns our peace, our security,
and our happiness?   Surely a thousand years is time
enough to teach that which is so plain, and of such

immense importance! We call ourselves civilized, yet we are daily perpetrating the grossest outrages; we boast of our knowledge, yet we do not know how to live one with another half so peaceably as wolves; we term ourselves Christians, yet the plainest injunction of Christ, "to love our neighbour as ourselves," we have yet, one thousand eight hundred and thirty-eight years after his death, to adopt! But most monstrous of all has been the moral blindness or the savage recklessness of ourselves as Englishmen.

> Secure from actual warfare, we have loved
> To swell the war-whoop, passionate for war!
> Alas! for ages ignorant of all
> Its ghastlier workings (famine or blue plague,
> Battle, or siege, or flight through wintry snows,)
> We, this whole people, have been clamorous
> For war and bloodshed; animating sports,
> The which we pay for as a thing to talk of,
> Spectators and not combatants! Abroad
> Stuffed out with big preamble, holy names,
> And adjurations of the God in heaven,
> We send our mandates for the certain death
> Of thousands and ten thousands! Boys and girls,
> And women, *that would groan to see a child*
> *Pull off an insect's leg*, all read of war,
> The best amusement for our morning's meal!
> The poor wretch who has learnt his only prayers
> From curses, who knows scarce words enough
> To ask a blessing from his heavenly Father,
> Becomes a fluent phraseman, absolute,
> Technical in victories, and deceit,
> *And all our dainty terms for fratricide;*
> Terms which we trundle smoothly o'er our tongues
> Like mere abstractions, empty sounds, to which
> We join no feeling, and attach no form!
> As if the soldier died without a wound;
> As if the fibres of this god-like frame
> Were gored without a pang; as if the wretch
> Who fell in battle, doing bloody deeds,

Passed off to heaven, translated and not killed;
As though he had no wife to pine for him,
No God to judge him!   Therefore evil days
Are coming on us, O my countrymen!
And what, if all-avenging Providence,
Strong and retributive, should make us know
The meaning of our words, force us to feel
The desolation and the agony of our fierce doings?

Coleridge.

This is the aspect of the Christian world in its most polished and enlightened quarter:—there surely is some need of serious inquiry; there must surely be some monstrous practical delusion here, that wants honestly encountering, and boldly dispersing.

But if such is the internal condition of Christian Europe, what is the phasis that it presents to the rest of the world? With the exception of our own tribes, now numerously scattered over almost every region of the earth, all are in our estimation barbarians. We pride ourselves on our superior knowledge, our superior refinement, our higher virtues, our nobler character. We talk of the heathen, the savage, and the cruel, and the wily tribes, that fill the rest of the earth; but how is it that these tribes know *us?* Chiefly by the very features that we attribute exclusively to them. They know us chiefly by our crimes and our cruelty. It is we who are, and must appear to them the savages. What, indeed, are civilization and Christianity? The refinement and ennoblement of our nature! The habitual feeling and the habitual practice of an enlightened justice, of delicacy and decorum, of generosity and affection to our fellow men. There is not one of these qualities that we have not violated for ever, and on almost all occasions, towards every single tribe with which we have come in contact. We have professed, indeed, to teach Christianity to them; but we had it not to teach, and we have carried them instead, all the curses and the horrors of a demon race. If the reign of Satan, in fact, were come,—if he were let loose with all his legions, to plague the earth for a thousand years, what would be the characteristics of his prevalence? Terrors and crimes; one wide pestilence of vice and obscenity; one fearful torrent of cruelty and wrath, deceit and oppression, vengeance and malignity; the passions of the strong would be inflamed—the weak would cry and implore in vain!

And is not that the very reign of spurious Christianity which has lasted now for these thousand years, and that during the last three hundred, has spread with discovery round the whole earth, and made the name of Christian synonymous with fiend? It is shocking that the divine and beneficent religion of Christ should thus have been libelled by base pretenders, and made to stink in the nostrils of all people to whom it ought, and would, have come as the opening of heaven; but it is a fact no less awful than true, that the European nations, while professing Christianity, have made it odious to the heathen. They have branded it by their actions as something breathed up, full of curses and cruelties, from the infernal regions. On them lies the guilt, the stupendous guilt of having checked the gospel in its career, and brought it to a full stop in its triumphant progress through the nations. They have done this, *and then wondered at their deed!* They have visited every coast in the shape of rapacious and unprincipled monsters, and then cursed the inhabitants as besotted with superstition, because they did not look on them as angels! People have wondered at the slow progress, and in many countries, the almost hopeless labours of the missionaries;—why should they wonder? The missionaries had Christianity to teach—and their countrymen had been there before them, and called themselves Christians! That was enough: what recommendations could a religion have, to men who had seen its professors for generations in the sole characters of thieves, murderers, and oppressors? The missionaries told them that in Christianity lay their salvation;—they shook their heads, they had already found it their destruction! They told them they were come to comfort and enlighten them;—they had already been comforted by the seizure of their lands, the violation of their ancient rights, the kidnapping of their persons; and they had been enlightened by the midnight flames of their own dwellings! Is there any mystery in the difficulties of the missionaries? Is there any in the apathy of simple nations towards Christianity?

The barbarities and desperate outrages of the so-called Christian race, throughout every region of the world, and upon every people that they have been able to subdue, are not to be paralleled by those of any other race, however fierce, however untaught, and however reckless of mercy and of shame, in any age of the earth. Is it fit that this horrible blending of the names of Christianity and outrage should continue? Yet it does continue, and must continue, till the genuine spirit of Christianity in this kingdom shall arouse itself, and determine that these villanies shall cease, or they who perpetrate them shall be

stripped of the honoured name of—Christian! If
foul deeds are to be done, let them be done in their
own foul name; and let robbery of lands, seizure of
cattle, violence committed on the liberties or the lives
of men, be branded as the deeds of devils and not of
Christians. The spirit of Christianity, in the shape of
missions, and in the teaching and beneficent acts of
the missionaries, is now sensibly, in many countries,
undoing the evil which wolves in the sheep's clothing
of the Christian name had before done. And of late
another glorious symptom of the growth of this divine
spirit has shown itself, in the strong feeling exhibited
in this country towards the natives of our colonies.
To fan that genuine flame of love, is the object of this
work. To comprehend the full extent of atrocities done
in the Christian name, we must look the whole wide
evil sternly in the face. We must not suffer ourselves to aim merely at the redress of this or that
grievance; but, gathering all the scattered rays of
aboriginal oppression into one burning focus, and
thus enabling ourselves to feel its entire force, we
shall be less than Englishmen and Christians if we do
not stamp the whole system of colonial usage towards
the natives, with that general and indignant odium
which must demolish it at once and for ever.

CHAPTER II.

THE DISCOVERY OF THE NEW WORLD.

The spoilers are come upon all high places through the wilderness.
Jeremiah xii. 12.
Forth rush the fiends as with the torrent's sweep,
And deeds are done that make the angels weep.—*Rogers.*

WE have thus in our first chapter glanced at the scene of crime and abomination which Europe through long ages presented, still daring to clothe itself in the fair majesty of the Christian name. It is a melancholy field of speculation—but our business is not there just now; we must hasten from it, to that other field of sorrow and shame at which we also glanced. For fifteen centuries, during which Christianity had been promulgated, Europe had become little aware of its genuine nature, though boastful of its profession; but during the latter portion of that period its nations had progressed rapidly in population, in strength, and in the arts of social life. They had, amid all their bickerings and butcherings, found sufficient leisure to become commercial, speculative, and ambitious of still greater wealth and power. Would to God, in their

improvements, they could have numbered that of
religious knowledge! Their absurd crusades, nevertheless, by which they had attempted to wrest the
Holy City from the infidels to put it into the possession of mere nominal Christians, whose very act of
seizing on the Holy Land proclaimed their ignorance
of the very first principles of the divine religion in
whose cause they assumed to go forth—these crusades,
immediately scandalous and disastrous as they were,
introduced them to the East; gave them knowledge of
more refined and immensely wealthy nations; and at
once raised their notions of domestic luxury and em-
bellishment; gave them means of extended knowledge ; and inspired them with a boundless thirst for
the riches of which they had got glimpses of astonishment. The Venetians and Genoese alternately grew
great by commerce with that East of which Marco
Polo brought home such marvellous accounts; and at
length, Henry of Portugal appeared, one of the noblest
and most remarkable princes in earth's annals! He
devoted all the energies of his mind and the resources
of his fortune to discovery! Fixing his abode by
the ocean, he sent across it not merely the eyes of
desire, but the far-glances of dawning science. Step by
step, year by year, spite of all natural difficulties, disasters and discouragements, he threw back the cloud
that had for ages veiled the vast sea; his ships brought
home news of isle after isle—spots on the wide waste
of waters, fairer and more sunny than the fabled
Hesperides; and crept along the vast line of the African coast to the very Cape of Hope. He died; but
his spirit was shed abroad in an inextinguishable
zeal, guided and made invincible by the Magnet,

" the spirit of the stone," the adoption of which he had suggested.*—At once arose Gama and Columbus, and as it were at once — for there were but five years and a few months between one splendid event and the other,—the East and the West Indies by the sea-path, and America, till then undreamed of, were discovered!

What an era of amazement was that! Worlds of vast extent and wonderful character, starting as it were into sudden creation before the eyes of growing, inquisitive, and ambitious Europe! Day after day, some news, astounding in its very infinitude of goodness, was breaking upon their excited minds; news which overturned old theories of philosophy and geography, and opened prospects for the future equally confounding by their strange magnificence! No single Paradise discovered; but countless Edens, scattered through the glittering seas of summer climes, and populous realms, stretching far and wide beneath new heavens, from pole to pole—

Another nature, and a new mankind.—*Rogers.*

Since the day of Creation, but two events of superior influence on the destinies of the human race had occurred—the Announcement of God's Law on Sinai, and the Advent of his Son! Providence had drawn aside the veil of a mighty part of his world, and submitted the lives and happiness of millions of his creatures to the arbitrium of that European race, which now boasted of superior civilization—and far more, of being the regenerated followers of his Christ. Never was so awful a test of sincerity presented to the professors of a heavenly creed!—never was such

* Mickle's Camoens.

opportunity allowed to mortal men to work in the eternal scheme of Providence! It is past! Such amplitude of the glory of goodness can never again be put at one moment into the reach of the human will. God's providence is working out its undoubted design in this magnificent revelation of

That maiden world, twin-sister to the old;—*Montgomery*.

But they who should have worked with it in the benignity and benevolence of that Saviour whose name they bore, have left to all futurity the awful spectacle of their infamy!

Had the Europeans really at this eventful crisis been instructed in genuine Christianity, and imbued with its spirit, what a signal career of improvement and happiness must have commenced throughout the vast American continent! What a source of pure, guiltless, and enduring wealth must have been opened up to Europe itself! Only let any one imagine the natives of America meeting the Europeans as they did, with the simple faith of children, and the reverence inspired by an idea of something divine in their visitors; let any one imagine them thus meeting them, and finding them, instead of what they actually were, spirits base and desperate as hell could have possibly thrown up from her most malignant regions — finding them men of peace instead of men of blood, men of integrity instead of men of deceit, men of love and generosity instead of men of cruelty and avarice—wise, enlightened, and just! Let any one imagine that, and he has before him such a series of grand and delightful consequences as can only be exhibited when Christianity shall *really* become the actuating spirit of nations; and they shall as the direct consequence, "beat their swords into ploughshares, and their spears into pruning-hooks." Imagine the Spaniards and the Portuguese to have been merely what they pretended to be,—men who had been taught in the divine law of the New Testament, that " God made of one blood all the nations of the earth ;" men who, while they burned to " plant the Cross," actually meant by it to plant in every new land the command, " thou shalt love thy neighbour as thyself;" and the doctrine, that the religion of the Christian is, to " do justice, to love mercy, and to walk humbly before God." Imagine that these men came amongst the simple people of the New World, clothed in all the dignity of Christian wisdom, the purity of Christian sentiment, and the sacred beauty of Christian benevolence; and what a contrast to the crimes and the horrors with which they devastated and depopulated that hapless continent! The historian would not then have had to say—" The bloodshed and attendant miseries which the unparalleled rapine and cruelty of the Spaniards spread over the New World, indeed disgrace human nature. The great and flourishing empires of Mexico and Peru, *steeped in the blood of* FORTY MILLIONS of their sons, present a melancholy prospect, which must excite the indignation of every good heart."* If, instead of that lust of gold which had hardened them into actual demons, they had worn the benign graces of true Christians, the natives would have found in them a higher image of divinity than any which they had before conceived, and the whole immense continent would have been laid open to them as a field of unexampled and limitless glory and

* Mickle.

felicity. They might have introduced their arts and sciences—have taught the wonders and the charms of household enjoyments and refinements—have shewn the beauty and benefit of cultivated fields and gardens; their faith would have created them confidence in the hearts of the natives, and the advantages resulting from their friendly tuition would have won their love. What a triumphant progress for civilization and Christianity! There was no wealth nor advantage of that great continent which might not have become legitimately and worthily theirs. They would have walked amongst the swarming millions of the south as the greatest of benefactors; and under their enlightened guidance, every species of useful produce, and every article of commercial wealth would have sprung up. Spain need not have been blasted, as it were, by the retributive hand of Divine punishment, into the melancholy object which she is this day. That sudden stream of gold which made her a second Tantalus, reaching to her very lips yet never quenching her thirst, and leaving her at length the poorest and most distracted realm in Europe, might have been hers from a thousand unpolluted sources, and bearing along with it God's blessing instead of his curse: and mighty nations, rivalling Europe in social arts and political power, might have been now, instead of many centuries hence, objects of our admiration, and grateful repayers of our benefits.

But I seem to hear many voices exclaiming, "Yes! these things *might* have been, had men been what they are not, nor ever were!" Precisely so !—that is the point I wish expressly to illustrate before I proceed to my narrative. These things might have been, and would have been, had men been merely what they professed. They called themselves Christians, and I merely state what Christians would and must, as a matter of course, have done. The Spaniards professed to be, and probably really believed that they were, Christians. They professed zealously that one of their most ardent desires was to bring the newly-discovered hemisphere under the cross of Christ. Columbus returned thanks to God for having made him a sort of modern apostle to the vast tribes of the West. Ferdinand and Isabella, when he returned and related to them the wonderful story of his discovery, fell on their knees before their throne, and thanked God too! They expressed an earnest anxiety to establish the empire of the Cross throughout their new and splendid dominions. The very Spanish adventurers, with their hands heavy with the plundered gold, and clotted with the blood of the unhappy Americans, were zealous for the spread of their faith. They were not more barbarous than they were self-deluded; and I shall presently shew whence had sprung, and how had grown to such a blinding thickness, that delusion upon them. But the truth which I am now attempting to elucidate and establish, is of far higher and wider concernment than as exemplified in the early adventurers of Spain and Portugal. This grand delusion has rested on Europe for a thousand years; and from the days of the Spaniards to the present moment, has gone on propagating crimes and miseries without end. For the last three hundred years, Europe has been boasting of its Christianity, and perpetrating throughout the vast extent of territories in every quarter of the globe subjected to

its power, every violence and abomination at which
Christianity revolts.   There is no nation of Europe
that is free from the guilt of colonial blood and oppression.   God knows what an awful share rests upon
this country !   It remains therefore for us simply to
consider whether we will abandon our national crimes
or our Christian name.   Whether Europe shall continue so to act towards what it pleases to term
"savage" nations, as that it must seem to be the very
ground and stronghold of some infernal superstition,
or so as to promote, what a large portion of the
British public at least, now sincerely desires,—the
Christianization, and with it the civilization, of the
heathen.

I shall now pass in rapid review, the treatment
which the natives of the greater portion of the regions
discovered since the days of Columbus and Gama,
have received at the hands of the nations styling
themselves Christian, that every one may see what
has been, and still is, the actual system of these nations ; and I shall first follow Columbus and his
immediate successors to the Western world, because
it was first, though only by so brief a period, reached
by the ships of the adventurers.

CHAPTER III.

THE PAPAL GIFT OF ALL THE HEATHEN WORLD TO THE PORTUGUESE AND SPANIARDS.

Woe is me, my mother, that thou hast born me a man of strife, and a man of contention to the whole earth.—*Jeremiah* xv. 10.

Also in their skirts is found the blood of the souls of the poor innocents. *Jeremiah* v. 16.

COLUMBUS, while seeking for a western track to the East Indies, on Friday, Oct. 12th, 1492, stumbled on a New World! The discoveries by Prince Henry of Portugal, of Madeira, and of a considerable extent of the African coast, had impressed him with a high idea of the importance of what yet was to be discovered, and of the possibility of reaching India by sea. This had led him to obtain a Bull from Pope Eugene IV. granting to the crown of Portugal all the countries which the Portuguese should discover from Cape Non to India. Columbus, having now discovered America, although unknown to himself, supposing it still to be some part of India, his monarchs, Ferdinand and Isabella, lost no time in applying for a similar grant. Alexander VI., a Spaniard, was equally generous with his predecessor, and accord-

ingly divided the world between the Spaniards and
Portuguese! "The Pope," says Robertson, "as the
vicar and representative of Jesus Christ, was supposed to have a right of dominion over all the kingdoms of the earth.   Alexander VI., a pontiff infamous
for every crime which disgraces humanity, filled the
papal throne at that time.   As he was born Ferdinand's subject, and very solicitous to procure the
protection of Spain, in order to facilitate the execution
of his ambitious schemes in favour of his own family,
he was extremely willing to gratify the Spanish
monarchs.   By an act of liberality, which cost him
nothing, and that served to establish the jurisdiction
and fortunes of the papal see, he granted in full right
to Ferdinand and Isabella, all the countries inhabited
by infidels which they had discovered, or should discover; and in virtue of that power which he derived
from Jesus Christ, he conferred on the crown of
Castile vast regions, to the possession of which he
himself was so far from having any title, that he was
unacquainted with their situation, and ignorant even
of their existence.   As it was necessary to prevent
this grant from interfering with that formerly made
to the crown of Portugal, he appointed that a line,
supposed to be drawn from pole to pole, a hundred
leagues to the westward of the Azores, should serve
as a limit between them; and, in the plenitude of his
power, bestowed all to the east of this imaginary line
upon the Portuguese, and all to the west of it, upon
the Spaniards.   Zeal for propagating the Christian
faith, was the consideration employed by Ferdinand
in soliciting this Bull, and is mentioned by Alexander
as his chief motive for issuing it."

It is necessary, for the right understanding of this history, to pause upon this remarkable fact, and to give it the consideration which it demands. In this one passage lies the key to all the atrocities, which from that hour to the present have been perpetrated on the natives of every country making no profession of Christianity, which those *making* such a profession have been able to subdue. An Italian priest,—as the unfortunate Inca, Atahualpa, afterwards observed with indignant surprise, when told that the pope had given his empire to the Spaniards,—here boldly presumes to give away God's earth as if he sate as God's acknowledged vicegerent. Splitting this mighty planet into two imaginary halves, he hands one to the Spanish and the other to the Portuguese monarch, as he would hand the two halves of an orange to a couple of boys. The presumption of the act is so outrageous, that at this time of day, and forgetting for a moment all the consequences which flowed from this deed, one is ready to burst into a hearty fit of laughter, as at a solemn farce, irresistibly ludicrous from its grave extravagance. But it was a farce which cost, and still costs the miserable natives of unproselyted countries dear. It was considered no farce—there was seen no burlesque in it at the time of its enactment. Not only the kings of Spain and Portugal, but the kings and people of all Europe bowed to this preposterous decision, and never dreamed for a moment of calling in question its validity.

Edward IV. of England, on receiving a remonstrance from John II. of Portugal on account of some English merchants attempting to trade within the limits assigned to the Portuguese by the pope's bull, so far from calling in question the right thus derived by the Portuguese from the pope, instantly ordered the merchants to withdraw from the interdicted scene.

Here then, we have the root and ground of that grand delusion which led the first discoverers of new lands, to imagine themselves entitled to seize on them as their own, and to violate every sacred right of humanity without the slightest perception of wrong, and even in many instances, in the fond belief that they were extending the kingdom of Christ. We have here the man of sin, the anti-Christ, so clearly foretold by St. Paul, — "the son of perdition, who opposeth and exalteth himself above all that is called God or that is worshipped; so that he as God, sitteth in the temple of God, shewing himself that he is God. . . . Even him, whose coming is after the working of Satan with all power, and signs and lying wonders; and *with all deceivableness of unrighteousness* in them that perish; because they received not the love of the truth that they might be saved. And for this cause *God shall send them a strong delusion, that they should believe a lie.*"—*Second Epistle to the Thessalonians*, ii. 3, 4, 9, 10, 11.

Strange and abounding in most singular transactions as is the history of the Papal church, there is not to be found in it one fact in which the son of perdition, the proud anti-Christ, is more characteristically shown than in this singular transaction. We have him here enacting the God indeed! and giving away a world in a breath. Vast and mighty nations, isles scattered through unknown oceans, continents stretching through all climates, and millions on millions of human beings, who never heard of his country or his religion, much less of his name, are disposed of with all their fortunes; given up as so many cattle to the sword or the yoke of the oppressor—the very ground given from beneath their feet, and no place left them on God's earth—no portion in his heritage, in time or in eternity, unless they acknowledged the mysterious dogmas and more mysterious power of this hoary and shaven priest! Never was "the son of perdition" more glaringly revealed; for perdition is the only word that can indicate that fulness of misery, devastation, and destruction, which went forth with this act, upon millions of innocent and unconscious souls. Never was "the deceivableness of unrighteousness" so signally exemplified; for here was all Europe,—monarchs, ministers,—whatever it possessed of wise, or learned, powerful, or compassionate, all blinded with such "a strong delusion," that they could implicitly "believe a lie" of so monstrous and flagrant a kind.

It is difficult for us now to conceive how so gross a delusion could have wrapped in darkness all the intellect of the most active and aspiring portion of the globe; but it is necessary that we should fix this peculiar psychological phenomenon firmly and clearly in our minds, for on it depends the explication of all that was done against humanity during the reign of Papacy, and much that still continues to be done to this very day by ourselves, even while we are believing ourselves enfranchised from this "strong delusion," and too much enlightened to "believe a lie."

We must bear in mind then, that this strange phenomenon was the effect of nearly a thousand years' labour of the son of perdition. For ages upon ages, every craft, priestly and political; every form of regal authority, of arms, and of superstition; every delusion of the senses, and every species of play upon the affections, hopes and fears of men, had been resorted to, and exerted, to rivet this "strong delusion" upon the human soul, and to make it capable of "believing a lie."

In the two preceding chapters, I have denied the possession of Christianity to multitudes and nations who had assumed the name, with a sternness and abruptness, which no doubt have startled many who have now read them; but I call earnestly upon every reader, to attend to what I am now endeavouring deeply to impress upon him ; for, I must repeat, that there is more of what concerns the progress of Christian truth, and consequently, the happiness of the human race, dependent on the thorough conception of the fact which I am going to state, than probably any of us have been sufficiently sensible of, and which we cannot once become really sensible of, without joining heart and hand in the endeavour to free our own great country, and Christendom in general, from the commission of cruelties and outrages that mock our profession of Christ's religion, and brand the national name with disgrace.

There is no fact then, more clearly developed and established past all controversy, in the history of the Papal church, than that from its very commencement it set aside Christianity, and substituted in the words of the apostle, "a strong delusion" and "the belief of a lie." The Bible—that treasury and depository of God's truth—that fountain of all pure and holy and kindly sentiments—that charter of all human rights—

that guardian of hope and herald of salvation, was withdrawn from the public eye. It was denounced as the most dangerous of two-edged instruments, and feared as the worst enemy of the Papal system. Christianity was no longer taught, the Bible being once disposed of; but an artful and deadly piece of machinery was put in action, which bore its name. Instead of the pure and holy maxims of the New Testament—its sublime truths, full of temporal and eternal freedom, its glorious knowledge, its animating tidings, its triumphant faith—submission to popes, cardinals, friars, monks and priests, was taught — a Confessional and a Purgatory took their place. Christianity was no longer existent; but the very religion of Satan—the most cunning invention, by which working on human cupidity and ambition, he was enabled to achieve a temporary triumph over the Gospel. Never was there a more subtle discovery than that of the Confessional and the Purgatory. Once having established a belief in confession and absolution, and who would not be religious at a cheap rate?—in the Confessional — the especial closet of Satan, every crime and pollution might be practised, and the guilty soul made to believe that its sin was that moment again obliterated. Even if death surprised the sinner, there was power of redemption from that convenient purgatory. Paid prayers were substituted for genuine repentance—money became the medium of salvation, and Beelzebub and Mammon sate and laughed together at the credulity of mankind!

Thus, as I have stated, Christianity was no longer taught; but a totally different system, usurping its name. Instead of simple apostles, it produced showy popes and cardinals; instead of humble preachers, proud temporal princes, and dignitaries as proud; instead of the Bible, the mass-book and the legends of saints; instead of one God and one Saviour Jesus Christ, the eyes of its votaries were turned for help on virgins, saints, and anchorites—instead of the inward life and purity of the gospel-faith, outward ceremonies, genuflexions, and pageantry without end. Every man, however desperate his nature or his deeds, knew that for a certain amount of coin, he could have his soul white-washed; and, instead of a healthy and availing piety, that spurious and diabolical devotion was generated, which is found at the present day amongst the bandits of Italy and Spain—who one moment plunge their stiletto or bury their bullet in the heart of the unsuspecting traveller, and the next kneel at the shrine of the Virgin, perform some slight penance, offer some slight gift to the church, and are perfectly satisfied that they are in the way of salvation. It is that spurious devotion, indeed, which marks every superstition—Hindoo, Mahometan, or Fetish—wherever, indeed, mere outward penance, or the offering of money, is substituted for genuine repentance and a new life.

Let any one, therefore, imagine the effect of this state of things on Europe through seven or eight centuries. The light of the genuine gospel withdrawn—all the purity of the moral law of Christ—all the clear and convincing annunciations of the rights of man—all the feelings of love and sympathy that glow alone in the gospel;—and instead of these an empty show; legends and masses, miracle-plays and holiday pageants; such doctrines of right and wrong, such maxims of worldly policy preached as suited ambitious dignitaries or luxurious friars—and it will account for that singular state of belief and of conscience which existed at the time of the discovery of the new countries of the East and West. It would have been impossible that such ignorance, or such shocking perversion of reason and faith, could have grown up and established themselves as the characteristics of the public mind, had every man had the Bible in his hand to refer to, and imbue himself daily with its luminous sense of justice, and its spirit of humanity.

We shall presently see what effects it had produced on even the best men of the 15th and 16th centuries; but what perhaps is not quite so much suspected, we shall have to learn in the course of this volume to what an extent the influence of this system still continues on the *Protestant* mind. So thoroughly had it debauched the public morality, that it is to this source that we alone can come to explain the laxity of opinion and the apathy of feeling that have ever since characterized Europe in its dealings with the natives of all new countries. To this day, we no more regard the clearest principles of the gospel in our transactions with them, than if such principles did not exist. The Right of Conquest, and such robber-phrases, have been, and even still continue to be, "as smoothly trundled from our tongues," as if we could find them enjoined on our especial approbation in the Bible. But genuine Christianity is at length powerfully awaking in the public mind of England; and I trust that even the perusal of this volume will strengthen our resolution to wash the still clinging stains of popery out of our garments, and to determine to stand by the morality of the Bible, and by that alone.

In closing this chapter, let me say that I should be very sorry to hurt the feelings of any modern Catholic. The foregoing strictures have no reference to them. However much or little of the ancient faith of the Papal church any of them may retain, I believe that, as a body, they are as sincere in their devotion as any other class of Christians; but the ancient system, character, and practice of the Church of Rome, are matters of all history, and too closely connected with the objects of this work, and with the interests of millions, to be passed without, what the author believes to be, a faithful exposition.

CHAPTER IV.

THE SPANIARDS IN HISPANIOLA.

The gathering signs of a long night of woe.—*Rogers.*

THE terms of the treaty between the Spanish monarchs and Columbus, on his being engaged as a discoverer, signed by the parties on the 17th of April, 1492, are sufficiently indicative of the firm possession which the doctrines of popery had upon their minds. The sovereigns constituted Columbus high-admiral of all the seas, islands, and continents which should be discovered by him, as a perpetual inheritance for him and his heirs. He was to be *their viceroy* in those countries, with a tenth of the free profits upon all the productions and the commerce of those realms. This was pretty well for monarchs professing to be Christians, and who ought to have been taught—" thou shalt not covet thy neighbour's house; thou shalt not covet thy neighbour's wife, nor his man-servant, nor his maid-servant, nor his ox, nor his ass, nor any thing that is thy neighbour's." But they had been brought up in another faith : the Pope had exclaimed—

Creation's heir! the world, the world is mine!

and they took him literally and really at his word. And it will soon be seen that Columbus, though naturally of an honorable nature, was not the less the dupe of this fearful system. He proceeded on his voyage, discovered a portion of the West Indies, and speedily plunged into atrocities against the natives that would have been pronounced shocking in Timour or Attila. James Montgomery, in his beautiful poem, the West Indies, has strongly contrasted the character of Columbus and that of his successors.

The winds were prosperous, and the billows bore
The brave adventurer to the promised shore ;
Far in the west, arrayed in purple light,
Dawned the New World on his enraptured sight.
Not Adam, loosened from the encumbering earth,
Waked by the breath of God to instant birth,
With sweeter, wilder wonder gazed around,
When life within, and light without he found ;
When all creation rushing o'er his soul,
He seemed to live and breathe throughout the whole.
So felt Columbus, when divinely fair
At the last look of resolute despair,
The Hesperian isles, from distance dimly blue,
With gradual beauty opened on his view.

In that proud moment, his transported mind
The morning and the evening worlds combined;
And made the sea, that sundered them before,
A bond of peace, uniting shore to shore.

Vain, visionary hope! rapacious Spain
Followed her hero's triumph o'er the main;
Her hardy sons in fields of battle tried,
Where Moor and Christian desperately died;—
A rabid race, fanatically bold,
And steeled to cruelty by lust of gold,
Traversed the waves, the unknown world explored;
The cross their standard, but their faith the sword;
Their steps were graves; o'er prostrate realms they trod;
They worshipped Mammon, while they vowed to God.

To estimate the effect of his theological education
on such a man as Columbus, we have only to pause a
moment, to witness the manner of his first landing in
the new world, and his reception there. On discovering the island of Guanahani, one of the Bahamas, the
Spaniards raised the hymn of *Te Deum.* At sunrise
they rowed towards land with colours flying, and the
sound of martial music; and amid the crowds of wondering natives assembled on the shores and hills
around, Columbus, like another Mahomet, set foot on
the beach, *sword in hand,* and *followed by a crucifix,*
which his followers planted in the earth, and then
prostrating themselves before it, *took possession of the
country* in the name of his sovereign. The inhabitants gazed in silent wonder on ceremonies so pregnant
with calamity to them, but without any suspicion of
their real nature. Living in a delightful climate, hidden through all the ages of their world from the other
world of labour and commerce, of art and artifice, of
avarice and cruelty, they appeared in the primitive

and unclad simplicity of nature. The Spaniards, says Peter Martyr,—"Dryades formossissimas, aut nativas fontium nymphas de quibus fabulatur antiquitas, se vidisse arbitrati sunt :"— they seemed to behold the most beautiful dryads, or native nymphs of the fountains, of whom antiquity fabled. Their forms were light and graceful, though dusky with the warm hues of the sun ; their hair hung in long raven tresses on their shoulders, unlike the frizzly wool of the Africans, or was tastefully braided. Some were painted, and armed with a light bow, or a fishing spear ; but their countenances were full of gentleness and kindness. Columbus himself, in one of his letters to Ferdinand and Isabella, describes the Americans and their country thus :—" This country excels all others, as far as the day surpasses the night in splendour : the natives love their neighbour as themselves; their conversation is the sweetest imaginable; their faces always smiling, and so gentle, so affectionate are they, that I swear to your highnesses there is not a better people in the world." The Spaniards indeed looked with as much amazement on the simple people, and the paradise in which they lived, as the natives did on the wonderful spectacle of European forms, faces, dress, arts, arms, and ships.— Such sweet and flowing streams; such sunny dales, scattered with flowers as gorgeous and beautiful as they were novel ; trees covered with a profusion of glorious and aromatic blossoms, and beneath their shade the huts of the natives, of simple reeds or palm-leaves ; the stately palms themselves, rearing their lofty heads on the hill sides ; the canoes skimming over the blue waters, and birds of most resplendent plumage flying from tree to tree. They walked

Through citron-groves and fields of yellow maize,
Through plantain-walks where not a sunbeam plays.
Here blue savannas fade into the sky ;
There forests frown in midnight majesty ;
Ceiba, and Indian fig, and plane sublime,
Nature's first-born, and reverenced by time!
There sits the bird that speaks ! there quivering rise
Wings that reflect the glow of evening skies!
Half bird, half fly, the fairy king of flowers,
Reigns there, and revels through the fragrant bowers ;
Gem full of life, and joy, and song divine,
Soon in the virgin's graceful ear to shine.
The poet sung, if ancient Fame speaks truth,
" Come ! follow, follow to the Fount of Youth !
I quaff the ambrosial mists that round it rise,
Dissolved and lost in dreams of Paradise !"
And there called forth, to bless a happier hour,
It met the sun in many a rainbow-shower !
Murmuring delight, its living waters rolled
'Mid branching palms, and amaranths of gold!

Rogers.

It were an absurdity to say that they were *Christians* who broke in upon this Elysian scene like malignant spirits, and made that vast continent one wide theatre of such havoc, insult, murder, and misery as never were before witnessed on earth. But it was not exactly in this island that this disgraceful career commenced. Lured by the rumour of gold, which he received from the natives, Columbus sailed southward first to Cuba, and thence to Hispaniola. Here he was visited by the cazique, Guacanahari, who was doomed first to experience the villany of the Spaniards. This excellent and kind man sent by the messengers which Columbus had despatched to wait on him, a curious mask of beaten gold, and when the vessel of Columbus was immediately afterwards wrecked in standing in to the coast, he appeared with all his people on the strand,—for the purpose of plundering and destroying them, as we might expect from *savages,* and as the Cazique would have been served had he been wrecked himself on the Spanish, or on our own coast at that time? No! but better Christian than most of those who bore that name, he came eagerly to do the very deed enjoined by Christ and his followers,—to succour and to save. " The prince," says Herrera, their own historian, " appeared all zeal and activity at the head of his people. He placed armed guards to keep off the press of the natives, and to keep clear a space for the depositing of the goods as they came to land: he sent out as many as were needful in their canoes to put themselves under the guidance of the Spaniards, and to assist them all in their power in the saving of their goods from the wreck. As they brought them to land, he and his nobles received them, and set sentinels over them, not suffering the people even to gratify that curiosity which at such a crisis must have been very great, to examine and inspect the curious articles of a new people; and his subjects participating in all his feelings, wept tears of sincere distress for the sufferers, and condoled with them in their misfortune. But as if this was not enough, the next morning, when Columbus had removed to one of his other vessels, the good Guacanahari appeared on board to comfort him, and to offer all that he had to repair his loss!"

This beautiful circumstance is moreover still more particularly related by Columbus himself, in his letter to his sovereigns; and it was on this occasion that he gave that character of the country and the people to which I have just referred. Truly had he a great

right to say that "they loved their neighbour as themselves." Let us see how the Spaniards and Columbus
himself followed up this sublime lesson.

Columbus being now left on the coast of the new
world with but one crazy vessel,— for Pinzon the commander of the other, had with true Spanish treachery,
set off on his way homewards to forestall the glory of
being the first bearer of the tidings of this great discovery to Europe,—he resolved to leave the number
of men which were now inconvenient in one small
crowded vessel, on the island. To this Guacanahari
consented with his usual good nature and good faith.
Columbus erected a sort of fort for them; gave them
good advice for their conduct during his absence, and
sailed for Spain. In less than eleven months he
again appeared before this new settlement, and found
it levelled with the earth, and every man destroyed.
Scarcely had he left the island when these men had
broken out in all those acts of insult, rapacity, and
oppression on the natives which only too soon became
the uniform conduct of the *Christians!* They laid
violent hands on the women, the gold, the food of the
very people who had even kindly received them;
traversed the island in the commission of every species
of rapacity and villany, till the astonished and outraged inhabitants now finding them fiends incarnate
instead of the superior beings which they had deemed
them, rose in wrath, and exterminated them.

Columbus formed a fresh settlement for his new-
comers, and having defended it with mounds and
ramparts of earth, went on a short voyage of discovery
among the West Indian isles, and came back to find
that the same scene of lust and rapine had been acted

over again by his colony, and that the natives were all in arms for their destruction. It is curious to read the relation of the conduct of Columbus on this discovery, as given by Robertson, a *Christian* and *Protestant* historian. He tells us, on the authority of Herrera, and of the son of Columbus himself, that the Spaniards had outraged every human and sacred feeling of these their kind and hospitable entertainers. That in the voracity of their appetites, enormous as compared with the simple temperance of the natives, they had devoured up the maize and cassado-root, the chief sustenance of these poor people; that their rapacity threatened a famine; that the natives saw them building forts and locating themselves as permanent settlers where they had apparently come merely as guests; and that from their lawless violence as well as their voracity, they must soon suffer destruction in one shape or another from their oppressors. Self preservation prompted them to take arms for the expulsion of such formidable foes. "*It was now,*" adds Robertson, "*necessary to have recourse to arms;* the employing of which against the Indians, Columbus had hitherto avoided with the greatest solicitude." Why necessary? Necessary for what? is the inquiry which must spring indignantly in every rightly-constituted mind. Because the Spaniards had been received with unexampled kindness, and returned it with the blackest ingratitude; because they had by their debauched and horrible outrages roused the people into defiance, those innocent and abused people must be massacred? That is a logic which might do for men who had been educated in the law of anti-Christ instead of Christ, and who went out with the Pope's bull as a title to seize on the property of other people, wherever the abused and degraded cross had not been erected; but it could never have been so coolly echoed by a *Protestant* historian, if it had not been for the spurious morality with which the Papal hierarchy had corrupted the world, till it became as established as gospel truth. Hear Robertson's relation of the manner in which Columbus repaid the *Christian* reception of these poor islanders.

"The body which took the field consisted only of two hundred foot, twenty horse, and twenty large dogs; and how strange soever it may seem to mention the last as composing part of a military force, they were not perhaps the least formidable and destructive on the whole, when employed against naked and timid Indians. All the caziques in the island, Guacanahari excepted, who retained an inviolable attachment to the Spaniards, were in arms, with forces amounting—if we may believe the Spanish historians —to a hundred thousand men. Instead of attempting to draw the Spaniards into the fastnesses of the woods and mountains, they were so improvident as to take their station in the Vega Real, the most open plain in the country. Columbus did not allow them to perceive their error, or to alter their position. He attacked them during the night, when undisciplined troops are least capable of acting with union and concert, and obtained *an easy and bloodless victory*. The consternation with which the Indians were filled by the noise and havoc made by the fire-arms, by the impetuous force of the cavalry, and the fierce onset of the dogs, was so great, that they threw down their weapons, and fled without attempting resistance. *Many were slain ; more were taken prisoners and reduced* to servitude; and so thoroughly were the rest intimidated, that, from that moment, they abandoned themselves to despair, relinquishing all thoughts of contending with aggressors whom they deemed invincible.

" *Columbus employed several months* in marching through the island, *and in subjecting it to the Spanish government, without meeting with any opposition.* He imposed a tribute upon all the inhabitants above the age of fourteen. Every person who lived in those districts where gold was found, was obliged to pay quarterly as much gold-dust as filled a hawk's bell; from those in other parts of the country, twenty-five pounds of cotton were demanded. This was the first regular taxation of the Indians, and served as a precedent for exactions still more intolerable."

This is a most extraordinary example of the Christian mode of repaying benefits! These were the very people thus treated, that a little time before had received with tears, and every act of the most admirable charity, Columbus and his people from the wreck. And a Protestant historian says that this was necessary! Again we ask, necessary for what? To shew that Christianity was hitherto but a name, and an excuse for the violation of every human right! There was no necessity for Columbus to repay good with evil; no necessity for him to add the crime of Jezebel, " to kill and take possession." If he really wanted to erect the cross in the new world, and to draw every legitimate benefit for his own country from it, he had seen that all that might be effected by legitimate means. Kindness and faith were only wanted to lay open the whole of the new world, and bring all its treasures to the feet of his countrymen. The gold

and gems might be purchased even with the toys of
European children; and commerce and civilization, if
permitted to go on hand in hand, presented prospects
of wealth and glory, such as never yet had been revealed to the world.   But Columbus, though he
believed himself to have been inspired by the Holy
Ghost to discover America,—thus commencing his
will, " In the name of the most Holy Trinity, who
inspired me with the idea, and who afterwards made
it clear to me, that by traversing the ocean west-
wardly, etc. ;" though Herrera calls him a man " ever
trusting in God ;" and though his son, in his history of
his life, thus speaks of him :—" I believe that he was
chosen for this great service ; and that because *he was
to be so truly an apostle*, as in effect he proved to be,
therefore was his origin obscure ; that therein he might
the more resemble those who were called to make
known the name of the Lord from seas and rivers,
and from courts and palaces.   And I believe also,
that *in most of his doings he was guarded by some*
special providence ; his very name was not without
some mystery ; for in it is expressed the wonder he
performed, inasmuch as *he conveyed to the new world*
the grace of the Holy Ghost."   Notwithstanding these
opinions—Columbus had been educated in the spurious Christianity, which had blinded his naturally
honest mind to every truly Christian sentiment.   It
must be allowed that he was an apostle of another
kind to those whom Christ sent out ; and that this
was a novel way of conveying the Holy Ghost to the
new world.   But he had got the Pope's bull in his
pocket, and that not only gave him a right to half the
world, but made all means for its subjection, however

diabolical, sacred in his eyes. We see him in this transaction, notwithstanding the superiority of his character to that of his followers, establishing himself as the apostle and founder of that system of destruction and enslavement of the Americans, which the Spaniards followed up to so horrible an extent. We see him here as the first to attack them, in their own rightful possessions, with arms—the first to pursue them with those ferocious dogs, which became so infamously celebrated in the Spanish outrages on the Americans, that some of them, as the dog Berezillo, received the full pay of soldiers; the first to exact gold from the natives; and to reduce them to slavery. Thus, from the first moment of modern discovery, and by the first discoverer himself, commenced that apostleship of misery which has been so zealously exercised towards the natives of all newly discovered countries up to this hour!

The immediate consequences of these acts of Columbus were these: the natives were driven to despair by the labours and exactions imposed upon them. They had never till then known what labour, or the curse of avarice was; and they formed a scheme to drive out their oppressors by famine. They destroyed the crops in the fields, and fled into the mountains. But there, without food themselves, they soon perished, and that so rapidly and miserably, that in a few months one-third of the inhabitants of the whole island had disappeared! Fresh succours arrived from Spain, and soon after, as if to realize to the afflicted natives all the horrors of the infernal regions, Spain, and at the suggestions of Columbus too, emptied all her gaols, and vomited all her malefactors on their devoted shores! A piece of policy so much admired in Europe, that it has been imitated by all other colonizing nations, and by none so much as by England! The consequences of this abominable system soon became conspicuous in the distractions, contentions, and disorders of the colony; and in order to soothe and appease these, Columbus resorted to fresh injuries on the natives, dividing their lands amongst his mutinous followers, and giving away the inhabitants—the real possessors—along with them as slaves! Thus he was the originator of those REPARTIMENTOS, or distribution of the Indians that became the source of such universal calamities to them, and of the extinction of more than fifty millions of their race.

Though Providence permitted these things, it did not leave them unavenged. If ever there was a history of the divine retribution written in characters of light, it is that of Spain and the Spaniards in America. On Spain itself the wrath of God seemed to fall with a blasting and enduring curse. From being one of the most powerful and distinguished nations of Europe, it began from the moment that the gold of America, gathered amidst the tears and groans, and dyed with the blood of the miserable and perishing natives, flowed in a full stream into it, to shrink and dwindle, till at once poor and proud, indolent and superstitious, it has fallen a prey to distractions that make it the most melancholy spectacle in Europe. On one occasion Columbus witnessed a circumstance so singular, that it struck not only him but every one to whom the knowledge of it came. After he himself had been disgraced and sent home in chains, being then on another voyage of discovery,—and refused entrance into the port of St. Domingo by the governor—he saw the approach of a tempest, and warned the governor of it, as the royal fleet was on the point of setting sail for Spain. His warning was disregarded; the fleet set sail, having on board Bovadillo, the ex-governor, Roldan, and other officers, men who had been not only the fiercest enemies of Columbus, but the most rapacious plunderers and oppressors of the natives. The tempest came; and these men, with sixteen vessels laden with an immense amount of guilty wealth, were all swallowed up in the ocean—leaving only two ships afloat, one of which contained the property of Columbus!

But the fortunes of Columbus were no less disastrous. Much, and perhaps deservedly as he has been pitied for the treatment which he received from an ungrateful nation, it has always struck me that, from the period that he departed from the noble integrity of his character; butchered the naked Indians on their own soil, instead of resenting and redressing their injuries; from the hour that he set the fatal example of hunting them with dogs, of exacting painful labours and taxes, that he had no right to impose,—from the moment that he annihilated their ancient peace and liberty, the hand of God's prosperity went from him. His whole life was one continued scene of disasters, vexations, and mortifications. Swarms of lawless and rebellious spirits, as if to punish him for letting loose on this fair continent the pestilent brood of the Spanish prisons, ceased not to harass and oppose him. Maligned by these enemies, and sent to Europe in chains; there seeking restoration in vain, he set out on fresh discoveries. But wherever he went misfortune pursued him. Denied entrance into the very countries he had discovered; defeated by the natives that his men unrighteously attacked ; shipwrecked in Jamaica, before it possessed a single European colony, he was there left for above twelve months, suffering incredible hardships, and amongst his mutinous Spaniards that threatened his life on the one hand, and Indians weary of their presence on the other. Having seen his authority usurped in the new world, he returned to the old,—there the death of Isabella, the only soul that retained a human feeling, extinguished all hope of redress of his wrongs; and after a weary waiting for justice on Ferdinand, he died, worn out with grief and disappointment. He had denied justice to the inhabitants of the world he had found, and justice was denied him; he had condemned them to slavery, and he was sent home in chains; he had given over the Indians to that thraldom of despair which broke the hearts of millions, and he himself died broken-hearted.

CHAPTER V.

THE SPANIARDS IN HISPANIOLA AND CUBA.

Her princes in the midst thereof are like wolves ravening for the prey; to shed blood, and to destroy souls, and to get dishonest gain.

Ezekiel xxii. 27.

BUT whether Columbus or others were in power, the miseries of the Indians went on. Bovadillo, the governor who superseded Columbus, and loaded him with irons, only bestowed allotments of Indians with a more liberal hand, to ingratiate himself with the fierce adventurers who filled the island. Raging with the quenchless thirst of gold, these wretches drove the poor Indians in crowds to the mountains, and compelled them to labour so mercilessly in the mines, that they melted away as rapidly as snow in the sun. It is true that the atrocities thus committed reaching the ears of Isabella, instructions were from time to time sent out, declaring the Indians free subjects, and enjoining mercy towards them; but like all instructions of the sort sent so far from home, they were resisted and set aside. The Indians, ever and anon, stung with despair, rose against their oppressors, but it was only to perish by the sword instead of the mine—they were pursued as rebels, their dwellings razed from the earth, and their caziques, when taken, hanged as male-factors.

> In vain the simple race
> Kneeled to the iron sceptre of their grace,
> Or with weak arms their fiery vengeance braved;
> They came, they saw, they conquered, they enslaved,
> And they destroyed! The generous heart they broke;
> They crushed the timid neck beneath the yoke;
> Where'er to battle marched their fell array,
> The sword of conquest ploughed resistless way;
> Where'er from cruel toil they sought repose,
> Around the fires of devastation rose.
> The Indian as he turned his head in flight,
> Beheld his cottage flaming through the night,
> And, mid the shrieks of murder on the wind,
> Heard the mute bloodhound's death-step close behind.
> The conquest o'er, the valiant in their graves,
> The wretched remnant dwindled into slaves;
> Condemned in pestilential cells to pine,
> Delving for gold amidst the gloomy mine.
> The sufferer, sick of life-protracting breath,
> Inhaled with joy the fire-damp blast of death,—
> Condemned to fell the mountain palm on high,
> That cast its shadow to the evening sky,
> Ere the tree trembled to his feeble stroke,
> The woodman languished, and his heart-strings broke;
> Condemned in torrid noon, with palsied hand,
> To urge the slow plough o'er the obdurate land,
> The labourer, smitten by the sun's fierce ray,
> A corpse along the unfinished furrow lay.
> O'erwhelmed at length with ignominious toil,
> Mingling their barren ashes with the soil,
> Down to the dust the Charib people past,
> Like autumn foliage withering in the blast;
> The whole race sunk beneath the oppressor's rod,
> And left a blank amongst the works of God.
>
> *Montgomery.*

In all the atrocities and indignities practised on these poor islanders, there were none which excite a

stronger indignation than the treatment of the generous female cazique, Anacoana. This is the narrative of
Robertson, drawn from Ovieda, Herrera, and Las
Casas. " The province anciently named Zaragua,
which extends from the fertile plain where Leogane
is now situated, to the western extremity of the island,
was subject to a female cazique, named Anacoana,
highly respected by the natives. She, from the par-
tial fondness with which the women of America were
attached to the Europeans, had always courted the
friendship of the Spaniards, and loaded them with
benefits. But some of the adherents of Roldan having
settled in her country, were so much exasperated at
her endeavouring to restrain their excesses, that they
accused her of having formed a plan to throw off the
yoke, and to exterminate the Spaniards. Ovando,
though he well knew what little credit was due to
such profligate men, marched without further inquiry
towards Zaragua, with three hundred foot, and seventy
horsemen. To prevent the Indians from taking alarm
at this hostile appearance, he gave out that his sole
intention was to visit Anacoana, to whom his countrymen had been so much indebted, in the most respectful manner, and to regulate with her the mode of
levying the tribute payable to the king of Spain.

"Anacoana, in order to receive this illustrious guest
with due honour, assembled the principal men in
her dominions, to the number of three hundred, and
advancing at the head of these, accompanied by a
great crowd of persons of inferior rank, she welcomed
Ovando with songs and dances, according to the
mode of the country, and conducted him to the place
of her residence. There he was feasted for some days,

with all the kindness of simple hospitality, and amused with the games and spectacles usual among the Americans upon occasions of mirth and festivity. But amid the security which this inspired, Ovando was meditating the destruction of his unsuspicious entertainer and her subjects; and the mean perfidy with which he executed this scheme, equalled his barbarity in forming it.

" Under colour of exhibiting to the Indians the parade of an European tournament, he advanced with his troops in battle array towards the house in which Anacoana and the chiefs who attended her were assembled. The infantry took possession of all the avenues which led to the village. The horsemen encompassed the house. These movements were the objects of admiration without any mixture of fear, until upon a signal which had been concerted, the Spaniards suddenly drew their swords and rushed upon the Indians, defenceless, and astonished at an act of treachery which exceeded the conception of undesigning men. In a moment, Anacoana was secured; all her attendants were seized and bound; fire was set to the house; and without examination or conviction, all these unhappy persons, the most illustrious in their country, were consumed in the flames. Anacoana was reserved for a more ignominious fate. She was carried in chains to St. Domingo, and after the formality of a trial before Spanish judges, was condemned upon the evidence of those very men who had betrayed her, *to be publicly hanged !* "

It is impossible for human treachery, ingratitude, and cruelty to go beyond that. All that we could relate of the deeds of the Spaniards in Hispaniola, would be but the continuance of this system of demon oppression. The people, totally confounded with this instance of unparalleled villany and butchery, sunk into the inanition of despair, and were regularly ground away by the unremitted action of excessive labour and brutal abuse. In fifteen years they sunk from one million to sixty thousand!—a consumption of *upwards of sixty thousand souls a-year in one island!* Calamities, instead of decreasing, only accumulated on their heads. Isabella of Spain died; and the greedy adventurers feeling that the only person at the head of the government that had any real sympathy with the sufferings of the natives was gone, gave themselves now boundless license. Ferdinand conferred grants of Indians on his courtiers, as the least expensive mode of getting rid of their importunities. Ovando, the governor, gave to his own friends and creatures similar gifts of living men, to be worked or crushed to death at their mercy—to perish of famine, or by the suicidal hand of despair. The avarice and rapacity of the adventurers became perfectly rabid. Nobles at home, farmed out these Indians given by Ferdinand to those who were going out to take part in the nefarious deeds—

> They sate at home, and turned an easy wheel,
> That set sharp racks at work to pinch and peel.

The small and almost nominal sum which had been allowed to the natives for their labour was now denied them; they were made absolute and unconditional slaves, and groaned and wasted away in mines and gold-dust streams, rapidly as those streams themselves flowed. The quantity of wealth drawn from their very vitals was enormous. Though Ovando had reduced the royal portion to one-fifth, yet it now amounted to above a hundred thousand pounds sterling annually— making the whole annual produce of gold in that island, five hundred thousand pounds sterling ; and considering the embezzlement and waste that must take place amongst a tribe of adventurers on fire with the love of gold, and fearing neither God nor man in their pursuit of it, probably nearer a million. Enormous fortunes sprung up with mushroom rapidity; luxury and splendour broke out with proportionate violence at home, and legions of fresh tormentors flocked like harpies to this strange scene of misery and aggrandizement. To add to all this, the sugar-cane—that source of a thousand crimes and calamities—was introduced! It flourished; and like another upas-tree, breathed fresh destruction upon this doomed people. Plantations and sugar-works were established, and became general; and the last and faintest glimmer of hope for the islanders was extinguished! Gold *might* possibly become exhausted, worked as the mines were with such reckless voracity; but the cane would spring afresh from year to year, and the accursed juice would flow for ever.

The destruction of human life now went on with such velocity, that some means were necessarily devised to obtain a fresh supply of victims, or the Spaniards must quit the island, and seek to establish their inferno somewhere else. But having perfected themselves in that part of Satan's business which consisted in tormenting, they now very characteristically assumed the other part of the fiend's trade—that of alluring and inveigling the unsuspicious into their snares. Were this not a portion of unquestionable history, related by the Spanish historians themselves, it is so completely an assumption of the art of the " father of lies," and betrays such a consciousness of the real nature of the business they were engaged in, that it would be looked upon as a happy burlesque of some waggish wit upon them. The fact however stands on the authority of Gomera, Herrera, Oviedo, and others. Ovando, the governor, seeing the rapidly wasting numbers of the natives, and hearing the complaints of the adventurers, began to cast about for a remedy, and at length this most felicitous scheme, worthy of Satan in the brightest moment of his existence, burst upon him.—There were the inhabitants of the Lucayo Isles, living in heathen idleness, and ignorant alike of *Christian* mines and *Christian* sugarworks. It was fitting that they should not be left in such criminal and damnable neglect any longer. He proposed, therefore, that these benighted creatures should be brought to the elysium of Hispaniola, and *civilized* in the gold mines, and *instructed in the Christian religion* in the sugar-mills! The idea was too happy, and too full of the milk of *Christian* kindness to be lost. At once, all the amiable gold-hunters clapped their hands with ecstasy at the prospect of so *many new martyrs to the Christian faith;* and Ferdinand, the benevolent and *most Catholic* Ferdinand, assented to it with the zeal of a royal nursing father of the church! A fleet was speedily fitted out for the benighted Lucayos; and the poor inhabitants there, wasting their existence in merely cultivating their maize, plucking their oranges, or fishing in their streams, just as their need or their inclination prompted them, were told by the Spaniards that they came from the heaven of their

ancestors—isles of elysian beauty and fertility; where
all pain and death were unknown, and where their
friends and relations, living in heavenly felicity,
needed only their society to render that felicity perfect!—that these beatified relatives had prayed them to
hasten and bring them to their own scene of enjoyment
—now waited impatiently for their arrival—and that
they were ready to convey them thither, to the
fields of heaven, in fact, without the black transit of
death! The simple creatures, hearing a story which
chimed in so exactly with their fondest belief, flocked
on board with a blind credulity, not even to be exceeded by the Bubble-dupes of modern England, and
soon found themselves in the grasp of fiends, and
added to the remaining numbers of the Hispaniolan
wretches in the mines and plantations. Forty thousand of these poor people were decoyed by this hellish
artifice; and Satan himself, on witnessing this Spanish
chef d'ouvre, must have felt ashamed of his inferiority
of tact in his own profession!*

* How affecting is Peter Martyr's account of these poor Lucayans,
thus fraudulently decoyed from their native countries. "Many of
them, in the anguish of despair, obstinately refuse all manner of sustenance, and retiring to desert caves and unfrequented woods, silently
give up the ghost. Others, repairing to the sea-coast on the northern
side of Hispaniola, cast many a longing look towards that part of the
ocean where they suppose their own islands to be situated; and as
the sea-breeze rises, they eagerly inhale it—fondly believing that it
has lately visited their own happy valleys, and comes fraught with the
breath of those they love, their wives and their children. With this
idea, they continue for hours on the coast, until nature becomes
utterly exhausted, when, stretching out their arms towards the ocean,
as if to take a last embrace of their distant country and relatives, they
sink down and expire without a groan. . . . . . One of them, who
was more desirous of life, or had greater courage than most of his

But the climax yet remained to be put to the inflictions on these islanders:—and that was found in the pearl fishery of Cubagua. Columbus had discovered this little wretched island—Columbus had suggested and commenced the slavery of the Indians,—and it seemed as though a Columbus was to complete the fabric of their misery. Don Diego, Columbus's son, had compelled an acknowledgment of his claims in the vice-royalty of the New World. He had enrolled himself by his marriage with the daughter of Don Ferdinand de Toledo, brother of the Duke of Alva, and a relative of the king, amongst the highest nobility of the land. Coming over to assume his hereditary station, he brought a new swarm of these proud and avaricious hidalgoes with him. He seized upon and distributed amongst them whatever portions of Indians remained unconsumed; and casting his eyes on this sand-bank of Cubagua, he established a colony of pearl-fishers upon it—where the Indians, and especially the wretched ones decoyed from the Lucayos, were compelled to find in diving the last extremity of their sufferings.

countrymen, took upon him a bold and difficult piece of work. Having been used to build cottages in his native country, he procured instruments of stone, and cut down a large spongy tree, called *jaruma* (the *bombax*, or wild cotton), the body of which he dexterously scooped into a canoe. He then provided himself with oars, some Indian corn, and a few gourds of water, and prevailed on another man and woman to embark with him on a voyage to the Lucayos. Their navigation was prosperous for near two hundred miles, and they were almost within sight of their long-lost shores, when unfortunately they were met by a Spanish ship, which brought them back to slavery and sorrow ! The canoe is still preserved in Hispaniola as a curiosity, considering the circumstances under which it was made."—*Decad.* vii.

And was there no voice raised against these dreadful enormities? Yes—and with the success which always attends the attempt to defend the weak against the powerful and rapacious in distant colonies. The Dominican monks, much to their honour, inveighed, from time to time, against them; but the Franciscans, on the other hand, sanctioned them, on the old plea of policy and necessity. It was *necessary* that the Spaniards should compel the Indians to labour, or they must abandon their grand source of wealth. That was conclusive. Where are the people that carry their religion or their humanity beyond their interest? The thing was not to be expected. One man, indeed, roused by the oppressions of Diego Columbus, and his notorious successor, Albuquerque, a needy man, actually appointed by Ferdinand to the office of Distributor of the Indians!—one man, Bartholomew de Las Casas, dared to stand forward as their champion, and through years of unremitting toil to endeavour to arrest from the government some mitigation of their condition. Once or twice he appeared on the eve of success. At one time Ferdinand declared the Indians free subjects, and to be treated as such; but the furious opposition which arose in the colony on this decision, soon drew from the king another declaration, to wit, that the Pope's bull gave a clear and satisfactory right to the Indians—that no man must trouble his conscience on account of their treatment, for the king and council would take all that on their own responsibility, and that the monks must cease to trouble the colony with their scruples. Yet the persevering Las Casas, by personal importunity at the court of Spain, painting the miseries and destruction of the Indians, now reduced from a million—not to sixty thousand as before,* but to *fourteen thousand*— again succeeded in obtaining a deputation of three monks of St. Jerome, as superintendents of all the colonies, empowered to relieve the Indians from thèir heavy yoke; and returned thither himself, in his official character of Protector of the Indians. But all his efforts ended in smoke. His coadjutors, on reaching Hispaniola, were speedily convinced by the violence and other persuasives of the colonies, that it was *necessary* that the Indians should be slaves; and the only resource of the benevolent Las Casas was to endeavour to found a new colony where he might employ the Indians as free men, and civilize and Christianize them. But this was as vain a project as the other. His countrymen were now prowling along every shore of the New World that they were acquainted with, kidnapping and carrying off the inhabitants as slaves, to supply the loss of those they had worked to death. The dreadful atrocities committed in these kidnapping cruizes, had made the name of the Spaniards terrible wherever they had been; and as the inhabitants could no longer anywhere be *decoyed*, he found the Spanish admiral on the point of laying waste with fire and sword, so as to seize on all its people in their flight, the very territory granted him in which to try his new experiment of humanity. The villany was accomplished; and amid the desolation of Cumana—the

* In less than fifty years from the arrival of the Spaniards, not more than two hundred Indians could be found in Hispaniola; and Sir Francis Drake states that when he touched there in 1585, not one was remaining; yet so little were the Spaniards benefited by their cruelty, that they were actually obliged *to convert pieces of leather into money!*—See Hakluyt's Voyages, vol. iii.

bulk of whose people were carried off as slaves to Hispaniola, and the rest having fled from their burning houses to the hills — the sanguine Las Casas still attempted to found his colony. It need not be said that it failed; the Protector of the Indians retired to a monastery, and the work of Indian misery went on unrestrained. To their oppression, a new and more lasting one had been added; from their destruction, indeed, had now sprung that sorest curse of both blacks and whites—that foulest stain on the Christian name—the Slave Trade. Charles V. of Spain, with that perfect freedom to do as they pleased with all heathen nations which the Papal church had given to Spain and Portugal, had granted a patent to one of his Flemish favourites, for the importation of negroes into America. This patent he had sold to the Genoese, and these worthy merchants were now busily employed in that traffic in men which is so *congenial* to *Christian* maxims, that it has from that time been the favourite pursuit of the *Christian* nations; has been defended by all the arguments of the most civilized assemblies in the world, and by the authority of Holy Writ, and is going on at this hour with undiminished horrors.

It has been charged on Las Casas, that with singular inconsistency he himself suggested this diabolical trade; but of that, and of this trade, we shall say more anon. We will now conclude this chapter with the brief announcement, that Diego Columbus had now conquered Cuba, by the agency of Diego Velasquez, one of his father's captains, and thus added another grand field for the consumption of natives, and the importation of slaves. We are informed that the Cubaans were so unwarlike that no difficulty was found in overrunning this fine island, except from a chief called Hatuey, who had fled from Hispaniola, and knew enough of the Spaniards not to desire their further acquaintance. His obstinacy furnishes this characteristic anecdote on the authority of Las Casas. " He stood upon the defensive at their first landing, and endeavoured to drive them back to their ships. His feeble troops, however, were soon broken and dispersed ; and he himself being taken prison, Velas-quez, according to the barbarous maxim of the Spaniards, considered him as a slave who had taken arms against his master, and condemned him to the flames."

When Hatuey was fastened to the stake, a Franciscan friar, *labouring to convert him,* promised him immediate admission into the joys of heaven,.if he could embrace the Christian faith. " Are there any Spaniards," says he, after some pause, " in that region of bliss which you describe ?" "Yes," replied the monk, " but such only as are worthy and good." "The best of them," returned the indignant Cazique, " have neither worth nor goodness! I will not go to a place where I may meet with that accursed race!"*

The torch was clapped to the pile—Hatuey perished—and the Spaniards added Cuba to the crown without the loss of a man on their own part.

* Las Casas, in his zeal for the Indians, has been charged with exaggerating the numbers destroyed, but no one has attempted to deny the following fact asserted by him : " I once beheld four or five principal Indians roasted alive at a slow fire ; and as the miserable victims poured forth dreadful screams, which disturbed the commanding officer in his afternoon slumbers—he sent word that they should be strangled ; but the officer on guard (I KNOW HIS NAME—I KNOW HIS RELATIVES IN SEVILLE) would not suffer it ; but causing their mouths to be gagged, that their cries might not be heard, he stirred up the fire with his own hands, and roasted them deliberately till they all expired. I SAW IT MYSELF!!!"

CHAPTER VI.

THE SPANIARDS IN JAMAICA AND OTHER WEST INDIAN ISLANDS.

THE story of one West India Island, is the story of all. Whether Spaniards, French, or English took possession, the slaughter and oppression of the natives followed. I shall, therefore, quit these fair islands for the present, with a mere passing glance at a few characteristic facts.

Herrera says that Jamaica was settled prosperously, because Juan de Esquival having brought the natives to submission *without any effusion of blood*, they laboured in planting cotton, and raising other commodities, which yielded great profit. But Esquival in a very few years died in his office, and was buried in Sevilla Nueva, a town which he had built and destined for the seat of government. There is a dark tradition connected with the destruction of this town, which would make us infer that the mildness of Esquival's government was not imitated by his successors. The Spanish planters assert that the place was destroyed by a vast army of ants, but the popular tradition still triumphs over this tradition of the planters. It maintains, that the injured and oppressed natives rose in their

despair and cut off every one of their tyrants, and laid
the place in such utter and awful ruin that it never
was rebuilt, but avoided as a spot of horror. The
city must have been planned with great magnificence,
and laid out in great extent, for Sloane, who visited
it in 1688, could discover the traces or remains of a
fort, a splendid cathedral and monastery, the one inhabited by Peter Martyr, who was abbot and chief
missionary of the island. He found a pavement at
two miles distance from the church, an indication of
the extent of the place, and also many materials for
grand arches and noble buildings that had never been
erected. The ruins of this city were now overgrown
with wood, and turned black with age. Sloane saw
timber trees growing within the walls of the cathedral
upwards of sixty feet in height; and General Vena-
bles in his dispatches to Cromwell, preserved in Thur-
low's State Papers, vol. iii., speaks of Seville as a town
that had existed *in times past.*

Both ancient tradition, and recent discoveries, says
Bryan Edwards, in his History of the West Indies,
give too much room to believe that the work of destruction proceeded not less rapidly in this island,
after Esquival's death, than in Hispaniola; for to this
day caves are frequently discovered in the mountains,
wherein the ground is covered almost entirely with
human bones; the miserable remains, without all
doubt, of some of the unfortunate aborigines, who,
immured in those recesses, were probably reduced to
the sad alternative of perishing with hunger or bleed-
ing under the swords of their merciless invaders.
That these are the skeletons of Indians is sufficiently
attested by the skulls, which are preternaturally com-

pressed. "When, therefore," says Edwards, "we are told of the fate of the Spanish inhabitants of Seville, it is impossible to feel any other emotion than an indignant wish that the story were better authenticated, and that heaven, in mercy, had permitted the poor Indians in the same moment to have extirpated their oppressors altogether! But unhappily this faint glimmering of returning light to the wretched natives, was soon lost in everlasting darkness, since it pleased the Almighty, for reasons inscrutable to finite wisdom, to permit the total destruction of this devoted people; who, to the number of 60,000, on the most moderate estimate, were at length wholly cut off and exterminated by the Spaniards—not a single descendant of either sex being alive when the English took the island in 1655, nor I believe for a century before."

The French historian, Du Tertre, informs us that his countrymen made a *lawful purchase* of the island of Grenada from the natives for *some glass beads, knives and hatchets, and a couple of bottles of brandy for the chief himself.* The nature of the bargain may be pretty well understood by the introduction of the brandy for the chief, and by the general massacre which followed, when Du Tertre himself informs us that Du Parquet, the very general who made this bargain, gave orders for extirpating the natives altogether, which was done with circumstances of the most savage barbarity, even to the women and children. The same historian assures us that St. Christopher's, the principal of the Caribbee Isles, was won by the joint exertions of Thomas Warner, an Englishman, and D'Esnambuc, the captain of a French privateer, who both seem to have entered with hearty good-will into the business of massacre and extermination; by which means, and by excessive labour, the total aboriginal population of the West Indian islands were speedily reduced from six millions, at which Las Casas estimated them, to nothing.

Let any one read the following account from Herrera and Peter Martyr, of the manner in which the Spaniards were received in these islands:—" When any of the Spaniards came near to a village, the most ancient and venerable of the Indians, or the cazique himself, if present, came out to meet them, and gently conducting them into their habitations, seated them on stools of ebony curiously ornamented. These benches seemed to be seats of honour reserved for their guests, for the Indians threw themselves on the ground, and kissing the hands and feet of the Spaniards, offered them fruits and the choicest of their viands, entreating them to prolong their stay with such solicitude and reverence as demonstrated that they considered them as beings of a superior nature, whose presence consecrated their dwellings, and brought a blessing with it. One old man, a native of Cuba, approaching Columbus with great reverence, and presenting a basket of fruit, thus addressed him:—' Whether you are divinities or mortal men we know not. You come into these countries with a force, against which, were we inclined to resist it, resistance would be a folly. We are all therefore at your mercy: but if you are men subject to mortality like ourselves, you cannot be unapprised that after this life there is another, wherein a very different portion is allotted to good and bad men. If, therefore, you expect to die, and believe with us that every one is to be rewarded in a future state according to his conduct in the present, you will do no hurt to those who do none to you.' "

Let the reader also, after listening to these exalted sentiments addressed by a *savage*, as we are pleased to term him, to a *Christian*, a term likewise used with as little propriety, read this account of the reception of Bartholomew Columbus by Behechio, a powerful cazique of Hispaniola. " As they approached the king's dwelling, they were met by his wives to the number of thirty, carrying branches of the palm-tree in their hands, who first saluted the Spaniards with a solemn dance, accompanied with a song. These matrons were succeeded by a train of virgins, distinguished as such by their appearance; the former wearing aprons of cotton cloth, while the latter were arrayed only in the innocence of pure nature. Their hair was tied simply with a fillet over their foreheads, or suffered to flow gracefully on their shoulders and bosoms. Their limbs were finely proportioned, and their complexions though brown, were smooth, shining and lovely. The Spaniards were struck with admiration, believing that they beheld the dryads of the woods, and the nymphs of the fountains realizing ancient fable. The branches which they bore in their hands, they now delivered with lowly obeisance to the lieutenant, who, entering the palace, found a plentiful, and according to the Indian mode of living, a splendid repast already provided. As night approached, the Spaniards were conducted to separate cottages, wherein each was accommodated with a cotton hammock, and the next morning they were again entertained with dancing and singing. This was followed by matches of wrest-

ling and running for prizes; after which two great
bodies of armed Indians suddenly appeared, and a
mock engagement ensued, exhibiting their modes of
warfare with the Charaibes. For three days were the
Spaniards thus royally entertained, and on the fourth
the affectionate Indians regretted their departure."

What beautiful pictures of a primitive age! what a
more than realization of the age of gold! and what a
dismal fall to that actual *age of gold* which was coming
upon them! To turn from these delightful scenes to
the massacres and oppressions of millions of these
gentle and kind people, and then to the groans of
millions of wretched Africans, which through three
long centuries have succeeded them, is one of the
most melancholy and amazing things in the criminal
history of the earth; nor can we wonder at the feelings
with which Bryan Edwards reviews this awful subject:—"All the murders and desolations of the most
pitiless tyrants that ever diverted themselves with the
pangs and convulsions of their fellow-creatures, fall
infinitely short of the bloody enormities committed by
the Spanish nation in the conquest of the New World
—a conquest, on a low estimate, effected by the
murder of ten millions of the species! After reading
these accounts, who can help forming an indignant
wish that the hand of Heaven, by some miraculous
interposition, had swept these European tyrants from
the face of the earth, who like so many beasts of prey,
roamed round the world only to desolate and destroy;
and more remorseless than the fiercest savage, thirsted
for human blood without having the impulse of natural appetite to plead in their defence!"

CHAPTER VII.

THE SPANIARDS IN MEXICO.

And he knew their desolate palaces, and he laid waste their cities.
Ezekiel xix. 7.

How Cortez conquered,—Montezuma fell.—*Montgomery.*

> Much of a Southern Sea they spake,
> And of that glorious city won,
> Near the setting of the sun,
> Throned in a silver lake:
> Of seven kings in chains of gold,
> And deeds of death by tongue untold,—
> Deeds such as breathed in secret there,
> Had shaken the confession-chair!—*Rogers.*

Six and twenty years had now elapsed since Columbus arrived in the New World. During this period the Spaniards had not merely committed the crimes we have been detailing, but they had considerably extended their discoveries. Columbus, who first discovered the West Indian islands, was the first also to discover the mainland of America. He reached the mouth of the Orinoca; traversed the coasts of Paria and Cumana; Yanez Pinzon, steering southward, had crossed the line to the river Amazon; the Portuguese under Alvarez Cabral had by mere accident made the coast of Brazil; Bastidas and De la Cosa had discovered the coast of Tierra Firmè; in his fourth voyage, Columbus had reached Porto Bello in Panama; Pinzon and De Solis discovered Yucatan, and in a second voyage extended their route southward beyond the Rio de la Plata; Ponce de Leon had discovered Florida; and Balboa in Darien had discovered the South Sea. These were grand steps in discovery towards those mighty kingdoms that were soon to burst upon them. Cordova discovered the mouth of the river Potonchan, beyond Campeachy; and finally, Grijalva ranged along the whole coast of Mexico from Tabasco to the river Panuco. Of their transactions on these coasts during their progress in discovery, nothing further need be said than that they were characterized by their usual indifference to the rights and feelings of the natives, and that, finding them for the most part of a more warlike disposition, several of these commanders had suffered severely from them, and some of them lost their lives.

But a strange and astounding epoch was now at hand. The names of Cortez and Pizarro, Mexico and Peru, are become sounds familiar to all ears— linked together as in a spell of wild wonder, and stand as the very embodiment of all that is marvellous, dazzling, and romantic in history. Here were vast empires, suddenly starting from the veil of ages into the presence of the European world, with the glitter of a golden opulence beyond the very extravagance of Arabian fable; populous as they were affluent; with a new and peculiar civilization; with arts and a literature unborrowed of other realms, and unlike

those of any other.　Here were those fairy and most
interesting kingdoms as suddenly assaulted and subdued by two daring adventurers with a mere handful
of followers; and as suddenly destroyed! Their
young civilization, their fair and growing fabric of
policy, ruthlessly dashed down and utterly annihilated;
their princes murdered in cold blood; their wealth
dissipated like a morning dream; and their swarming
people crushed into slaves, or swept from their cities
and their fair fields, as a harvest is swept away by the
sickle!

It is difficult, amid the intoxication of the imagination on contemplating such a spectacle,—for there is
nothing like it in the history of the whole world—it
is difficult, dazzled by military triumph, and seduced
by the old sophisms of glory and adventure, to bring
the mind steadily to contemplate the real nature and
consequences of these events.　The names of Cortez
and Pizarro, indeed, through all the splendour of that
renown with which the acclamations of their interested
cotemporaries, and the false morality of their historians have surrounded them, still retain the gloom
and terror of their cruelties.　But this is derived
rather from particular acts of outrageous atrocity,
than from a just estimate of the total villany and
unrighteous nature of their entire undertakings.
Their entrance, assault, and subduction of the kingdoms of Mexico and Peru, were from first to last,
in limine et in termino, the acts of daring robbers, on
flame with the thirst of gold, and of a spurious and
fanatical renown,—setting at defiance every sentiment of justice, mercy and right, and bound by no
scruples of honour or conscience, in the pursuit of

their object. It is not to be denied that in the prosecution of their schemes, they displayed the most
chivalrous courage, and Cortez the most consummate
address,—but these are the attributes of the arch-fiend
himself—boundless ambition, gigantic talent, the most
matchless and successful address without one feeling
of pity, or one sentiment of goodness! These surely
are not the qualities for which Christians ought to
applaud such men as Cortez and Pizarro! They are
these false and absurd notions, derived from the spirit
of gentile antiquity, that have so long mocked the
progress of Christianity, and held civilization in abey-
ance. It is to these old sophisms that we owe all
the political evils under which we groan, and under
which we have made all nations that have felt our
power groan too. To every truly enlightened and
Christian philosopher can there be a more melancholy
subject of contemplation, than these romantic empires
thus barbarously destroyed by an irruption of worse
than Goths and Vandals? But that melancholy must
be tenfold augmented, when we reflect what *would*
have been the fate of these realms if Europe had been
not nominally, but *really* Christianized at the moment
of their discovery. If it had learned that the " peace on
earth and good-will towards men," with which the children of heaven heralded the gospel into the world, was
not a mere flourish of rhetoric,—not a mere phrase of
eastern poetry, " beautiful exceedingly;" but actually
the promulgation of the grandest and most pregnant
axiom in social philosophy, that had ever been, or
should be made known to mankind, or that it was
possible for heaven itself from the infinitude of its
blessedness to send down to it. That in it lay con-

centrated the perfection of civil policy, the beauty of
social life, the harmony of nations, and the prosperity
of every mercantile adventure. That it was the
triumphant basis, on which arts and sciences, literature and poetry, should raise their proudest fabrics,
and society from its general adoption, date its genuine
civilization and a new era of glory and enjoyment.
Suppose that to have been the mind and feeling of
Europe at that time—and it is merely to suppose it to
be what it pretended to be—in possession of Christianity—what would have been the simple consequence? To the wonder that thrilled through Europe at the tidings of such discovered states, an admiration as lively would have succeeded. Vast kingdoms in the heart of the new world, with cities and
cultivated fields; with temples and palaces; monarchs
of great state and splendour; vessels of silver and
gold in gorgeous abundance; municipal police; national couriers; and hieroglyphic writing, and records
of their own invention! Why, what interesting
intelligence to every lover of philosophy, of literature,
and of the study of human nature! Genuine intelligence, and enlightened curiosity would have flocked
thither to look and admire; genuine philanthropy, to
give fresh strength and guidance to this germinating
civilization,—and Christian spirits would have glowed
with delight at the thought of shewing, in the elevated
virtues, the justice, generosity and magnanimity derived by them from their faith, the benefits which it
could confer on these growing states.

But to have expected anything of this kind from
the Spaniards, would have been the height of folly.
They had no more notion of what Christianity is, than

the Great Mogul had. They knew no more than what Rome chose to tell them. They were not distinguished by one Christian virtue,—for they had been instructed in none. They were not more barbarous to the Americans, than they were faithless, jealous, malignant, and quarrelsome amongst each other. Disorderly and insubordinate as soldiers, nothing but the terrors of their destructive arms, and the fatal paralysis of mind which singular prophesies had cast on the Americans, could have prevented them from being speedily swept away in the midst of their riot and contention. The idea which the Spaniards had of Christianity, is best seen in the form of proclamation which Ojeda made to the inhabitants of Tierra Firme, and which became the Spanish model in all future usurpations of the kind. After stating that the popes, as the successors of St. Peter, were the possessors of the world, it thus went on:

" One of these pontiffs, as lord of the world, hath made a grant of these islands, and of Tierra Firmè of the ocean sea, to the Catholic kings of Castile, Don Ferdinand and Donna Isabella of glorious memory, and their successors, our sovereigns, with all they contain, as is more fully expressed in certain deeds passed upon that occasion, which you may see if you desire it, (Indians, who neither knew Latin, Spanish, nor the art of reading!). Thus his majesty is king and lord of these islands, and of the continent, in virtue of this donation; and as king and lord aforesaid, most of the islands to which his title hath been notified, have recognised his majesty, and now yield obedience and subjection to him as their lord, *voluntarily and without resistance!* and instantly, as soon as they received information (from the sword and musket!) they obeyed the religious men sent by the king to preach to them, and *to instruct them in our holy faith!* . . . . . You *are bound and obliged* (true enough!) to act in the same manner . . . . . . If you do this, you act well, and perform that to which you are bound and obliged; his majesty, and I in his name, *will receive you with love and kindness,* and *will leave you and your children free and exempt from servitude, and in the enjoyment of all you possess, in the same manner as the inhabitants of the islands!* (ay, love and kindness, *such* as they had shewn to the islanders. Satan's genuine glozing— " lies like truth, and yet most truly lies.") Besides this, his majesty *will bestow upon you many privileges, exemptions, and rewards!* (Ay, such as they had bestowed on the islanders—but here begins the simple truth.) But if you will not comply, or maliciously delay to obey my injunctions, then, *with the help of God,* I will enter your country by force; I will carry on war against you with the utmost violence; I will subject you to the yoke of the church and the king; I will take your wives and children, and will make slaves of them, and sell or dispose of them according to his majesty's pleasure; I will seize your goods, and do all the mischief in my power to you as rebellious subjects, who will not acknowledge or submit to their lawful sovereign. And I protest that all the bloodshed and calamities which shall follow are to be imputed to you, and not to his majesty, or to me, or to the gentlemen who serve under me, etc."—*Herrera.*

Here then we have the romance stripped away from such ruffians as Cortez and Pizarro. We have here the very warrant under which they acted—a tissue of such most impudent fictions, and vindictive truths, as could only issue from that great office of delusion and oppression which corrupted all Europe with its abominable doctrine. The last sentence, however, betrays the inward feeling and consciousness of those who used it, that blood-guiltiness was not perfectly removed to their satisfaction, and is a miserable attempt at further self-delusion. These apostles' of the sword, before whose proclamation our sarcasms against Mahomet and his sword-creed, fall to the ground, knew only too well that all their talk of love and kindness to the islanders was the grossest falsehood. The Pope's bull could not blind them to that; and though the misery they inflicted is past, Europe still needs the warning of their deeds, to open its eyes to the nature of much of its own morality.

Cortez commenced his career against Mexico with breach of faith to his employer. It was villain using villain, and with the ordinary results. Velasquez, the governor of Cuba, who had sent out Grijalva, roused by the description of the new and beautiful country which he had 'coasted, now sought for a man, so humble in his pretensions and so destitute of alliance, that he might trust him with a fleet and force for the acquisition of it. Such a man he believed he had found in Hernando Cortez,—a man, like many other men in Spain, of noble blood, but very ignoble fortune—poor, proud, so hot and overbearing in his disposition and so dissipated in his habits, that his father was glad to send him out as an adventurer. Ovando, governor of Hispaniola, the notorious betrayer of Anacoana, and murderer of her chiefs, was his relation, and received him with open arms as a fit instrument in such work as he had to do. Cortez attended Velasquez in that expedition to Cuba in which the cazique Hatuey was burnt at the stake for his resistance to their invasion, and died bearing that memorable testimony to Spanish Christianity. Velasquez, who had acted the traitor towards Diego Columbus, whose deputy in the government of Cuba he was, had however scarcely sent out Cortez, when he conceived a suspicion that he would show no better faith than he himself had done. Scarcely had Cortez sailed for Trinidad, when Velasquez sent instructions after him, to deprive him of his commission. Cortez eluded this by hastening to the Havanna, where an express also to arrest him was forwarded. Cortez, fully justified the suspicions of Velasquez; for, from the moment that he found himself at the head of a fleet, he abandoned every idea of acknowledging the authority which had put it into his command. He boldly avowed his intentions to his fellow adventurers, and as their views, like his own, were plunder and dominion, he received their applause and their vows of adherence. Thus supported in his schemes of ambition, he set sail for the Mexican coast, with eleven vessels of various burdens and characters. His own, or admiral's ship, was of a hundred tons, three of seventy or eighty tons, and the others were open boats. He carried with him six hundred and seventeen men; amongst whom were to be found only thirteen muskets, thirty-two cross-bows, sixteen horses, ten small field-pieces, and four falconets. Behold Cortez and his comrades thus on their way to conquer the great kingdom of Mexico, bearing on their great banner the figure of a large cross, and this inscription,—LET US FOLLOW THE CROSS, FOR UNDER THIS SIGN WE SHALL CONQUER!

" So powerfully," says Robertson, — to whose curious remarks I shall occasionally draw the attention of my readers,—" were Cortez and his followers animated with both these passions (religion and avarice) that no less eager to plunder the opulent country whither they were bound, than *zealous to propagate the Christian faith (!)* among its inhabitants, they set out, not with the solicitude natural to men going upon dangerous services, but with that confidence which arises from security of success, and certainty of the divine protection." No doubt they believed the cross which they followed was the cross of Christ, but every one now will be quite as well satisfied that it was the cross of one of the two thieves, a most fitting ensign for such an expedition. Cortez, indeed, was a fiery zealot, and frequently endangered the success of his enterprise by his assault on the gods and temples of the natives, just as Mahomet or Omar would have done; for there was not a pin to choose between the faith in which he had been educated, and that of the prophet of Mecca. One followed the cross, the other the crescent, but their faith alike was—the sword.*

After touching at different spots, to remind the natives of the Christian faith by " routing them with great slaughter," and carrying off provisions, cotton garments, gold, and twenty female slaves, one of whom was the celebrated woman, called by the Spa-

* Clavigero gives a curious account of the mode in which Cortez took possession of the province of Tabasco, on the plains of Coutla, where he killed eight hundred of the natives, and founded a small city in memory thereof, calling it *Madonna della Victoria!* Here he put on his shield, unsheathed his sword, and gave three stabs with it to a large tree which was in the principal village, declaring that if any person durst oppose his possession, he would defend it with that sword.

niards Donna Marina, who rendered them such services as interpreter, they entered, on the 2nd of April 1519, the harbour of St. Juan de Ulua. Here we are told by the Spanish historians, that the natives came on board in the most friendly and unsuspicious manner. Two of them were officers from the local government, sent to inquire what was the object of Cortez in coming thither, and offering any assistance that might be necessary to enable him to proceed in his voyage. Cortez assured them that *he came with the most friendly intentions*, to seek an interview with the king, of great importance to the welfare of their country; and next morning, in proof of the sincerity and friendliness of his views, landed his troops and ammunition, and began a fortification. This brought Teutile and Pilpatoe, as Robertson calls them, or Teuhtlile and Cuitlalpita, according to Clavigero, himself a Mexican, the local governors, into the camp with a numerous attendance. Montezuma, the emperor, had been alarmed, as well he might, by the former appearance of the Spaniards on his coast, and these officers urged Cortez to take his departure. He persisted, however, that he must see Montezuma, being come as an ambassador from the king of Spain to him, and charged with communications that could be opened to no one else—falsehoods worthy of a robber, for he not only had no commission from the king of Spain, but was in open rebellion to the Spanish government at the moment. To induce him to depart, these simple people resorted to the same unlucky policy as our ancestors the Saxons did with the Danes, and presented him with a present of ten loads of fine cotton cloth, plumes of various colours, and articles in gold and silver of rich and curious workmanship, besides a quantity of provisions. These not only inflamed his cupidity to the utmost, but another circumstance served to convince him that he had stumbled upon a different country to what any of his countrymen had yet found in America; and stimulated equally his ambition to conquer it. He observed painters at work in the train of Teuhtlile and Pitalpatoe,* sketching on cotton cloth, himself, his men, his horses, ships and artillery. To give more effect to these drawings, he sounded his trumpets, threw his army into battle array, put it through a variety of striking military movements, and tore up the neighbouring woods with the discharge of his cannon. The Mexicans, struck with terror and admiration at these exhibitions, dispatched speedy information of all these particulars by the couriers, and in seven days received the answer of the emperor, though his capital was one hundred and eighty miles off, that Cortez must instantly depart the country. But had he had the slightest intention of the kind, the unlucky courtesy of the emperor would have changed his resolve. To render his command the more palatable, he sent an ambassador of rank, with a hundred men of burden carrying presents, and they again poured out before Cortez such a flood of treasures, as astonished him and his greedy followers.

* Thus called by Herrera. Bernal Diaz also calls Teuhtlile, Teudili. It is singular that scarcely two writers, ancient or modern, call the same South American person by the same name. Our modern travellers not only differ from the Spanish historians, but from one another. Even the familiar name of Montezuma, is Moctezuma and Motezuma; that of Guatimozin, Guatimotzin and Quauhtemotzin. The same confusion prevails amongst our authors, in nearly all the proper names of America, Asia, or Africa.

There were boxes full of pearls and precious stones; gold in its native state, and gold wrought into the richest trinkets; two wheels, the one of gold, the other of silver. That of gold, representing the Mexican century, had the image of the sun engraved in the middle, round which were different figures in bass-relief. Bernal Diaz says the circumference was thirty palms of Toledo, and the value of it ten thousand sequins. The one of silver, in which the Mexican year was represented, was still larger, with a moon in the middle, surrounded also with figures in bass-relief.* Thirty loads or bales of cotton cloths of the most exquisite fineness, and pictures in feather-work of surprising brilliancy and art. These were all opened out on mats in the most tempting manner; and besides these, was a vizor, which Cortez had desired at the last interview might be filled with gold dust, telling the officer most truly—that "the Spaniards had a disease of the heart which could only be cured by gold."

Cortez took the presents, and coolly assured the ambassador that he should not quit the country till he had seen the emperor. A third message, accompanied by a third and more peremptory order for his departure, producing no greater effect, the officers left the camp in displeasure, and Cortez prepared to march into the country.

But before he commenced his expedition there were a few measures to be taken. He was a traitor to the governor of Cuba who had sent him out; and the governor had still adherents in the army, who objected to what appeared to them this rash enter-

* Engravings of these may be seen in Clavigero.

prise against so powerful and populous an empire.
It was necessary to silence these people, and his mode
of doing this reminds one of the solemn artifices of
Oliver Cromwell. He held out to the soldiers such
prospects of booty as secured them to his interests,
and on the discontented remonstrating with him, he
appeared to fall in with their views, and gave instant
orders for the return home, at the same time sending
his emissaries amongst the soldiers to exasperate them
against the return. When the order for re-embarka-
tion the next day was therefore issued, the whole army
seemed in a fury against it, and Cortez feigning to
have believed the order for the return was their own
desire, now declared that he was ready to lead them
forwards. But this was not sufficient. Knowing that
he was a traitor to the trust reposed in him, he
resorted to one of those grave farces by which usurpers
often attempt to give an appearance of title to their
power, though they know well enough the emptiness
of it. He laid out the plan of a town,—named it
Villa Rica de la Vera Cruz, or the Rich Town of
the True Cross, established magistrates and a municipal council, and then appeared before them and
resigned his command into their hands, having taken
good care that the magistrates were so much his
creatures as instantly to re-invest him with it. Assuming now this command, not as flowing from the
governor of Cuba, but from the constituted authorities
under the crown, and therefore from the crown itself,
he immediately seized on the officers who had mur-
mured at his breach of faith, clapped them in chains,
and sent them aboard the fleet! So far so good; but
the reflection still came, how would all these deeds

sound at home? and Cortez therefore took the only
means that could secure him in that quarter.   He
collected all the gold that could be procured by any
means, and sent it by the hand of two of the mock
magistrates of Vera Cruz to the King of Spain, giving
a plausible colouring to their assumption of power independent of Cuba, and soliciting a confirmation of it.

These were the measures of an adventurer not more
daring than artful; yet a single circumstance shewed
him still his insecurity.   At the moment that his
magistrates were about to sail for Spain, he discovered
that a conspiracy was in existence to seize one of the
vessels in the harbour, and to sail to Cuba, and give
the alarm to Velasquez.   This startling fact determined him to put the *coup de grace* to his measures,—
to destroy his fleet, and let his followers see that there
was no longer any resource but to follow him boldly
in his attack upon Mexico, or perish.   He had the
address to bring his men to commit this act themselves:
they dragged the vessels ashore—stripped them of
sails, rigging, iron-work—whatever might be useful,
and then broke them up.   A more daring and politic
action is not upon record.   Cortez, in fact, had nothing
to hope from his fleet, and had cast his life and fortune on the conquest of this great and wealthy realm.

When we contemplate him at this juncture, we are
however not more struck with his daring and determined policy, than as Christians we are indignant at
the real nature of the act that he meditated.   This
was no other than to ravage this young and growing
empire, to plunder it of its gold, and consume its
millions of inhabitants in mines and plantations, by
the sword and by the lash, as his countrymen had con-

sumed the wealth and the people of the islands,—and all this on pretence of planting the Cross! It was the cool speculation of a daring robber, hardened by a false faith, and by witnessing deeds of blood and outrage, to a total insensibility to every feeling but the diseased overgrowth of selfish ambition.

The attempt to subdue a kingdom stretching from the Atlantic to the Pacific Ocean in a breadth of above five hundred leagues from east to west, and of upwards of two hundred from north to south—a kingdom populous, fertile, and of a warlike reputation; and that with a force of not seven hundred men, appears at first view an act of madness: but Cortez was too well acquainted with American warfare to know that it was not impracticable. In the first place, he knew that the weapons of the natives had very little effect upon the quilted cotton dress which the Spaniards adopted on these expeditions, and that by the terror of their fire-arms and their union of movement, they could in almost all cases and situations keep them at that distance which took away even that little effect, while it left them open to the full play of the European missives. He knew the terror that the natives had of the Spanish horses, dogs, and artillery; and moreover he had speedily discovered, through the means of one of the women slaves brought from Darien who proved to be a Mexican by birth, that Mexico was a kingdom newly cemented by the arms of Montezuma and his immediate predecessors, and therefore full of provinces still smarting under the sense of their subjugation, and ready to seize on an occasion of revenge. In fact, he had speedily practical evidence of this, for the cazique of Chempoalla, a neighbouring town, sent an embassy to him soliciting his friendship, and offering to join him in his designs against Montezuma, whom he represented as a haughty and exacting tyrant to the provinces. Cortez of course caught gladly at this alliance, and removing his settlement, planted it at Quiabislan, near Chempoalla. The hint was given him of the real condition of the empire, and he was too crafty to neglect it. He immediately gave himself out as the champion of the aggrieved and oppressed, come to redress all their wrongs, and restore them to their liberties !

But there was another and most singular cause which gave Cortez a fair prospect of success. Throughout the American kingdoms ancient prophecies prevailed,—that a new race was to come in, and seize upon the reins of power, and before it the American tribes were to quail and give place. In the islands, in Mexico, in Peru,—far and wide,—this mysterious tradition prevailed. Everywhere these terrible people were expected to come from towards the rising of the sun: they were to be completely clad, and to lay waste every country before them;—circumstances so entirely verified in the Spaniards, that the spirit of the American natives died within them at the rumour of their approach, as the natives of Canaan did at that of the Israelites coming with the irresistible power and the awful miracles of God. For ages these prophecies had weighed on the public mind, and had been sung with loud lamentations at their solemn festivals. Cazziva, a great cazique, declared that in a supernatural interview with one of the Zemi, this terrible event had been revealed to him. " The demons which they worshipped," says Acosta, " in this instance, told them true." Montezuma therefore, though naturally haughty, warlike, and commanding, on so appalling an event as the fulfilment of these ancient prophecies, lost his courage, his decision, his very power of mind, and exhibited nothing but the most utter vacillation and weakness, while Cortez was advancing towards his capital in defiance of his orders.

Having strengthened himself by the alliance of the Chempoallans, and others of the Totonacas, and chastised the Tlascalans, a fierce people who gave no credit to his pretences, he advanced to Cholula, a place of great importance, consisting, according to Cortez's account, of forty thousand houses and many populous suburban villages. Montezuma had now consented to his reception, and he was received in this city by his orders. It was a sacred city,—" the Rome of Anahuac or Mexico," says Clavigero, full of temples, and visited by hosts of pilgrims. Here, suspecting treachery, he determined to strike terror into both the emperor and the people. " For this purpose," says Robertson, " the Spaniards and Zempoallans were drawn up in a large court which had been allotted for their quarters near the centre of the town. The Tlascalans had orders to advance; the magistrates, and several of the chief citizens, were sent for, under various pretences, and seized. On a signal given, the troops rushed out, and fell upon the multitude destitute of leaders, and so much astonished, that the weapons dropping from their hands, they stood motionless and incapable of defence. While the Spaniards pressed them in front, the Tlascalans attacked them in the rear. The streets were filled with bloodshed and death; the temples, which afforded a retreat to the priests and some of the leading men, were set on fire, and they perished in the flames. This scene of horror continued two days, during which the wretched inhabitants suffered all that the destructive rage of the Spaniards, or the implacable revenge of their Indian allies, could inflict. At length the carnage ceased, after the slaughter of six thousand Cholulans, without the loss of a single Spaniard! Cortez then released the magistrates, and reproaching them bitterly for their intended treachery, declared that as justice was now appeased he forgave the offence, but required them to recall the citizens who had fled, and reestablish order in the town. Such was the ascendant which the Spaniards had acquired over this superstitious race of men, and so deeply were they impressed with an opinion of their superior discernment, as well as power, that in obedience to this command, the city was in a few days again filled with people, who amidst the ruins of their sacred buildings, yielded respectful service to men whose hands were stained with the blood of their relatives and fellow-citizens.

" From Cholula," adds Robertson, "Cortez marched directly towards Mexico, which was only twenty leagues distant:"—and that is all the remark that he makes on this brutal butchery of an innocent people, by a man on his march to plant the cross! A Christian historian sees only in this most savage and infernal action, a piece of necessary policy—so obtuse become the perceptions of men through the ordinary principles of historic judgment. But the Christian mind asks what business Cortez had there at all? The people were meditating his destruction? True;—and it was natural and national that they should get rid of so audacious and lawless an enemy, who entered their country with the intentions of a robber, set at defiance the commands of their king, and stirred up rebellion at every step he took. The Mexicans would have been less than men if they had not resolved to cut him off. What right had he there? What right to disturb the tranquillity of their country, and shed the blood of its people? These are questions that cannot be answered on any Christian principles, or on any principles but those of the bandit and the murderer. *Six thousand people butchered in cold blood—two days employed in hewing down trembling wretches, too fearful to even raise a single weapon against the murderers!* Heavens! are these the deeds that we admire as heroic and as breathing of romance? Yet, says Clavigero, " He ordered the great temple to be cleaned from the gore of his murdered victims; and raised there the standard of the cross; *after giving the Cholulans, as he did all the other people among whom he stopped,* SOME IDEA OF THE CHRISTIAN RELIGION!!! What *idea* had the Abbé Don Francesco Saverio Clavigero of Christianity himself?

But Cortez had plunged headlong into the enterprise—he had set his life and that of his followers at stake on the conquest of Mexico, and there was no action, however desperate, that he was not prepared to commit. And sure enough his hands became well filled with treachery and blood. It is not my business to dwell particularly upon these atrocities, but merely to recall the memory of them; yet it may be as well to give, in the words of Robertson, the manner in which the Spaniards were received into the capital, because it contrasts strongly with the manner in which the Christians behaved in this same city, and to this same monarch.

"In descending from the mountains of Chalco,* across which the road lay, the vast plain of Mexico opened gradually to their view. When they first beheld this prospect, one of the most striking and beautiful on the face of the earth—when they observed fertile and cultivated fields stretching further than the eye could reach—when they saw a lake resembling the sea in extent, encompassed with large towns; and discovered the capital city, rising upon an island in the middle, adorned with its temples and turrets—the scene so far exceeded their imagination, that some believed the fanciful dreams of romance were realized, and that its enchanted palaces and gilded domes were presented to their sight. Others could hardly persuade themselves that this wonderful spectacle was anything more than a dream. As they advanced, their doubts were removed; but their amazement increased. They were now fully satisfied that the country was rich beyond any conception which they had formed of it, and flattered themselves that at length they should obtain an ample recompense for all their services and sufferings.

" When they drew near the city, about a thousand persons, who appeared to be of distinction, came forth to meet them, adorned with plumes, and clad in mantles of fine cotton. Each of these, in his order, passed by Cortez, and saluted him according to the mode deemed most respectful and submissive in their country. They announced the approach of Montezuma

* The Ithualco of other authors.

himself, and soon after his harbingers came in sight. There appeared first, two hundred persons in an uniform dress, with large plumes of feathers alike in fashion, marching two and two in deep silence, barefooted, with their eyes fixed on the ground. These were followed by a company of higher rank, in their most showy apparel; in the midst of whom was Montezuma, in a chair or litter, richly ornamented with gold and feathers of various colours. Four of his principal favourites carried him on their shoulders; others supported a canopy of curious workmanship over his head. Before him marched three officers with rods of gold in their hands, which they lifted up on high at certain intervals, and at that signal all the people bowed their heads, and hid their faces, as unworthy to look on so great a monarch. When he drew near, Cortez dismounted, advancing towards him with officious haste, and in a respectful posture. At the same time Montezuma alighted from his chair, and leaning on the arms of two of his near relatives, approached with a slow and stately pace, his attendants covering the street with cotton cloths that he might not touch the ground. Cortez accosted him with profound reverence after the European fashion. He returned the salutation according to the mode of his country, by touching the earth with his hand, and then kissing it. This ceremony, the customary expression of veneration from inferiors towards those who were above them in rank, appeared such amazing condescension in a proud monarch, who scarcely deigned to consider the rest of mankind as of the same species with himself, that all his subjects firmly believed those persons before whom he humbled himself in this manner, to be something more than

human. Accordingly, as they marched through the
crowd, the Spaniards frequently, and with much satisfaction, heard themselves denominated *Teules*, or divinities. Montezuma conducted Cortez to the quarter
which he had prepared for his reception, and immediately took leave of him, with a politeness not unworthy of a court more refined. ' You are now,' says he,
' with your brothers in your own house ; refresh yourselves after your fatigue ; and be happy till I return."

The Spanish historians give some picturesque particulars of this interview, which Robertson has not
copied. The dress of Montezuma is thus described :
As he rode in his litter, a parasol of green feathers
embroidered with fancy-work of gold was held over
him. He wore hanging from his shoulders a mantle
adorned with the richest jewels of gold and precious
stones ; on his head a thin crown of the same metal ;
and upon his feet shoes of gold, tied with strings
of leather worked with gold and gems. The persons
on whom he leaned, were the king of Tezcuco and the
lord of Iztapalapan. Cortez put on Montezuma's neck
a thin cord of gold strung with glass beads, and would
have embraced him, but was prevented by the two
lords on whom the king leaned. In return for this
paltry necklace, Montezuma gave Cortez two of
beautiful mother-of-pearl, from which hung some large
cray-fish of gold in imitation of nature.

Here, then, to their own wonder and admiration,
were this handful of Spanish adventurers in the "glorious city,".

> Near the setting of the sun,
> Throned in a silver lake.

Generous minds would have rejoiced in the glory

of such a discovery, and have exulted in the mutual benefits to be derived from an honourable intercourse between their own country and this new and beautiful one,—but Cortez and his men were merely gazing on the novel splendour of this interesting city with the greedy eyes of robbers, and thinking how they might best seize upon its power, and clutch its wealth. Who is not familiar with their rapid career of audacious villany, in this fairy capital? Scarcely were they received as guests,* when they seized on the monarch, and that at the very moment that he gave to Cortez his own daughter, and heaped on him other favours—and compelled him, under menaces of instantly stabbing him to the heart, to quit his palace, and take up his residence in their own quarters. The astonished and distressed king, now a puppet in their hands, was made to command every thing which they desired to be done; and they were by no means scrupulous in their exercise of this power, knowing that the people looked on the person of the monarch as sacred, and would not for a moment refuse to obey his least word, though in the hands of his enemies. The very first thing which they required him to do, was to order to be delivered up to them Qualpopoca, one of his generals, who had been employed in quelling one of the insurrections that the Spaniards had raised near Villa Rica, and who being attacked by the Spanish officer Escalante, left in command there, had killed him, with seven of his men, and taken one other alive. The order was obeyed, and the brave general, his son, and five of his principal officers, were burnt alive by these Christian heroes! To add to

---

* Clavigero says only six days.

the cruelty and indignity of the deed, Montezuma himself was put into irons during the transaction, accompanied by threats of a darker kind.

The simplicity of Robertson's remarks on this affair are singular: " In these transactions, as represented by the Spanish historians, we search in vain for the qualities which distinguish other parts of Cortez's conduct." What qualities? " To usurp a jurisdiction which could not belong to a stranger, who assumed no higher character than that of an ambassador from a foreign prince, and under colour of it, to inflict a capital punishment on men whose conduct entitled them to esteem, appears an act of barbarous cruelty."

Why, the whole of Cortez's conduct, from the moment that he entered with arms the kingdom of Mexico, was a usurpation that " could not belong to a stranger assuming merely the title of an ambassador." What ambassador comes with armed troops; or when the monarch orders him to quit his realm, marches further into it; or foments rebellion as he goes along; or massacres the inhabitants by wholesale? Was the butchery of six thousand people at Cholula, no act of barbarous cruelty?

Well, by what Robertson complacently terms " the fortunate temerity in seizing Montezuma," the Spaniards had suddenly usurped the sovereign power, and they did not pause here. They sent out some of their number to survey the whole kingdom; to spy out its wealth, and pitch on fitting stations for colonies. They put down such native officers as were too honest or able for them; they compelled Montezuma, though with tears and groans, to acknowledge himself the

vassal of the Spanish crown. They divided the
Mexican treasures amongst them; and finally drove
the Mexicans to desperation.

The arrival of the armament from Cuba under
Narvaez, sent by Velasquez to punish Cortez for his
treason, and his victory over Narvaez, and the union
of those troops with his own, belong to the general
historian—my task is to exhibit his treatment to the
natives; and his next exploit, is that of exposing
Montezuma to the view of his exasperated subjects
from the battlements of his house, in the hope that his
royal puppet might have authority enough to appease
them; a scheme which proved the death of the
emperor—for his own subjects, indignant at his tame
submission to the Spaniards, let fly their arrows at him.
The fury of the Mexicans on this catastrophe, the
terrible nocturnal retreat of Cortez from the city, still
called amongst the inhabitants of Mexico, *La Noche
Triste*, the sorrowful night,—the strange battle of
Otumba, where Cortez, felling the standard-bearer of
the army, dispersed in a moment tens of thousands
like a mist,—the flight to Tlascala, and the return
again to the siege,—the eight thousand *Tamenes*, or
servile Indians, bearing through the hostile country
to the lake the brigandines in parts, ready to put
together on their arrival,—Father Olmedo blessing
the brigandines as they were launched on the lake
in the presence of wondering multitudes,—and the
desperate siege and assault themselves, all are full of
the most stirring interest, and display a sort of satanic
grandeur in the man, amidst the horrors into which
his ambitious guilt had plunged him, that are only to
be compared to that of Napoleon in Russia, beset, in

his extremity, by the vengeful warriors of the north. But the crowning disgrace of Cortez, is that of putting to the torture the new emperor, Guatimotzin, the nephew and son-in-law of Montezuma, whom the Mexicans, in admiration of his virtues and talents, had placed on the throne. The bravery with which Guatimotzin had defended his city, the frankness with which he yielded himself when taken, would have made his person sacred in the eyes of a generous conqueror; but Guatimotzin had committed the crime, unpardonable in the eyes of a Spaniard, of casting the treasures for which the Spaniards harassed his country into the lake,—and Cortez had him put to the severest torture to force from him the avowal of where they lay. Even *he* is said at length to have been ashamed of so base and horrid a business; yet he afterwards put him to death, and the manner in which this, and other barbarities are related by Robertson, is worthy of observation.

"It was not, however, without difficulty that the Mexican empire could be entirely reduced to the form of a Spanish province. Enraged and rendered desperate by oppression, the natives forgot the superiority of their enemies, and ran to arms in defence of their liberties. In every contest, however, the European valour and discipline prevailed. But fatally for the honour of their country, the Spaniards sullied the glory redounding from these repeated victories, by their mode of treating the vanquished people. After taking Guatimotzin, and becoming masters of his capital, they supposed that the king of Castile entered on possession of all the rights of the captive monarch, and affected to consider every effort of the

Mexicans to assert their own independence, as the rebellion of vassals against their sovereign, or the mutiny of slaves against their master. Under the sanction of these ill-founded maxims, they violated every right that should be held sacred between hostile nations. After each insurrection, they reduced the common people, in the provinces which they subdued, to the most humiliating of all conditions, that of personal servitude. Their chiefs, supposed to be more criminal, were punished with greater severity, and put to death in the most ignominious or the most excruciating mode that the insolence or the cruelty of their conquerors could devise. In almost every district of the Mexican empire, the progress of the Spanish arms is marked with blood, and with deeds so atrocious, as disgrace the enterprising valour that conducted them to success. In the country of Panuco, sixty caziques, or leaders, and four hundred nobles were burnt at one time. Nor was this shocking barbarity perpetrated in any sudden sally of rage, or by a commander of inferior note. It was the act of Sandoval, an officer whose name is entitled to the second rank in the annals of New Spain; and executed after a solemn consultation with Cortez; and to complete the horror of the scene, the children and relatives of the wretched victims were assembled, and compelled to be spectators of their dying agonies.

" It seems hardly possible to exceed in horror this dreadful example of severity; but it was followed by another, which affected the Mexicans still more sensibly, as it gave them a more feeling proof of their own degradation, and of the small regard which their haughty masters retained for the ancient dignity and

splendour of their state.　On a slight suspicion, confirmed by a very imperfect evidence, that Guatimotzin
had formed a scheme to shake off the yoke, and to
excite his former subjects to take arms, Cortez, without the formality of a trial, ordered the unhappy
monarch, together with the caziques of Tezeuco and
Tacuba, the two persons of the greatest eminence in
the empire, to be hanged; and the Mexicans, with
astonishment and horror, beheld this disgraceful punishment inflicted upon persons to whom they were
accustomed to look up with reverence hardly inferior
to that which they paid to the gods themselves.　The
example of Cortez and his principal officers, encouraged and justified persons of subordinate rank to
venture upon committing greater excesses."

It is not easy to see how Cortez and his men " sullied the glory of their repeated victories," by these
actions—for these very victories were gained over a
people who had no chance against European arms,—
and were infamous in themselves, being violations of
every sacred right of humanity.　What, indeed, could
sully the reputation of the man after the butchery of
six thousand Cholulas in cold blood?　The notions
of glory with which Robertson, in common with many
other historians, was infected, are mere remnants of
that corrupted morality which Popery disseminated,
and which created the Cortezes and Pizarros of those
days, and the Napoleons of our own.　No truth can
be plainer to the sound sense of a real Christian, than
that true glory can only be the result of great deeds
done in a just cause.　But Cortez's whole career was
one perpetual union of perfidy and blood.　His
words were not to be relied on for a moment.　His

promises of kindness and of restoration to both Montezuma and Guatimotzin, were followed only by fetters,
tortures, and hanging.

Such were the horrors of the siege of Mexico, that
Bernal Diaz says, they can be compared to nothing
but those of the destruction of Jerusalem. According
to Bernal Diaz, the slain exceeded one hundred thousand; and those who died of famine, bad food and
water, and infection, Cortez himself asserts, were
more than fifty thousand. Cortez, on gaining possession of the city, ordered all the Mexicans out of it;
and Bernal Diaz, an eye-witness, says, that " for
three days and three nights, all the three roads leading from the city, were seen full of men, women, and
children; feeble, emaciated, and forlorn, seeking
refuge where they could find it. The fetid smell
which so many thousands of putrid bodies emitted was
intolerable, and occasioned some illness to the general
of the conquerors. The houses, streets, and canals,
were full of disfigured carcases; the ground of the
city was in some places dug up by the citizens in
search of roots to feed on; and many trees stripped
of bark for the same purpose. The general caused
the dead bodies to be buried, and large quantities of
wood to be burnt through all the city, as much in
order to purify the infected air, as to celebrate his
victory."

But Providence failed not to visit the deeds of Cortez
on himself, as he had done on Columbus. Bernal Diaz
says, that "after the death of Guatimotzin, he became
gloomy and restless; rising continually from his bed,
and wandering about in the dark." That "nothing
prospered with him, and that it was ascribed to the

curses he was loaded with." His government was
acknowledged late by the crown, and soon divided
with other authorities. He returned, like Columbus,
to Europe to seek redress of wrongs heaped on *him ;*
like him, not obtaining this redress, he sought to
amuse his mind by fresh discoveries, and added Cali-
fornia to the known regions; but the attempt to soothe
his uneasy spirit was vain. Neglected, and even insulted
by the crown, to which he had thus guiltily added vast
dominions, he ended his days in the same fruitless
and heart-wearing solicitation of the court which Columbus had done before.

CHAPTER VIII.

THE SPANIARDS IN PERU.

Their quiver is an open sepulchre; they are all mighty men.
Jeremiah v. 16.
They are cruel and have no mercy, their voice roareth like the sea;
and they ride upon horses set in array as men of war.
Jeremiah vi. 23.

THE scene widened, and with it the rapacity and rage
for gold in the Spaniards. The possession and the
plunder of Mexico only served to whet their appetite
for carnage, and for one demon of avarice and cruelty
to raise up ten. They had seen enough to convince

them that the continent which they had reached was immense, and Mexico filled their imagination with abundance of wealthy empires to seize upon and devour. Into these very odd Christians, not the slightest atom of Christian feeling or Christian principle ever entered. They were troubled with no remorse for the horrible excesses of crime and ravage which they had committed. The cry of innocent nations that they had plundered, enslaved, and depopulated, and which rose to heaven fearfully against them, never seemed to pierce the proud brutishness of their souls. They had but one idea: that all these swarming nations were revealed to them by Providence for a prey. The Pope had given them up to them; and they had but one feeling,—a fiery, quenchless, rabid lust of gold. That they might enlighten and benefit these nations—that they might establish wise and beneficent relations with them; that they might enrich themselves most innocently and legitimately in the very course of dispensing equivalent advantages, never came across their brains. It was the spirit of the age, coolly says Robertson—but he does not tell us how such came to be its spirit, after a thousand years of the profession of Christianity. We have seen how that came to pass; and we must go on from that time to the present, tracing the dreadful effects of the substitution of Popery for Christian truth and mercy.

Rumours of lands lying to the south came ever and anon upon the eager ears of the Spaniards,—lands still more abundant in gold, and vast in extent. On all hands the locust-armies of Moloch and Mammon were swarming, "seeking whom they might devour:"

and amongst these beautiful specimens of the teaching of the infallible and holy Mother Church, were three individuals settled in Panama, who were busily employed in concocting a scheme of discovery and of crime, of blood and rapine, southward; and who were destined to succeed to a marvellous degree. These worthy personages, who were occupied with so commendable and truly Catholic a speculation as that of finding out some peaceful or feeble people whom they might, as a matter of business, fall upon, plunder, and if necessary, assassinate, for their own aggrandizement—were no other than Francis Pizarro, the bastard of a Spanish gentleman, by a very low woman, who had been employed by his father in keeping his hogs till he run away and enlisted for a soldier; Diego de Almagro, a foundling; and Hernando de Luque, schoolmaster, and priest! a man who, by means which are not related, but may be imagined, had scraped together sufficient money to inspire him with the desire of getting more.

Pizarro was totally uneducated, except in hog-keeping, and the trade of a mercenary. He could not even read; and was just one of the most hardened, unprincipled, crafty, and base wretches which history in its multitudinous pages of crime and villany, has put on record. Almagro was equally daring, but had more honesty of character; and as for Luque, he appears to have been a careful, cunning attender to the main chance. Having clubbed together their little stock of money, and their large one of impudent hardihood, they procured a small vessel and a hundred and twelve men, and Pizarro taking the command, set out in quest of whatever good land fortune and the Pope's bull might put in their way. For some time their fortune was no better than their object deserved; they were tossed about by tempestuous weather, exposed to great hardships, and discouraged by the prudential policy of the governor of Panama; but at length, in 1526, about seven years after Cortez had entered Mexico, they came in sight of the coast of Peru, and landing at a place called Tumbez, where there was a palace of the Incas, were delighted to find that they were in a beautiful and cultivated country, where the object of their desires—gold, was in wonderful abundance.

Having found the thing they were in quest of—a country to be harried, and having the Pope's authority to seize on it, they were now in haste to get that of the emperor. The three speculators agreed amongst themselves on the manner in which they would share the country they had in view. Pizarro was to be governor; Almagro, lieutenant-governor; and Luque, having the apostle's warrant, that he who desires a bishopric, desires a good thing, desired that—he was to be bishop of this new country. These preliminaries being agreed upon, Pizarro was sent off to Spain. Here he soon shewed his associates what degree of faith they were to put in him. He procured the governorship for himself, and not being ambitious of a bishopric, he got that for Luque; but poor Almagro was dignified with the office of commandant of the fortress of Tumbez—when such fortress should be raised. Almagro was, as might be expected, no little enraged at this piece of cool villany, especially when he compared it with the titles and the powers which Pizarro had secured to himself, viz.—a country of two hundred leagues in extent, in which he was to exercise the supreme authority, both civil and military, with the title of Governor, Adelantado and Captain-general. To appease this natural resentment, the greedy adventurer agreed to surrender the office of Adelantado to Almagro; and having thus parcelled out the poor Peruvians and their country in imagination, they proceeded to do it in reality. But before we follow them to the scene of their operations, let us for a moment pause, and note exactly what was the actual affair which they were thus comfortably proposing to themselves as a means of making their fortunes, and for which they had thus the ready sanction of Pope and Emperor.

Peru,—a splendid country, stretching along the coast of the Pacific from Chili to Quito, a space of fifteen hundred miles. Inland, the mighty Andes lifted their snowy ridges, and at once cooled and diversified this fine country with every variety of scene and temperature. Like Mexico, it had once consisted of a number of petty and savage states, but had been reduced into one compact and well-ordered empire by the Incas, a race of mysterious origin, who had ruled it about four hundred years. The first appearance of this race in Peru is one of the most curious and inexplicable mysteries of American history. Manco Capac and Mama Ocollo, a man and woman of commanding aspects, and clad in garments suitable to the climate, appeared on the banks of the lake Titiaca, declaring that they were the children of the Sun, sent by him, who was the parent of the human race, to comfort and instruct them. They were received by the Peruvians with all the reverence which their claims demanded. They taught the men agriculture, and the women spinning and weaving, and other domestic arts. Who these people might be, it is in vain to imagine; but if we are to judge from the nature of their institutions, they must have been of Asiatic origin, and might by some circumstances of which we now can know nothing, be driven across the Pacific to these shores. The worship of the sun, which they introduced; the perfect despotism of the government; the inviolable sanctity of the reigning family, all point to Asia for their origin. They soon, however, raised the Peruvians above all the barbarous nations by whom they were surrounded; and one by one they added these nations to their own kingdom, till Peru had grown into the wide and populous realm that the Spaniards found it. That they had made great progress in the arts of smelting, refining, and working in the precious metals, the immense quantity of gold and silver vessels found by the Spaniards testify. Their agriculture was admirable: they had introduced canals and reservoirs for irrigating the dry and sandy parts of the country; and employed manures with the greatest judgment and effect. They had separated the royal family from the public, it is true, by the very singular constitution of marrying only in the family, but they had given to all the people a common proportion of labour in the lands, and a common benefit in their produce. They had established public couriers, like the Mexicans, and constructed bridges of ropes, formed of the cord-like running plants of the country, and thrown them across the wildest torrents. They had at the time the Spaniards entered the country, two roads running the whole length of the kingdom; one along the mountains, which must have cost incalculable labour, in hewing through rocks and filling up the deepest chasms, the other along the lower country. These roads had at that time no equals in Europe, and are said by the Inca, Garcillasso de la Vega, to have been constructed in the reign of Huana Capac, the father of Atahualpa, the Inca whom they found on the throne. In some of the finest situations, he says that the Indians had cut steps up to the summits of the Andes, and constructed platforms, so that when the Inca was travelling, the bearers of his litter could carry him up with ease, and allow him to enjoy a survey of the splendid views around and below. These were evidences of great advances in civilization, but there were particulars in which they were far more civilized than their invaders, and far more Christian too. Their Incas conquered only to civilize and improve the adjoining states. They were advocates for peace, and the enjoyment of its blessings. They even forbad the fishing for pearls, because, says Garcillasso, they preferred the preservation of their people, rather than the accumulation of wealth, and would not consent to the sufferings which the divers must necessarily undergo. When did the Christians ever shew so much true philanthropy and human feeling?

And these are the people whom Robertson, falling miserably in with the views, or rather, the pretensions of the Spaniards, says, appeared so feeble in intellect as to be incapable of receiving Christianity. The idea is a gross absurdity. What! a people who, like the Mexicans and Peruvians, had cities, temples, palaces, a regular form of government; who cultivated the ground, and refined metals, and wrought them into trinkets and vessels, not capable of receiving the simple truths of Christianity which "the wayfaring man though a fool cannot err in?" The Mexicans had introduced their hieroglyphic writing, the Peruvians their quipos, or knotted and coloured cords, by which they made calculations, and transmitted intelligence, and handed down history of facts, yet they could not understand so plain a thing as Christianity! It is the base policy of those who violate the rights of men, always to add to their other injuries that of calumniating their victims as mere brutes in capacity and in the scale of being. By turns, Negroes, Hottentots, and the whole race of the Americans, have been declared incapable of freedom, and of embracing that simple religion which was sent for the good of the whole human family. If such an absurdity needed any refutation, it has had it amply in the reception of this religion by great numbers of all these races : but the fact is, that it would have been a disgrace to the understanding of the American Indians to have embraced the wretched stuff which was presented to them by the Spaniards as Christianity. A wooden cross was presented to the wondering natives, and they were expected instantly to bow down to it, and to acknowledge the pope, a person they had never heard of till that moment, or they were to be instantly cut to pieces, or burnt alive. No pains were taken to explain the beautiful truths of the Christian revelation —those truths, in fact, were lost in the rubbish of papal mummeries, and violent dogmas; and what could the astonished people see in all this but a species of Moloch worship in perfect keeping with the despe-

rate and rapacious character of the invaders? Garcillasso de la Vega, the Inca, tells us that Huana Capac, a
prince whose life had more of the elements of true
Christianity in it than those of the Spaniards altogether, being full of love and humanity, was accustomed to say, that he was convinced that the sun was
not God, because he always went on one track through
the heavens,—that he had no liberty to stop, or to
turn out of his ordinary way, into the wide fields of
space around him; and that it was clear that he was
therefore only a servant, obeying a higher power.
The Peruvians had, like the Athenians, an unknown
god, to whom they had a temple, and whom they
called Pachacamac, but as he was invisible and
was everywhere, they could not conceive any shape
for him, and therefore worshipped him in the secret of
their hearts. How ridiculous to say that people who
had arrived at such a pitch of reasoning, and at such
practice of the beneficent principles of love and humanity which Christianity inculcates, were incapable
of embracing doctrines so consonant to their own
views and habits.

How lamentable, that a British historian should
suffer himself to follow the wretched calumnies of
Buffon and De Paw against the Americans, with the
examples of Mexico and Peru, and the effects of the
Jesuit missions staring him in the face. The Spaniards and Portuguese, as we shall presently see, and as
Robertson must have known, soon found that the
Indians were delighted to embrace Christianity, even
in the imperfect form in which it was presented to
them, and by thousands upon thousands exhibited the
beauty of Christian habits as strikingly as these Europeans did the most opposite qualities.

But the strangest remark of Robertson is, " that the fatal defect of the Peruvians was their unwarlike character." Fatal, indeed, their inability to contend with the Europeans proved to them; but what a burlesque on the religion of the Europeans—that the *peaceful* character of an innocent people should prove fatal to them only from—*the followers of the Prince of Peace!*

But the fact is, that the Peruvians as well as the Mexicans were not unwarlike. On the contrary, by their army they had extended and consolidated their empire to a surprising extent. They had vanquished all the nations around them; and it was only the bursting upon them of a new people, with arts so novel and destructive as to confound and paralyse their minds, that they were so readily overcome. A variety of circumstances combined to prostrate the Americans before the Europeans. Those prophecies to which we have alluded, the fire-arms, the horses, the military movements, and the very art of writing, all united their influence to render them totally powerless. The Inca, Garcillasso, says that at the period of Pizarro's appearance in Peru, many prodigies and omens troubled the public mind, and prepared them to expect some terrible calamity. There was a comet— the tides rose and fell with unusual violence—the moon appeared surrounded by three bands of different colours, which the priests interpreted to portend civil war, and total change of dynasty. He says that the fire-arms, which vomited thunder and lightning, and mysteriously killed at a distance—the neighing and prancing of the war-horses, to people who had never seen creatures larger than a llama, and the art of conveying their thoughts in a bit of paper above all, gave them notions of the spiritual intercourse of these invaders, that it was totally hopeless to contend against. The very cocks, birds which were unknown there before their introduction by the Spaniards, were imagined to pronounce the name of Atahualpa, as they crew in triumph over him, and became called Atahualpas, or Qualpas, after him. He assures us that even after the Spaniards had become entire masters of the country, the Indians on meeting a horseman on the highway, betrayed the utmost perturbation, running backward and forward several times, and often falling on their faces till he was gone past. And he relates an anecdote, which amusing as it is, shews at once what was the effect of the art of writing, and that the humblest natives did not want natural ingenuity even in their deepest simplicity. The steward of Antonio Solar, a gentleman living at a distance from his estate, sent one day by two Indians ten melons to him. With the melons he gave them a letter, and said at the same time — "now mind you don't eat any of these, for if you do this letter will tell." The Indians went on their way; but as it was very hot, and the distance four leagues, they sate down to rest, and becoming very thirsty, longed to eat one of the melons. "How unhappy are we that we cannot eat a melon that grows in our master's ground."—"Let us do it," says one—"Ah," said the other, "but then the letter."—"Oh," replied the first speaker, "we can manage that—we will put the letter under a stone, and what it does not see it cannot tell." The thing was done; the melon eaten, and afterwards another, that they might take in an equal number. Antonio Solar read the letter, looked at the melons, and instantly exclaimed—" But where are the other two ?" The confounded Indians declared, that those were all they had received. " Liars," replied Antonio Solar, " I tell you, the letter says you had ten, and you have eaten two !" It was no use persisting in the falsehood—the frightened Indians ran out of the house, and concluded that the Spaniards were more than mortal, while even their letter watched the Indians, and told all that they did.

Such were the Peruvians ; children in simplicity, but possessing abundant ingenuity, and principles of human action far superior to their invaders, and capable of being ripened into something peculiarly excellent and beautiful. Twelve monarchs had reigned over them, and all of them of the same beneficent character. Let us now see how the planters of the Cross conducted themselves amongst them.

CHAPTER XI.

THE SPANIARDS IN PERU—CONTINUED.

For gold the Spaniard cast his soul away :
His gold and he were every nation's prey.—*Montgomery*.

THE three speculators of Panama had made up their
band of mercenaries, or what the Scotch very expres-
sively term " rank rievers," to plunder the Peruvians.
These consisted of one hundred and eighty men,
thirty of whom were horsemen. These were all they
could raise; and these were sufficient, as experience
had now testified, to enable them to overrun a vast
empire of Americans. Almagro, however, remained
behind, to gather more spoilers together as soon as
circumstances would permit, and Pizarro took the
command, of his troop, and landed in the Bay of
St. Matthew, in the north of the kingdom. He resolved to conduct his march southward so near to the
coast as to keep up the communication with his vessels ;
and falling upon the peaceable inhabitants, he went
on fighting, fording rivers, wading through hot sands,
and inflicting so many miseries upon his own followers and the natives, as made him look more like an

avenging demon than a man. It is not necessary
that we should trace very minutely his route. In
the province of Coaque they plundered the people of
an immense quantity of gold and silver. From the
inhabitants of the island of Puna,, he met with a
desperate resistance, which cost him six months to
subdue, and obliged him to halt at Tumbez, to restore
the health of his men. Here he received a reinforce-
ment of troops from Nicaragua, commanded by Sebastian Benalcazor, and Hernando Soto. Having also his
brothers, Ferdinand, Juan, and Gonzalo, and his uncle
Francisco de Alcantara, with him in this expedition,
he pushed forwards towards Caxamalca, destroying and
laying waste before him. Fortunately for him, that
peace and unity which had continued for four hundred
years in Peru, was now broken by two contending
monarchs, and as unfortunately for the assertion of
Robertson, that the Peruvians were unwarlike, they
were at this moment in the very midst of all the fury
of a civil war. The late Inca, Huana Capac, had
added Quito to the realm, and at his death, had left
that province to Atahualpa, his son by the daughter
of the conquered king of Quito. His eldest son, who
ascended the throne of Peru, demanded homage of
Atahualpa or surrender of the throne of Quito; but
Atahualpa was too bold and ambitious a prince for
that, and the consequence was a civil contest. So
engrossed were the combatants in this warfare, that
they had no time to watch, much less to oppose, the
progress of the Spaniards. Pizarro had, therefore,
advanced into the very heart of the kingdom when Atahualpa had vanquished his brother, put him in prison,
and taken possession of Peru. Having been solicited

during the latter part of his march by both parties to espouse their cause, and holding himself in readiness to act as best might suit his interests, he no sooner found Atahualpa in the ascendant, than he immediately avowed himself as his partizan, and declared that he was hastening to his aid. Atahualpa was in no condition to repulse him. He was in the midst of the confusions necessarily existing on the immediate termination of a civil war. His brother, though his captive, was still held by the Peruvians to be their rightful monarch, and it might be of the utmost consequence to his security to gain such extraordinary and fearful allies. The poor Inca had speedy cause to rue the alliance. Pizarro determined, on the very first visit of Atahualpa to him in Caxamalca, to seize him as Cortez had seized on Montezuma. He did not wait to imitate the more artful policy of Cortez, but trusted to the now too well known ascendency of the Spanish arms, to take him without ceremony. He and his followers now saw the amazing wealth of the country, and were impatient to seize it. The capture of the unsuspecting Inca is one of the most singular incidents in the history of the world; a mixture of such naked villany, and impudent mockery of religion, as has scarcely a parallel even in the annals of these Spanish missionaries of the sword—these red-cross knights of plunder. He invited Atahualpa to an interview in Caxamalca, and having drawn up his forces round the square in which he resided, awaited the approach of his victim. The following is Robertson's relation of the event:—

"Early in the morning the Peruvian camp was all in motion. But as Atahualpa was solicitous to appear with the greatest splendour and magnificence in his first interview with the strangers, the preparations for this were so tedious, that the day was far advanced before he began his march. Even then, lest the order of the procession should be deranged, he moved so slowly, that the Spaniards became impatient, and apprehensive that some suspicion of their intention might be the cause of this delay. In order to remove this, Pizarro dispatched one of his officers with fresh assurances of his friendly disposition. At length the Inca approached. First of all appeared four hundred men, in an uniform dress, as harbingers to clear the way before him. He himself, sitting on a throne or couch, adorned with plumes of various colours, and almost covered with plates of gold and silver, enriched with precious stones, was carried on the shoulders of his principal attendants. Behind him came some chief officers of his court, carried in the same manner. Several bands of singers and dancers accompanied this cavalcade; and the whole plain was covered with troops, amounting to more than thirty thousand men.

" As the Inca drew near to the Spanish quarters, Father Vincent Valverde, chaplain to the expedition, advanced with a crucifix in one hand and a breviary in the other, and in a long discourse explained to him the doctrine of the creation; the fall of Adam; the incarnation, the sufferings, and resurrection of Jesus Christ; the appointment of St. Peter as God's vicegerent on earth; the transmission of his apostolic power by succession to the Popes; the donation made to the king of Castile by Pope Alexander, of all the regions in the New World. In consequence of all this, he required Atahualpa to embrace the Christian faith; to acknowledge the supreme jurisdiction of the Pope, and to submit to the king of Castile as his lawful sovereign; promising, if he complied instantly with his requisition, that the Castilian monarch would protect his dominions, and permit him to continue in the exercise of his royal authority; but if he should impiously refuse to obey this summons, he denounced war against him in his master's name, and threatened him with the most dreadful effect of his vengeance.

"This strange harangue, unfolding deep mysteries, and alluding to unknown facts, of which no powers of eloquence could have conveyed at once a distinct idea to an American, was so lamely translated by an unskilful interpreter, little acquainted with the idiom of the Spanish tongue, and incapable of expressing himself with propriety in the language of the Inca, that its general tenor was altogether incomprehensible to Atahualpa. Some parts of it, of more obvious meaning, filled him with astonishment and indignation. His reply, however, was temperate. He began with observing, that he was lord of the dominions over which he reigned by hereditary succession; and added, that he could not conceive how a foreign priest should pretend to dispose of territories which did not belong to him; that if such a preposterous grant had been made, he, who was the rightful possessor, refused to confirm it. That he had no inclination to renounce the religious institutions established by his ancestors; nor would he forsake the service of the Sun, the immortal divinity whom he and his people revered, in order to worship the God of the Spaniards who was subject to death. That, with re-·

spect to other matters contained in this discourse, as he had never heard of them before, and did not understand their meaning, he desired to know where the priest had learned things so extraordinary. " In this book," answered Valverde, reaching out to him his Breviary. The Inca opened it eagerly, and turning over the leaves, lifted it to his ear. " This," said he, " is silent; it tells me nothing;" and threw it with disdain to the ground. The enraged monk, running towards his countrymen, cried out, ' To arms! Christians, to arms! The word of God is insulted; avenge this profanation on these impious dogs!'

" Pizarro, who, during this long conference, had with difficulty restrained his soldiers, eager to seize the rich spoils of which they had now so near a view, immediately gave the signal of assault. At once the martial music struck up, the cannon and muskets began to fire, the horses sallied out fiercely to the charge; the infantry rushed on, sword in hand. The Peruvians, astonished at the suddenness of an attack which they did not expect, and dismayed with the destructive effects of the fire-arms, and the irresistible impression of the cavalry, fled with universal consternation on every side, without attempting either to annoy the enemy or to defend themselves. Pizarro, at the head of his chosen band, advanced directly towards the Inca; and though his nobles crowded round him with officious zeal, and fell in numbers at his feet, while they vied with one another in sacrificing their own lives that they might cover the sacred person of their sovereign, the Spaniards soon penetrated to the royal seat, and Pizarro seizing the Inca by the arm, dragged him to the ground, and carried him as a prisoner to his quarters. The fate of the monarch increased the precipitate flight of his followers. The Spaniards pursued them towards every quarter, and, with deliberate and unrelenting barbarity, continued to slaughter the wretched fugitives, who never once offered to resist. The carnage did not cease till the close of the day. *Above four thousand Peruvians were killed. Not a single Spaniard fell, nor was one wounded,* but Pizarro himself, whose hand was slightly hurt by one of his own soldiers, while struggling eagerly to lay hold on the Inca.

" The plunder of the field was rich beyond any idea which the Spaniards had yet formed concerning the wealth of Peru, and they were so transported with the value of their acquisition, as well as the greatness of their success, that they passed the night in the extravagant exultation natural to indigent adventurers on such an extraordinary change of fortune."

Daring, perfidious, and every way extraordinary as this capture of the Inca was, his ransom was still more extraordinary. Observing the insatiable passion of the Spaniards for gold, he offered to fill the room in which he was kept with vessels of gold as high as he could reach. This room was twenty-two feet in length, and sixteen in breadth ; and the proposal being immediately agreed to, though never for a moment meant on the part of the Spaniards to be fulfilled, a line was drawn along the walls all round the room to mark the height to which the gold was to rise. Instantly the Inca, in the simple joy of his heart at the hope of a liberty which he was never to enjoy, issued orders to his subjects to bring in the gold; and from day to day the faithful Indians came in laden from all quarters with the vessels of gold. The sight must have been more like a fairy dream, than any earthly reality. The splendid and amazing mass, such as no mortal eyes on any other occasion probably ever witnessed, soon rose to near the stipulated height, and the avarice of the soldiers, and the joy of Atahualpa rose rapidly with it. But the exultation of the Inca received a speedy and cruel blow. He learned that fresh troops of Spaniards had arrived, and that those in whose hands he was, had been tampering with Huascar, his brother, in his prison. Alarmed lest, after all, they should, on proffer of a higher price, liberate his brother, and detain himself, the wretched Inca was driven in desperation to the crime of dooming his brother to death. He issued his order, and it was done. Scarcely was this effected, when the Spaniards, unable to wait for the gold quite reaching the mark, determined to part it; and orders were given to melt the greater portion of it down. They chose the festival of St. James, the patron saint of Spain, as the most suitable to distinguish by this act of national plunder, and proceeded to appropriate the following astonishing sums.—Certain of the richest vessels were set aside first for the crown. Then the fifth claimed by the crown was set apart. Then a hundred thousand pesos, equal to as many pounds sterling, were given to the newly arrived army of Almagro. Then Pizarro and his followers divided amongst them, one million five hundred and twenty-eight thousands five hundred pesos: every horseman obtained above eight thousand, and every footman four!

Imagine the privates of an army of foot soldiers pocketing for prize-money, each four thousand pounds!

the troopers each eight thousand! But enormous as
this seems, there is no doubt that it would have been
vastly more had the natives been as confident in the
faith of the Spaniards as they had reason to be of the
reverse. The Inca, Garcillasso, and some of the Spanish historians, tell us that on the Spaniards displaying
their greedy spirit of plunder, vast quantities of treasure vanished from public view, and never could be
discovered again. Amongst these were the celebrated
emerald of Manta, which was worshipped as a divinity; was as large as an ostrich egg, and had smaller
emeralds offered to it as its children; and the chain of
gold made by order of Huana Capac, to surround the
square at Cuzco on days of solemn dancing, and was
in length seven hundred feet, and of the thickness of a
man's wrist.

The Inca having fulfilled, as far as the impatience of
the Spaniards would permit him, his promises, now
demanded his freedom. Poor man! his tyrants never
intended to give him any other freedom than the freedom of death. They held him merely as a lure, by
which to draw all the gold and the power of his kingdom
into their hands. But as, after this transaction, they
could not hope to play upon him much further, they
resolved to dispatch him. The new adventurers who
had arrived with Almagro were clamorous for his destruction, because they looked upon him as a puppet
in the hands of Pizarro, by which he would draw away
gold that might otherwise fall into their hands. The
poor Inca too, by an unwitting act, drew this destruction more suddenly on his own head. Struck with
admiration at the art of writing, he got a soldier to
write the word Dios (God) on his thumb-nail, and

shewing it to everybody that came in, saw with surprise that every man knew in a moment the meaning of it. When Pizarro, however, came, he could not read it, and blushed and shewed confusion. Atahualpa saw, with a surprise and contempt which he could not conceal, that Pizarro was more ignorant than his own soldiers; and the base tyrant, stung to the quick with the affront which he might suppose designed, resolved to rid himself of the Inca without delay. For this purpose, he resorted to the mockery of a trial; appointed himself, and his companion in arms, Almagro, the very man who had demanded his death, judges, and employed as interpreter, an Indian named Philippillo, who was notoriously desirous of the Inca's death, that he might obtain one of his wives. This precious tribunal charged the unfortunate Inca with being illegitimate; with having dethroned and put to death his brother; with being an idolater—the faith of the country; with having a number of concubines—the custom of the country too ; with having embezzled the royal treasures, which he had done to satisfy these guests, and for which he ought now to have been free, had these wretches had but the slightest principle of right left in them. On these and similar charges they condemned him to be burnt alive! and sent him instantly to execution, only commuting his sentence into strangling instead of burning, on his agreeing, in his terror and astonishment, to acknowledge the Christian faith! What an idea he must have had of the Christian faith !

The whole career of Pizarro and his comrades, and especially this last unparalleled action, exhibit them as such thoroughly desperado characters—so har-

dened into every thing fiendly, so utterly destitute of
every thing human, that nothing but the most fearful
scene of misery and crime could follow whenever they
were on the scene; and Peru, indeed, soon was one
wide field of horror, confusion, and oppression. The
Spaniards had neither faith amongst themselves, nor
mercy towards the natives, and therefore an army of
wolves fiercely devouring one another, or Pandemo-
nium in its fury can only present an image of Peru
under the herds of its first invaders. It is not my
province to follow the quarrels of the conquerors
further than is necessary to shew their effect on the
natives; and therefore I shall now pass rapidly over
matters that would fill a volume.

Pizarro set up a son of Atahualpa as Inca, and held
him as a puppet in his hands; but the Peruvians set
up Manco Capac, brother of Huana; and as if the
example of the perfidy of the Spaniards had already
communicated itself to the heretofore orderly Peruvians, the general whom Atahualpa had left in Quito,
rose and slew the remaining family of his master, and
assumed that province to himself. The Spaniards
rejoiced in this confusion, in which they were sure to
be the gainers. The adventurers who had shared
amongst them the riches of the royal room, had now
reached Spain with Ferdinand Pizarro at their head,
bearing to the court the dazzling share which fell to
its lot. Honours were showered on Pizarro and his
fellow-marauders,—fresh hosts of harpies set out for
this unfortunate land, and Pizarro marching to Cuzco,
made tremendous slaughter amongst the Indians, and
took possession of that capital and a fresh heap of
wealth more enormous than the plunder of Atahu-

alpa's room. To keep his fellow officers, thus flushed with intoxicating deluges of affluence, in some degree quiet, he encouraged them to undertake different expeditions against the natives. Benalcazar fell on Quito,—Almagro on Chili; but the Peruvians were now driven to desperation, and taking the opportunity of the absence of those forces, they rose, and attacked their oppressors in various quarters. The consequence was what may readily be supposed—after keeping the Spaniards in terror for some time, they were routed and slaughtered by thousands. But no sooner was this over than the Spaniards turned their arms against each other. " Civil discord," says Robertson, " never raged with a more fell spirit than amongst the Spaniards in Peru. To all the passions which usually envenom contests amongst countrymen, avarice was added, and rendered their enmity more ravenous. Eagerness to seize the valuable forfeitures expected upon the death of every opponent, shut the door against mercy. To be wealthy, was of itself sufficient to expose a man to accusation, or to subject him to punishment. On the slightest suspicions, Pizarro condemned many of the most opulent inhabitants in Peru to death. Carvajal, without seeking for any pretext to justify his cruelty, cut off many more. The number of those who suffered by the hand of the executioner, was not much inferior to what fell in the field; and the greater part was condemned without the formality of any legal trial."

Providence exhibited a great moral lesson in the fate of these discoverers of the new world. As they shewed no regard to the feelings or the rights of their fellow men, as they outraged and disgraced every principle of the sacred religion which they professed, scarcely one of them but was visited with retributive vengeance even in this life; and many of them fell miserably in the presence of the wretched people they had so ruthlessly abused, and not a few by each other's hands. We have already shewn the fortunes of Columbus and Cortez; that of Pizarro and his lawless accomplices is still more striking and awful. Almagro, one of the three original speculators of Panama, was the first to pay the debt of his crimes. A daring and rapacious soldier, but far less artful than Pizarro, he had, from the hour that Pizarro deceived him at the Spanish court, and secured honours and commands to himself at his expense, always looked with suspicious eyes upon his proceedings, and sought advancement rather from his own sword than from his old but perfidious comrade. Chili being allotted to him, he claimed the city of Cuzco as his capital;—a bloody war with the Pizarros was the consequence; Almagro was defeated, taken prisoner, and put to death, being strangled in prison and afterwards publicly beheaded. But Pizarro's own fate was hastened by this of his old comrade. The friends of Almagro rallied round young Almagro his son. They suddenly attacked Pizarro in his house at noon, and on a Sunday; slew his maternal uncle Alcantara, and several of his other friends, and stabbed him mortally in the throat. The younger Almagro was taken in arms against the new governor, Vaca de Castro, and publicly beheaded in Cuzco; five hundred of these adventurers falling in the battle itself, and forty others perishing with him on the scaffold. Gonzalo Pizarro, after maintaining a war against the viceroy Nugnez Vela, defeating and killing him, was himself defeated by Gasca, and put to death, with Carvajal and some other of the most notorious offenders.

Such were the crimes and the fate of the Spaniards in Peru. Robertson, who relates the deeds of the Spanish adventurers in general with a coolness that is marvellous, thus describes the character of these men.

" The ties of honour, which ought to be held sacred amongst soldiers, and the principle of integrity, interwoven as thoroughly in the Spanish character as in that of any nation, seem to have been equally forgotten. Even the regard for decency, and the sense of shame were totally lost. During their dissensions, there was hardly a Spaniard in Peru who did not abandon the party which he had originally espoused, betray the associates with whom he had united, and violate the engagements under which he had come. The viceroy Nugnez Vela was ruined by the treachery of Cepeda and the other judges of the royal audience, who were bound by the duties of their function to have supported his authority. The chief advisers and companions of Gonzalo Pizarro's revolt were the first to forsake him, and submit to his enemies. His fleet was given up to Gasca by the man whom he had singled out among his officers to entrust with that important command. On the day that was to decide his fate, an army of veterans, in sight of the enemy, threw down their arms without striking a blow, and deserted a leader who had often led them to victory... It is only where men are far removed from the seat of government, where the restraints of law and order are little felt; where the prospect of gain is unbounded, and where immense wealth may cover the crimes by which it is acquired, that we can find any parallel to the cruelty, the rapaciousness, the perfidy and corruption prevalent amongst the Spaniards in Peru."

While such was their conduct to each other, we may very well imagine what it was to the unhappy natives. These fine countries, indeed, were given up to universal plunder and violence. The people were everywhere pursued for their wealth, their dwellings ransacked without mercy, and themselves seized on as slaves. As in the West Indian Islands and in Mexico, they were driven to the mines, and tasked without regard to their strength,—and like them, they perished with a rapidity that alarmed even the Court of Spain, and induced them to send out officers to inquire, and to stop this waste of human life. Las Casas again filled Spain with his loud remonstrances, but with no better success. When their viceroys, visitors, and superintendents arrived, and published their ordinances, requiring the Indians to be treated as free subjects, violent outcries and furious remonstrances, similar to what England has in modern times received from the West Indies when she has wished to lighten the chains of the negro, were the immediate result. The oppressors cried out that they should all be ruined,—that they were " robbed of their just rights," and there was no prospect but of general insurrection, unless they might continue to devour the blood and sinews of the unfortunate Indians. One man, the President Gasca, a simple ecclesiastic, exhibited a union of talents and integrity most remarkable and illustrious amid such general corruption; he went out poor and he returned so, from a country where the temptations to wink at evil were boundless;

and he effected a great amount of good in the reduction of civil disorder; but the protection of the Indians was beyond even his power and sagacity, and he left them to their fate.

CHAPTER X.

THE SPANIARDS IN PARAGUAY.

ONE more march in the bloody track of the Spaniards, and then, thank God! we have done with them—at least, in this hemisphere. In this chapter we shall, however, have a new feature presented. Hitherto we have seen these human ogres ranging through country after country, slaying, plundering, and laying waste, without almost a single arm of power raised to check their violence, or a voice of pity to plead successfully for their victims. The solitary cry of Las Casas, indeed, was heard in Hispaniola; but it was heard in vain. The name of Christianity was made familiar to the natives, but it was to them a terrible name, for it came accompanied by deeds of blood, and lust and infamy. It must have seemed indeed, to them, the revelation of some monstrous Moloch, more horrible, because more widely and indiscriminately destructive than any war-god of their own. How dreadful must have appeared the very rites of this religion of the white-men! They baptized thousands upon thousands, and then sent them to the life-in-death of slavery—to the consuming pestilence of the plantation and the mine. We are assured by their own authors, that the moment after they had baptized numbers of these unhappy creatures, they cut their throats that they might prevent all possibility of a relapse, and send them straight to heaven! Against these profanations of the most humane of religions, what adequate power had arisen? What was there to prove that Christianity was really the very opposite in nature to what those wretches, by their deeds, had represented it? Nothing, or next to nothing. The remonstrances and the enactments of the Spanish crown were non-existent to the Indians, for they fell dead before they reached those distant regions where such a tremendous power of avarice and despotism had raised itself in virtual opposition to authority, human or divine. Some of the ecclesiastics, indeed, denounced the violence and injustice of their countrymen; but they were few, and disconnected in their efforts, and abodes; and their assurances that the religion of Christ was in reality merciful and kind, were belied by the daily and hourly deeds of their kindred; and were doubly belied by the lives of the far greater portion of their own order, who yielded to none in unholy license, avarice, and cruelty. How could the Indians be persuaded of its divine power?—for it exhibited no power over nine-tenths of all that they saw professing it. But now there came a new era. There came an order of men who not only displayed the effects of Christian principle in themselves, but who had the sagacity to combine their efforts, till they became sufficiently powerful to make Christianity practicable, and capable of conferring some of its genuine benefits on its neophytes. These were the Jesuits—an order recent in its origin, but famous above all others for the talent, the ambition and the profound policy of its members. We need not here enter further into its general history, or inquire how far it merited that degree of odium which has attached to it in every quarter of the globe—for in every quarter of the globe it has signalised its spirit of proselytism, and has been expelled with aversion. I shall content myself with stating, that I have formerly ranked its operations in Paraguay and Brazil amongst those of its worst ambition; but more extended inquiry has convinced me that, in this instance, I, in common with others, did them grievous wrong. A patient perusal of Charlevoix's History of Paraguay, and of the vast mass of evidence brought together by Mr. Southey from the best Spanish authorities in his History of Brazil, must be more than sufficient to exhibit their conduct in these countries as one of the most illustrious examples of Christian devotion—Christian patience—Christian benevolence and disinterested virtue upon record. It gives me the sincerest pleasure, having elsewhere expressed my opinion of the general character of the order, amid the bloody and revolting scenes of Spanish violence in the New World, to point to the Jesuits as the first to stand collectively in the very face of public outrage and the dishonour of the Christian religion, as the friends of that religion and of humanity.

I do not mean to say that they exhibited Christianity in all the splendour of its unadulterated truth;—no, they had enough of the empty forms and legends, and false pretences, and false miracles of Rome, about them; but they exhibited one great feature of its spirit—love to the poor and the oppressed, and it was at once acknowledged by them to be divine. I do not mean to say that they adopted the soundest system of policy in their treatment of the Indians; for their besetting sin, the love of power and the pride of intellectual dominance, were but too apparent in it; and this prevented their labours from acquiring that permanence which they otherwise would: but they did this, which was a glorious thing in that age, and in those countries—they showed what Christianity, even in an imperfect form, can accomplish in the civilization of the wildest people. They showed to the outraged Indians, that Christianity was really a blessing where really embraced; and to the Spaniards, that their favourite dogmas of the incapacity of the Indians for the reception of divine truth, and for the patient endurance of labour and civil restraint, were as baseless as their own profession of the Christian faith. They stood up against universal power and rapacity, in defence of the weak, the innocent, and the calumniated; and they had the usual fate of such men—they were the martyrs of their virtue, and deserve the thanks and honourable remembrance of all ages.

In strictly chronological order we should have noticed the Portuguese in Brazil, before following the Spaniards to Paraguay; as Paraguay was not taken possession of by the Spaniards till about twenty years after the Portuguese had seized upon Brazil: but it is of more consequence to us to take a consecutive view of the conduct of the Spaniards in South America, than to take the settlement of different countries in exact order of time. Having with this chapter dismissed the Spaniards, we shall next turn our attention to the Portuguese in the neighbouring regions of Brazil, and then pursue our inquiries into their treatment of the natives in their colonies in the opposite regions of the world.

The Spaniards entered this beautiful country with the same spirit that they had done every other that they had hitherto discovered;—but they found here a different race. They had neither creatures gentle as those of the Lucayo Islands, nor of Peru, nor men so far civilized as these last, nor as the Mexicans to contend with. They did not find the natives of these regions appalled with their wonder, or paralysed with prophecies and superstitious fears; but like the Charaib natives, they were fierce and ferocious—tattooed and disfigured with strange gashes and pouches for stones in their faces; quick in resentment, and desperate cannibals. When Juan Diaz de Solis discovered the Plata in 1515, he landed with a party of his men in order to seize some of the natives; but they killed, roasted, and devoured, both him and his companions. Cabot, who was sent out to form a settlement there ten years afterwards, treated the natives with as little ceremony, and found them as quick to return the insult. Diego Garcia, who soon followed Cabot, came with the intention of carrying off *eight hundred slaves to Portugal*, which he actually accomplished, putting them and his vessel into the charge of a Portuguese of St. Vincente. Garcia made war on the great tribe of the Guaranies for this purpose, and thus made them hostile to the settlement of the Spaniards. In 1534, the powerful armament of Don Pedro de Mendoza, consisting of eleven ships and eight hundred men, entered the Plata, and laid the foundation of Buenos Ayres. One of his first acts was to murder his deputy-commandant, Juan Osorio; and one of the next to make war on the powerful and vindictive tribe of the Quirandies, who possessed the country round his new settlement: the consequences of which were, that they reduced him to the most horrid state of famine, burnt his town about his ears, and eventually obliged him to set sail homeward, on which voyage he died.

These were proceedings as impolitic as they were wicked, in the attempt to colonize a new, a vast, and a warlike country; but it was the mode which the Spaniards had generally practised. They seemed to despise the natives alike as enemies and as men; and they went on fighting, and destroying, and enslaving, as matters of course. As they were now in a great country, abounding with martial tribes, we must necessarily take a very rapid glance at their proceedings. They advanced up the Paraguay, under the command of Ayolas, whom Mendoza had left in command, and seized on the town of Assumpcion, a place which, from its situation, became afterwards of the highest consequence. This noble country, stretching through no less than twenty degrees of south latitude, and surrounded by the vast mountains of Brazil to the east, of Chili to the west, and of Moxos and Matto Grosso to the north, is singularly watered with some of the noblest rivers in the world, descending from the mountains on all sides, and as they traverse it in all its quarters, fall southward, one after another, into the great central stream, till they finally *debouche* in the great estuary of the Plata. Assumpcion, situated at the junction of the Paraguay and the Pilcomayo, besides the advantages of a direct navigation, was so centrally placed as naturally to be pointed out as a station of great importance in the discovery and settlement of the country.

Ayolas, whom Mendoza had left in command, having subdued several tribes of the natives to the Spanish yoke, set out up the river Paraguay in quest of the great lure of the Spaniards, gold, where he and all his men were cut off by the Indians of the Payagoa tribe. His deputy, Yrala, after sharing his fate, caught two of the Payagoas, tortured and burnt them alive; and then, spite of the fate of their comrades, and only fired by the same news of gold, resolved to follow in the same track; fresh forces in the mean time arriving from Spain, and committing fresh aggressions on the natives along the course of the river. Cabeza de Vaca being appointed Adelantado in the place of Mendoza, arrived at Assumpcion in 1542, and after subduing the two great tribes of the Guaranies and Guaycurus, set off also in the great quest of gold. He sent out expeditions, moreover, in various directions; but Vaca, though he had no scruples in conquering the Indians, was too good for the people about him. He would not suffer them to use the men as slaves, and to carry off the women. So they mutinied against him, and shipped him off for Spain. Yrala was thus again left in power, and to keep his soldiers in exercise, actually marched across the country three hundred and seventy-two leagues, and reached the confines of Peru. Returning from this stupendous march, he next attacked the Indians on the borders of Brazil, and defined the limits of the

provinces of Portugal and Spain. He then divided
the land into *Repartimientos*, as the Spaniards had
done every where else; thus giving the country to the
adventurers, and the people upon it as a part of the
property. "The settlers," says Southey, "in the
mean time, went on in those habits of lasciviousness
and cruelty which characterize the Creoles of every
stock whatever. He made little or no attempt to
check them, perhaps because he knew that any attempt would be ineffectual, . . . perhaps because he
thought all was as it should be, . . . that the Creator
had destined the people of colour to serve those of a
whiter complexion, and be at the mercy of their lust
and avarice."

By such men, Yrala, Veyaor who founded Ciudad
Real on the Parana, Chaves who founded the town of
Santa Cruz de la Sierra in Moxos, and the infamous
Zarate, were the name, power, and crimes of the Spa-
niards spread in Paraguay, when the Jesuits were
invited thither from Brazil and Peru in 1586.

This is one of the greatest events in the history of
the Spaniards in the New World. With these men
they introduced a power, which had it been permitted
to proceed, would have speedily put a stop to their
cruelties on the natives, and would eventually have
civilized all that mighty continent. But the Spaniards
were not long in perceiving this, and such a storm of
vengeance and abuse was raised, as ultimately broke
up one of the most singular institutions that ever existed, and dispersed those holy fathers and their works
as a dream.

They were, indeed, received at first with unbounded
joy. Those from Peru, says Southey, came from

Potosi; and were received at Salta with incredible joy as though they had been angels from heaven. For although the Spaniards were corrupted by plenty of slaves and women whom they had at command, they, nevertheless, regretted the want of that outward religion, the observance of which was so easily made compatible with every kind of vice. At Santiago de Estero, which was then the capital and episcopal city, triumphal arches were erected; the way was strewn with flowers; the governor, with the soldiers and chief inhabitants went out to meet them, and solemn thanksgiving was celebrated, at which the bishop chanted the Te Deum. At Corduba, they met with five brethren of their order who had arrived from Brazil: Leonardo Armenio, the superior, an Italian; Juan Salernio; Thomas Filds, a Scotchman; Estevam de Grao, and Manoel de Ortiga, both Portuguese. The Jesuits found, wherever the Spaniards had penetrated, the Indians groaning under their oppressions and licentiousness, ready to burst out, and take summary vengeance at the first opportunity; and they were on all sides surrounded by tribes of others in a state of hostile irritation, regarding the Spaniards as the most perfidious as well as powerful enemies, from whom nothing was to be hoped, and against whom every advantage was to be seized. Yet amongst these fierce tribes, the Jesuits boldly advanced, trusting to that principle which ought always to have been acted upon by those calling themselves Christians, that where no evil is intended evil will seldom be received. It is wonderful how successful this system was in their hands. With his breviary in his hand, and a cross of six feet high, which served him for a staff, the Jesuit missionary set

out to penetrate into some new region.   He was accompanied by a few converted Indians who might act
as guides and interpreters.   They took with them a
stock of maize as provision in the wilderness, where
the bows of the Indians did not supply them with
game; for they carefully avoided carrying fire-arms,
lest they should excite alarm or suspicion.   They
thus encountered all the difficulties of a wild country;
climbing mountains, and cutting their way through
pathless woods with axes; and at night, if they reached
no human habitation, they made fires to keep off the
wild beasts, and reposed beneath the forest trees.
When they arrived amongst the tribes they sought,
they explained through their interpreters, that they
came thus and threw themselves into their power, to
prove to them that they were their friends; to teach
them the arts, and to endow them with the advantages
of the Europeans.   In some cases they had to suffer for
the villanies of their countrymen—the natives being
too much exasperated by their wrongs to be able to
conceive that some fresh experiment of evil towards
them was not concealed under this peaceful shew.
But, in the far greater number of cases, their success
was marvellous.   They speedily inspired the Indians
with confidence in their good intentions towards them;
for the natives of every country yet discovered, have
been found as quick in recognizing their friends as they
have been in resenting the injuries of their enemies.
The following anecdote given by Charlevoix, is peculiarly indicative of their manner of proceeding.—
Father Monroy, with a lay-brother Jesuit, called Juan
de Toledo, had at length reached the Omaguacas,
whose cacique Piltipicon had once been baptized, but,

owing to the treatment of the Spaniards, had renounced their religion, and pursued them with every possible evil; massacred their priests; burnt their churches; and ravaged their settlements. Father Monroy was told that certain and instant death would be the consequence of his appearing before Piltipicon; but armed with all that confidence which Jesus Christ has so much recommended to the preachers of his gospel, he entered the house of the terrible cacique, and thus addressed him: " The good which I desire you, has made me despise the terrors of almost certain death; but you cannot expect much honour in taking away the life of a naked man. If, contrary to my expectation, you will consent to listen to me, all the advantage of our conversation will be yours; whereas, if I die by your hands, an immortal crown in heaven will be my reward." Piltipicon was so amazed, or rather softened by the missionary's boldness, that he immediately offered him some of the beer brewed from maize, which the Omaguacas use; and not only granted his request to proceed further up his country, but furnished him with provisions for the journey. The end of it was, that Piltipicon made peace with the Spaniards, and ultimately embraced Christianity, with all his people.

The Jesuits, once admitted by the Indians, soon convinced them that they could have no end in view but their good; and the resistance which they made to the attempts of the Spaniards to enslave them, gave them such a fame amongst all the surrounding nations as was most favourable to the progress of their plans. When they had acquired an influence over a tribe, they soon prevailed upon them to come into their settlements, which they called REDUCTIONS, and where they gradually accustomed them to the order and comforts of civilized life. These Reductions were principally situated in Guayra, on the Parana, and in the tract of country between the Parana and the Uruguay, the great river which, descending from the mountains of Rio Grande, runs southward parallel with the Parana, and debouches in the Plata. In process of time they had established thirty of these Reductions in La Plata and Paraguay, thirteen of them being in the diocese of the Assumpcion, besides those amongst the Chiquitos and other nations. In the centre of every mission was the Reduction, and in the centre of the Reduction was a square, which the church faced, and likewise the arsenal, in which all the arms and ammunition were laid up. In this square the Indians were exercised every week, for there were in every town two companies of militia, the officers of which had handsome uniforms laced with gold and silver, which, however, they only wore on those occasions, or when they took the field. At each corner of the square was a cross, and in the centre an image of the Virgin. They had a large house on the right-hand of the church for the Jesuits, and near it the public workshops. On the left-hand of the church was the public burial-ground and the widows' house. Every necessary trade was taught, and the boys were taken to the public workshops and instructed in such trades as they chose. To every family was given a house, and a piece of ground sufficient to supply it with all necessaries. Oxen were supplied from the common stock for cultivating it, and while this family was capable of doing the necessary work, this land never was taken away. Besides this private property, there were two larger portions, called Tupamba, or God's Possession, to which all the community contributed the necessary labour, and raised provisions for the aged, sick, widows, and orphans, and income for the public service, and the payment of the national tribute. The boys were employed in weeding, keeping the roads in order, and various other offices. They went to work with the music of flutes and in procession. The girls were employed in gathering cotton, and driving birds from the fields. Every one had his or her proper avocation, and officers were appointed to superintend every different department, and to see that all was going on well in shops and in fields. They had, however, their days and hours of relaxation. They were taught singing, music, and dancing, under certain regulations. On holidays, the men played at various games, shot at marks, played with balls of elastic gum, or went out hunting and fishing. Every kind of art that was innocent or ornamental was practised. They cast bells, and carved and gilded with great elegance. The women, beside their other domestic duties, made pottery, and spun and wove cotton for garments. The Jesuits exported large quantities of the Caa, or Paraguay tea, and introduced valuable improvements in the mode of its preparation.

Such were some of the regulations which the Jesuits had established in these settlements; and notwithstanding the regular system of employment kept up, the natives flocked into them in such numbers, that it required all the ingenuity of the fathers to accommodate them all. The largest of their Reductions contained as many as eight thousand inhabitants; the smallest fifteen hundred ; the average was about three thousand. To preserve that purity of morals which was inculcated, it was found necessary to obtain a royal mandate, that no Spaniard should enter these Reductions except when going to the bishop or superior. " And one thing," says Charlevoix, "greatly to their honour, was universally allowed by all the Europeans settled in South America : the converted Indians inhabiting them, no longer exhibited traces of their former proneness to vengeance, cruelty, and the grosser vices. They were no longer, in any respect, the same men they formerly were. The most cordial love and affection for each other, and charity for all men, delighted all who visited them, the infidels especially, whom their behaviour served to inspire with the most favourable opinion of the Christian religion." " It is," he adds, "no ways surprising that God should work such wonders in such pure souls; nor that those very Indians, to whom some learned doctors would not allow reason enough to be received into the bosom of the church, should be at this day one of its greatest ornaments, and perhaps the most precious portion of the flock of Christ."

There is nothing more wonderful in all the inscrutable dispensations of Providence, than that this beautiful scene of innocence and happiness should have been suffered to be broken in upon by the wolves of avarice and violence, and all dispersed as a morning dream. But the Jesuits, by their advocacy and civilization of these poor people, had raised up against them three hostile powers,—the Spaniards—the man-hunters of Santo Paulo—and political demagogues.

The Spaniards soon hated them for standing between them and their victims. They hated them for presuming to tell them that they had no right to enslave, to debauch, to exterminate them. They hated them because they would not suffer them to be given up to them as property—mere live stock—beasts of labour, in their Encomiendas. They regarded them as robbing them of just so much property, and as setting a bad example to the other Indians who were already enslaved, or were yet to be so. They hated them because their refusing them entrance into their Reductions was a standing and perpetual reproof of the licentiousness of their lives. They foresaw that if this system became universal, the very pillars of their indolent and debased existence would be thrown down: "for," says Charlevoix, " the Spaniards here think it beneath them to exercise any manual employment. Those even who are but just landed from Spain, put every stitch they have brought with them upon their backs, and set up for gentlemen, above serving in any menial capacity."

Whoever, therefore, sought to seize upon any unauthorized power in the colony, began to flatter these lazy people, by representing the Jesuits as their greatest enemies, who were seeking to undermine their fortunes, and deprive them of the services of the Indians. Such men were, Cardenas the bishop of Assumpcion, and Antequera ;—Cardenas, entering irregularly into his office in 1640, and Antequera who was sent as judge to Assumpcion in 1721, more than eighty years afterwards, and who seized on the government itself. Both attacked the Jesuits as the surest means of winning the popular favour. They knew the jealousy with which their civilization of the Indians was regarded, and they had only to thunder accusations in the public ears calculated to foment that jealousy, in order to secure the favour of the people. Accordingly, these ambitious, intriguing, and turbulent persons, made not only South America, but Europe itself ring with alarms of the Jesuits. They contended that they were ruining the growing fortunes of the Spanish states,—that they were aiming at an independent power, and were training the Indians for the purpose of effecting it. They talked loudly of wealthy mines, which the Jesuits worked while they kept their location strictly secret. These mines could never be found. They represented that they dwelt in wealthy cities, adorned with the most magnificent churches and palaces, and lived in a condition the most sensual with the Indians. These calumnies, only too well relished by the lazy and rapacious Spaniards, did not fail of their effect—the Jesuits were attacked in their Reductions, harassed in a variety of modes, and eventually driven out of the country; where circumstances connected with the less worthy members of their order in Europe, added their fatal influence to the odium already existing here. But of that anon.

During their existence in this country, the greatest curse and scourge of their Reductions were the Paulistas, or Man-hunters, of Santo Paulo in Brazil. These people were a colony of Mamelucoes, or descendants of Portuguese and Indians; and a more dreadful set of men are not upon record. Their great business was to hunt for mines, and for Indians. For this purpose they ranged through the interior, sometimes in large troops, armed and capable of reducing a strong town, at others, they were scattered into smaller parties prowling through the woods, and pouncing on all that fell into their clutches. They were fierce, savage, and merciless. They seemed to take a wild delight in the destruction of human settlements, and in the blaze of human abodes. They maintained themselves in the wilds by hunting, fishing, the plunder of the natives; and when that failed, they could subsist on the pine-nuts, and the flour prepared from the carob, or locust-tree, termed by them war-meal.

Their abominable practices had been vehemently denounced by the Jesuits of Santo Paulo, and in consequence they became bitter enemies of the order. One of their favourite stratagems, was to appear in small parties, led by commanders in the habits of Jesuits, in those places which they knew the Jesuits frequented in the hopes of making proselytes. The first thing they did there, was to erect crosses. They next made little presents to the Indians they met; distributed remedies amongst the sick; and as they were masters of the Guarani language, exhorted them to embrace the Christian religion, of which they explained to them in a few words, the principal articles. When they had, by these arts, assembled a great number of them, they proposed to them to remove to some more convenient spot, where they assured them they should want for nothing. Most of these poor creatures permitted themselves to be thus led by these wolves in sheeps' clothing, till the traitors, dropping the mask, began to tie them, cutting the throats of those who endeavoured to escape, and carried the rest into slavery. Some, however, escaped from time to time, and alarmed the whole country. This scheme served two purposes; it for a time procured them great numbers of Indians, and it cast an odium on the Jesuits, to whom it was attributed, which long operated against them. But it was not long that these base miscreants were contented with this mischief. It struck them, that the Reductions of the Jesuits in Guayra, a province adjoining their own, might be made an easy prey; and would furnish them with a rich booty of human flesh at a little cost of labour. They accordingly soon fell upon them, and the relation of the miseries and desolation inflicted on these peaceful and flourishing settlements, as given by Charlevoix, is heart-rending. Nine hundred Mamelucoes, accompanied by two thousand Indians, under one of their most famous commanders Anthony Rasposo, broke into Guayra, and beset the reduction of St. Anthony, which was under the care of Father Mola. They put to the sword all the Indians that attempted to resist; butchered, even at the foot of the altar, such as fled there for refuge; loaded the principal men with chains, and plundered the church. Some of them having entered the missionary's house, in hopes of a rich booty, finding nothing but a threadbare soutane and a few tattered shirts, told the Indians they must be very foolish to take for masters, strangers who came into their country because they had not wherewith to live in their own; that they would be much happier in Brazil, where they would want for nothing, and would not be obliged to maintain their pastors.

These were, no doubt, fine speeches to be made to

people loaded with chains, and whose relatives and countrymen had been but that instant butchered before their eyes. Father Mola in vain threw himself at the commander's feet; represented to him the innocence and simplicity of these poor Indians; conjured him by all that was most sacred, to set bounds to the fury of the soldiers; and at last, threatened them with the indignation of heaven: but these savages answered him, that it was enough to be baptized again to be admitted into heaven, and that they would make their way into it though God himself should oppose their entrance.* They carried away into slavery two thousand five hundred Indians.

Some of the prisoners escaped, and returned to join Father Mola and such of their brethren as had fled to the woods. The father, they found amid the ruins of his Reduction sunk in the deepest sorrow. However, he roused himself and persuaded them to retire with him to the Reduction of the Incarnation. The Reductions of St. Michael and of Jesus-Maria, were speedily treated in the same manner; and they set out for Santo Paulo, driving their victims before them as so many cattle. Nine months the march continued. The merciless wretches urged them for-

---

* Charlevoix gives another instance of that sort of Catholic *piety* which such ruffians as these find quite compatible with the commission of the blackest crimes. During these expeditions these man-hunters surprised the Reduction of St. Theresa, and carried off all the inhabitants. This happened a few days before Christmas; yet on Christmas day these banditti came to church, every man with a taper in his hand, in order to hear mass. The minute the Jesuit had finished, he mounted the pulpit, and reproached them in the bitterest terms for their injustice and cruelty; to all which they listened with as much calmness as if it did not at all concern them.

ward till numbers fell by the way, worn out with
fatigue and famine. The first who gave way were
sick women and aged persons; who begged in vain
that their husbands, wives, or children, might remain
with them in their dying hours. All that could be
forced on by goading and blows, were, and when
they fell, they were left to perish by the wild beasts.
Two Jesuit fathers, Mansilla and Maceta, however,
followed their unhappy people, imploring more gentleness towards the failing, and comforting the dying.
When Father Maceta first beheld his people chained
like galley slaves, he could not contain himself. He
ran up to embrace them, in spite of the cocked
muskets, with which he was threatened, and volleys
of blows poured upon him at every step. Seeing in
the throng the cazique Guiravara and his wife chained
together, he ran up to the cazique, who before his
conversion had used Father Maceta very cruelly, and
kissing his chain, told him that he was overjoyed to
be able to shew him that he entertained no resentment
of his ill usage, and would risk his life to procure his
liberty. He procured both their freedom, and that
of several other Indians, on promise of a ransom.
Thus these noble men followed their captive people
through the whole dreadful journey, administering
every comfort and hope of final liberation in their
power; and their services and sympathy, we may well
imagine, were sufficiently needed, for out of the whole
number of captives collected in Guayra, fifteen hundred only arrived in life at Santo Paulo.

But the journey of the fathers did not end here.
They could get no redress; and therefore hastened to
Rio Janeiro; and succeeding no better there, went

on to the Bay of All-Saints, to Don Diego Lewis Oliveyra, governor and captain-general of the kingdom. The governor ordered an officer to repair with them to Santo Paulo; but it was too late, the prisoners were distributed far and wide, and the commissary could not or dared not attempt to recall them. News also of fresh enterprises meditated against the Paraguay Reductions, by these hideous man-hunters, made the fathers hasten away to put their brethren upon their guard.

The story of the successive devastation of the Reductions is long. The Jesuits were compelled to retreat southward from one place to another with their wretched neophytes. The magistrates and governors gave them no aid, for they entertained no good-will towards them; and they were, even in the central ground between the Parana and Uruguay, compelled to train their people to arms, and defend themselves. It is not only a long but sorrowful recital, both of the injuries received from the Paulistas and from their own countrymen—we must therefore pass it over, and merely notice the manner of their final expulsion.

The court of Spain ordered the banishment of the Jesuits, and the authorities, only too happy to execute the order, surrounded their colleges in the night with soldiers, seized the persons of the missionaries,—their libraries and manuscripts, which in time became destroyed, an irreparable loss to historical literature. Old men in their beds even were not suffered to remain and die in peace, but were compelled to accompany the rest, till they died on their mules in the immense journey from some of the settlements, and across the wildest mountains to the sea. The words of Mr.

Southey may well close this strange and melancholy history.

" Bucarelli shipped off the Jesuits of La Plata, Tucuman, and Paraguay, one hundred and fifty-five in number, before he attacked the Reductions. This part of the business he chose to perform in person; and the precautions which he took for arresting seventy eight defenceless missionaries, will be regarded with contempt, or with indignation, as they may be supposed to have proceeded from ignorance of the real state of things, or from fear, basely affected for the purpose of courting favour by countenancing successful calumnies. He had previously sent for all the Caciques and Corregidores to Buenos Ayres, and persuaded them that the king was about to make a great change for their advantage. Two hundred soldiers from Paraguay were ordered to guard the pass of the Tebiquary; two hundred Corrientines to take post in the vicinity of St. Miguel; and he defended the Uruguay with threescore dragoons, and three companies of grenadiers. They landed at the Falls; one detachment proceeded to join the Paraguay party, and seize the Parana Jesuits; another incorporated itself with the Corrientines, and marched against those on the eastern side of the Uruguay; and the Viceroy himself advanced upon Yapeyen, and those which lay between the two rivers. The Reductions were peaceably delivered up. The Jesuits, without a murmur, followed their brethren into banishment; and Bucarelli was vile enough to take credit in his dispatches for the address with which he had so happily performed a dangerous service; and to seek favour by loading the persecuted Company with charges of the grossest and foulest calumnies.

The American Jesuits were sent from Cadiz to Italy, where Faenza and Ravenna were assigned for their places of abode. Most of the Paraguay brethren settled at Faenza. There they employed the melancholy hours of age and exile in preserving, as far as they could from memory alone (for they had been deprived of all their papers), the knowledge which they had so painfully acquired of strange countries, strange manners, savage languages, and savage man. The Company originated in extravagance and madness; in its progress it was supported and aggrandized by fraud and falsehood; and its history is stained by actions of the darkest dye. But it fell with honour. No men ever behaved with greater equanimity, under undeserved disgrace, than the last of the Jesuits; and the extinction of the order was a heavy loss to literature, a great evil to the Catholic world, and an irreparable injury to the tribes of South America.

" Bucarelli replaced the exiled missionaries by priests from the different Mendicant orders; but the temporal authority was not vested in their hands—this was vested in lay-administrators. . . . . . . Here ended the prosperity of these celebrated communities —here ended the tranquillity and welfare of the Guaranies. The administrators, hungry ruffians from the Plata, or fresh from Spain, neither knew the language nor had patience to acquire it. It sufficed for them that they could make their commands intelligible by the whip. The priests had no authority to check the enormities of these wretches; nor were they always irreproachable themselves. A year had scarce elapsed before the Viceroy discovered that the Guaranies, for the sake of escaping from this intoler-

able state of oppression, were beginning to emigrate
into the Portuguese territories, and actually soliciting
protection from their old enemies.   Upon the first
alarm of so unexpected an occurrence, Bucarelli dis-
placed all the administrators; but the new administrators were as brutal and rapacious as their predecessors; the governor was presently involved in a violent
struggle with the priests, touching their respective
powers, and the confusion which ensued, evinced how
wisely the Jesuits had acted in combining the spiritual
and temporal authorities. . . . . . . The Viceroy then
instituted a new form of administration.   The Indians
were declared exempt from all personal service, not
subject to the Encomienda system, and entitled to
possess property—a right of which, Bucarelli said,
they had been deprived by the Jesuits ; for this
governor affected to emancipate the Guaranies, and
talked of placing them under the safeguard of the law,
and purifying the Reductions from tyranny ! They
were to labour for the community under the direction
of the administrators ; and as an encouragement to
industry, the Reductions were opened to traders during
the months of February, March, and April.   The end
of all this was, that compulsory and cruel labour left
the Indians neither time nor inclination—neither heart
nor strength—to labour for themselves.   The arts
which the Jesuits had introduced, were neglected and
forgotten; their gardens lay waste ; their looms fell to
pieces ; and in these communities, where the inhabitants for many generations had enjoyed a greater
exemption from physical and moral evil than any other
inhabitants of the globe, the people were now made
vicious and miserable.   Their only alternative was to

remain, and to be treated like slaves, or fly to the woods, and take their chance as savages."

Here we must close our review of the Spaniards in the New World. Our narrative has been necessarily brief and rapid, for the history of their crimes extends over a vast continent, and through three centuries; and would, related at length, fill a hundred volumes. We have found them, however, everywhere the same —cruel, treacherous, and regardless of the feelings of humanity and the sense of justice. They have wreaked alike their vengeance on the natives of every country they have entered, and on those of their own race who dared to espouse the cause of the sufferers. This spirit continued to the last. In all their colonies, the natives, whether of Indian blood, or the Creoles descended of their own, were carefully excluded from the direction of their own affairs, and the emoluments of office. Spaniards from the mother country were sent over in rapacious swarms, to fatten on the vitals of these vast states, and return when they had sucked their fill. The retribution has followed; and Spain has not now left a single foot of all these countries which she has drenched in the blood, and filled with the groans of their native children.

Mr. Ward, in his "Mexico in 1827," says that in 1803, the number of Indians remaining in Mexico was two millions and a half; but that their history is everywhere a blank. Some have become habituated to civil life, and are excellent artizans, but the greater portion are totally neglected. That, during the Revolution, the sense of the injuries which the race had received from the Spaniards, and which seemed to have slumbered in their bosoms for three centuries, blazed up and shewed itself in the eager and burning enthusiasm with which they flocked to the revolutionary standard to throw off the yoke of their ancient oppressors. He adds, " Whatever may be the advantages which they may derive from the recent changes, and the nature of these time alone can determine, the fruits of the introduction of boasted civilization into the New World have been hitherto bitter indeed. Throughout America the Indian race has been sacrificed; nor can I discover that in New Spain any one step has been taken for their improvement. In the neighbourhood of the capital nothing can be more wretched than their appearance; and although under a republican form of government, they must enjoy, in theory at least, an equality of rights with every other class of citizens, they seemed practically, at the period of my first visit, to be under the orders of every one, whether officer, soldier, churchman, or civilian, who chose to honour them with a command."—vol. ii. p. 215.

CHAPTER XI.

THE PORTUGUESE IN BRAZIL.

THOUGH we now make our first inquiry into the conduct of the Portuguese towards the natives of their
colonies, and enter upon so immense a scene of action
as that of the vast empire of Brazil, our notice may
happily be condensed into a comparatively small
space, because the features of the settlement of Paraguay by the Spaniards, and that of Brazil by the
Portuguese are wonderfully similar. The natives
were of a like character, bold and warlike, and were
treated in like fashion. They were destroyed, enslaved, given away in Encomiendos, just as it suited
the purpose of the invaders; the Jesuits arrived, and
undertook their defence and civilization, and were
finally expelled, like their brethren of Paraguay, as
pestilential fellows, that would not let the colonists
"do as they pleased with their own."

Yanez Pinzon, the Spaniard, was the first who discovered the coast of Brazil, in A.D. 1500, and coasting northward from Cape Agostinho, he gave the
natives such a taste of the faith and intentions of the
whites as must have prepared them to resist them to

the utmost on their reappearance. Betwixt Cape Agostinho and the river Maranham, seeing a party of the natives on a hill near the shore, they landed, and endeavoured to open some degree of intercourse; but the natives not liking their appearance, attempted to drive them away, killed eight of them, wounded more, and pursued them with fury to their boat. The Spaniards, of course, did not spare the natives, and soon afterwards shewed that the natives were very much in the right in repelling them, for on entering the Maranham, where the natives *did* receive them cordially, they seized about thirty of these innocent people and carried them off for slaves.

Scarcely had Pinzon departed, when Cabral, with the Portuguese squadron, made his accidental visit to the same coast. In the following year Amerigo Vespucci was sent thither to make further discoveries, and having advanced as far southward as 52°, returned home. In 1503, he was sent out again, and effected a settlement in 18° S. in what was afterwards called the Captaincy of Porto Seguro. One of the very first acts of Portugal was to ship thither as colonists the refuse of her prisons, as Spain had done to her colonies, and as Portugal also had done to Africa and India; a horrible mode of inflicting the worst curses of European society on new countries, and of presenting to the natives under the name of Christians, men rank and fuming with every species of brutal vice and pestiferous corruption.

Ten years after the discovery of Brazil, a young noble, Diego Alvarez, who was going out on a voyage of adventure, was wrecked on the coast of Bahia, and was received with cordiality by the natives, and named

Caramuru, or the Man of Fire, from the possession of fire-arms. Here he married the daughter of the chief, and finally became the great chief himself, with a numerous progeny around him. Another man, Joam Ramalho, who also had been shipwrecked, married a daughter of the chief of Piratininga, and these circumstances gave the Portuguese a favourable reception in different places of this immense coast. In about thirty years after its discovery the country was divided into captaincies, the sugar-cane was introduced, and the work of colonization went rapidly on. The natives were attacked on all sides; they defended themselves with great spirit, but were compelled to yield before the power of fire-arms. But while the natives suffered from the colonists, the colonists suffered too from the despotism of the governors of the captaincies; a Governor-general was therefore appointed just half a century after the discovery, in the person of Thome de Sousa, and some Jesuits were sent out with him to civilize the natives.

Amongst these was Father Manoel de Nobrega, chief of the mission, who distinguished himself so nobly in behalf of the Indians. The city of Salvador, in the bay of All-Saints, was founded as the seat of government, and the Jesuits immediately began the work of civilization. There was great need of it both amongst the Indians and their own countrymen. "Indeed, the fathers," says Southey, "had greater difficulties to encounter in the conduct of their own countrymen than in the customs and disposition of the natives. During half a century, the colonization of Brazil had been left to chance; the colonists were almost without law and religion. Many settlers had never either

confessed or communicated since they entered the
country; the ordinances of the church were neglected
for want of a clergy to celebrate them, and the moral
precepts had been forgotten with the ceremonies.
Crimes which might easily at first have been prevented, had become habitual, and the habit was now
too strong to be overcome.   There were indeed individuals in whom the moral sense could be discovered,
but in the majority it had been utterly destroyed.
They were of that description of men over whom the
fear of the gallows may have some effect; the fear of
God has none.   A system of concubinage was practised among them, worse than the loose polygamy of
the savages.   The savage had as many women as
consented to become his wives—the colonist as many
as he could enslave.   There is an ineffaceable stigma
upon the Enropeans in their intercourse with those
whom they treat as inferior races—there is a perpetual contradiction between their lust and their avarice.
The planter will one day take a slave for his harlot,
and sell her the next as a being of some lower species
—a beast of labour.   If she be indeed an inferior
animal, what shall be said of the one action?   If she
be equally with himself an human being and an immortal soul, what shall be said of the other?   Either
way there is a crime committed against human nature.
Nobrega and his companions refused to administer
the sacraments of the church to those persons who
retained native women as concubines, or men as slaves.
Many were reclaimed by this resolute and Christian
conduct; some, because their consciences had not
been dead, but sleeping; others, for worldly fear,
because they believed the Jesuits were armed with

secular as well as spiritual authority. The good effect which was produced on such persons was therefore only for a season. Mighty as the Catholic religion is, avarice is mightier; and in spite of all the best and ablest men that ever the Jesuit order, so fertile of great men, has had to glory in, the practice of enslaving the natives continued."

Yet, according to the same authority, the country had not been entirely without priests; but they had become so brutal that Nobrega said, " No devil had persecuted him and his brethren so greatly as they did. These wretches encouraged the colonists in their abominations, and openly maintained that it was lawful to enslave the natives, because they were beasts; and then lawful to use the women as concubines, because they were slaves. This was their public doctrine! Well might Nobrega say they did the work of the devil. They opposed the Jesuits with the utmost virulence. Their interest was at stake. They could not bear the presence of men who said mass and performed all the ceremonies of religion gratuitously." Much less, it may be believed, who maintained the freedom of the natives.

Such were the people amongst which the Jesuits had to act, yet they set to work with their usual alacrity. Fresh brethren came out to their aid; and Nobrega was appointed Vice-provincial of Brazil. They soon ingratiated themselves with the natives by their usual affability and kindness. They zealously acquainted themselves with the language; gave presents to the children; visited the sick; but above all, stood firmly between them and the atrocities of their countrymen. When the Jesuits arrived, these atrocities had driven many tribes into the fiercest hostility, and so evident was it that nothing but these atrocities had made, or kept them hostile, that when they heard the joyful report that the Jesuits were come as friends and protectors of the Indians, and when they saw their conduct so consonant to these tidings, *they brought their bows to the governor, and solicited to be received as allies!* How universally, on the slightest opportunity, have those called savage nations shamed the Europeans styling themselves civilized, by proofs of their greater faith and disposition to peace! Amicable intercourse and civilization are the natural order of things between the powerful and enlightened, and the weak and simple, if avarice and lust did not intervene.

Nobrega and his brethren soon produced striking changes on these poor people. They persuaded them to live in peace, to abandon their old habits, to build churches and schools. The avidity of the children to learn to read was wonderful. One of the natives soon was able to make a catechism in the Tupi tongue, and to translate prayers into it. They taught them not only reading, writing, and arithmetic, but to sing in the church; an accomplishment which perfectly enchanted them. " Nobrega usually took with him four or five of these little choristers on his preaching expeditions. When they approached an inhabited place, one carried the crucifix before them, and they began singing the Litany. The savages, like snakes, were won by the voice of the charmer. They received him joyfully; and when he departed with the same ceremony, the children followed the music. He set the catechism, creed, and ordinary prayers to *sol fa;* and the pleasure of learning to sing was such a temptation, that the little Tupis sometimes ran away from their parents to put themselves under the care of the Jesuits."

Fresh coadjutors arrived, and with them the celebrated Joseph de Anchieta, who became more celebrated than Nobrega himself. Nobrega now established a college in the plains of Piratininga, and sent thither thirteen of the brethren, with Anchieta as schoolmaster. If our settlers, in the different new nations where they have located themselves, had imitated the conduct of this great man, what a world would this be now! what a history of colonization would have to be written! how different to the scene I am doomed to lay open. " Day and night," says the historian, " did this indefatigable man labour in discharging the duties of his office. There were no books for the pupils; he wrote for every one his lesson on a separate leaf, after the business of the day was done, and it was sometimes day-light before his task was completed. The profane songs that were in use, he parodied into hymns in Portugueze, Castilian, Latin and Tupinamban. The ballads of the natives underwent the same travesty in their own tongue." He did not disdain to act as physician, barber, nor even shoemaker, to win them and to benefit them.

But it was not merely in such peaceful and blessed acts that the Jesuits were obliged to employ themselves. They were soon called upon to save the very colonies from their enemies. The French entered the country, and the native tribes smarting under the wrongs which the Portuguese had heaped plentifully on them, were only too glad to unite with them against their merciless oppressors. The Jesuits defended their own settlements, and then proceeded to give one of the most splendid examples in history of the power there is in Christian principle to suspersede wars, and to extort attention and protection even from men in the fiercest irritation and resentment of injuries. While the Portuguese were making war on the Tamoyos, and other martial tribes, Nobrega denounced their proceedings as heaping injustice upon injustice, for the natives would, he said, trust in the Portuguese if they saw any hope of fair treatment—any safety from the man-hunters. But when the Indians were triumphant, and had surrounded Espirito Santo, and threatened the very existence of the place, Nobrega and Anchieta set sail for that port, everybody looking upon them as madmen rushing upon certain destruction. A more fearful, and to all but that noble faith in truth and justice which is capable of working wonders, a more hopeless enterprise never was undertaken. As they entered the port, a host of war-canoes came out to meet them; but the moment they saw that they were Jesuits, the Indians knew that they came with peaceful intentions, and dropped their hostile attitude. Spite of all the exasperation of their wrongs, and the natural presumption of success, they carried the vessel without injury or insult into port, and listened with attention to the words of the fathers.

For two months these excellent men lived in the midst of those exasperated Indians, nay, one of them remained there alone for a considerable time, labouring to soothe their wrath, to convince them of better treatment, and dispose them to peace. The fiercer natives threatened them daily with death, and with being devoured, but the better spirits and their own blameless lives protected them. They built a little church, and thatched it with palm-leaves, where they preached and celebrated mass daily, and at length effected a peace, and the salvation of the colonies; for they found that a wide-spread coalition was forming amongst the Indian tribes to sweep their oppressors out of the land.

One would have thought that such instances as these of the wisdom and sound policy of virtue, would have been enough to persuade the Portuguese to adopt more righteous measures towards the natives; but avarice and cruelty are not easily eradicated—a famine broke out—they purchased the Indians for slaves with provisions! Nothing can equal the blindness of base minds. Whenever affairs went wrong with them, the Portuguese had recourse to the Jesuits, and the Jesuits by their influence with the Indians, achieved the most signal service for them. They marched against the French, and drove them out. They built towns; they protected the state from hostile tribes. A Jesuit, with his crucifix in his hand, was of more avail at the head of armies than the most able general; but these things once accomplished, all these services were forgotten—the slave-hunters were at work again, and the colonies fell again as rapidly into troubles and consequent decline. By the end of the century, from the discovery of Brazil, the Jesuits had collected all the natives along the coast as far as the Portuguese territories reached, into their aldeas, or villages, and were busy in the work of civilization. Nothing indeed would have been easier than for them to civilize the whole country, had it been possible to civilize the Portuguese first. But their conduct to the natives was but one continued practice of treachery and outrage. When they needed their aid to defend them from their enemies, out marched the natives under their Jesuit leaders, and fought for them; and the first act of the colonists, when the victory was won, was to seize on their benefactors and portion them out as slaves. The man-hunters broke into the villages and caried off numbers, having, in fact, depopulated the whole country besides. There is no species of kidnapping, no burnings of huts, no fomenting of wars between different tribes; no horror, in short, which has made the names of Christians so infamous for the last three hundred years in Africa that had not its parallel then in Brazil.

Besides, for more than a hundred years, Brazil was the constant scene of war and contention between the European powers terming themselves Christian. French, English, and Dutch, were in turn endeavouring to seize upon one part or other of it; and every description of rapine, bloodshed, and treachery which can disgrace nations pretending to any degree of civilization was going on before the eyes of the astonished natives. What notions of Christianity must the Indians have had, when these people called themselves Christians? They saw them assailing one another, fighting like madmen for what in reality belonged to none of them; burning towns, destroying sugar plantations; massacring all, native or colonist, that fell into their hands, or seizing them for slaves. They saw bishops contending with governors, priests contending with one another; they saw their beautiful country desolated from end to end (down to 1664), and every thing which is sacred to heaven or honourable or valuable to men, treated with contempt.

—What was it possible for them to believe of Christianity, than that it was some devilish compact, which at once invested men with a terrible power, and with the will to wield it, for the accomplishment of the widest ruin and the profoundest misery?

Through all this, under all changes, whoever were masters, or whoever were contending—the Indians experienced but one lot, slavery and ruin. Laws indeed were repeatedly enacted in Portugal on their behalf—they were repeatedly declared free—but as everywhere else, they were laughed at by the colonists, or resisted with rebellious fury.

Amid this long career of violence, the only thing which the mind can repose on with any degree of pleasure, is the conduct of the Jesuits, the steady friends of justice and the Indians; and towards the latter part of this period there arrived in Maranham one of the most extraordinary men, which not only that remarkable order, but which the world has produced. This was Antonio Vieyra, a young Jesuit, who had left the favour of the king and court, and the most brilliant prospects, for the single purpose of devoting himself to the cause of the Indians. His boldness, his honesty of speech and purpose, his resolute resistance to the system of base oppression, operating through the whole mass of society around him—were perhaps equalled by his fellows; but the greatness of his talents, and the vehement splendour of his eloquence, have few equals in any age. Mr. Southey has given the substance of a sermon preached by him before the governor at St. Lewis, which so startled and moved the whole people, by the novel and fearful view in which he exhibited to them their treatment of the

Indians, that with one accord they resolved to set them free.

It is worth while here to give a slight specimen or two of this extraordinary discourse. His text was, the offer of Satan:—" All these things will I give thee, if thou wilt fall down and worship me." —" Things," said he, " are estimated at what they cost. What then did the world cost our Saviour, and what did a soul cost him ? The world cost him a word—He spoke, and it was made. A soul cost Him his life, and his blood. But if the world cost only a word of God, and a soul cost the blood of God, a soul is worth more than all the world. This Christ thought, and this the devil confessed. Yet you know how cheaply we value our souls ? you know at what rate we sell them ? We wonder that Judas should have sold his Master and his soul for thirty pieces of silver; but how many are there who offer their own to the devil for less than fifteen ! Christians ! I am not now telling you that you ought not to sell your souls, for I know that you must sell them ;—I only entreat that you will sell them by weight. Weigh well what a soul is worth, and what it cost, and then sell it and welcome ! But in what scales is it to be weighed ? You think I shall say, In those of St. Michael the archangel, in which souls are weighed. I do not require so much. Weigh them in the devil's own balance, and I shall be satisfied ! Take the devil's balance in one hand, put the whole world in one scale and a soul in the other, and you will find that your soul weighs more than the world.—' All this will I give thee, if thou wilt fall down and worship me.' . . . . . But at what a different price now does the devil purchase souls from that which he formerly offered for them? I mean in this country. The devil has not a fair in the world where they go cheaper! In the Gospel he offers all the kingdoms of the world to purchase a single soul;—he does not require so large a price to purchase all that are in Maranham. It is not necessary to offer worlds; it is not necessary to offer kingdoms, nor cities, nor towns, nor villages;—it is enough for the devil to point at a plantation, and a couple of Tapuyas, and down goes the man upon his knees to worship him! Oh what a market! A negro for a soul, and the soul the blacker of the two! The negro shall be your slave for the few days you have to live, and your soul shall be my slave through all eternity—as long as God is God! This is the bargain which the devil makes with you."

Amazing as was the effect of this celebrated sermon, of course it did not last long. But Vieyra did not rest here. He hastened to Portugal, and stated the treatment of the Indians to the king. He obtained an order, that all the Indian settlements in the state of Maranham should be under the direction of the Jesuits; that Vieyra should direct all expeditions into the interior, and settle the reduced Indians where he pleased; and that all ransomed Indians should be slaves for five years and no longer, their labour in that time being an ample compensation for their original cost. Here was a sort of apprenticeship system more favourable than the modern British one, but destined to be just as little observed.

CHAPTER XII.

THE PORTUGUESE IN BRAZIL,—CONTINUED.

I regret that my limits will not permit me to follow
further the labours and enterprises of Vieyra and
his brethren in behalf of the Indians, whom they
sought far and wide in that immense region, and
brought in thousands upon thousands into settlements, only to arouse afresh the furious opposition,
and bring down upon themselves the vengeance of
the colonists. But the history of this great strife between Christianity and Injustice, in Brazil, fills three
massy quarto volumes, and runs through three centuries. It is full of details of the deepest interest;
but there is no chapter, either in that history or any
other, more heart-rending, than that of the transfer of
the seven Reductions of the Jesuits lying east of the
Uruguay. These were ceded by Spain to Portugal
in 1750, in a treaty of demarcation.

" They contained," to use the words of Mr.
Southey, " thirty thousand Guaranies, not fresh from
the woods or half reclaimed, and therefore willing to
revert to a savage state, and capable of enduring its
exposure, hardships, and privations; but born as their

fathers and grandfathers had been, in easy servitude, and bred up in the comforts of regular domestic life. These persons, with their wives and their children, their sick and their aged, their horses, and their sheep and their oxen, were to turn out, like the children of Israel from Egypt, into the wilderness; not to escape from bondage, but in obedience to one of the most tyranical commands that ever were issued in the reck-lessness of unfeeling power." Mr. Southey adds, " Yet Ferdinand must be acquitted of intentional injustice. His disposition was such, that he would have rather suffered martyrdom than have issued so wicked an edict, had he been sensible of its inhu-manity and wickedness."

This might more readily be credited, if, when the abominable enormity of the measure was made mani-fest to him, any disposition was shewn to stop the proceedings, or make reparation for the misery in-flicted. But nothing of the kind took place. The Jesuits made immediate and earnest representations; the Indians cried out vehemently against their expatria-tion; the colonists of both countries were averse to the measure; the very governors and officers proceeded tardily with it, in the hope that the moment the evil was discovered it would be countermanded; but no such countermand was ever issued. And what was there to hinder it? The King of Spain and the Queen of Portugal, were man and wife, dwelling in one palace, and of the greatest accord in life and sen-timent; it had only to be willed by one of them, and it might, and would have been, speedily done. If ever there was a cold-blooded transaction, in which the lives and happiness of thirty thousand innocent

people were reckoned of no account in the mere tracing of a boundary line between two countries, this
appears to be one; and if ever the retribution of
heaven was displayed in this world, it would seem to
have been in the persons of the monarchs who issued
this brutal order, and suffered it to stand, spite of the
cries of the thousands of sufferers. Happy in each
other, while they thus remained insensible to the
happiness of these poor Indians, the queen was consumed by a slow and miserable malady, and the king,
a weak man of a melancholy temperament, sunk heart-
broken for her loss.

But meantime, commissioners and armies of both
Spanish and Portuguese were drawing towards the
confines of the doomed land, to carry into effect the
expulsion of its rightful inhabitants. The Jesuits
behaved with the utmost submission and propriety.
Finding that they could do nothing by remonstrance,
they offered to yield up the charge of the Reductions
to whatever parties might be appointed to receive it.
The natives appealed vehemently to the Spanish
governor. "Neither we nor our forefathers," said
they, "have ever offended the king, or ever attacked
the Spanish settlements. How then, innocent as we
are, can we believe that the best of princes would
condemn us to banishment? Our fathers, our forefathers, our brethren, have fought under the king's
banner, often against the Portuguese, often against
the savages. Who can tell how many of them have
fallen in battle, or before the walls of Nova Colonia,
so often besieged? We ourselves can shew in our
scars, the proofs of our fidelity and our courage. We
have ever had it at heart to extend the limits of the

Spanish empire, and to defend it against all enemies;
nor have we ever been sparing of our blood, or our
lives. Will then the Catholic king requite these
services by the bitter punishment of expelling us
from our native land, our churches, our homes, and
fields, and fair inheritance? This is beyond all belief! By the royal letters of Philip V., which, according to his own injunctions, were read to us from
the pulpits, we were exhorted never to suffer the
Portuguese to approach our borders, because they
were his enemies and ours. Now we are told that
the king will have us yield up, to these very Portuguese, this wide and fertile territory, which for a
whole century we have tilled with the sweat of our
brows. Can any one be persuaded that Ferdinand
the son should enjoin us to do that which was so frequently forbidden by his father Philip? But if time
and change have indeed brought about such friendship between old enemies, that the Spaniards are
desirous to gratify the Portuguese, there are ample
tracts of country to spare, and let those be given
them. What! shall we resign our towns to the Portuguese? The Portuguese!—by whose ancestors so
many hundred thousands of ours have been slaughtered, or carried away into cruel slavery in Brazil?
This is as intolerable to us, as it is incredible that it
should be required. When, with the Holy Gospels
in our hands, we promised and vowed fidelity to God
and the king of Spain, his priests and governors promised us on his part, friendship and perpetual protection,—and now we are commanded to give up our
country! Is it to be believed that the promises, and
faith, and friendship of the Spaniards can be of so
little stability?"

But the Spaniards and Portuguese advanced with their troops into their country. The poor people, driven frantic by their grief and indignation, determined to resist. They brought out their cannon, made of pieces of large cane, covered with wet hides and bound with iron hoops, and determined with such arms even, to oppose those more dreadful ones, of which they had too often witnessed the effect. For some time they repelled their enemies, and even obliged them to retire from the territory; but in the next campaign, the allied army made dreadful havoc amongst them. Yet they still remained in arms; and their sentiments may be well understood by the following characteristic extract, sent from one of their officers to an officer of the Spanish troops,—"Sir, look well; it is a well-known thing, that since our Lord God in his infinite wisdom created the heavens and the earth, with all which beautifies it, which is to endure till the day of judgment, we have not known that God, who is the Lord of these lands, gave them to the Spaniards before he came into the world. Three parts of the earth are for them; namely, Europe, Asia, and Africa, which are to the east; and this remaining part in which we dwell, our Lord Jesus Christ, as soon as he died, set apart for us. We poor Indians have fairly possessed this country during all these years, as children of God, according to his will, not by the will of any other living being. Our Lord God permitted all this that it might be so. We of this country remember our unbelieving grandfathers, and we are greatly amazed when we think that God should have pardoned so many sins as we ourselves have committed. Sir, consider that which you are about is a thing which we poor Indians have never seen done amongst Christians!"

Poor people! how little did they know how feeble are the strongest reasons drawn from the Christian faith, when addressed to those who would resent as a deadly insult the true charge that they are no Christians at all. In this case the Indians were the only Christians concerned in this melancholy affair. Well might they say, "Your actions are so different from your words, that we are more amazed than if we saw two suns in the firmament." Well might they ask, "What will God say to you after your death on this account? What answer will you make in the day of judgment when we shall all be gathered together?" Like all other Europeans when doing their will on the natives of their colonies, they cared neither for God, nor the day of judgment; they went on and drove the genuine Christians, the poor simple-hearted Indians, to the woods, or compelled them to submit. Their lands were laid waste, their towns burnt; many were slain, many were dispersed, many died heart-broken in the homeless woods,—and scarcely was all this misery and wickedness completed,—when the news of the king's death arrived, and soon after, the annulment of this very treaty; so that these lands were not to be yielded to the Portuguese, and all this evil had been done, even politically, in vain. The poor people were invited to return to their possessions, and the Jesuits to their sorrowful labour of repairing the ravages so foolishly and heartlessly committed.

Mr. Southey thinks that the Portuguese in Brazil were more lenient to the natives than the Spaniards

in their South-American colonies.   I must confess
that his own History of Brazil does not give me that
impression.   It is true that they did not succeed in so
speedily depopulating the country; but that in part,
must be attributed to the more warlike and hardy
character of the people, and to the fact that Brazil did
not for a long time become a mining country.   By
the time that it did, all the Indians that the horrible
man-hunters of San Paulo could seize in their wild
excursions, were wanted in the cultivated lands and
sugar plantations, and negroes were imported in
abundance—the English for a long time supplying
by contract four thousand annually.   The final expulsion of the Jesuits deprived the Indians of the only
body of real friends that they ever knew.   Finer
materials than those poor people for civilization, no
race on the earth ever presented.   Had the Jesuits
been permitted to continue their peaceful labours, the
whole continent would have become one wide scene of
peace, fertility, and happiness.   What a contrast does
Brazil present, after the lapse of three centuries, and
even after the introduction of European royalty!
The people are described by modern travellers as living
in the utmost filth, idleness, licentiousness, and dis-
honesty.   " The Indians are driven into the interior,
where," says Mr. Luccock, " they form a great bar to
civilization; their animosity to the whites being of the
bitterest sort, and their purposes of vengeance for
injuries received, so long bequeathed from father to
son, as to be rooted in their hearts as firmly as the
colour is attached to their skin.   Under the influence
of this passion, they destroy every thing belonging to
the Europeans or their descendants, which falls in their

way; even the cow and the dog are not spared. For such outrages they pay dearly; small forts, or military stations, being placed around the colonized parts of the district, from whence a war of plunder and extermination is carried on against them. In this warfare not only are fire-arms made use of, but the lasso, dogs, and all the stratagems which are usually employed against beasts of prey." Mr. Luccock met with one man who had been thus engaged against the Indians *forty years, and was on his way to ask some honorary distinction from the sovereign for his services!*

Instead of a country swarming with labourers and good citizens, as it would have been under a Christian policy, Brazil now suffers for want of inhabitants, and the barbarous slave-trade is made to supply the whole country with servants. Ten thousand negroes are annually brought into Rio alone, whence we may infer how vast must be the demand for the whole empire; and of the estimation in which they are held, and of the sort of religion which still bears the abused name of Christianity there, one anecdote will give us sufficient idea. "Two negroes," says Mr. Luccock, "being extremely ill, a clergyman was sent for, who on his arrival found one of them gone beyond the reach of his art; and the other, having crawled off his bed, was lying on the floor of his cabin. As we entered, the priest was jesting and laughing in the most volatile manner—then filled both his hands with water, and dropped it on the poor creature's head, pronouncing the form of baptism. The dying man, probably experiencing some little relief from the effusion, exclaimed, 'Good—very good.' 'Oh,' said the priest, 'it is very good, is it?—then there is more for you;' dashing upon him what remained in the basin. Without delay he resumed his jokes, and in the midst of them the man expired."

We must now quit South America, to follow the European *Christians* in their colonial career in another quarter of the globe. And in thus taking leave of this immense portion of the New World, where such cruelties have been perpetrated, and so much innocent blood shed by the avarice and ambition of Europe, we may ask,—What has been done by way of atonement; or what is the triumph of civilization? We have already quoted Mr. Ward on the present state of the aborigines of Mexico, and Mr. Luccock on those of Rio Janeiro. Baron Humboldt can furnish the reader with ample indications of a like kind in various parts of South America. Maria Graham tells us, so recently as 1824, that in Chili, Peru, and the provinces of La Plata, the system of Spain, which had driven those realms to revolt, had diffused "sloth and ignorance" as their necessary consequences. That in Brazil, "the natives had been either exterminated or wholly subdued. The slave-hunting, which had been systematic on the first occupation of the land, and more especially after the discovery of the mines had so diminished the wretched Indians, that the introduction of negroes was deemed necessary: *they* now people the Brazilian fields; and if here and there an Indian aldea is to be found, the people are wretched, with less than negro comforts, and much less than negro spirit or industry: *the Indians are nothing in Brazil.*"

That the system of exterminating the Indians has been continued to the latest period where any remained, we may learn from a horrible fact, which she tells us she relates on good authority. " In the Captaincy of Porto Seguro, *within these twenty years,* an Indian tribe had been so troublesome that the Capitam Môr resolved to get rid of it. It was attacked, but defended itself so bravely, that the Portuguese resolved to desist from open warfare ; but with unnatural ingenuity exposed ribbons and toys, infested with small-pox matter, in the places where the poor savages were likely to find them. The plan succeeded. The Indians were so thinned that they were easily overcome !"—*Voyage to Brazil,* p. 9.

But if any one wishes to learn what are the wretched fruits of all the bloodshed and crimes perpetrated by the Spaniards in America, he has only to look into Sir F. B. Head's " Rough Notes on the Pampas," made in 1826. What a scene do these notes lay open ! Splendid countries, overrun with a most luxuriant vegetation, and with countless troops of wild horses and herds of wild cattle, but thinly peopled, partly with Indians and partly with the Gauchos, or descendants of the Spanish, existing in a state of the most hideous hostility and hatred one towards another. The Gauchos, inflamed with all the ancient demoniacal cruelty and revenge of the Spaniards,—the Indians, educated, raised, and moulded by ages of the most inexpiable wrongs into an active and insatiable spirit of vengeance, coming, like the whirlwind from the deserts, as fleet and unescapable, to burn, destroy, and exterminate—in a word, to inflict on the Gauchos all the evils of injury and death that they and their fathers have inflicted on them. As Captain Head scoured across those immense plains, from Buenos

Ayres, and across the Andes to Chili, he was ever and anon coming to the ruins of huts where the Indians had left the most terrible traces of their fury. It may be well to state, in his own words, what every family of the Gauchos is liable to :—

" In invading the country, the Pampas Indians generally ride all night, and hide themselves on the ground during the day; or if they do travel, crouch almost under the bellies of their horses, who, by this means, appear to be dismounted and at liberty. They usually approach the huts at night, at a full gallop, with their usual shriek, striking their mouths with their hands; and this cry, which is to intimidate their enemies, is continued through the whole of the dreadful operation.

" Their first act is to set fire to the roof c⸗ the hut, and it is almost too dreadful to fancy wl.⸗ .e feelings of a family must be, when, after having been alarmed by the barking of the dogs, which the Gauchos always keep in great numbers, they first hear the wild cry which announces their doom, and in an instant afterwards find the roof burning over their heads.

" As soon as the families rush out, which they of course are obliged to do, the men are wounded by the Indians with their lances, which are eighteen feet long; and as soon as they fall, they are stripped of their clothes; for the Indians, who are very desirous to get the clothes of the Christians, are careful not to have them spotted with blood. While some torture the men, others attack the children, and will literally run the infants through the body with their lances, and raise them to die in the air. The women are also attacked; and it would form a true but dreadful picture to describe their fate, as it is decided by the momentary gleam which the burning roof throws upon their countenances.

"The old women, and the ugly young ones, are instantly butchered; but the young and beautiful are idols by whom even the merciless hand of the savage is arrested. Whether the poor girls can ride or not, they are instantly placed upon horses, and when the hasty plunder of the hut is concluded, they are driven away from its smoking ruins, and from the horrid scene which surrounds it. At a pace which in Europe is unknown, they gallop over the trackless regions before them, feed upon mare's flesh, sleeping on the ground, until they arrive in the Indian's territory, when they have instantly to adopt the wild life of their captors."

Scenes of such horrors, where the mangled remains of the victims were still lying around the black ruins of their huts, which Captain Head passed, are too dreadful to transcribe. But what are the feelings of the Gaucho towards these terrible enemies? Captain Head asked a Gaucho what they did with their Indian prisoners when they took any.—"To people accustomed to the cold passions of England, it would be impossible to describe the savage, inveterate, furious hatred which exists between the Gauchos and the Indians. The latter invade the country for the ecstatic pleasure of murdering the Christians, and in the contests which take place between them, mercy is unknown. Before I was quite aware of those feelings, I was galloping with a very fine-looking Gaucho who had been fighting with the Indians, and after listening to his report of the killed and wounded, I happened, very simply, to ask him how many prisoners they had taken. The man replied with a look which I shall never forget—he clenched his teeth, opened his lips, and then sawing his fingers across his bare throat for a quarter of a minute, bending towards me, with his spurs sticking into his horse's sides, he said, in a sort of low, choking voice, ' Se matan todas,'—we kill them all!"

Here then we have a thinly populated country inhabited, so far as it is inhabited at all, by men that are inspired towards each other by the spirit of fiends. It is impossible that civilization can ever come there except by some fresh and powerful revolution. We hear of the new republics of South America, and naturally look for more evidences of good from the spirit of liberty: but in the towns we find the people indolent, ignorant, superstitious, and most filthy; and in the country naked Indians on horseback, scouring the wilds, and making use of the very animals by which the Spaniards subjugated them, to scourge and exterminate their descendants. In the opinion of Captain Head, they only want fire-arms, which one day they may get, to drive them out altogether! And what are they whom they would drive out? Only another kind of savages. People who, calling themselves Christians, live in most filthy huts swarming with vermin—sit on skeletons of horses' heads instead of chairs—lie during summer out of doors in promiscuous groups—and live entirely on beef and water; the beef, chiefly mare's flesh, being roasted on a long spit, and every one sitting round and cutting off pieces with long knives. The cruelty and beastliness of their nature exceeding even that of the Indians themselves.

This then is the result of three centuries of blood-shed and tyranny in those regions—one species of barbarism merely substituted for another. What a different scene to that which the same countries would now have exhibited, had the Jesuits not been violently expelled from their work of civilization by the lust of gold and despotism. " When we compare," says Captain Head, " the relative size of America with the rest of the world, it is singular to reflect on the history of these fellow-creatures, who are the aborigines of the land; and after viewing the wealth and beauty of so interesting a country, it is painful to consider what the sufferings of the Indians have been, and still may be. Whatever may be their physical or natural character*. . . still they are the human beings placed there by the Almighty; the country belonged to them; and they are therefore entitled to the regard of every man who has religion enough to believe that God has made nothing in vain, or whose mind is just enough to respect the persons and the rights of his fellow-creatures."

The view I have been enabled in my space to take of the treatment of the South Americans by their invaders, is necessarily a mere glance,—for, unfor-

---

* " I sincerely believe they are as fine a set of men as ever existed, under the circumstances in which they are placed. In the mines I have seen them using tools which our miners declared they had not strength to work with, and carrying burdens which no man in England could support; and I appeal to those travellers who have been carried over the snow on their backs, whether they were able to have returned the compliment; and if not, what can be more grotesque than the figure of a civilized man riding upon the shoulders of a fellow-creature whose physical strength he has ventured to despise?"

Head's Rough Notes, p. 112.

tunately for the Christian name and the name of
humanity, the history of blood and oppression there is
not more dreadful than it is extensive. I have not
staid to describe the conduct of the French, Dutch,
and English, in their possessions on the southern continent, simply because they are only too much like
those of the Spaniards and Portuguese—they form
no bright exception, and we shall only too soon meet
with these refined nations in other regions.

Note.—The fate of Venezuela ought not to be
quite passed over. It is a striking instance of the
indifference with which the lives and fortunes ot a
whole nation are often handed over by great kings to
destruction as a mere matter of business. Charles V.
of Spain being deeply indebted to a trading house of
Augsburgh, the Welsers, gave them this province.
They, in their turn, made it over to some German
military mercenaries, who overrun the whole country
in search of mines, and plundered and oppressed the
people with the most dreadful rapacity. In the course
of a few years their avarice and exactions had so completely exhausted and ruined the province that the
Germans threw it up, and it fell again into the hands
of the Spaniards, but in such a miserable condition
that it continued to languish and drag on a miserable
existence, if it has even recovered from its fatal injuries at the present time.

CHAPTER XIII.

THE PORTUGUESE IN INDIA.

Son mui buenos Catolicos, pero mui malos Christianos;—They are very good Catholics, but nevertheless very bad Christians indeed.
Saying of an old Catholic priest. Ward's Mexico.

Most of the countries in India have been filled with tyrants who prefer piracy to commerce—who acknowledge no right but that of power ; and think that whatever is practicable is just.
The Abbé Raynal.

SCARCELY had Columbus made known the New World when the Portuguese, under Vasco de Gama, opened the sea-path to the East Indies. Those affluent and magnificent regions, which had so long excited the wonder and cupidity of Europe, and whose gems, spices, and curious fabrics, had been introduced overland by the united exertions of the Arabs, the Venetians, and Genoese, were now made accessible by the great highway of the ocean; and the Pope generously gave all of them to the Portuguese! The language of the Pontiff was like the language of another celebrated character to our Saviour, and founded on about as much real right: "All these kingdoms will I give unto thee, if thou wilt fall down and worship me." The Portuguese were nothing loath. They were, in the expressive language of a great historian, "all on fire for plunder and the propagation of their religion!" Away, therefore, they hastened, following the sinuous guidance of those African coasts which they had already traced out—on which they had already commenced that spoliation and traffic in men which for three centuries was to grow only more and more extensive, dreadful, and detestable—"those countries where," says M. Malte Brun, "tyranny and ignorance have not had the power to destroy the inexhaustible fecundity of the soil, but have made them, down to the present times, the theatre of eternal robbery, and one vast market of human blood."

They landed in Calicut, under Gama, in 1498, and speedily gave sufficient indications of the object of their visit, and the nature of their character. But in India they had more formidable obstacles to their spirit of dominance and extermination than they and the Spaniards had found in the New World. They beheld themselves on the limits of a vast region, inhabited by a hundred millions of people—countries of great antiquity, of a higher civilization, and under the rule of active and military princes. Populous cities, vast and ancient temples, palaces, and other public works; a native literature, science handed down from far-off times, and institutions of a fixed and tenacious caste, marked them as a people not so easily to be made a prey of as the Mexicans or Peruvians. Peaceful as were the habits, and bloodless as were the religion and the social principles of a vast body of the Hindoos, their rulers, whether the de-

scendants of the great Persian and Tartar conquerors,
and Mahomedans in faith, or of their own race and
religion, were disposed enough to resist any foreign
aggression. At sea, indeed, swarmed the Moorish
fleets, which had long enjoyed the monopoly of the
trade of these rich and inexhaustible regions; but
these they soon subdued. Their conquests and cruelties were therefore necessarily confined chiefly to the
coasts and to the paradisiacal islands which stud the
Indian seas, and, as Milton has beautifully expressed
it, cast their spicy odours abroad, till

> Many a league
> Cheered with the grateful smell, old Ocean smiles.

We must take a rapid view of the Portuguese in
India,—for our object is not a history of European conquests, but of European treatment of the natives of
the countries they have entered; and the atrocities of
the Portuguese in the East are too notorious to require tracing minutely, and step by step in their progress. Every reader is familiar with the transactions
between Gama and the Zamorin of Calicut, through
the splendid poem of Camoens. Alvarez Cabral, the
discoverer of Peru, who succeeded him, was by no
means particular in his policy. On the slightest suspicion of evil intention, he fell upon the people and
made havoc amongst them. The inhabitants of Calicut, between the intrigues of the Moorish merchants
and those of the Portuguese adventurers, were always
the dupes and the sufferers. They attempted to drive
out the Portuguese, and Cabral, in revenge, burnt all
the Arabian vessels in the harbour, cannonaded the
town, and then sailed, first to Cochin, and then to
Cananor. These and other places being tributary to

the Zamorin, received them as saviours, and enabled them to build forts, to gain command of the seas, and drive from them the ships of the Zamorin and the Moors.   But the celebrated Alphonso Albuquerque made the most rapid strides, and extended the conquests of the Portuguese there beyond any other commander.   He narrowly escaped with his life in endeavouring to sack and plunder Calicut.   He seized on Goa, which thenceforward became the metropolis of all the Portuguese settlements in India.   He conquered Molucca, and gave it up to the plunder of his soldiers.   The fifth part of the wealth thus thievishly acquired, was reserved for the king, and was purchased on the spot by the merchants for 200,000 pieces of gold.   Having established a garrison in the conquered city, he made a traitor Indian, who had deserted from the king of Molucca, and had been an instrument in the winning of the place, supreme magistrate; but again finding Utimut, the renegade, as faithless to himself, he had him and his son put to death, even though 100,000 pieces of gold, a bait that was not easily resisted by these Christian marauders, was offered for their lives.   He then proceeded to Ormuz in the Persian Gulph, which was a great harbour for the Arabian merchants; reduced it, placed a garrison in it, seized on fifteen princes of the blood, and carried them off to Goa.   Such were some of the deeds of this celebrated general, whom the historians in the same breath in which they record these unwarrantable acts of violence, robbery and treachery, term an excellent and truly glorious commander.   He made a descent on the isle of Ceylon, and detached a fleet to the Moluccas, which established a settlement in those delightful regions of the cocaa, the sago-tree, the nutmeg, and the clove. The kings of Persia, of Siam, Pegu, and others, alarmed at his triumphant progress, sought his friendship; and he completed the conquest of the Malabar coast. With less than forty thousand troops the Portuguese struck terror, says the historian, "into the empire of Morocco, the barbarous nations of Africa, the Mamelucs, the Arabians, and all the eastern countries from the island of Ormuz to China." How much better for their pretensions to Christianity, and for their real interests, if they had struck them with admiration of that faith and integrity, and of those noble virtues which Christianity can inspire, and which were never yet lost on the attention of nations where they have been righteously displayed. But the Portuguese unfortunately did not understand what Christianity was. Their notions of religion made avarice, lust, and cruelty, all capable of dwelling together in one heart; and, in the language of their own historians, the vessels bound for the east were crowded with adventurers who wanted to enrich themselves, secure their country, and make proselytes. They were on the eve of opening a most auspicious intercourse with China, when some of these adventurers, under Simon Andrada, appeared on the coast. This commander treated the Chinese in the same manner as the Portuguese had been in the habit of treating all the people of Asia. He built a fort without permission, in the island of Taman, from whence he took opportunities of pillaging, and extorting money from all the ships bound from, or to, all the ports of China. He carried off young girls from the coast; he seized upon the men and made them slaves;

he gave himself up to the most licentious acts of piracy, and the most shameful dissoluteness. His soldiers and sailors followed his example with avidity; and the Chinese, enraged at such outrages, fell upon them, drove them from the coast, and for a long time refused all overtures of trade from them.

In Japan, they were for a time more fortunate. They exported, in exchange for European goods or commodities, from India, gold, silver, and copper to the value of about 634,000*l.* annually. They married the richest heiresses, and allied themselves to the most powerful families.

" With such advantages," says the Abbé Raynal, " the avarice as well as the ambition of the Portuguese might have been satisfied. They were masters of the coast of Guinea, Arabia, Persia, and the two peninsulas of India. They were possessed of the Moluccas, Ceylon, and the isles of Sunda, while their settlement at Macao insured to them the commerce of China and Japan. Throughout these immense regions, the will of the Portuguese was the supreme law. Earth and sea acknowledged their sovereignty. Their authority was so absolute, that things and persons were dependent upon them, and moved entirely by their directions. No native, nor private person dared to make voyages, or carry on trade, without obtaining their permission and passport. Those who had this liberty granted them, were prohibited trading in cinnamon, ginger, pepper, timber, and many other articles, of which the conquerors reserved to themselves the exclusive benefit.

" In the midst of so much glory, wealth, and conquest, the Portuguese had not neglected that part of

Africa which lies between the Cape of Good Hope
and the Red Sea, and in all ages has been famed for
the richness of its productions. The Arabians had been
settled there for several ages; they had formed along
the coast of Zanguebar several small independent
states, abounding in mines of silver and gold. To
possess themselves of this treasure was deemed by the
Portuguese an indispensable duty. Agreeable to this
principle, these Arabian merchants were attacked and
subdued about the year 1508. Upon their ruin was
established an empire extending from Sofala as far
as Melinda, of which the island of Mozambique was
made the centre.

"These successes properly improved, might have
formed a power so considerable that it could not have
been shaken; but the vices and follies of some of their
chiefs, the abuse of riches and power, the wantonness
of victory, the distance of their own country, changed
the character of the Portuguese. Religious zeal,
which had added so much force and activity to their
courage, now produced in them nothing but ferocity.
They made no scruple of pillaging, cheating, and
enslaving the idolaters. They supposed that the
pope, in bestowing the kingdoms of Asia on the
Portuguese monarchs, had not withholden the property of individuals from their subjects. Being absolute masters of the Eastern seas, they extorted a tribute
from the ships of every country; they ravaged the
coasts, insulted the princes, and became the terror and
scourge of all nations.

"The king of Sidor was carried off from his own
palace, and murdered, with his children, whom he
had entrusted to the care of the Portuguese.

" At Ceylon, the people were not suffered to cultivate the earth, except for their new masters, who treated them with the greatest barbarity.

" At Goa they established the inquisition, and whoever was rich became a prey to the ministers of that infamous tribunal.

" Faria, who was sent out against the pirates from Malacca, China, and other parts, made a descent on the island of Calampui, and plundered the tombs of the Chinese emperors.

" Sousa caused all the pagodas on the Malabar coast to be destroyed, and his people inhumanly massacred the wretched Indians who went to weep over the ruins of their temples.

" Correa terminated an obstinate war with the king of Pegu, and both parties were to swear on the books of their several religions to observe the treaty. Correa swore on a collection of songs, and thought by this vile stratagem to elude his engagement.

" Nuno d' Acughna attacked the isle of Daman on the coast of Cambaya. The inhabitants offered to surrender to him if he would permit them to carry off their treasures. This request was refused, and Nuno put them all to the sword.

" Diego de Silveira was cruizing in the Red Sea. A vessel richly laden saluted him. The captain came on board, and gave him a letter from a Portuguese general, which was to be his passport. The letter contained only these words: *I desire the* captains of ships belonging to the king of Portugal, to seize upon this Moorish vessel as lawful prize.

" Henry Garcias, when governor of the Moluccas, was requested by the king of Tidore, who was ill, to

send him a physician. Garcias accordingly sent one
who villanously poisoned him. He then made a descent upon the island; besieged the capital, took it,
plundered it, and used the inhabitants very cruelly.
This event happening in time of peace, and without
the least provocation, caused an implacable hatred to
the Portuguese amongst all the people, not only of
that island, but of all the Moluccas.

" In a short time the Portuguese preserved no
more humanity or good faith with each other than
with the natives. Almost all the states, where they
had the command, were divided into factions. There
prevailed everywhere in their manners, a mixture of
avarice, debauchery, cruelty, and devotion. They had
most of them seven or eight concubines, whom they
kept to work with the utmost rigour, and forced from
them the money they gained by their labour. Such
treatment of women was very repugnant to the spirit
of chivalry. The chiefs and principal officers admitted
to their tables a multitude of those singing and dancing women, with which India abounds. Effeminacy
introduced itself into their houses and armies. The
officers marched to meet the enemy in palanquins.
That brilliant courage which had confounded so many
nations, existed no longer amongst them. They were
with difficulty brought to fight, except for plunder.
In a short time, the king no longer received the
tribute which was paid him by one hundred and fifty
eastern princes. It was lost on its way from them to
him. Such corruption prevailed in the finances, that
the tributes of sovereigns, the revenues of provinces,
which ought to have been immense, the taxes levied on
gold, silver, and spices, on the inhabitants of the con-

tinent and islands, were not sufficient to keep up a
few citadels, and to fit out the shipping necessary for
the protection of trade."

Some gleams of valour blazed up now and then;
Don Juan de Castro revived the spirit of the settlers
for awhile; Ataida, and fresh troops from Portugal
repelled the native powers, who, worn out with endurance of outrages and indignities, and alive to the
growing effeminacy of their oppressors, rose against
them on all hands. But these were only temporary
displays. The island of Amboyna was the first to
avenge itself; and the words addressed to them by
one of its citizens are justly descriptive of their real
character. A Portuguese had, at a public festival,
seized upon a very beautiful woman, and regardless
of all decency, had proceeded to the grossest of outrages. One of the islanders, named Genulio, armed
his fellow-citizens; after which he called together the
Portuguese, and addressed them in the following
manner:—" To revenge affronts so cruel as those we
have received from you, requires actions, not words;
yet we will speak to you. You preach to us a Deity,
who delights, you say, in generous actions; but theft,
murder, obscenity, and drunkenness are your common
practice: your hearts are inflamed with every vice.
Our manners can never agree with yours. Nature
foresaw this when she separated us by immense seas,
and you have overleaped her barriers. This audacity,
of which you are not ashamed to boast, is a proof of
the corruption of your hearts. Take my advice;
leave to their repose those nations that resemble you
so little; go, fix your habitations amongst those who
are as brutal as yourselves; an intercourse with you

would be more fatal to us than all the evils which it is in the power of your God to inflict upon us. We renounce your alliance for ever. Your arms are more powerful than ours; but we are more just than you, and we do not fear them. The Itons are from this day your enemies;—fly from this country, and beware how you approach it again."

Equally detested in every quarter, they saw a confederacy forming to expel them from the east. All the great powers of India entered into the league, and for two or three years carried on their preparations in secret. Their old enemy, the Zamorin, attacked Manjalor, Cochin, and Cananor. The king of Cambaya attacked Chaul, Daman, and Baichaim. The king of Achen laid siege to Malacca. The king of Ternate made war on them in the Moluccas. Agalachem, a tributary to the Mogul, imprisoned the Portuguese merchants at Surat; and the queen of Gareopa endeavoured to drive them out of Onor. The exertions of Ataida averted immediate destruction; but a more formidable power was now preparing to expel them from their ill-acquired and ill-governed possessions,—the Dutch. In little more than a century from the appearance of the Portuguese in India, this nation drove them from Malacca and Ceylon; from most of their possessions on the coast of Malabar; and had, moreover, made settlements on the Coromandel coast. It was high time that this reign of crime and terror came to an end, had a better generation succeeded them. After the death of Sebastian, and the reduction of Portugal by Philip II., the last traces of order or decency seemed to vanish from the Indian settlements. Portugal itself exhibited, with the usual

result of ill-gotten wealth, a scene of miserable ex-
tremes—profusion and poverty. Those who had been
in India were at once indolent and wealthy; the
farmer and the artizan were reduced to the most abject
condition. " In the colonies the Portuguese gave
themselves," says Raynal, " up to all those excesses
which make men hated, though they had not courage
enough left to make them feared. They were monsters. Poison, fire, assassination, every sort of crime
was become familiar to them; nor were they private
persons only who were guilty of such practices,—men
in office set them the example ! They massacred the
natives; they destroyed one another. The governor
just arrived, loaded his predecessor with irons, that he
might deprive him of his wealth. The distance of the
scene, false witnesses, and large bribes secured every
crime from punishment."

CHAPTER XIV.

THE DUTCH IN INDIA.

A free nation, which is its own master, is born to command the ocean. It cannot secure the dominion of the sea without seizing upon the land, which belongs to the first possessor ; that is, to him who is able to drive out the ancient inhabitants. They are to be enslaved by force or fraud, and exterminated in order to get their possessions.

Raynal.

WE come now to the conduct of a Protestant people towards the natives of their colonies; and happy would it be if we came with this change to a change in their policy and behaviour. But the Dutch, though zealous Protestants at home, were zealous Catholics abroad in cruelty and injustice. Styling themselves a reformed people, there was no reformation in their treatment of Indians or Caffres. They, as well as other Protestant nations, cast off the outward forms and many of the inward superstitions of the Roman church: but they were far, far indeed from comprehending Christianity in its glorious greatness ; in the magnificence of its moral elevation ; in the sublimity of its objects; in the purity of its feeling, and the

beautiful humanity of its spirit. The temporal yoke
of Rome was cast off, but the mental yoke still lay
heavy on their souls, and it required ages of bitter
experience to restore sufficiently their intellectual
sensibility to permit them even to feel it. Popery
was dethroned in them, but not destroyed. They
recognized their rights as men, and the slavery under
which they had been held; but their vision was not
enough restored to allow them to recognize the rights
of others, and to see that to hold others in slavery,
was only to take themselves out of the condition of
the victim, to put themselves into the more odious,
criminal, and eventually disastrous one of the tyrant.
They were still infinitely distant from the condition
of freemen. They were free from the immediate
compulsion of their spiritual task-masters, but they
were not free from the iron which they had thrust
into their very souls,—from the corrupt morals, the
perverted principles, the debased tone of feeling and
perception, which the Papal church had inflicted on
them. The wretched substitution of ceremonies,
legends, and false maxims, for the grand and rege-
nerating doctrines of Christian truth, which had existed for more than a thousand years, had generated a
spurious morality, which ages only could obliterate.
It is a fallacy to suppose that the renunciation of the
Romish faith, carried with it a renunciation of the
habits of mind which it had created,—or that those
who called themselves reformers were thoroughly
reformed, and rebaptized with the purity and fulness
of Christianity. Many and glorious examples were
given of zeal for the right, even unto death; of the
love of truth, which cast out all fear of flames and

scaffolds; of that devotion to the dictates of conscience that shrunk from no sacrifice, however severe;—but even in the instance of the noblest of those noble martyrs, it would be self-delusion for us to suppose that they had sprung from the depth of darkness to perfect light at one leap; that they rose instantaneously from gross ignorance of Christian truths, to the perfection of knowledge; that they had miraculously cast off at one effort all slavery of spirit, and the dimness of intellectual vision, which were the work of ages. They had regained the wish and the will to explore the regions of truth; they had made some splendid advances, and shewn that they descried some of the most prominent features of the genuine faith: but they were, the best of them, but babes in Christ. To become full-grown men required the natural lapse of time; and to expect them to start up into the full standard of Christian stature, was to expect an impossibility. And if the brightest and most intrepid, and most honest intellects were thus circumstanced, what was the condition of the mass? That may be known by calling to mind how readily Protestants fell into the spirit of persecution, and into all the cruelties and outrages of their Popish predecessors. Ages upon ages were required, to clear away the dusty cobwebs of error, with which a spurious faith had involved them; and to raise again the Christian world to the height of Christian knowledge. We are yet far and very far from having escaped from the one, or risen to the other. There are yet Christian truths, of the highest import to humanity, that are treated as fables and fanatic dreams by the mass of the Christian world; and we shall see as we proceed, that to this hour the most sacred principles of Christianity are outraged; and the worst atrocities of the worst ages of Rome are still perpetrated on millions of millions of human beings, over whom we vaunt our civilization, and to whom we present our religion as the spirit of heaven, and the blessing of the earth.

When, therefore, we see the Dutch, ay, and the English, and the Anglo-Americans, still professing truth and practising error; still preaching mercy, and perpetrating the basest of cruelties; still boasting of their philosophy and refinement, and enacting the savage; still vapouring about liberty, with a whip in one hand and a chain in the other; still holding the soundness of the law of conquest, and the equal soundness of the commandment, Not to covet our neighbour's goods; the soundness of the belief that Negroes, Indians, and Hottentots, are an inferior species, and the equal soundness of the declaration that " God made of one blood all the nations of the earth ;" still declaring that LOVE, the love of our neighbour as of ourselves, is the great distinction of Christians ;—and yet persisting in slavery, war, massacres, extermination of one race, and driving out of others from their ancient and hereditary lands—we must bear in mind that we behold only the melancholy result of ages of abandonment of genuine Christianity for a base and accommodating forgery of its name,— and the humiliating spectacle of an inconsistency in educated nations unworthy of the wildest dwellers in the bush, entailed on us by the active leaven of that very faith which we pride ourselves in having renounced. We have, indeed, renounced mass and the confessional, and the purchase of indulgences; but have tenaciously retained the mass of our tyrannous propensities. We practise our crimes without confessing them; we indulge our worst desires without even having the honesty to pay for it; and the old, spurious morality, and political barbarism of Rome, are as stanchly maintained by us as ever—while we claim to look back on Popery with horror, and on our present condition as the celestial light of the nineteenth century.

What a glorious thing it would have been, if when the Dutch and English had appeared in America and the Indies, they had come there too as Protestants and Reformed Christians! If they had protested against the cruelties and aggressions of the popish Spaniards and Portuguese—if they had reformed all their rapacious practices, and remedied their abuses—if they had, indeed, shown that they were really gone back to the genuine faith of Christ, and were come to seek honest benefit by honest means; to exchange knowledge for wealth, and to make the Pagans and the Mahomedans *feel* that there was in Christianity a power to refine, to elevate, and to bless, as mighty as they professed. But that day was not arrived, and has only partially arrived yet, and that through the missions. For anything that could be discovered by their practice, the Dutch and English might be the papists, and the Spaniards and Portuguese the reformed. From their deeds the natives, wherever they came, could only imagine their religion to be something especially odious and mischievous.

The Dutch having thrown off the Spanish yoke at home, applied themselves diligently to commerce; and they would have continued to purchase from the

Spaniards and Portuguese, the commodities of the
eastern and western worlds, to supply their customers
therewith ;—but Philip II., smarting under the loss of
the Netherlands, and being master of both Spain and
Portugal, commanded his subjects to hold no dealings
with his hated enemies.   Passion and resentment are
the worst of counsellors, and Philip soon found it so
in this instance.   The Dutch, denied Indian goods in
Portugal, determined to seek them in India itself.
They had renounced papal as well as Spanish authority, and had no scruples about interfering with the
pope's grant of the east to the Portuguese. They soon,
therefore, made their appearance in the Indian seas,
and found the Portuguese so thoroughly detested
there, that nothing was easier for them than to avenge
past injuries and prohibitions, by supplanting them.
It was only in 1594 that Philip issued his impolitic
order that they should not be permitted to receive
goods from Portuguese ports,—and by 1602, under
their admirals, Houtman and Van Neck, they had
visited Madagascar, the Maldives, and the isles of
Sunda ; they had entered into alliance with the principal sovereigns of Java; established factories in several
of the Moluccas, and brought home abundance of pepper, spices, and other articles. Numerous trading companies were organized ; and these all united by the
policy of the States-general into the one memorable
one of the East India Company, the model and original
of all the numerous ones that sprung up, and especially
of the far greater one under the same name, of England.   The natives of India had now a similar spectacle
exhibited to their eyes, which South America had
about the same period—the Christian nations, boasting

of their superior refinement and of their heavenly religion, fighting like furies, and intriguing like fiends one against another. But the Portuguese were now become debauched and effeminate, and were unsupported by fresh reinforcements from Europe; the Dutch were spurred on by all the ardour of united revenge, ambition, and the love of gain. The time was now come when the Portuguese were to expiate their perfidy, their robberies, and their cruelties; and the prediction of one of the kings of Persia was fulfilled, who, asking an ambassador just arrived at Goa, how many governors his master had beheaded since the establishment of his power in India, received for answer—"none at all." "So much the worse," replied the monarch, "his authority cannot be of long duration in a country where so many acts of outrage and barbarity are committed."

The Dutch commenced their career in India with an air of moderation that formed a politic contrast with the arrogance and pretension of the Portuguese. They fought desperately with the Portuguese, but they kept a shrewd eye all the time on mercantile opportunities. They sought to win their way by duplicity, rather than by decisive daring. By these means they gradually rooted their rivals out of their most important stations in Java, the Moluccas, in Ceylon, on the Coromandel and Malabar coasts. Their most lucrative posts were at Java, Bantam, and the Moluccas. No sooner had they gained an ascendency than they assumed a haughtiness of demeanor that even surpassed that of the Portuguese; and in perfidy and cruelty, they became more than rivals. All historians have remarked with astonishment the fearful metamorphosis which the Dutch underwent in their colonies. At home they were moderate, kindly, and liberal; abroad their rapacity, perfidy, and infamous cruelty made them resemble devils rather than men. Whether contending with their European rivals, or domineering over the natives, they showed no mercy and no remorse. Their celebrated massacre of the English in Amboyna has rung through all lands and languages, and is become one of the familiar horrors of history. There is, in fact, no narrative of tortures in the annals of the Inquisition, that can surpass those which the Dutch practised on their English rivals on this occasion. The English had five factories in the island of Amboyna, and the Dutch determined to crush them. For this purpose they got up a charge of conspiracy against the English—collected them from all their stations into the town of Amboyna, and after forcing confessions of guilt from them by the most unheard-of torture, put them to death. The following specimen of the agonies which Protestants could inflict on their fellow-protestants, may give an idea of what sort of increase of religion the Reformation had brought these men.

"Then John Clark, who also came from Hitto, was fetched in, and soon after was heard to roar out amain. They tortured him with fire and water for two hours. The manner of his torture, as also that of Johnson's and Thompson's, was as followeth:—

"They first hoisted him by the hands against a large door, and there made him fast to two staples of iron, fixed on both sides at the top of the door-posts, extending his arms as wide as they could stretch them. When thus fastened, his feet, being two feet from the ground, were extended in the same manner, and made fast to the bottom of the door-trees on each side. Then they tied a cloth about the lower part of his face and neck, so close that scarce any water could pass by. That done, they poured water gently upon his head till the cloth was full up to his mouth and nostrils, and somewhat higher, so that he could not draw breath but he must swallow some, which being continually poured in softly, forced all his inward parts to come out at his nose, ears, and eyes, and often, as it were choking him, at length took away his breath, and caused him to faint away. Then they took him down in a hurry to vomit up the water, and when a little revived, tied him up again, using him as before. In this manner they served him three or four times, till his belly was as big as a tun, his cheeks like bladders, his eyes strutting out beyond his forehead; yet all this he bore without confessing anything, insomuch that the fiscal and tormentors reviled him, saying he was a devil, and no man; or was enchanted, that he could bear so much. Hereupon they cut off his hair very short, supposing he had some witchcraft hidden therein. Now they hoisted him up again, and burnt him with lighted candles under his elbows and arm-pits, in the palms of his hands, and at the bottoms of his feet, even till the fat dropped out on the candles. Then they applied fresh ones; and under his arms they burnt so deep that his inwards might be seen."—*History of Voyages to the East and West Indies.*

And all this that they might rule sole kings over the delicious islands of cloves and cinnamon, nutmegs and mace, camphor and coffee, areca and betel, gold, pearls and precious stones; every one of them more

precious in the eyes of the thorough trader, whether
he call himself Christian or Infidel, than the blood of
his brother, or the soul of himself.

To secure the dominion of these, they compelled
the princes of Ternate and Tidore to consent to the
rooting up of all the clove and nutmeg trees in the
islands not entirely under the jealous safeguard of
Dutch keeping. For this they utterly exterminated
the inhabitants of Banda, because they would not
submit passively to their yoke. Their lands were
divided amongst the white people, who got slaves
from other islands to cultivate them. For this Malacca was besieged, its territory ravaged, and its navigation interrupted by pirates; Negapatan was twice
attacked; Cochin was engaged in resisting the kings
of Calicut and Travancore; and Ceylon and Java
have been made scenes of perpetual disturbances.
These notorious dissensions have been followed by as
odious oppressions, which have been practised at Japan,
China, Cambodia, Arracan, on the banks of the
Ganges, at Achen, Coromandel, Surat, in Persia, at
Bassora, Mocha, and other places. For this they
encouraged and established in Celebes a system of
kidnapping the inhabitants for slaves which converted
that island into a perfect hell.

Sir Stamford Raffles has given us a most appalling
picture of this system, and the miseries it produced, in
an official document in his History of Java. In this
document it is stated that whole villages were made
slaves of; that there was scarcely a state or a family
that had not its assortment of these unhappy beings,
who had been reduced to this condition by the most
cruel and insidious means. There are few things in

history more darkly horrible than this kidnapping system of the Celebes. The Vehme Gerichte, or secret tribunals of Germany, were nothing to the secret prisons of the Celebes. In Makásar, and other places, these secret prisons existed; and such was the dreadful combination of power, influence, and avarice, in this trade,—for the magistrates and princes were amongst the chief dealers in it,—that no possibility of exposing or destroying these dens of thieves existed. Any man, woman, or child might be suddenly pounced on, and immured in one of these secret prisons till there were sufficient victims to send to the slave-ships. They were then marched out chained at midnight, and put on board. Any one may imagine the terror and insecurity which such a state of things occasioned. Everybody knew that such invisible dungeons of despair were in the midst of them, and that any moment he might be dragged into one of them, beyond the power or any hope of rescue.

"A rich citizen," says this singular official report, "who has a sufficient number of emissaries called bondsmen, carries on this trade of kidnapping much more easily than a poor one does. The latter is often obliged to go himself to the *Kámpong Búgis*, or elsewhere, to take a view of the stolen victim, and to carry him home; while the former quietly smokes his pipe, sure that his thieves will in every corner find out for him sufficient game without his exerting himself at all. The thief, the interpreter, the seller, are all active in his service, because they are paid by him. In some cases the purchaser unites himself with the seller to deceive the interpreter, while in others the interpreter agrees with the thief and pretended seller to put the victim into the hands of the purchaser. What precautions, what scrutiny can avail, when we reflect, that the profound secresy of the prisons is equalled only by the strict precautions in carrying the person on board ?"

The man-stealers were trained for the purpose. They marked out their victims, watched for days, and often weeks, endeavoured to associate themselves with them, and beguile them into some place where they might be easily secured. Or they pounced on them in the fields or woods. They roved about in gangs during the night, and in solitary places. None dare cry for help, or they were stabbed instantly, even though it were before the door of the purchaser.

What hope indeed could there be for anybody, when the authorities were in this diabolical league? and this was the custom of legalizing a kidnapping : "A person calling himself an interpreter, repairs, at the desire of one who says that he has bought a slave, to the secretary's office, accompanied by any native who, provided with a note from the purchaser, gives himself out as the seller. For three rupees, a certificate of sale in the usual form is immediately made out; three rupees are paid to the notary; two rupees are put into the hands of the interpreter; the whole transaction is concluded, and the purchaser has thus become the owner of a free-born man, who is very often stolen without his (the purchaser's) concurrence; but about this he does not trouble himself, for the victim is already concealed where nobody can find him; nor can the transaction become public, because there never were found more faithful receivers than the slave-traders. It is a maxim with them, in their own phrase, " never to betray their prison." Both purchaser and seller are often fictitious—the public officers being in league with the interpreters. By such means it is obvious a stolen man is as easily procured as if he were already pinioned at the door of his purchaser. You have only to give a rupee to any one to say that he is the seller, and plenty are ready to do that. Numbers maintain themselves on such profits, and slaves are thus often bribed against their own possessors. The victims are never examined, nor do the Dutch concern themselves about the matter, so that at any time any number of orders for transport may, if necessary, be prepared before-hand with the utmost security.

"Let us," continues the report, "represent to ourselves this one town of Makásar, filled with prisons, the one more dismal than the other, which are stuffed with hundreds of wretches, the victims of avarice and tyranny, who, chained in fetters, and taken away from their wives, children, parents, friends, and comforts, look to their future destiny with despair."

On the other hand, wives missing their husbands, children their parents, parents their children, with their hearts filled with rage and revenge, were running through the streets, if possible, to discover where their relatives were concealed. It was in vain. They were sometimes stabbed, if too troublesome in their inquiries; or led on by false hopes of ransom, till they were themselves thrown into debt, and easily made a prey of too. Such was the terror universally existing in these islands when the English conquered them, that the inhabitants did not dare to walk the streets, work in the fields, or go on a journey, except in companies of five or six together, and well armed.

Such were some of the practices of the Protestant Dutch. But their sordid villany in gaining possession of places was just as great as that in getting hold of people. Desirous of becoming masters of Malacca, they bribed the Portuguese governor to betray it into their hands. The bargain was struck, and he introduced the enemy into the city in 1641. They hastened to his house, and massacred him, to save the bribe of 500,000 livres—21,875*l.* of English money! The Dutch commander then tauntingly asked the commander of the Portuguese garrison, as he marched out, when he would come back again to the place. The Portuguese gravely replied—" *When your crimes are greater than ours!*"

Desirous of seizing on Cochin on the coast of Malabar, they had no sooner invested it than the news of peace between Holland and Portugal arrived; but they kept this secret till the place was taken, and when reproached by the Portuguese with their base conduct, they coolly replied—" Who did the same on the coast of Brazil ?"

Like all designing people, they were as suspicious of evil as they knew themselves capable of it. On first touching at the isle of Madura, the prince intimated his wish to pay his respects to the commander on board his vessel. It was assented to; but when the Dutch saw the number of boats coming off, they became alarmed, fired their cannon on the unsuspicious crowd, and then fell upon the confounded throng with such fury that they killed the prince, and the greater part of his followers.

Their manner of first gaining a footing in Batavia is thus recorded by the Javan historians. " In the first place they wished to ascertain the strength of *Jákatra* (the native town on the ruins of which Batavia was built). They therefore landed like màta-mátas (peons or messengers); the captain of the ship disguising himself with a turban, and accompanying several *Khójas*, (natives of the Coromandel coast.) When he had made his observations, he entered upon trade; offering however much better terms than were just, and making more presents than were necessary. A friendship thus took place between him and the prince: when this was established, the captain said that his ship was in want of repairs, and the prince allowed the vessel to come up the river. There the captain knocked out the planks of the bottom, and sunk the vessel, to obtain a pretence for further delay, and then requested a very small piece of ground on which to build a shed for the protection of the sails and other property during the repair of the vessel. This being granted, the captain raised a wall of mud, so that nobody could know what he was doing, and continued to court the favour of the prince. He soon requested as much more land as could be covered by a buffalo's hide, on which to build a small *póndok*. This being complied with, he cut the hide into strips, and claimed all the land he could inclose with them. He went on with his buildings, engaging to pay all the expenses of raising them. When the fort was finished, he threw down his mud wall, planted his cannon, and refused to pay a *doit!*"

But the whole history of the Dutch in Java is too long for our purpose. It may be found in Sir Stamford Raffles's two great quartos, and it is one of the most extraordinary relations of treachery, bribery, massacre and meanness. The slaughter of the Chinese traders there is a fearful transaction. On pretence of conveying those who yielded out of the country, they took them to sea, and threw them overboard. On one occasion, they demanded the body of *Surapáti*—a brave man, who rose from the rank of a slave to that of a chief, and a very troublesome one to them—from the very grave. They placed it upright in a chair, the commandant approached it, made his obeisance, treated it as a living person, with an expression of ironical mockery, and the officers followed his example. They then burnt the body, mixed it with gun-powder, and fired a salute with it in honour of the victory.

Such was their treatment of the natives, that the population of one province, *Banyuawngi*, which in 1750 amounted to upwards of 80,000 souls, in 1811 was reduced to 8,000. It is no less remarkable, says Sir Stamford Raffles, that while in all the capitals of British India the population has increased, wherever the Dutch influence has prevailed the work of depopulation has followed. In the Moluccas the oppressions and the consequent depopulation was monstrous. Whenever the natives have had the opportunity they have fled from the provinces under their power to the native tracts. With the following extract from Sir Stamford Raffles we will conclude this dismal notice of the deeds of a European people, claiming to be Christian, and what is more, Protestant and Reformed.

" Great demands were at all times made on the peasantry of Java for the Dutch army. Confined in unhealthy garrisons, exposed to unnecessary hardships and privations, extraordinary casualties took place amongst them, and frequent new levies became necessary, while the anticipation of danger and suffering produced an aversion to the service, which was only aggravated by the subsequent measures of cruelty and oppression. The conscripts raised in the provinces were usually sent to the metropolis by water; and though the distance be short between any two points of the island, a mortality similar to that of a slave-ship in the middle passage took place on board these receptacles of reluctant recruits. They were generally confined in the stocks till their arrival at Batavia. . . . Besides the supply of the army, one half of the male population of the country was constantly held in readiness for other public services, and thus a great portion of the effective hands were taken from their families, and detained at a distance from home in labours which broke their spirit and exhausted their strength. During the administration of Marshal Daendals, it has been calculated that the construction of public roads alone destroyed the lives of at least ten thousand workmen. The transport of government stores, and the capricious requisitions of government agents of all classes, perpetually harassed, and frequently carried off numbers of the people. If to these drains we add the waste of life occasioned by insurrections which tyranny and impolicy excited in Chéribon; the blighting effects of the coffee monopoly, and forced services in the Priáng'en Regencies, and the still more desolating operations of the policy pursued, and the consequent anarchy produced, in Bantam, we shall have some idea of the depopulating causes which existed under the Dutch administration."

CHAPTER XV.

THE ENGLISH IN INDIA.—SYSTEM OF TERRITORIAL ACQUISITION.

" And Ahab came into his house, heavy and displeased, because of the word which Naboth the Jezreelite had spoken to him; for he had said, I will not give thee the inheritance of my fathers. And he laid him down upon his bed, and turned away his face, and would eat no bread. But Jezebel his wife came to him and said unto him, Why is thy spirit so sad that thou eatest no bread? And he said unto her, Because I spoke unto Naboth the Jezreelite, and said unto him, give me thy vineyard for money; or else if it please thee, I will give thee *another* vineyard for it; and he answered I will not give thee my vineyard.

And Jezebel, his wife, said unto him, Dost thou now govern the kingdom of Israel? Arise, and eat bread, and let thine heart be merry; I will give thee the vineyard of Naboth the Jezreelite.

*　　*　　*　　*　　*　　*　　*

And the word of the Lord came to Elijah the Tishbite, saying, Arise, go down to meet Ahab king of Israel, which is in Samaria; behold he is in the vineyard of Naboth, whither he is gone down to possess it. And thou shalt speak unto him, saying, Thus saith the Lord, Hast thou killed, and also taken possession?' 1 *Kings* xxi. 4-19.

THE appearance of the Europeans in India, if the inhabitants could have had the Bible put into their hands, and been told that that was the law which these strangers professed to follow, must have been a curious spectacle. They who professed to believe the com-

mands that they should not steal, covet their neighbour's goods, kill, or injure—must have been seen
with wonder to be the most covetous, murderous, and
tyrannical of men. But if the natives could have read
the declaration of Christ—" By this shall men know
that ye are my disciples, that ye love one another,"—
the wonder must have been tenfold; for never did men
exhibit such an intensity of hatred, jealousy, and
vengeance towards each other. Portuguese, Dutch,
French, English, and Danes, coming together, or one
after the other, fell on each other's forts, factories, and
ships with the most vindictive fury. They attacked
each other at sea or at land; they propagated the most
infamous characters of each other wherever they came,
in order to supersede each other in the good graces of
the people who had valuable trading stations, or were
in possession of gold or pearls, nutmegs or cinnamon,
coffee, or cotton cloth. They loved one another to that
degree that they were ready to join the natives any
where in the most murderous attempts to massacre
and drive away each other. What must have seemed
most extraordinary of all, was the English expelling
with rigour those of their own countrymen who ventured there without the sanction of the particular trading company which claimed a monopoly of Indian
commerce. The rancour and pertinacity with which
Englishmen attacked and expelled Englishmen, was
even more violent than that which they shewed to
foreigners. The history of European intriguers, especially of the Dutch, Portuguese, English, and French,
in the East, in which every species of cruelty and bad
faith have been exhibited, is one of the most melancholy and humiliating nature. Those of the English

and French did not cease till the very last peace. At every outbreak of war between these nations in Europe, the forts and factories and islands which had been again and again seized upon, and again and again restored by treaties of peace in India, became immediately the scene of fresh aggressions, bickerings, and enormities. The hate which burnt in Europe was felt hotly, even to that distance; and men of another climate, who had no real interest in the question, and to whom Europe was but the name of a distant region which had for generations sent out swarms of powerful oppressors, were called upon to spill their blood and waste their resources in these strange deeds of their tyrants. It is to be hoped that the bulk of this evil is now past. In the peninsula of India, to which I am intending in the following chapters to confine my attention, the French now retain only the factories of Chandernagore, Caricall, Mahee, and Pondicherry; the Portuguese Goa, Damaun, and Diu; the Dutch, Serampore and Tranquebar; while the English power had triumphed over the bulk of the continent—over the vast regions of Bengal, Madras, Bombay, the Deccan and the Carnatic—over a surface of upwards of five hundred thousand square miles, and a population of nearly a hundred millions of people! These states are either directly and avowedly in British possession, or are as entirely so under the name of allies. We may well, therefore, leave the history of the squabbles and contests of the European Christians with each other for this enormous power, disgraceful as that history is to the name of Christianity—to inquire how we, whose ascendency has so wonderfully prevailed there, have gained this dominion and how we have used it.

When Europe sought your subject-realms to gain,
And stretched her giant sceptre o'er the main,
Taught her proud barks the winding way to shape,
And braved the stormy spirit of the Cape;
Children of Brama! then was Mercy nigh,
To wash the stain of blood's eternal dye?
Did Peace descend to triumph and to save,
When free-born Britons crossed the Indian wave?
Ah no!—to more than Rome's ambition true,
The muse of Freedom gave it not to you!
She the bold route of Europe's guilt began,
And, in the march of nations, led the van!

Pleasures of Hope.

We are here to witness a new scene of conquest. The Indian natives were too powerful and populous to permit the Europeans to march at once into the heart of their territories, as they had done into South America, to massacre the people, or to subject them to instant slavery and death. The old inhabitants of the empire, the Hindoos, were indeed, in general, a comparatively feeble and gentle race, but there were numerous and striking exceptions; the mountaineers were, as mountaineers in other countries, of a hardy, active, and martial character. The Mahrattas, the Rohillas, the Seiks, the Rajpoots, and others, were fierce and formidable tribes. But besides this, the ruling princes of the country, whether Moguls or Hindoos, had for centuries maintained their sway by the same power by which they had gained it, that of arms. They could bring into the field immense bodies of troops, which though found eventually unable to compete with European power and discipline, were too formidable to be rashly attacked, and have cost oceans of blood and treasure finally to reduce them to subjection. Moreover, the odium which the Spa-

niards and Portuguese had everywhere excited by
their unceremonious atrocities, may be supposed to
have had their effect on the English, who are a re-
flecting people; and it is to be hoped also that the
progress of sound policy and of Christian knowledge,
however slow, may be taken into the account in some
degree. They went out too under different circumstances—not as mere adventurers, but as sober traders,
aiming at establishing a permanent and enriching
commerce with these countries; and if Christianity, if
the laws of justice and of humanity were to be violated,
it must be under a guise of policy, and a form of law.

We shall not enter into a minute notice of the
earliest proceedings of the English in India, because
for upwards of a century from the formation of their
first trading association, those proceedings are comparatively insignificant. During that period Bombay had
been ceded as part of a marriage-portion by the Portuguese to Charles II.; factories had been established
at Surat, Madras, Masulipatam, Visigapatam, Calcutta, and other places; but it was not till the different
chartered companies were consolidated into one grand
company in 1708, styled "The United Company of
Merchants trading to the East Indies," that the
English affairs in the east assumed an imposing
aspect. From that period the East India Company
commenced that career of steady grasping at dominion
over the Indian territories, which has never been
relaxed for a moment, but, while it has for ever worn
the grave air of moderation, and has assumed the language of right, has gone on adding field to field and
house to house—swallowing up state after state, and
prince after prince, till it has finally found itself the

sovereign of this vast and splendid empire, as it would fain persuade itself and the world, by the clearest claims, and the most undoubted justice. By the laws and principles of modern policy, it may be so; but by the eternal principles of Christianity, there never was a more thorough repetition of the hankering after Naboth's vineyards, of the " slaying and taking possession " exhibited to the world. It is true that, as the panegyrists of our Indian policy contend, it may be the design of Providence that the swarming millions of Indostan should be placed under our care, that they may enjoy the blessings of English rule, and of English knowledge: but Providence had no need that we should violate all his most righteous injunctions to enable him to bring about his designs. Providence, the Scriptures tell us, intended that Jacob should supersede Esau in the heritage of Israel: but Providence had no need of the deception which Rebecca and Jacob practised,—had no need of the mess of pottage and the kid-skins, to enable Him to effect his object. We are much too ready to run the wilful career of our own lusts and passions, and lay the charge at the door of Providence. It is true that English dominion is, or will become, far better to the Hindoos than that of the cruel and exacting Moguls; but who made us the judge and the ruler over these people? If the real object of our policy and exertions in India has been the achievement of wealth and power, as it undoubtedly has, it is pitiful and hypocritical to endeavour to clothe it with the pretence of working the will of Providence, and seeking the good of the natives. We shall soon see which objects have been most zealously and undeviatingly pursued, and by

what means. If our desires have been, not to enrich
and aggrandize ourselves, but to benefit the people and
rescue them from the tyranny of bad rulers, heaven
knows what wide realms are yet open to our benevolent exertions; what despots there are to pull down;
what miserable millions to relieve from their oppressions;—and when we behold Englishmen levelling their
vengeance against such tyrants, and visiting such unhappy people with their protective power, where
neither gold nor precious merchandise are to be won
at the same time, we may safely give the amplest credence and the profoundest admiration to their claims of
disinterested philanthropy. If they present themselves
as the champions of freedom, and the apostles of social
amelioration, we shall soon have opportunities of asking how far they have maintained these characters.

Mr. Auber, in his " History of the British Power in
India," has quoted largely from letters of the Board of
Directors of the Company, passages to shew how sincerely the representatives of the East India Company
at home have desired to arrest encroachment on the
rights of the natives; to avoid oppressive exactions;
to resist the spirit of military and political aggression.
They have from year to year proclaimed their wishes
for the comfort of the people; they have disclaimed all
lust of territorial acquisition; have declared that they
were a mercantile, rather than a political body; and
have rebuked the thirst of conquest in their agents,
and endeavoured to restrain the avidity of extortion in
them. Seen in Mr. Auber's pages, the Directors
present themselves as a body of grave and honorable
merchants, full of the most admirable spirit of moderation, integrity, and benevolence; and we may give

them the utmost credit for sincerity in their professions and desires. But unfortunately, we all know
what human nature is. Unfortunately the power, the
wealth, and the patronage brought home to them by
the very violation of their own wishes and maxims
were of such an overwhelming and seducing nature,
that it was in vain to resist them. Nay, in such
colours does the modern philosophy of conquest and
diplomacy disguise the worst transactions between one
state and another, that it is not for plain men very
readily to penetrate to the naked enormity beneath.
When all the world was applauding the success of
Indian affairs,—the extension of territory, the ability
of their governors, the valour of their troops; and
when they felt the flattering growth of their greatness,
it required qualities far higher than mere mercantile
probity and good intentions, to enable them to strip
away the false glitter of their official transactions, and
sternly assure themselves of the unholiness of their
nature. We may therefore concede to the Directors
of the East India Company, and to their governors
and officers in general, the very best intentions, knowing as we do, the force of influences such as we have
already alluded to, and the force also of modern diplomatic and military education, by which a policy and
practices of the most dismal character become gradually to be regarded not merely unexceptionable,
but highly honorable. We may allow all this, and
yet pronounce the mode by which the East India
Company has possessed itself of Hindostan, as the
most revolting and unchristian that can possibly be
conceived. The most masterly policy, regarded independent of its *morale*, and a valour more than Roman

have been exhibited by our governors-generals and armies on the plains of Hindostan: but if there ever was one system more Machiavelian—more appropriative of the shew of justice where the basest injustice was attempted—more cold, cruel, haughty and unrelenting than another,—it is the system by which the government of the different states of India has been wrested from the hands of their respective princes and collected into the grasp of the British power. Incalculable gainers as we have been by this system, it is impossible to review it without feelings of the most poignant shame and the highest indignation. Whenever we talk to other nations of British faith and integrity, they may well point to India in derisive scorn. The system which, for more than a century, was steadily at work to strip the native princes of their dominions, and that too under the most sacred pleas of right and expediency, is a system of torture more exquisite than regal or spiritual tyranny ever before discovered; such as the world has nothing similar to shew.

Spite of the repeated instructions sent out by the Court of Directors to their servants in India, to avoid territorial acquisitions, and to cultivate only honest and honorable commerce; there is evidence that from the earliest period the desire of conquest was entertained, and was, spite of better desires, always too welcome to be abandoned. In the instructions forwarded in 1689, the Directors expounded themselves in the following words: "The increase of our revenue is the subject of our care, as much as our trade:—'t is that must maintain our force when twenty accidents may interrupt our trade;—'t is that must make us a

nation in India. Without that, we are but as a great
number of interlopers, united by his Majesty's royal
charter, fit only to trade where nobody of power
thinks fit only to prevent us; and upon this account
it is that the wise Dutch, in all their general advices
which we have seen, write ten paragraphs concerning
their government, their civil and military policy, warfare, and the increase of their revenue, for one para-
graph they write concerning trade."*

Spite of all pretences to the contrary—spite of all
advices and exhortations from the government at
home of a more unambitious character, this was the
spirit that never ceased to actuate the Company, and
was so clearly felt to be it, that its highest servants,
in the face of more peaceful injunctions, and in the
face of the Act of Parliament strictly prohibiting
territorial extension, went on perpetually to add conquest to conquest, under the shew of necessity or
civil treaty; and they who offended most against the
letter of the law, gratified most entirely the spirit of
the company and the nation. Who have been looked
upon as so eminently the benefactors and honourers
of the nation by Indian acquisition as Lord Clive,
Warren Hastings, and the Marquess Wellesley? It
is for the determined and successful opposition to the
ostensible principles and annually reiterated advices
of the Company, that that very Company has heaped
wealth and distinctions upon these and other persons,
and for which it has just recently voted an additional
pension to the latter nobleman.

What then is this system of torture by which the
possessions of the Indian princes have been wrung

* Mills's Hist. of British India, i. 74. Bruce, iii. 78.

from them ?   It is this—the skilful application of the
process by which cunning men create debtors, and
then force them at once to submit to their most exorbitant demands.   From the moment that the English
felt that they had the power in India to "divide and
conquer," they adopted the plan of doing it rather by
plausible manœuvres than by a bold avowal of their
designs, and a more honest plea of the right of conquest—the ancient doctrine of the strong, which they
began to perceive was not quite so much in esteem as
formerly.   Had they said at once, these Mahomedan
princes are arbitrary, cruel, and perfidious—we will
depose them, and assume the government ourselves—
we pretend to no other authority for our act than our
ability to do it, and no other excuse for our conduct
than our determination to redress the evils of the people :
that would have been a candid behaviour.   It would
have been so far in accordance with the ancient doctrine
of nations that little would have been thought of it ;
and though as Christians we could not have applauded
the " doing evil that good might come of it," yet had
the promised benefit to more than eighty millions of
people followed, that glorious penance would have
gone far in the most scrupulous mind to have justified
the crime of usurpation.   But the mischief has been,
that while the exactions and extortions on the people
have been continued, and in many cases exaggerated,
the means of usurpation have been those glozing and
hypocritical arts, which are more dangerous from their
subtlety than naked violence, and more detestable because wearing the face, and using the language, of
friendship and justice.   A fatal friendship, indeed,
has that of the English been to all those princes that

were allured by it. It has pulled them every one from their thrones, or has left them there the contemptible puppets of a power that works its arbitrary will through them. But friendship or enmity, the result has been eventually the same to them. If they resisted alliance with the encroaching English, they were soon charged with evil intentions, fallen upon, and conquered; if they acquiesced in the proffered alliance, they soon became ensnared in those webs of diplomacy from which they never escaped, without the loss of all honour and hereditary dominion—of every thing, indeed, but the lot of prisoners where they had been kings. The first step in the English friendship with the native princes, has generally been to assist them against their neighbours with troops, or to locate troops with them to protect them from aggression. For these services such enormous recompense was stipulated for, that the unwary princes, entrapped by their fears of their native foes rather than of their pretended friends, soon found that they were utterly unable to discharge them. Dreadful exactions were made on their subjects, but in vain. Whole provinces, or the revenues of them, were soon obliged to be made over to their grasping *friends;* but they did not suffice for their demands. In order to pay them their debts or their interest, the princes were obliged to borrow large sums at an extravagant rate. These sums were eagerly advanced by the English in their private and individual capacities, and securities again taken on lands or revenues. At every step the unhappy princes became more and more embarrassed, and as the embarrassment increased, the claims of the Company became proportionably pressing. In the technical phraseology of money-lenders, "the screw was then turned," till there was no longer any enduring it. The unfortunate princes felt themselves, instead of being relieved by their artful friends, actually introduced by them into

> Regions of sorrow, doleful shades, where peace
> And rest can never dwell ; hope never comes
> That comes to all ; but torture without end
> Still urges.

To escape it, there became no alternative but to throw themselves entirely upon the mercy of their inexorable creditors, or to break out into armed resistance. In the one case they found themselves speedily stripped of every vestige of their power — their revenues and management of their territories given over to these creditors, which still never were enough to liquidate their monstrous and growing demands; so that the next proposition was that they should entirely cede their territories, and become pensioners on their usurpers. In the other case, they were at once declared perfidious and swindling,—no faith was to be kept with them,—they were assaulted by the irresistible arms of their oppressors, and inevitably destroyed or deposed.

If they sought aid from another state, that became a fortunate plea to attack that state too; and the English were not contented to chastise the state thus aiding its ancient neighbour, it was deemed quite sufficient ground to seize and subjugate it also. There was no province that was for a moment safe from this most convenient system of policy, which feared public opinion sufficiently to seek arguments to make a case before it, but resolved still to seize, by hook or by crook, all that it coveted. It did not suffice that a province merely refused an alliance, if the proper time was deemed to be arrived for its seizure—some plea of danger or suspicion was set up against it. It was called good policy not to wait for attack, but to charge it with hostile designs, though not a hostile indication was given—it was assailed with all the forces in the empire. Those princes that were once subjected to the British power or the British *friendship*, were set up or pulled down just as it suited their pleasure. If necessary, the most odious stigmas were fixed on them to get rid of them—they were declared weak, dissolute, or illegitimate. If a prince or princess was suspected of having wealth, some villanous scheme was hatched to plunder him or her of it. For more than a century this shocking system was in operation, every day growing more daring in its action, and more wide in its extent. Power both gave security and augmented audacity—for every British subject who was not belonging to the Company, and therefore interested in its operations, was rigidly excluded from the country, and none could therefore complain of the evil deeds that were there done under the sun. It is almost incredible that so abominable an influence could be for a century exercised over a great realm, by British subjects, many of whom were in all other respects worthy and most honourable men; and, what is more, that it could be sanctioned by the British parliament, and admired by the British nation. But we have yet the proofs to adduce, and unfortunately they are only too abundant and conclusive. Let us see them.

We will for the present pass the operations of Clive

in the Carnatic at once to destroy the French influence there, and to set up ·Mahomet Ali, a creature of the English. We shall anon see the result of that: we will observe in the first place the manner of obtaining Bengal, as it became the head of the English empire in India, and the centre of all future transactions.

In 1756, Suraja Dowla, the Subahdar of Bengal, demanded an officer belonging to him who, according to the custom amongst the colonists there, had taken refuge at Calcutta. The English refused to give him up. The Subahdar attacked and took the place. One hundred and forty-six of the English fell into the conqueror's hands, and were shut up for the night in the celebrated *Black-hole*, whence only twenty-three were taken out alive in the morning. It may be said in vindication of the Subahdar, that the act of immuring these unfortunate people in this horrible den was not his, but that of the guards to whom they were entrusted for the night, and who put them there as in a place of the greatest security; and it may be added, not to the credit of the English, that this very *black-hole* was the *English* prison, where they were in the habit of confining *their* prisoners. As Mr. Mills very justly asks—" What had they to do with a *black-hole?* Had no *black-hole* existed, as none ought to exist anywhere, least of all in the sultry and unwholesome climate of Bengal, those who perished in the *black-hole* of Calcutta would have experienced a different fate."

On the news of the capture of Calcutta arriving at Madras, a body of troops was dispatched under Admiral Watson and Colonel Clive, for its recovery;

which was soon effected, and Hoogly, a considerable
city about twenty-three miles further up the river,
was also attacked and reduced. A treaty was now
entered into with Suraja Dowla, the Subahdar, which
was not of long continuance; for, lest the Subahdar,
who was not at bottom friendly to the English, as he
had in reality no cause, should form an alliance with
the French at Chandernagore, they resolved to depose
him! This bold and unwarrantable scheme of depos-
ing a prince in his own undoubted territories, and that
by mere strangers and traders on the coast, is the
beginning of that extraordinary and unexampled assumption which has always marked the conduct of the
English in India. Scarcely had they entered into
the treaty with this Subahdar than they resolved to
depose him because he would protect the French, who
were also permitted to hold a factory in his territory
as well as they. This audacious scheme was Clive's.
Admiral Watson, on the contrary, declared it an extraordinary thing to depose a man they had so lately
made a solemn treaty with. But Clive, as he afterwards avowed, when examined before the House of
Commons, declared that " they must now go further;
they could not stop there. *Having established themselves by force and not by consent of the Nabob,* he would
endeavour to drive them out again." This is the
robber's doctrine;—having committed one outrage, a
second, or a series of outrages must be committed, to
prevent punishment, and secure the booty. But
having once entertained the idea of pulling the Subahdar from his throne, they did not scruple to add
treason and rebellion to the crime of invading the
rights of the sovereign. They began by debauching

his own officers. They found out one Meer Jaffier Khan, a man of known traitorous mind, who had been paymaster-general under the former Subahdar, and yet retained great power in the army. This wretch, on condition of being placed on the throne, agreed to betray his master, and seduce as many of the influential of his officers as possible. The terms of this diabolical confederacy between this base traitor and the baser *Christian English*, as they stand in the first parliamentary report on Indian affairs, and as related by Orme in his History of India (ii. 153), and by Mills (ii. 110), are very instructive.

The English had got an idea which wonderfully sharpened their desire to depose Suraja Dowla, that he had an enormous treasure. The committee (of the council of Calcutta) really believed, says Mr. Orme, the wealth of Suraja Dowla much greater than it possibly could be, even if the whole life of the late Nabob Aliverdi had not been spent in defending his dominions against the invasions of ruinous enemies; and even if Suraja Dowla had reigned many, instead of one year. They resolved, accordingly, not to be sparing in their commands; and the situation of Meer Jaffier, and the manners and customs of the country, made him ready to promise whatever they desired. In the name of compensation for losses by the capture of Calcutta, 10,000,000 rupees were promised to the English Company; 5,000,000 rupees to English inhabitants; 2,000,000 to the Indians, and 700,000 to the Armenian merchants. These sums were specified in the formal treaty. Besides this, the Committee resolved to ask 2,500,000 rupees for the squadron, and the same amount for the army. " When this was settled," says Lord Clive, "Mr. Becher (a member) suggested to the committee, that he thought that committee, who managed the great machine of government, was entitled to some consideration, as well as the army and navy." Such a proposition in such an assembly, could not fail to appear eminently reasonable. It met with a suitable approbation. Mr. Becher informs us, that the sums received were 280,000 rupees by Mr. Drake the governor; 280,000 by Col. Clive; and 240,000 each by himself, Mr. Watts, and Major Kilpatrick, the inferior members of the committee. The terms obtained by favour of the Company were, that all the French factories and effects should be given up; that the French should be for ever excluded from Bengal; that the territory surrounding Calcutta to the distance of 600 yards beyond the Mahratta ditch, and all the land lying south of Calcutta as far as Culpee, should be granted them on Zemindary tenure, the Company paying the rent in the same manner as the other Zemindars.

Thus did these Englishmen bargain with a traitor to betray his prince and country,—the traitor, for the bribe of being himself made prince, not merely sell his master, but give two millions three hundred and ninety-eight thousand pounds sterling,* with valuable privileges and property of the state,—while these dealers in treason and rebellion pocketed each, from two hundred and forty to two hundred and eighty thousand pounds sterling! A more infamous transaction is not on record.

To carry this wicked conspiracy into effect, the

* According to Orme, 2,750,000*l.*

English took the field against their victim Suraja
Dowla; and Meer Jaffier, the traitor, in the midst of
of the engagement moved off, and went over to the
English with his troops—thus determining the fate of
a great kingdom, and of thirty millions of people, with
the loss of twenty Europeans killed and wounded, of
sixteen Sepoys killed, and only thirty-six wounded.
The unfortunate prince was soon afterwards seized
and assassinated by the son of this traitor Meer Jaffier.
The vices and inefficiency of this bad man soon compelled the English to pull him down from the throne
into which they had so criminally raised him. They
then set up in his stead his son-in-law, Meer Causim.
This man for a time served their purpose, by the
activity with which he raised money to pay their claims
upon him. He resorted to every species of cruelty
and injustice to extort the necessary funds from his
unfortunate subjects. But about three years, nearly the
same period as their former puppet-nabob had reigned,
sufficed to weary them of him. He was rigorous
enough to raise money to pay them, but he was not tool
enough, when that was done, to humour every scheme
of rapacity which they dictated to him. They complained of his not allowing their goods to pass duty-
free through his territories; he therefore abolished all
duties, and thus laid open the trade to everybody.
This enraged them, and they determined to depose
him. Meer Causim, however, was not so readily dismissed as Meer Jaffier had been. He resisted vigo-
rously; massacred such of their troops as fell into his
hands, and fleeing into Oude, brought them into war
with its nabob. What is most remarkable, they again
set up old Meer Jaffier, whom they had before deposed

for his crimes and his imbecility. But probably, from their experience of Meer Causim, they now preferred an easy tool to one with more self-will. In their treaty with him they made a claim upon him for ten lacs of rupees; which demand speedily grew to twenty, thirty, forty, and finally to fifty-three lacs of rupees. All delicacy was laid aside in soliciting the payment, and one half of it was soon extorted from him. The Subahdar, in fact, was now become the merest puppet in their hands. They were the real lords of Bengal, and in direct receipt of more than half the revenues. Within less than ten years from the disgraceful bargain with the traitor Meer Jaffier, they had made Bengal their own, though they still hesitated to avow themselves as its sovereigns; they had got possession of Benares; they had acquired that power over the Nabob of Oude, in consequence of the successful war brought upon him by his alliance with the deposed nabob Meer Causim, that would at any time make them entirely his masters; the Mogul himself was ready and anxious to obtain their friendship; they were, in short, become the far greatest power in India.

Here then is an opening instance of the means by which we acquired our territories in India; and the language of Lord Clive, when he returned thither as governor of Bengal in 1765, may shew what other scenes were likely to ensue. " We have at last arrived at that critical period which I have long foreseen; I mean that period which renders it necessary for us to determine whether we can or shall take the whole to ourselves. Jaffier Ali Khan is dead. His natural son is a minor; but I know not whether he is yet declared successor. Sujah Dowla is beat from his dominions. We are in possession of it; and it is scarcely hyperbole to say—to-morrow the whole Mogul empire is in our power. The inhabitants of the country, we know by long experience, have no attachment to any obligation. Their forces are neither disciplined, commanded, nor paid like ours. Can it then be doubtful that a large army of Europeans will effectually preserve us sovereigns ?"

The scene of aggression and aggrandizement here indicated, soon grew so wide and busy, that it would far exceed the whole space of this volume to trace even rapidly its great outlines. The Great Mogul, the territories of Oude and Arcot, Mysore, Travancore, Benares, Tanjore, the Mahrattas, the whole peninsula in fact, speedily felt the effect of these views, in diplomatic or military subjection. We can point out no fortunate exception, and must therefore content ourselves with briefly touching upon some of the more prominent cases.

The first thing that deserves attention, is the treatment of the Mogul himself. This is the statement of it by the French historian: " The Mogul having been driven out of Delhi by the Pattans, by whom his son had been set up in his room, was wandering from one province to another in search of a place of refuge in his own territories, and requesting succour from his own vassals, but without success. Abandoned by his subjects, betrayed by his allies, without support and without an army, he was allured by the power of the English, and implored their protection. They promised to conduct him to Delhi, and re-establish him on his throne; but they insisted that he should previously cede to them the absolute sovereignty over Bengal. This cession was made by an authentic act, attended by all the formalities usually practised throughout the Mogul empire. The English, possessed of this title, which was to give a kind of legitimacy to their usurpation, at least in the eyes of the vulgar, soon forgot the promises they had made. They gave the Mogul to understand, that particular circumstances would not suffer them to be concerned in such an enterprise ; but some better opportunity was to be hoped for; and to make up for his losses, they assigned him a pension of six millions of rupees, (262,500*l.*), with the revenue of Allahabad, and Sha Ichanabad, or Delhi, upon which that unfortunate prince was reduced to subsist himself, in one of the principal towns of Benares, where he had taken up his residence."—*Raynal.*

Hastings, in fact, made it a reason for depriving him again even of this pension, that he had sought the aid of the Mahrattas, to do that which he had vainly hoped from the English—to restore him to his throne. This is Mills's relation of this fact, founded on the fifth Parliamentary Report.—" Upon receiving from him the grant of the duannee, or the receipt and management of the revenues of Bengal, Bahar, and Orissa, it was agreed that, as the royal share of these revenues, twenty-six lacs of rupees should be annually paid to him by the Company. His having accepted of the assistance of the Mahrattas to place him on the throne of his ancestors, was now made use of as a reason for telling him, that the tribute of these provinces should be paid to him no more. Of the honour, or the discredit, however, of this transaction, the principal share belongs not to the governor, but to the Directors themselves; who, in their letter to Bengal, of the 11th of November 1768, had said, ' If the emperor flings himself into the hands of the Mahrattas, or any other power, we are disengaged from him, *and it may open a fair opportunity of withholding* the twenty-six lacs we now pay him.'" Upon the whole, indeed, of the measure dealt out to this unhappy sovereign,—depriving him of the territories of Corah and Allahabad; depriving him of the tribute which was due to him from these provinces of his which they possessed—the Directors bestowed unqualified approbation; and though they condemned the use which had been made of their troops in subduing the country of the Rohillas, they frankly declare, "We, upon the maturest deliberation, confirm the treaty of Benares." "Thus," adds Mills, "they had plundered the unhappy emperor of twenty-six lacs per annum, and the two provinces of Corah and Allahabad, which they had sold to the Vizir for fifty lacs of rupees, on the plea that he had forfeited them by his alliance with the Mahrattas;" as though he was not free, if one party would not assist him to regain his rights, to seek that assistance from another.

Passing over the crooked policy of the English, in seizing upon the isles of Salsette and Bassein, near Bombay, and treating for them afterwards, and all the perfidies of the war for the restoration of Ragabah, the Peshwa of the Mahrattas, the fate of the Nabob of Arcot, one of their earliest allies, is deserving of particular notice, as strikingly exemplifying their policy. They began by obtaining a grant of land in 1750, surrounding Madras. They then were only too happy to assist the Nabob against the French. For these military aids, in which Clive distinguished himself, the English took good care to stipulate for their usually monstrous payments. Mahomed Ali, the nabob, soon found that he was unable to satisfy the demands of his allies. They urged upon him the maintenance of large bodies of troops for the defence of his territories against these French and other enemies. This threw him still more inextricably into debt, and therefore more inextricably into their power. He became an unresisting tool in their hands. In his name the most savage exactions were practised on his subjects. The whole revenues of his kingdom, however, proved totally inadequate to the perpetually accumulating demands upon them. He borrowed money where he could, and at whatever interest, of the English themselves. When this interest could not be paid, he made over to them, under the name of *tuncaus*, the revenues of some portion of his domains. These assignments directly decreasing his resources, only raised the demands of his other creditors more violently, and the fleecing of his subjects became more and more dreadful. In this situation, he began to cast his eyes on the neighbouring states, and to incite his allies, by the assertion of various claims upon them, to join him in falling upon them, and thus to give him an opportunity of paying them. This exactly suited their views. It gave them a prospect of money, and of conquest too, under the plausible colour of assisting their ally in urging his just claims. They first joined him in falling on the Rajah of Tanjore, whom the Nabob claimed as a tributary, and indebted to him in a large amount of revenue. The Rajah was soon reduced to submission, and agreed to pay thirty lacs and fifty thousand rupees, and to aid the Nabob in all his wars. Scarcely, however, was this treaty signed, than they repented of it; thought they had not got enough; hoped the Rajah would not be exact to a day in his payment, in which case they would fall on him again for breach of treaty. It so happened;—they rushed out of their camp, seized on part of Vellum, and the districts of Coiladdy and Elangad, to the retention of which the poor Rajah was obliged to submit.

This affair being so fortunately adjusted, the Nabob called on his willing allies to attack the Marawars. They too, he said, owed him money; and money was what the English were always in want of. They readily assented, though they declared that they believed the Nabob to have no real claim on the Marawars whatever. But then, they said, the Nabob has made them his enemies, and it is necessary for his security that they should be reduced. They did not pretend it was just—but then, it was politic. The particulars of this war are barbarous and disgraceful to the English. The Nabob thirsted for the destruction of these states : he and his Christian-allies soon reduced Ramnadaporam, the capital of the great Marawar, seized the Polygar, a minor of twelve years old, his mother, and the Duan; they came suddenly upon the Polygar of the lesser Marawar while he was trusting to a treaty just made, and killed him; and pursued the inhabitants of the country with severities that can only be represented by the language of one of the English officers addressed to the Council. Speaking of the animosity of the people against them, and their attacking the baggage, he says, " I can only determine it by reprisals, which will oblige me to plunder and burn the villages; kill every man in them; and take prisoners the women and children. These are actions which the nature of this war will require." *

Such were the unholy deeds into which the Nabob and the great scheme of acquisition of territory had led our countrymen in 1773; but this was only the beginning of these affairs. This bloody campaign ended, and large sums of money levied, the Nabob proposed *another* war on the Rajah of Tanjore! There was not the remotest plea of injury from the Rajah, or breach of treaty. He had paid the enormous sum demanded of him before, by active levies on his subjects, and by mortgaging lands and jewels; but the Nabob had now made him a very dangerous enemy— he *might* ally himself with Hyder Ali, or the French, or some power or other—therefore it was better that he should be utterly destroyed, and his country put into the power of the Nabob! "Never," exclaims Mr. Mills, "I suppose, was the resolution taken to make war upon a lawful sovereign, with the view of reducing him entirely, that is, stripping him of his dominions, and either putting him and his family to death, or making them prisoners for life, upon a more accommodating reason! We have done the Rajah great injury—we have no intention of doing him right—this is a sufficient reason for going on to his destruction." But it was not only thought, but done; and this was the bargain: The Nabob was to advance money and all due necessaries for the war, and to pay 10,000 instead of 7,000 sepoys. The unhappy Rajah was speedily defeated, and taken prisoner with his

* Tanjore Papers. Mills' History.

family; and his country put into the hands of his mortal enemy. There were men of honour and virtue enough amongst the Directors at home, however, to feel a proper disgust, or at least, regard for public opinion, at these unprincipled proceedings, and the Rajah, through the means of Lord Paget was restored, not however without having a certain quantity of troops quartered upon him; a yearly payment of four lacs of pagodas imposed; and being bound not to make any treaty or assist any power without the consent of the English. He was, in fact, put into the first stage of that process of subjection which would, in due time, remove from him even the shadow of independence.

Such were the measures by which the Nabob of Arcot endeavoured to relieve himself from his embarrassments with the English; but they would not all avail. Their demands grew faster than he could find means to satisfy them. Their system of action was too well devised to fail them; their victims rarely escaped from their toils: he might help them to ruin his neighbours, but he could not escape them himself. During his life he was surrounded by a host of cormorant creditors; his country, harassed by perpetual exactions, rapidly declined; and the death of his son and successor, Omdut ul Omrah, in 1801, produced one of the strangest scenes in this strange history. The Marquis Wellesley was then Governor-general, and, pursuing that sweeping course which stripped away the hypocritical mask from British power in India, threw down so many puppet princes, and displayed the English dominion in Indostan in its gigantic nakedness. The revenues of the Carnatic had been before taken in the hands of the English, but Lord Wellesley resolved to depose the prince; and the manner in which this deposition was effected, was singularly despotic and unfeeling. They had come to the resolution to depose the Nabob, and only looked about for some plausible pretence. This they professed to have found in a correspondence which, by the death of Tippoo Saib, had fallen into their hands —a correspondence between Tippoo and some officers of the Nabob. They alleged, that this correspondence contained injurious and even treasonable language towards the English. When, therefore, the Nabob lay on his death-bed they surrounded his house with troops, and immediately that the breath had departed from him they demanded to see his will. This rude and unfeeling behaviour, so repugnant to the ideas of every people, however savage and brutal, at a moment so solemn and sacred to domestic sorrow, was respectfully protested against—but in vain. The will they insisted upon seeing, and it accordingly was put into their hands by the son of the Nabob, now about to mount the throne himself. Finding that the son was nominated as his heir and successor by the Nabob, the Commissioners immediately announced to him the charge of treason against his father, and that the throne was thereby forfeited by the family. This charge, of course, was a matter of surprise to the family; especially when the papers said to contain the treason were produced, and they could find in them nothing but terms of fidelity and respect towards the English government. But the English had resolved that the charge should be a sufficient charge, and the young prince manfully resisting it, they then declared him to be of illegitimate birth,—a very favourite and convenient plea with them. On this they set him aside, and made a treaty with another prince, in which for a certain provision the Carnatic was made over to them for ever. The young nabob, Ali Hussein, did not long survive this scene of indignity and arbitrary deposition —his death occurring in the spring of the following year.

Such was the English treatment of their friend the Nabob of Arcot;—the Nabob of Arcot, whose name was for years continually heard in England as the powerful ally of the British, as their coadjutor against the French, against the ambitious Hyder Ali, as their zealous, and accommodating friend on all occasions. It was in vain that either the old Nabob, or the young one, whom they so summarily deposed, pleaded the faith of treaties, their own hereditary right, or ancient friendship. Arcot had served its turn; it had been the stalking-horse to all the aggressions on other states that they needed from it,—they had exacted all that could be exacted in the name of the Nabob from his subjects—they had squeezed the sponge dry; and moreover the time was now come that they could with impunity throw off the stealthy crouching attitude of the tiger, the smiling meek mask of alliance, and boldly seize upon undisguised sovereign powers in India. Arcot was but one state amongst many that were now to be so treated. Benares, Oude, Tanjore, Surat, and others found themselves in the like case.

Benares had been a tributary of Oude; but in 1764, when the English commenced war against the Nabob of Oude, the Rajah of Benares joined the English, and rendered them the most essential services. For these he was taken under the English protection. At first with so much delicacy and consideration was he treated, that a resident was not allowed, as in the case of other tributaries, to reside in his capital, lest in the words of the minute of the Governor-general in command in 1775: "such resident might acquire an improper influence over the Rajah and his country, which would in effect render him master of both; lest it should end," as they knew that such things as a matter of course did end, "in reducing him to the mean and depraved state of a mere Zemindar." The council expressed its anxiety that the Rajah's independence should be in no way compromised than by the mere fact of the payment of his tribute, which, says Mills, continued to be paid with an exactness rarely exemplified in the history of the tributary princes of Hindustan. But unfortunately, the Rajah gave some offence to the powerful Warren Hastings, and there was speedily a requisition made upon him for the maintenance of three battalions of Sepoys, estimated at five lacs of rupees. The Rajah pleaded inability to pay it forthwith; but five days only were given him. This was followed by a third and fourth requisition of the same sort. Seeing how the tide was running against him, the unhappy Rajah sent a private gift of two lacs of rupees to Mr. Hastings,—the pretty sum of 20,000*l.*, in the hope of regaining his favour, and stopping this ruinous course of exaction. That unprincipled man took the money, but exacted the payment of the public demand with unabated rigour, and even fined him 10,000*l.* for delay in payment, and ordered troops, as he had done before, to march into his country to enforce the iniquitous exaction!

The work of diplomatic robbery on the Rajah now went on rapidly. " The screw was now turned" with vigour,—to use a homely but expressive phrase, the nose was held desperately to the grind-stone. No bounds were set to the pitiless fury of spoliation, for the Governor's revenge had none; and besides, there was a dreadful want of money to defray the expenses of the wars with Hyder into which the government had plunged. " I was resolved," says Hastings, " to draw from his guilt" (his having offended Mr. Hastings—the guilt was all on the other side) " the means of relief to the Company's distresses. In a word, I had determined to make him pay largely for his pardon, or to exact a severe vengeance for his past delinquency."* What this delinquency could possibly be, unless it were not having sent Mr. Hastings a *second* present of *two lacs*, is not to be discovered; but the success of the first placebo was not such as to elicit a second. The Rajah, therefore, tried what effect he could produce upon the council at large; he sent an offer of TWENTY LACS *for the public service.* It was scornfully rejected, and a demand of FIFTY *lacs* was made! The impossibility of compliance with such extravagant demands was what was anticipated; the Governor hastened to Benares, arrested the Rajah in his own capital; set at defiance the indignation of the people at this insult. The astounded Rajah made his escape, but only to find himself at war with his insatiable despoilers. In vain did he propose every means of accommodation. Nothing would now serve but his destruction. He was attacked, and compelled to fly. Bidgegur, where,

* Governor-general's own Narrative. Second Report of Select Committee, 1781.

says Hastings himself, " he had left his wife, a woman
of amiable character, his mother, all the other women
of his family, and the survivors of the family of his
father, Bulwant Sing," was obliged to capitulate; and
Hastings, in his fell and inextinguishable vengeance,
even, says Mills, "in his letters to the commanding
officer, employed expressions which implied that the
plunder of these women was the due reward of the
soldiers; and which suggested one of the most dreadful outrages to which, in the conception of the country, a human being could be exposed."

The fort was surrendered on express stipulation for
the safety, and freedom from search, of the females;
but, adds Mills, "the idea suggested by Mr. Hastings
diffused itself but too perfectly amongst the soldiery;
and when the princesses, with their relatives and
attendants, to the number of three hundred women,
besides children, withdrew from the castle, the capitu-
lation was shamefully violated; they were plundered of
their effects, and their persons otherwise rudely and
disgracefully treated by the licentious people, and followers of the camp." He adds, "one is delighted for
the honour of distinguished gallantry, that in no part
of the opprobrious business the commanding officer
had any share. He leaned to generosity and the protection of the princesses from the beginning. His utmost endeavours were exerted to restrain the outrages
of the camp; and he represented them with feeling
to Mr. Hastings, who expressed his concurrence, etc."

The only other consolation in this detestable affair is,
that the soldiers, in spite of Hastings, got the plunder
of the Rajah, and that the Court of Directors at home
censured his conduct. But these are miserable drops

of satisfaction in this huge and overflowing cup of bitterness,—of misery to trusting, friendly, and innocent
people; and of consequent infamy on the British name.

We must, out of the multitudes of such cases, confine ourselves to one more. The atrocities just re-
cited had put Benares into the entire power of the
English, but it had only tended to increase the pecu-
niary difficulties. The soldiery had got the plunder
—the expenses of the war were added to the expenses
of other wars;—some other kingdom must be plundered, for booty must be had: so Mr. Hastings continued his journey, and paid a visit to the Nabob of
Oude. It is not necessary to trace the complete progress of this Nabob's friendship with the English. It
was exactly like that of the other princes just spoken
of. A treaty was made with him; and then, from time
to time, the usual exactions of money and the maintenance of troops for his own subjection were heaped
upon him. As with the Nabob of Arcot, so with him,
they were ready to sanction and assist him in his most
criminal views on his neighbours, to which his need of
money drove him. He proposed to Mr. Hastings, in
1773, to assist him in *exterminating the Rohillas,* a people bordering on his kingdom; "a people," says Mills,
"whose territory was, by far, the best governed part
of India: the people protected, their industry encouraged, and the country flourishing beyond all parallel."
It was by a careful neutrality, and by these acts, that
the Rohillas sought to maintain their independence;
and it was of such a people that Hastings, sitting at
table with his tool, the Nabob of Oude, coolly heard
him offer him a bribe of forty lacs of rupees (400,000*l.*)
and the payment of the troops furnished, to as-

sist him to destroy them utterly! There does not seem to have existed in the mind of Hastings one human feeling: a proposition which would have covered almost any other man with unspeakable horror, was received by him as a matter of ordinary business. "Let us see," said Hastings, "we have a heavy bonded debt, at one time 125 lacs of rupees. By this a saving of near one third of our military expenses would be effected during the period of such service; the forty lacs would be an ample supply to our treasury; and the Vizir (the Nabob of Oude) would be freed from a troublesome neighbour." These are the monster's own words; the bargain was struck, but it was agreed to be kept secret from the council and court of Directors. In one of Hastings' letters still extant, he tells the Nabob, "should the Rohillas be guilty of a breach of their agreement (a demand of forty lacs suddenly made upon them—for in this vile affair everything had a ruffian character—they first demanded their money, and then murdered them), *we will thoroughly exterminate them*, and settle your excellency in the country."* The extermination was conducted to the letter, as agreed, as far as was in their power. The Rohillas defended themselves most gallantly; but were overpowered,—and their chief, and upwards of a hundred thousand people fled to the mountains. The whole country lay at the mercy of the allies, and the British officers themselves declared that perhaps never were the rights of conquest more savagely abused. Colonel Champion, one of them, says in a letter of June 1774, published in the Report alluded to below, "the inhumanity and dishonour with which the late proprie-

* Fifth Parliamentary Report.—Appendix, No. 21.

tors of this country and their families have been used, is known all over these parts. A relation of them would swell this letter to an enormous size. I could not help compassionating such unparalleled misery, and my requests to the Vizir to shew lenity were frequent, but as fruitless as even those advices which I almost hourly gave him regarding the destruction of the villages; with respect to which he always promised fair, but did not observe one of his promises, nor cease to overspread the country with flames, till three days after the fate of Hafez Rhamet was decided." The Nabob had frankly and repeatedly assured Hastings that his intention was to *exterminate* the Rohillas, and every one who bore the name of Rohilla was either butchered, or found his safety in flight and in exile. Such were the diabolical deeds into which our government drove the native princes by their enormous exactions, or encouraged them in, only in the end to enslave them the more.

Before the connexion between the English and Oude, its revenue had exceeded three millions sterling, and was levied without being accused of deteriorating the country. In the year 1779, it did not exceed one half of that sum, and in the subsequent years it fell far below it, while the rate of taxation was increased, and the country exhibited every mark of oppressive exaction.* In this year the Nabob represented to the council the wretched condition to which he was reduced by their exactions : that the children of the deceased Nabob had subsisted in a very distressed manner for two years past; that the attendants, writers, and servants, had received no pay for that period;

* Mills, ii. 624.

that his father's private creditors were daily pressing him, and there was not a foot of country which could be appropriated to their payment; that the revenue was deficient fifteen lacs, (a million and a half sterling); that the country and cultivation were abandoned; the old chieftains and useful attendants of the court were forced to leave it; that the Company's troops were not only useless, but caused great loss to the revenue and confusion in the country; and that the support of his household, on the meanest scale, was beyond his power.

This melancholy representation produced—what? —pity, and an endeavour to relieve the Nabob?—no, exasperation. Mr. Hastings declared that, both it and the crisis in which it was made were equally alarming. The only thing thought of was what was to be done if the money did not come in? But Mr. Hastings, on his visit to the Nabob at Lucknow, made a most lucky discovery. He found that the mother and widow of the late Nabob were living there, and possessed of immense wealth. His rapacious mind, bound by no human feeling or moral principle, and fertile in schemes of acquisition, immediately conceived the felicitous design of setting the Nabob to strip those ladies, well known to English readers since the famous trial of Mr. Hastings, as "the Begums." It was agreed between the Nabob and Mr. Hastings, that his Highness should be relieved of the expense which he was unable to bear, of the English troops and gentlemen; and he, on his part, engaged to strip the Begums of both their treasure and their jaghires (revenues of certain lands), delivering to the Governor-general the proceeds. As a plea for this most abominable transaction, in which a prince was compelled by his cruel necessities and the grinding exactions and threats of the English to pillage forcibly his near relatives, a tale of treason was hatched against these poor women. When they refused to give up their money, the chief eunuchs were put to the torture till the ladies in compassion gave way: 550,000*l.* sterling were thus forced from them: the torture was still continued, in hope of extracting more; the women of the Zenana were deprived of food at various times till they were on the point of perishing for want; and every expedient was tried that the most devilish invention could suggest, till it was found that they had really drawn the last doit from them. But what more than all moves one's indignation against this base English Inquisitor, was, that he received as his share of these spoils the sum of ten lacs, or 100,000*l.*! —and that notwithstanding the law of the Company against the receipt of presents; its avowed distress for want of money; and the poverty of the kingdom of Oude, which was thus plundered and disgraced from the very inability to pay its debts, if debts such shameful exactions can be called. Hastings did not hesitate to apprise the council of what he had received, and requested their permission to retain it for himself.

Of the numerous transactions of a most wicked character connected with these affairs; of the repugnance of the Nabob to do the dirty work of Hastings on his relatives, the Begums; of the haughty insolence by which his tyrant compelled him to the compact; of the restoration of the jaghires, but not the moneys to the Begums; of the misery and desolation which forced itself even upon the horny eyes of Hastings as he made his second progress through the territories of Oude, the work of his own oppressions and exactions; of the twelve and a half millions which he added by his wars and political manœuvres to the Indian debt— we have not here room to note more than the existence of such facts, which are well known to all the readers of Indian history, or of the trial of Warren Hastings, where every artifice of the lawyers was employed to prevent the evidence of these things being brought forward; and where a House of Peers was found base or weak enough to be guided by such artifices, to refuse the most direct evidence against the most atrocious transactions in history; and thus to give sanction and security to the commission of the most dreadful crimes and cruelties in our distant colonies. Nothing could increase from this time the real power of the English over Oude, though circumstances might occasion a more open avowal of it. Even during the government of Lord Cornwallis and Sir John Shore, now Lord Teignmouth, two of the most worthy and honourable rulers that British India ever had, the miseries and exactions continued, and the well-intentioned financial measures of Lord Cornwallis even tended to increase them. In 1798, the governor, Sir John Shore, proceeded to depose the ruling Nabob as illegitimate (a plea on which the English set aside a number of Indian princes), and elevated another in his place, and that upon evidence, says the historian, "upon which an English court of law would not have decided against him a question of a few pounds."

It was not, however, till 1799, under the government of the Marquis Wellesley, that the hand of British power was stretched to the utmost over this devoted district. That honest and avowed usurper, who disdained the petty acts of his predecessors, but declared that the British dominion over the peninsula of India must be frankly avowed and fearlessly asserted — certainly a much better doctrine than the cowardly and hypocritical one hitherto acted upon ;—that every Englishman who did not belong to the Company must and should be expelled from that country; and that the English power and the Corporate monopoly should be so strenuously and unflinchingly exerted, that foreign aggression or domestic complaint should be alike dispersed;—this straightforward Governor - general soon drove the Nabob of Oude to such desperation, by the severity of his measures and exactions, that he declared his wish to abdicate. Nothing could equal the joy of the Governor-general at the prospect of this easy acquisition of this entire territory: but that joy was damped by discovering that the Nabob only wished to resign in favour of — his own son ! The chagrin of the Governor-general on this discovery is not to be expressed ; and the series of operations then commenced to force the Nabob to abdicate in favour of the Company; when that could not be effected, to compel him to sacrifice one half of his territories to save the rest; when that sacrifice was made, to inform him that he was to have no independent power in his remaining half—is one of the most instructive lessons in the art of diplomatic fleecing, of forcing a man out of his own by the forms of treaty but with the iron-hand of irresistible power, which any despot who wishes to do a desperate deed handsomely, and in the most approved style, can desire. It was in vain that the Nabob de-

clared his payment of exactions ; his hereditary right;
his readiness shewn on all occasions to aid and oblige;
the force of treaties in his favour.   It was in vain that
he asked to what purpose should he give up one half
of his dominions if he were not to have power over the
other, when it was to secure this independent power
that he gave up that half?   What are all the arguments of right, justice, reason, or humanity, when
Ahab wants the vineyard of Naboth, and the Jezebel
of political and martial power tells him that she will
give it him?   The fate of Oude was predetermined,
along with that of various other states, by the Governor-general, and it was decided as he determined it
should be.

Before we close this chapter, we will give one instance of the manner in which the territories of those
who held aloof, and did not covet the fatal friendship
of the English were obtained, and the most striking of
these are the dominions of Hyder Ali—the kingdom
of Mysore.

Hyder was a soldier of fortune.   He had risen by
an active and enterprising disposition from the condition of a common soldier to the head of the state.
The English considered him as an ambitious, able,
and therefore very dangerous person in India.   There
can be no doubt that he considered them the same.
He was an adventurer; so were they.   He had acquired a great territory by means that would not bear
the strictest scrutiny; so had they;—but there was
this difference between them, Hyder acted according
to the customs and maxims in which he had been
educated, and which he saw universally practised by all
the princes around him.   He neither had the advan-

tage of Christian knowledge and principle, nor pretended to them. The English, on the contrary, came
there as merchants; they were continually instructed
by their masters at home not to commit military
aggressions.   They were bound by the laws of their
country not to do it. They professed to be in possession of a far higher system of religion and morals than
Hyder and his people had. They pretended to be the
disciples of the Prince of Peace. Their magnanimous creed they declared to be, " To do to others as
they would wish to be done by."   But neither Hyder
nor any other Indian ever saw the least evidence of
any such superiority of morals, or of faith, in their
conduct. They were as ambitious, and far more
greedy of money than the heathen that they pretended to despise for their heathenism. They ought
to have set a better example—but they did not.
There never was a people that grasped more convul-
sively at dominion, or were less scrupulous in the
means of obtaining it. They declared Hyder cruel
and perfidious. He knew them to be both. This
was the ground on which they stood. There were
reasons why the English should avoid interfering with
Hyder.   There were none why he should avoid encroaching on them, for he did not profess any such
grand principles of action as they did. If they were
what they pretended to be, they ought to preach peace
and union amongst the Indian princes : but union was
of all things in the world the very one which they
most dreaded ; for they *were not* what they pretended
to be; but sought on the divisions of the natives to
establish their own power. Had Hyder attacked
them in their own trading districts, there could have

been no reason why they should not chastise him for it. But it does not appear that he ever did attack them at all till they fell upon him, and that with the avowed intention to annihilate his power as dangerous. No, say they, but he attacked the territories of our ally the Subahdar of Deccan, which we were bound to defend. And here it is that we touch again upon that subtle policy by which it became impossible, when they had once got a footing in the country that, having the will and the power, they should not eventually have the dominion. While professing to avoid conquest, we have seen that they went on continually making conquests. But it was always on the plea of aiding their allies. They entered knowingly into alliances on condition of defending with arms their allies, and then, when they committed aggressions, it was *for* these allies. In the end the allies were themselves swallowed up, with all the additional territories thus gained. It was a system of fattening allies as we fatten oxen, till they were more worthy of being devoured. They cast their subtle threads of policy like the radiating filaments of the spider's web, till the remotest extremity of India could not be touched without startling them from their concealed centre into open day, ready to run upon the unlucky offender. It was utterly impossible, on such a system, but that offences should come, and wo to them by whom they did come.

The English were unquestionably the aggressors in the hostilities with Hyder. They entered into a treaty with Nizam Ali, the Subahdar of Deccan, offensive and defensive; and the very first deed which they were to do, was to seize the fort of Bangalore, which belonged to Hyder. They had actually marched in 1767 into his territories, when Hyder found means to draw the Nizam from his alliance, and in conjunction with him fell upon them, and compelled them to fly to Trincomalee. By this unprovoked and voluntary act they found themselves involved at once in a war with a fierce and active enemy, who pursued them to the very walls of Madras; scoured their country with his cavalry; and compelled them to a dishonourable peace in 1769, by which they bound themselves to assist *him* too in his defensive wars! To enter voluntarily into such conditions with such a man, betrayed no great delicacy of moral feeling as to what wars they engaged in, or no great honesty in their intentions as regarded the treaty itself. They must soon either fight with some of Hyder's numerous enemies, or break faith with him. Accordingly the very next year the Mahrattas invaded his territories; he called earnestly on his English allies for aid, and aid they did not give. Hyder had now the justest reason to term them perfidious, and to hold them in distrust. Yet, though deeply exasperated by this treachery, he would in 1778 most willingly have renewed his alliance with them; and the presidency of Madras acknowledged their belief that, had not the treaty of 1769 been evaded, Hyder would never have sought other allies than themselves. * There were the strongest reasons why they should have cultivated an amicable union with him, both to withdraw him from the French, and on account of his own great power and revenues. But they totally neglected him, or insulted him with words of mere cold courtesy; and

* Mills, ii. 480.

a new aggression upon the fortress of Mahé, a place tributary to Hyder, which they attacked in order to expel the French, and which Hyder resented on the same principle as they would resent an attack upon any tributary of their own, well warranted the declaration of Hyder, that they " were the most faithless and usurping of mankind." They were these arbitrary and impolitic deeds which brought down Hyder speedily upon them, with an army 100,000 strong; and soon showed them Madras menaced, the Carnatic overrun, Arcot taken, and a war of such a desperate and bloody character raging around them, as they had never yet seen in India, and which might probably have expelled them thence, had not death released them in 1782 from so formidable a foe, who had been so wantonly provoked.

Tippoo Sultaun, with all his activity and cunning, had not the masterly military genius of his father,—but he possessed all the fire of his resentment, and it was not to be expected that, after what had passed, there could be much interval of irritation between him and the English. They had roused Hyder as a lion is roused from his den, and he had made them feel his power. They would naturally look on his son with suspicion, and Tippoo had been taught to regard them as " the most faithless and usurping of mankind." Whatever, therefore, may be said for or against him, on the breaking out of the second war with him, the original growth of hostility between the British and the Mysorean monarchs, must be charged to the former, and in the case of the last war, there appears to have been no real breach of treaty on the part of Tippoo. He had been severely punished for any act of irritation

which he might have committed against any of the
British allies, by the reduction of his capital, the surrender of his sons as hostages, and the stripping away
of one half of his territories to be divided amongst his
enemies, each of whom had enriched himself with half
a million sterling of annual revenue at his expense.
Tippoo must have been nothing less than a madman
in his shattered condition, and with his past experience, to have lightly ventured on hostilities with the
English. But it was charged on him that he was
seeking an alliance with the French. What then?
He had the clearest right so to do. So long as he
maintained the terms of his treaty, the English had
no just right to violate theirs towards him. The
French were his ancient and hereditary friends. Tippoo persisted to the last that he had done nothing to
warrant an attack upon him; but Lord Mornington
had adopted his notions about consolidating the British
power in India, and every possible circumstance, or
suspicion of a circumstance, was to be seized upon as
a plea for carrying his plans into effect. It was
enough that a fear *might* be entertained of Tippoo's
designs. It became good policy to get the start; and
when once that forestalling system in hostilities, that
outstripping in the race of mischief, is adopted, there
is no possible violence nor enormity which may not
be undertaken, or defended upon it. Tippoo was assailed by the British, and their ally the Nizam; and
though he again and again protested his innocence,
again and again asked for peace, he was pursued to
his capital, and killed bravely defending it. His
territories were divided amongst those who had divided the former half of them in like manner, the

English, the Nizam, and the Mahrattas, with a little state appropriated to a puppet-rajah. Thus did the English shew what they would do to those who dared to decline their protection. Thus did they pursue, beat down, and destroy with all their mighty resources an independent prince, whose whole revenue, after their first partition of his realm, did not much exceed a million sterling. We have heard a vast deal in Europe of the partition of Poland, but how much better was the forcible dismemberment of Mysore? The injury of this dismemberment of his kingdom is, however, not the least heaped upon Tippoo. On his name have been heaped all the odious crimes that make us hate the worst of tyrants. Cruelty, perfidy, low cunning, and all kinds of baseness, make up the idea of Tippoo which we have derived from those who profited by his destruction. But what say the most candid historians? "That the accounts which we have received from our countrymen, who dreaded and feared him, are marked with exaggeration, is proved by this circumstance, that his servants adhered to him with a fidelity which those of few princes in any age or country have displayed. Of his cruelty we have heard the more, because our own countrymen were amongst the victims of it. But it is to be observed, that unless in certain instances, the proof of which cannot be regarded as better than doubtful, their sufferings, however intense, were only the sufferings of a very rigorous imprisonment, of which, considering the manner in which it is lavished upon them by their own laws, Englishmen ought not to be very forward to complain. At that very time, in the dungeons of Madras or Calcutta, it is probable that unhappy sufferers were enduring calamities for debts of 100*l.*, not less atrocious than those which Tippoo, a prince born and educated in a barbarous country, and ruling over a barbarous people, inflicted upon imprisoned enemies, part of a nation, who, by the evils they had brought upon him, exasperated him almost to frenzy, and whom he regarded as the enemies both of God and man. Besides, there is among the papers relating to the intercourse of Tippoo with the French, a remarkable proof of his humanity, which, when these papers are ransacked for matters to criminate him, ought not to be suppressed. In a draught of conditions on which he desired to form a treaty with them, these are the words of a distinct article :—' I demand that male and female prisoners, as well English as Portuguese, who shall be taken by the republican troops, or by mine, shall be treated with humanity; and, with regard to their persons, that they shall (their property becoming the right of the allies) be transported, at our joint expense, out of India, to places far distant from the territories of the allies.'

" Another feature in the character of Tippoo was his religion, with a sense of which his mind was most deeply impressed. He spent a considerable part of every day in prayer. He gave to his kingdom a particular religious title, *Cudadad*, or God-given ; and he lived under a peculiarly strong and operative conviction of the superintendence of a Divine Providence. To one of his French advisers, who urged him zealously to obtain the support of the Mahrattas, he replied, ' I rely solely on Providence, expecting that I shall be alone and unsupported; but God and my courage will accomplish everything.' . . . . He had

the discernment to perceive, what is so generally hid
from the eyes of rulers in a more enlightened state of
society, that it is the prosperity of those who labour
with their hands which constitutes the principle and
cause of the prosperity of states.   He therefore made
it his business to protect them against the intermediate
orders of the community, by whom it is so difficult to
prevent them from being oppressed. His country
was, accordingly, at least during the first and better
part of his reign, the best cultivated, and his population the most flourishing, in India: while under the
English and their pageants, the population of Carnatic
and Oude, hastening to the state of deserts, was the
most wretched upon the face of the earth; and even
Bengal itself, under the operations of laws ill adapted
to their circumstances, was suffering almost all the
evils which the worst of governments could inflict. . .
For an eastern prince he was full of knowledge. His
mind was active, acute, and ingenious. But in the
value which he set upon objects, whether as means,
or as an end, he was almost perpetually deceived.
Besides, a conviction appears to have been rooted in
his mind that the English had now formed a resolution
to deprive him of his kingdom, and that it was useless
to negotiate, because no submission to which he could
reconcile his mind, would restrain them in the gratification of their ambitious designs."—*Mills*.

Tippoo was right. The great design of the English, from their first secure footing in India, was
to establish their control over the whole Peninsula.
The French created them the most serious alarm in
the progress of their career towards this object; and
any native state which shewed more than ordinary

energy, excited a similar feeling. For this purpose
all the might of British power and policy was exerted
to expel these European rivals, and to crush such
more active states. The administration of the Marquis Wellesley was the exhibition of this system full
blown. For this, all the campaigns against Holkar
and Scindia; the wars from north to south, and from
east to west of India, were undertaken; and blood was
made to flow, and debts to accumulate to a degree
most monstrous. Yet the admiration of this system
of policy in England has shewn how little human life
and human welfare, even to this day, weigh in the
scale against dominion and avarice. We hear nothing
of the horrors and violence we have perpetrated, from
the first invasion of Bengal, to those of Nepaul and
Burmah; we have only eulogies on the empire
achieved:—" See what a splendid empire we have
won!" True,—there is no objection to the empire, if
we could only forget the means by which it has been
created. But amid all this subtle and crooked policy
—this creeping into power under the colour of allies—
this extortion and plunder of princes, under the name
of protection—this forcible subjection and expatriation
of others, we look in vain for the generous policy of
the Christian merchant, and the Christian statesman.*

---

* Sir Thomas Roe was sent in 1614, on an embassy to the Great
Mogul. In his letters to the Company, he strongly advised them
against the expensive ambition of acquiring territory. He tells them,
"It is greater than trade can bear; for to maintain a garrison will cut
out your profit: a war and traffic are incompatible. The Portuguese,
notwithstanding their many rich residences, are beggared by keeping
of soldiers : and yet their garrisons are but mean. They never made
advantage of the Indies since they defended them ;—observe this well.
It has also been the error of the Dutch, who seek plantations here by

The moderation of a Teignmouth, a Cornwallis, or a Bentinck, is deemed mere pusillanimity. Those divine maxims of peace and union which Christianity would disseminate amongst the natives of the countries that we visit, are condemned as the very obstacles to the growth of our power. When we exclaim, " what might not Englishmen have done in India had they endeavoured to pacify and enlighten, instead of to exact and destroy ?" we are answered by a smile, which informs us that these are but romantic notions,—that the only wisdom is to get rich !

the sword. They turn a wonderful stock ; they prowl in all places ; they possess some of the best : yet their dead pays consume all the gain. Let this be received as a rule, that if you will profit, seek it at sea, and in quiet trade : for without controversy, it is an error to affect garrisons, and land-wars in India."

Had Sir Thomas been inspired, could he have been a truer prophet? The East India Company, after fighting and conquering in India for two centuries, have found themselves, at the dissolution of their charter, nearly fifty millions in debt ; while their trade with China, a country in which they did not possess a foot of land, had become the richest commerce in the world ! The article of tea alone returning between three and four millions annually, and was their sole preventive against bankruptcy. Can, indeed, any colonial acquisition be pointed out that is not a loss to the parent state ?

CHAPTER XVI.

THE ENGLISH IN INDIA—CONTINUED.
TREATMENT OF THE NATIVES.

Rich in the gems of India's gaudy zone,
And plunder, piled from kingdoms not their own,
Degenerate trade! thy minions could despise,
The heart-born anguish of a thousand cries;
Could lock, with impious hands their teeming store,
While famished nations died along the shore;
Could mock the groans of fellow-men; and bear
The curse of kingdoms peopled with despair;
Could stamp disgrace on man's polluted name,
And barter, with their gold, eternal shame.

Pleasures of Hope.

WE have in some degree caught a glimpse of the subject of this chapter in the course of the last. The treatment of the native chiefs in our pursuit of territorial possession is in part the treatment of the natives, but it is unhappily a very small part. The scene of exaction, rapacity, and plunder which India became in our hands, and that upon the whole body of the population, forms one of the most disgraceful portions of human history; and while the temptations to it existed in full force, defied all the powers of legislation, or the moral influence of public opinion to check the evil. In vain the East India Company itself, in vain the British Parliament legislated on the subject; in vain did the Court of Directors from year to year, send out the most earnest remonstrances to their servants,—the allurement was too splendid, the opportunities too seducing, the example too general, the security too great, to permit any one to attend to either law, remonstrance, or the voice of humanity. The fame of India, as a vast region of inexhaustible wealth, had resounded through the world for ages; the most astonishing notions of it floated through Europe, before the sea-track to it was discovered; and when that was done, the marvellous fortunes made there by bold men, as it were in a single day, and by a single stroke of policy, seemed more than to warrant any previous belief. Men in power received their presents of ten, twenty, or a hundred thousand pounds. Clive, for the assistance of the British army, was presented with the magnificent gift of a jaghire, or hereditary revenue of 30,000*l.* a year! On another occasion he received his 28,000*l.*, and his fellow-rulers each a similar sum. Hastings received his twenty and his hundred thousand pounds, as familiarly as a gold snuff-box or a piece of plate would be given as a public testimony of respect for popular services, in England. Every man, according to his station and his influence, found the like golden harvest. Who could avoid being inflamed with the thirst for Indian service?— who avoid the most exaggerated anticipations of fortune? It was a land, and a vast land, hedged about with laws of exclusion to all except such as went through the doors of the Company. There were there no interlopers,—no curious, because obstructed observers. There was but one object in going thither, and one interest when there. It was a soil made sacred, or rather, doomed, to the exclusive plunder of a privileged number. The highest officers in the government had the strongest motives to corruption, and therefore could by no possibility attempt to check the the same corruption in those below them. When the power and influence of the Company became considerably extended over Bengal, Bahar, Orissa, Oude, the Carnatic, and Bombay, the harvest of presents grew into a most affluent one. Nothing was to be expected, no chance of justice, of attention, of alleviation from the most abominable oppression, but through the medium of presents, and those of such amounts as fairly astonish European ears. Every man, in every department, whether civil, military, or mercantile, was in the certain receipt of splendid presents. When the government had found it necessary to forbid the receipt of presents by any individual in the service, not only for themselves, but for the Company, the highest officers set the laws at defiance, and the mischief was made more secret, but not less existent.

But besides presents and official incomes, there were the farming of the revenues, and domestic trade, which opened up boundless sources of profit. The revenues were received in each district by zemindars from the ryots or husbandmen, and handed, after a fixed deduction, to the chief office of the revenue. But between these zemindars and the ryots were aumils, or other inferior officers, who farmed the revenues in each lesser district or village; that is, contracted with the zemindars for the revenues at a certain sum, and took the trouble of exacting them from the ryots, who paid a rate fixed by law or ancient custom, and could not be turned out of their lands while such rate was regularly paid. Wherever the English obtained a claim over the revenues of a prince, which we have seen they speedily did, they soon became the zemindars, or their agents, the aumils, or other middlemen between them and the ryots. Anciently, the ryots paid one tenth of their produce, for all their taxes were paid in kind, but in time the rate grew to more than half. When the English power became more fixed and open, and it was found that under the native zemindars the exactions of the revenues did not at all satisfy their demands, they took on themselves the whole business of collecting these revenues. This, as we shall see, on the evidence of the Company's own officers, became a dreadful system to the people. The Mahomedan exactions had been generally regarded more considerate than those of the native Hindu chiefs; but the grinding pressure of the English system brought on the unfortunate ryot the most unexampled misery. Of this, however, anon. It only requires here to be pointed out as one of the various sources of enormous profits and jobbing which made India so irresistibly attractive to Englishmen.

The private trade was another grand source of revenue. The public trade, that is, the transit of goods to and from Europe, was the peculiar monopoly of the Company; but all coasting trade—trade to and between the isles, and in the interior of India, became a monopoly of the higher servants of the Company, who were at once engaged in the Company's concerns and their own. The monopoly of salt, opium, betel, and other commodities became a mine of wealth. The Company's servants could fix the price at whatever rate they pleased, and thus enhance it to the unfortunate people so as to occasion them the most intense distress. Fortunes were made in a day by this monopoly, and without the advance of a single shilling. The very Governor-general himself engaged in this private trade; and contracts were given to favourites on such terms, that two or three fortunes were made out of them before they reached the merchant. In one case that came out on the trial of Warren Hasings, a contract for opium had been given to Mr. Sullivan, though he was going into quite a different part of India, and on public business; this, of course, he sold again, to Mr. Benn, for 40,000*l.*; and Mr. Benn immediately sold it again for 60,000*l.*, clearing 20,000*l.* by the mere passing of the contract from one hand to the other; and the purchaser then declared that he made a large sum by it.

All these things put together, made India the theatre of sure and splendid fortune to the adventurer, and of sore and abject misery to the native. We have only to look about us in any part of England, but especially in the metropolis, and within fifty miles round it, to see what streams of wealth have flowed into this country from India. What thousands of splendid mansions and estates are lying in view, which, when the traveller inquires their history, have been purchased by the gold of India. We are told that those days of magical accumulation of wealth are over; that this great fountain of affluence is drained comparatively dry; that fortunes are not now readily made in India; yet the Company, though they have lost their monopoly of trade, and their territories are laid open to the free observation of their countrymen, are in possession of the government with a revenue of twenty millions. But all this time, what has been doing with and for the natives. We shall see that anon; yet it may here be asked, What *could* be doing? For what did men go to India? For what did they endure its oppressive and often fatal climate? Was it from philanthropical or personal motives? Did they seek the good of the Indians or their own? The latter, assuredly: and it was not to be expected that the majority of men should be so high-minded or disinterested as to seek the good of others at the expense of their own. The temptations to visit India were powerful, but not the less powerful were the motives to hasten away at the very earliest possible period. It was not to be expected from human nature that the natives could be much thought of. What *has* been done for them by the devoted few, we shall recognise with delight; at present we must revert to the evil influences of nearly two hundred years.

Amongst the first to claim our attention, are those doings in high places which have excited so strongly the cupidity of thousands, and especially those dazzling presents which became the direct causes of the most violent exactions on the people, for out of them had all these things to be drawn. The Company could, indeed, with a very bad grace, condemn bribery in its officers, for it has always been accused of this evil practice at home in order to obtain its exclusive privileges from government; and so early as 1693, it appeared from parliamentary inquiry, that its annual expenditure under the head of gifts to men in power previous to the Revolution, seldom exceeded 1,200*l.*, but from that period to that year it had grown to nearly 90,000*l.* annually. The Duke of Leeds was impeached for a bribe of 5,000*l.*, and 10,000*l.* were even said to be traced to the king.* Besides this, whenever any rival company appeared in the field, government was tempted with the loans of enormous sums, at the lowest interest. Like fruits were to be expected in India, and were not long wanting. We cannot trace this subject to its own vast extent—it would require volumes—we can only offer a few striking examples:—

None can be more remarkable than the following list, which, besides sums that we may suppose it to have been in the power of the receivers to conceal, and of the amount of which it is not easy to form a conjecture, were detected and disclosed by the Committee of the House of Commons in 1773.

The rupees are valued according to the rate of exchange of the Company's bills at the different periods.

*Account of such sums as have been proved or acknowledged
    before the Committee to have been distributed by the
    Princes and other natives of Bengal, from the year
    1757 to the year 1766, both inclusive; distinguishing
    the principal times of the said distributions, and
    specifying the sums received by each person respectively:—*

Resolution in favour of Meer Jaffier—1757.

	Rupees.	Rupees.	£.
Mr. Drake (Governor) - - -		280,000	31,500
Col. Clive, as second in the Select Committee }	280000		
Ditto, as Commander-in-Chief -	200,000		
Ditto, as a private donation - -	1,600,000		
		2,080,000	234,000

* Macpherson's Annals, ii. 652, 662.

	Rupees.	Rupees.	£
Mr. Watts, as a Member of the Committee	240,000		
Ditto, as a private donation	800,000		
		1,040,000	117,000
Major Kilpatrick		240,000	27,000
Ditto, as a private donation		300,000	33,750
Mr. Maningham		240,000	27,000
Mr. Becher		240,000	27,000
Six Members of Council, one lac each		600,000	68,000
Mr. Walsh		500,000	56,250
Mr. Scrafton		200,000	22,500
Mr. Lushington		50,000	5,625
Captain Grant		100,000	11,250
Stipulation to the Navy and Army			600,000
			1,261,075

Memorandum—the sum of two lacs to Lord
Clive, as Commander-in-Chief, must be deducted from this account, it being included in
the donation to the army -   -   -   -   22,500

                                                      1,238,575

Resolution in favour of Causim in 1760.

	Rupees.	£
Mr. Sumner		28,000
Mr. Holwell	270,000	30,937
Mr. M'Guire	180,000	20,628
Mr. Smyth	130,300	15,354
Major Yorke	134,000	15,354
General Caillaud	200,000	22,916
Mr. Vansittart, 1762, received seven lacs, but the two lacs to Gen. Caillaud are included; so that only five lacs must be accounted for here	500,000	58,333
Mr. M'Guire 5,000 gold morhs	75,000	8,750
		200,269

Resolution in favour of Jaffier in 1763.

	Rupees.	£
Stipulation to the Army	2,500,000	291,666
Ditto to the Navy	1,250,000	145,833
		437,499

	Rupees.	£
Major Munro, in 1764, received from Bulwant Sing - - - - - - -		10,000
Ditto, from the Nabob - - - -		3,000
The Officers belonging to Major Munro's family from ditto - - - - -		3,000
The Army, from the merchants at Benares -	400,000	46,666
		62,666

Nudjeem ul Dowla's Accession, 1765.

	Rupees.	£
Mr. Spencer - - - - - - -	200,000	23,333
Messrs. Pleydell, Burdett, and Grey, one lac each	300,000	35,000
Mr. Johnstone - - - - - -	237,000	27,650
Mr. Leycester - - - - - -	112,500	13,125
Mr. Senior - - - - - -	172,500	20,125
Mr. Middleton - - - - - -	122,500	14,291
Mr. Gideon Johnstone - - - - -	50,000	5,833
		139,357

	Rupees.	£
General Carnac received from Bulwant Sing, in 1765 - - - - - -	80,000	9,333
Ditto from the king - - - - -	200,000	23,333
Lord Clive received from the Begum, in 1766 -	500,000	58,333
		90,999

Restitution.—Jaffier, 1757.

	Rupees.
East India Company - - - - - - -	1,200,000
Europeans - - - - - - - - -	600,000
Natives - - - - - - - - -	250,000
Armenians - - - - - - - -	100,000
	2,150,000

Causim. 1760.

	Rupees.
East India Company - - - - - - -	62,500

Jaffier. 1763.

	Rupees.
East India Company - - - - - - -	375,000
Europeans, Natives, etc. - - - - - -	600,000
	975,000

Peace with Sujah Dowla.

	Rupees.	£
East India Company - - - - -	5,000,000	583,333

Total of Presents, £2,169,665. Restitution, etc., £3,770,833.
Total amount, exclusive of Lord Clive's Jaghire, £5,940,498.

These are pretty sums to have fallen into the pockets of the English, chiefly *douceurs*, in ten years. Let the account be carried on for all India at a similar rate for a century, and what a sum! Lord Clive's jaghire alone was worth 30,000*l.* per annum. And, besides this, it appears from the above documents that he also pocketed in these transactions 292,333*l.* No wonder at the enormous fortunes rapidly made; at the enormous debts piled on the wretched nabobs, and the dreadful exactions on the still more wretched people. No man could more experimentally than Clive thus address the Directors at home, as he did in 1765: "Upon my arrival, I am sorry to say, I found your affairs in a condition so nearly desperate as would have alarmed any set of men whose sense of honour and duty to their employers had not been estranged by the too eager pursuit of their own immediate advantages. The sudden, and among many, the unwarrantable acquisition of riches (who was so entitled to say this?) had introduced luxury in every shape, and in its most pernicious excess. These two enormous evils went hand in hand together through the whole presidency, infecting almost every member of every department. Every inferior seemed to have grasped at wealth, that he might be enabled to assume that spirit of profusion which was now the only distinction between him and his superiors. Thus all distinction ceased, and every rank became, in a manner, upon an equality. Nor was this the end of the mischief; for a contest of such a nature amongst our servants necessarily destroyed all proportion between their wants and the honest means of satisfying them. In a country *where money is* *plenty, where fear is the principle of government, and where your arms are ever victorious, it is no wonder that the lust of riches should readily embrace the proffered means of its gratification, or that the instruments of your power should avail themselves of their authority, and proceed even to extortion in those cases where simple corruption could not keep pace with their rapacity.* Examples of this sort, set by superiors, could not fail being followed, in a proportionate degree, by inferiors. The evil was contagious, and spread among the civil and military, down to the writer, the ensign, and the free merchant."—Clive's Letter to the Directors, Third Report of Parliamentary Committee, 1772.

The Directors replied to this very letter, lamenting their conviction of its literal truth.—" We have the strongest sense of the deplorable state to which our affairs were on the point of being reduced, from the corruption and rapacity of our servants, and *the universal depravity of manners throughout the settlement.* The general relaxation of all discipline and obedience, both military and civil, was hastily tending to a dissolution of all government. Our letter to the Select Committee expresses our sentiments of what has been obtained by way of donations; and to that we must add, that we think the vast fortunes acquired in the inland trade *have been obtained by a scene of the most tyrannic and oppressive conduct that was ever known in any age or country!*"

But however the Directors at home might lament, they were too far off to put an end to this "scene of the most tyrannic and oppressive conduct that was ever known in any age or country." This very same grave and eloquent preacher on this oppression and corruption, Clive, was the first to set the example of contempt of the Directors' orders, and commission of those evil practices. The Directors had sent out fresh covenants to be entered into by all their servants, both civil and military, binding them not to receive presents, nor to engage in inland trade; but it was found that the governor had not so much as brought the new covenants under the consideration of the council. The receipt of presents, and the inland trade by the Company's servants went on with increased activity. When at length these covenants were forwarded to the different factories and garrisons, General Carnac, and everybody else signed them. General Carnac however delayed his signing of them till he had time to obtain a present of two lacs of rupees (upwards of 20,000l.) from the reduced and impoverished Emperor. Clive appointed a committee to inquire into these matters, which brought to light strange scenes of rapacity, and of " threats to extort gifts." But what did Clive? He himself entered largely into private trade and into a vast monopoly of salt, an article of the most urgent necessity to the people; and this on the avowed ground of wishing some gentlemen whom he had brought out to make a fortune. His committee sanctioned the private trade in salt, betel-nut, and tobacco, out of which nearly all the abuses and miseries he complained of had grown, only confining it to the *superior servants* of the Company: and he himself, when the orders of the Directors were laid before him in council, carelessly turned them aside, saying, the Directors, when they wrote them, could not know what changes had taken place in India. No! they did not know that he and his council were now partners in the salt trade, and realizing a profit, including interest, of upwards of fifty per cent.! Perhaps Clive thought he had done a great service when he had attempted to lessen the number of harpies by cutting off the trading of the juniors, and thus turning the tide of gain more completely into his own pockets, and those of his fellows of the council. It must have been a very provoking sight to one with a development of acquisitiveness so ample as his own, to witness what Verelst, in his "View of Bengal," describes as then existing. "At this time many black merchants found it expedient to purchase the name of any young writer in the Company's service by loans of money, and under this sanction harassed and oppressed the natives. So plentiful a supply was derived from this source, that many young writers were enabled to spend 1500*l.* and 2000*l.* per annum, were clothed in fine linen, and fared sumptuously every day." What were the miseries and insolent oppressions under which the millions of Bengal were made to groan by such practices, and by the lawless violence with which the revenues were collected about that period by the English, may be sufficiently indicated by the following passages. Mr. Hastings, in a letter to the President Vansittart, dated Bauglepore, April 25th, 1762, says—"I beg to lay before you a grievance which loudly calls for redress, and will, unless duly attended to, render ineffectual any endeavour to create a firm and lasting harmony between the Nabobs and the Company: I mean the oppressions committed under the sanction of the English name, and through the want of spirit to oppose them. The evil, I am well assured, is not confined to our dependents alone, *but is practised all over the country, by people falsely assuming the habit of our sepoys, or calling themselves our gomastahs.* On such occasions, the great power of the English intimidates the people from making any resistance; so, on the other hand, the indolence of the Bengalees, or the difficulty of gaining access to those who might do them justice, prevents our having knowledge of the oppressions. I have been surprised to meet with several English flags flying in places which I have passed; and on the river I do not believe I passed a boat without one. By whatever title they have been assumed, I am sure their frequency can boast no.good to the Nabob's revenues, the quiet of the country, or the honour of our nation. A party of sepoys, who were on the march before us, afforded sufficient proofs of the rapacious and insolent spirit of these people when they are left to their own discretion. Many complaints against them were made to us on the road; *and most of the petty towns and serais were deserted at our approach, and the shops shut up, from the apprehension of the same treatment from us.*"

Mr. Vansittart endeavoured zealously to put a stop to such abominable practices; but what could he do? The very members of the council were deriving vast emoluments from this state of things, and audaciously denied its existence. Under such sanction, every inferior plunderer set at defiance the orders of the president and the authority of the officers appointed to prevent the commission of such oppressions on the natives. The native collectors of the revenue, when they attempted to levy, under the express sanction of the governor, the usual duties on the English, were not only repelled by them, but seized and punished as enemies of the Company and violatĕrs of its privileges. The native judges and magistrates were resisted in the discharge of their duties; and even their functions usurped. Everything was in confusion, and many of the zemindars and other collectors refused to be answerable for the revenues. Even the nabob's own officers were refused the liberty to make purchases on his account. One of them, of high connexions and influence, was seized for having purchased from the nabob some saltpetre; the trade in which they claimed as belonging exclusively to them. He was put in irons and sent to Calcutta, where some of the council voted for having him publicly whipped, others desired that his ears might be cut off, and it was all that the president could effect to get him sent back to his own master to be punished. In Mr. Vansittart's own narrative, is given a letter from one officer to the nabob, complaining that though he was furnished with instructions to send away Europeans who were found committing disorders to Calcutta, notwithstanding any pretence they shall make for so doing; he had used persuasions, and conciliated, and found them of no avail. That he had then striven by gentle means to stop their violences; upon which he was threatened that if he interfered with them or their servants, they would treat him in such a manner as should cause him to repent. That all their servants had boasted publicly, that this was what would be done to him did he presume to meddle. He adds, " Now sir, I am to inform you what I have obstructed them in. *This place (Backergunge) was of great trade formerly, but now brought to nothing by the following practices.* A gentleman sends a gomastah here to buy or sell. He immediately looks upon himself as sufficient to force every inhabitant either to buy his goods, or to force them to sell him theirs; and on refusal, or non-capacity, a flogging or confinement immediately ensues. This is not sufficient even when willing; but a second force is made use of, which is, to engross the different branches of trade to themselves, and not to suffer any persons to buy or sell the articles they trade in. They compel the people to buy or sell at just what rate they please, and my interfering occasions an immediate complaint. These, *and many other oppressions which are daily practised*, are the reasons that this place is growing destitute of inhabitants. . . . Before, justice was given in the public cutcheree, but now every gomastah is become a judge; they even pass sentence on the zemindars themselves; and draw money from them for pretended injuries."

Such was the state of the country in 1762, as witnessed by Mr. Hastings, and such it continued till Clive's government,—Clive, who so forcibly described it to the Directors; and what did Clive do? He aggravated it, enriched himself enormously by the very system, and so left it. Such it continued till Mr. Hastings,—this Mr. Hastings, who so feelingly had written his views and abhorrence of it to the President Vansittart, came into supreme power, and what did the wise and benevolent Mr. Hastings? He became the Aaron's-rod of gift-takers; the prince of exactors, and the most unrelenting oppressor of the natives that ever visited India, or perhaps any other country. In the mean time this system of rapacity and extortion had reduced the people to the most deplorable condition of poverty and wretchedness imaginable. The monopoly of trade, and the violent abduction of all their produce in the shape of taxes, dispirited them to the most extreme degree, and brought on the country those famines and diseases for which that period is so celebrated. In 1770 occurred that dreadful famine, which has throughout Europe excited so much horror of the English. They have been accused of having directly created it, by buying up all the rice, and refusing to sell any of it except at the most exorbitant price. The author of the " Short History of the English Transactions in the East Indies," thus boldly states the fact. Speaking of the monopoly just alluded to, of salt, betel-nut, and tobacco, he says, " Money in this current came but by drops. It could not quench the thirst of those who waited in India to receive it. An expedient, such as it was, remained to quicken it. The natives could live with little salt, but could not want food. Some of the agents saw themselves well situated for collecting the rice into stores; they did so. They knew that the Gentoos would rather die than violate the principles of their religion by eating flesh. The alternative would therefore be between *giving what they had*, or *dying!* The inhabitants sunk. They that cultivated the land, and saw the harvest at the disposal of others, planted in doubt; scarcity ensued. Then the monopoly was easier managed,—sickness ensued. In some districts, the languid living left the bodies of their numerous dead unburied."—p. 145.

Many and ingenious have been the attempts to remove this awful opprobrium from our national character. It has been contended that famines are, or

were of frequent occurrence in India;—that the
natives had no providence; and that to charge the
English with the miserable consequences of this
famine is unreasonable, because it was what they could
neither foresee nor prevent. Of the drought in the
previous autumn there is no doubt; but there is unhappily as little, that the regular rapacity of the
English had reduced the natives to that condition of
poverty, apathy, and despair, in which the slightest
derangement of season must superinduce famine;
—that they were grown callous to the sufferings of
their victims, and were as alive to their gain by the
rising price through the scarcity, as they were in all
other cases. Their object was sudden wealth, and they
cared not, in fact, whether the natives lived or died,
so that that object was effected. This is the relation
of the Abbé Raynal, a foreign historian, and the light
in which this event was beheld by foreign nations.

"It was by a drought in 1769, at the season when
the rains are expected, that there was a failure of the
great harvest of 1769, and the less harvest of 1770.
It is true that the rice on the higher grounds did not
suffer greatly by this disturbance of the seasons, but
there was far from a sufficient quantity for the nourishment of all the inhabitants of the country; add to
which the English, who were engaged beforehand to
take proper care of their subsistence, as well as of the
Sepoys belonging to them, did not fail to keep locked
up in their magazines a part of the grain, though the
harvest was insufficient. . . . This scourge did not
fail to make itself felt throughout Bengal. Rice,
which is commonly sold for one sol ($\frac{1}{2}$d.) for three
pounds, was gradually raised so high as four or even

six sols (3d.) for one pound; neither, indeed, was there any to be found, except in such places where the Europeans had taken care to collect it for their own use.

" The unhappy Indians were perishing every day by thousands under this want of sustenance, without any means of help and without any revenue. They were to be seen in their villages; along the public ways; in the midst of our European colonies,—pale, meagre, emaciated, fainting, consumed by famine— some stretched on the ground in expectation of dying; others scarce able to drag themselves on to seek any nourishment, and throwing themselves at the feet of the Europeans, entreating them to take them in as their slaves.

" To this description, which makes humanity shudder, let as add other objects, equally shocking. Let imagination enlarge upon them, if possible. Let us represent to ourselves, infants deserted, some ex- piring on the breasts of their mothers; everywhere, the dying and the dead mingled together; on all sides, the groans of sorrow and the tears of despair; and we shall then have some faint idea of the horrible spec- tacle which Bengal presented for the space of six weeks.

" During this whole time, the Ganges was covered with carcases; the fields and highways were choked up with them; infectious vapours filled the air, and diseases multiplied; and one evil succeeding another, it appeared not improbable that the plague would carry off the total population of that unfortunate king- dom. It appears, by calculations pretty generally acknowledged, that the famine carried off a fourth

part, that is to say—*about three millions!* What is
still more remarkable, is, that such a multitude of
human creatures, amidst this terrible distress, remained
in absolute inactivity. All the Europeans, especially the English, were possessed of magazines. These
were not touched. Private houses were so too. No
revolt, no massacre, not the least violence prevailed.
The unhappy Indians, resigned to despair, confined
themselves to the request of succours they did not
obtain; and peacefully awaited the relief of death.

"Let us now represent to ourselves any part of
Europe afflicted with a similar calamity. What disorder! what fury! what atrocious acts! what crimes
would ensue! How should we have seen amongst us
Europeans, some contending for their food, dagger in
hand, some pursuing, some flying, and without remorse
massacring one another! How should we have seen
men at last turn their rage on themselves; tearing
and devouring their own limbs; and, in the blindness
of despair, trampling under foot all authority, as well
as every sentiment of nature and reason!

"Had it been the fate of the English to have had
the like events to dread on the part of the people of
Bengal, perhaps the famine would have been less
general and less destructive. For, setting aside, as
perhaps we ought, every charge of monoply, no one
will undertake to defend them against the reproach
of negligence and insensibility. And in what a crisis
have they merited that reproach? In the very instant
of time in which the life or death of several millions
of their fellow-creatures was in their power. One
would think that in such alternative, the very love of
humankind, that sentiment innate in all hearts, might
have inspired them with resources."—i. 460-4.

CHAPTER XVII.

THE ENGLISH IN INDIA, CONTINUED.—TREATMENT OF THE NATIVES, CONTINUED.

" IF," says the same historian, in whose language we concluded the last chapter, " to this picture of public oppressions we were to add that of private extortions, we should find the agents of the Company almost everywhere exacting their tribute with extreme rigour, and raising contributions with the utmost cruelty. We should see them carrying a kind of inquisition into every family, and sitting in judgment on every fortune; robbing indiscriminately the artizan and the labourer; imputing it often to a man, as a crime, that he is not sufficiently rich, and punishing him accordingly. We should view them selling their favour and their credit, as well to oppress the innocent as to oppress the guilty. We should find, in consequence of these irregularities, despair seizing every heart, and an universal dejection getting the better of every mind, and uniting to put a stop to the progress and activity of commerce, agriculture, and population." This, which is the language of a foreigner, was also the language of the Directors at the same period, addressed to their servants in India. They complained that their "orders had been disregarded; that oppression pervaded the whole country; that youths had been suffered with impunity to exercise sovereign jurisdiction over the natives, and to acquire rapid fortunes by monopolizing commerce." They ask "whether there be a thing which had not been made a monopoly of? whether the natives are not more than ever oppressed and wretched?" They were just then appointing Mr. Hastings their first Governor-general, and expressed a hope that he would "set an example of temperance, economy, and application." Unfortunately Mr. Hastings set an example of a very different kind. It was almost immediately after his appointment to his high station that he entered into that infamous bargain with the Nabob of Oude for the extermination of the Rohillas; and during his government scarcely a year passed without the most serious charges being preferred against him to the supreme council, of which he himself was the head, of his reception of presents and annuities contrary to the express injunctions of the Company, and for the purpose of corrupt appointments. In 1775 he was charged with the receipt of 15,000 rupees, as a bribe for the appointment of the Duan of Burdwan, or manager of the revenues; in 1776, of receiving an annual salary from the Phousdar of Hoogly of 36,000 rupees for a similar cause. About the same time it came out too, that in 1772, that is, immediately on entering the governorship, he received from the Munny Begum a present of one lac and a half of rupees, for appointing her the guardian and superintendent of the

affairs of the Nabob of Bengal, a minor; and the
same sum had been received by Mr. Middleton, his
agent.   The council felt itself bound to receive evidence on these charges.   The Maha Rajah Nundcomar, who had been appointed to various important
offices by Mr. Hastings himself, came forward and
accused the governor of acquitting Mahmud Reza
Khan, the Naib Duan of Bengal, and Rajah Shitabroy
the Naib Duan of Bahar, of vast embezzlements in
their accounts, and also offered proof of the bribe of
upwards of three and a half lacs from Munny Begum
and Rajah Gourdass.   What answer did he make to
these charges?   He refused to enter into them; but
immediately commenced a prosecution of Nundcomar,
on a charge of conspiracy; which failing, he had him
tried on a charge of forgery, said to be committed five
years before.   On this he was convicted by a jury of
Englishmen, and hanged, though the crime was not
capital by the laws of his country.   This was a circumstance that cast the foulest suspicions upon him.   It was
said that a man standing in the position and peculiar circumstances of the governor, accused of the high crimes
of bribery and corruption, would, had he been innocent,
have used every exertion to have saved the life of an
accuser, had he been prosecuted by others, instead of
himself hastening him out of the way; which must
leave the irresistible conviction in the public mind, of
his own guilt.   But on the celebrated trial of Mr.
Hastings, this was exactly the mode in which every
accusation was met.   When the most celebrated men
of the time had united to reiterate these and other
charges; when he stood before the House of Peers,
impeached by the Commons, instead of standing for-

ward as a man conscious of his innocence, and glad of the opportunity to clear his name from such foul taint, every technical obstruction which the ingenuity of his council could devise was thrown in the way of evidence. When the evidence of this Rajah Nundcomar, as taken by the supreme council of Calçutta, was tended, it was rejected because it was not given in the council upon oath; though Mr. Hastings well knew that the Hindoos never gave evidence upon oath, being contrary to their religion; that it was never required,—that this very evidence had been received by the council as legal; and that he himself had always contended during his own government, that such evidence was legal. When a letter of Munny Begum was presented, proving the reception of her bribe by Mr. Hastings, that letter was not admitted because it was merely a copy, though an attested one; the original letter itself was however produced, and persons high in office in India at the time of the transaction, came forward to swear to the hand and seal as those of the Begum. And what then? the original letter itself was rejected because it made part of the evidence before the council, which had been rejected before on other grounds!

Such was the manner in which these and the other great charges against this celebrated governor, which we have noticed in a former chapter, were met. Every piece of decisive evidence against him was resisted by every possible means: so that had he been the most innocent man alive, the only conviction that could remain on the mind of the public must have been that of his guilt. He had neither acted like an innocent, high-minded man, to whom the imputation of guilt is intolerable, himself in India, nor had his advocates in England been instructed to do so. Evidence on every charge, of the most conclusive nature, was offered, and resolutely rejected; and spite of all the endeavours to clear the memory of Warren Hastings of cruelty and corruption, the very conduct of himself and his counsel on the trial, must stamp the accusing verdict indelibly on his name.

But his individual conduct is here of no further concern than to shew what must have been the contagion of his example, and what the license given by the House of Peers, by the rejection of evidence in such a case, to all future adventurers in India. Well might Burke exclaim, "That it held out to all future governors of Bengal the most certain and unbounded impunity. Peculation in India would be no longer practised, as it used to be, with caution and with secresy. It would in future stalk abroad at noon-day, and act without disguise; because, after such a decision as had just been made by their lordships, there was no possibility of bringing into a court the proofs of peculation." And indeed every misery which the combined evils of war, official plunder, and remorseless exaction could heap upon the unhappy natives, seems to have reigned triumphant through the British provinces and dependencies of India at this period. The destructive contests with Hyder Ali, the ravages of the English and their ally, the Nabob of Arcot, in Tanjore and the Marawars, were necessarily productive of extreme ruin and misery. During Mr. Hastings' government the duannee, or management of the revenues was assumed in Bengal by the English. Reforms both in the mode of collecting the taxes and in the administration of justice were attempted. The lands were offered on leases of five years, and those leases put up to auction to the best bidders. The British Parliament in 1773 appointed a Supreme Court of Judicature, in which English judges administered English law. But as the great end aimed at was not the relief of the people, but the increase of the amount of taxation, these changes were only disastrous to the natives. Native officers were in many cases removed, and the native ryots only the more oppressed. Every change, in fact, seemed to be tried except the simple and satisfactory one of reducing the exactions and cultivating the blessings of peace. Ten years after these changes had been introduced, and had been all this time inflicting unspeakable calamities on the people, Mr. Dundas moved inquiry into Indian affairs, and pronounced the most severe censures on both the Indian Presidencies and the Court of Directors. He accused the Presidencies, and that most justly, of plunging the nation into wars for the sake of conquest, of contemning and violating treaties, and plundering and oppressing the people of India. The Directors he charged with blaming the misconduct of their servants only when it was unattended with profit, and exercising a very constant forbearance as often as it was productive of gain or territory.

Of the effects of his own military and financial changes Mr. Hastings had a good specimen in his journey through the province of Benares in 1784. This was only three years after he had committed the atrocities in this province, related in a former chapter, and driven the Rajah from his throne; and these are his own words, in a letter to the Council, dated Lucknow, April, 1784:—"From the confines of Buxar to Benares, I was followed and fatigued by the clamours of the discontented inhabitants. The distresses which were produced by the long-continued drought unavoidably tended to heighten the general discontent: yet I have reason to fear that the cause principally existed in a defective, if not a corrupt and oppressive administration. From Buxar to the opposite boundary I have seen nothing but traces of complete devastation in every village." And what had occasioned those devastations? The wars and the determined resolve introduced by Mr. Hastings himself, to have the very uttermost amount that could be wrung from the people.

For the sort of persons to whom Mr. Hastings was in the habit of farming out the revenues of the provinces, and the motives for which they were appointed, we must refer to particulars which came out on his trial respecting such men as Kelleram, Govind Sing, and Deby Sing; but nothing can give a more lively idea of the horrid treatment which awaited the poor natives under such monsters as these collectors, than the statements then made of the practices of the last mentioned person, Deby or Devi Sing. This man was declared to have been placed on his post for corrupt ends. He was a man of the most infamous character; yet that did not prevent Mr. Hastings placing him in such a responsible office, though he himself declared on the trial that he " so well knew the character and abilities of Rajah Deby Sing that he could easily conceive it was in his power both to commit great enormities and to conceal the real grounds of them from the British collectors in the district."—

Well, notwithstanding this opinion, the Rajah offered a very convenient sum of money, four lacs of rupees—upwards of 40,000*l.*—and he was appointed renter of the district of Dinagepore. Complaints of his cruelties were not long in arriving at Calcutta. Mr. Patterson, a gentleman in the Company's service, was sent as a commissioner to inquire into the charges against him; and the account of them, as given by Mr. Patterson, is thus quoted by Mills, from "The History of the Trial of Warren Hastings, Esq."

"The poor ryots, or husbandmen, were treated in a manner that would never gain belief if it was not attested by the records of the Company: and Mr. Burke thought it necessary to apologize to their lordships for the horrid relation with which he would be obliged to harrow their feelings. The worthy Commissioner Patterson, who had authenticated the particulars of this relation, had wished, that for the credit of human nature, he might have drawn a veil over them; but as he had been sent to inquire into them, he must, in the discharge of his duty state those particulars, however shocking they were to his feelings. The cattle and corn of the husbandmen were sold for a third of their value, and their huts reduced to ashes ! The unfortunate owners were obliged to borrow from usurers, that they might discharge their bonds, which had unjustly and illegally been extorted from them while they were in confinement; and such was the determination of the infernal fiend, Devi Sing, to have these bonds discharged, that the wretched husbandmen were obliged to borrow money, not at twenty, or thirty, or forty, or fifty, but at six hundred per cent. to satisfy him ! Those who could not raise the money were most cruelly tortured. *Cords were drawn tight round their fingers, till the flesh of the four on each hand was actually incorporated, and became one solid mass. The fingers were then separated again by wedges of iron and wood driven in between them!* Others were tied, two and two, by the feet, and thrown across a wooden bar, upon which they hung with their feet uppermost. They were then beat on the soles of the feet till the toe-nails dropped off! They were afterwards beat about the head till the blood gushed out at the mouth, nose, and ears. They were also flogged upon the naked body with bamboo canes, and prickly bushes, and above all, with some poisonous weeds, which were of a caustic nature, and burnt at every touch. The cruelty of the monster who had ordered all this, had contrived how to tear the mind as well as the body. He frequently had a father and son tied naked to one another by the feet and arms, and then flogged till the skin was torn from the flesh; and he had the devilish satisfaction to know, that every blow must hurt; for if one escaped the son, his sensibility was wounded by the knowledge he had, that the blow had fallen upon his father. The same torture was felt by the father, when he knew that every blow that missed him had fallen upon his son.

"The treatment of the females could not be described. Dragged from the inmost recesses of their houses, which the religion of the country had made so many sanctuaries, they were exposed naked to public view. The Virgins were carried to the Court of Justice, where they might naturally have looked for protection, but they now looked for it in vain; for in the face of the ministers of justice, in the face of the spec-

tators, in the face of the sun, those tender and modest
virgins were brutally violated. The only difference
between their treatment and that of their mothers was,
that the former were dishonoured in the face of day,
the latter in the gloomy recesses of their dungeon.
Other females had the nipples of their breasts put in
a cleft bamboo, and torn off." What follows is too
shocking and indecent to transcribe! It is almost
impossible, in reading of these frightful and savage
enormities, to believe that we are reading of a country
under the British government, and that these unmanly
deeds were perpetrated by British agents, and for the
purpose of extorting the British revenue. Thus were
these innocent and unhappy people treated, because
Warren Hastings wanted money, and sold them to a
wretch whom he knew to be a wretch, for a bribe;
thus were they treated, because Devi Sing had paid
his four lacs of rupees, and must wring them again
out of the miserable ryots, though it were with their
very life's blood, and with fire and torture before
unheard of even in the long and black catalogue of
human crimes. And it should never be forgotten,
that though Mr. Burke pledged himself, if permitted,
under the most awful imprecations, to prove every
word of this barbarous recital, such permission was
stoutly refused; and that, moreover, the evidence of
the Commissioner Patterson stands in the Company's
own records.

But it was not merely the commission of these outrages which the poor inhabitants had to endure. The
English courts of justice, which should have protected
them, became an additional means of torture and ruin.
The writs of the supreme court were issued at the

suit of individuals against the zemindars of the country in ordinary actions of debt. They were dragged from their families and affairs, with the frequent certainty of leaving them to disorder and ruin, any distance, even as great as 500 miles, to give bail at Calcutta; a thing, which, if they were strangers, and the sum more than trifling, it was next to impossible they should have in their power. In default of this, they were consigned to prison for all the many months which the delays of English judicature might interpose between this calamitous stage and the termination of the suit. Upon the affidavit, into the truth of which no inquiry was made, upon the unquestioned affidavit of any person whatsoever—a person of credibility, or directly the reverse, no difference—the natives were seized, carried to Calcutta, and consigned to prison, where, even when it was afterwards determined that they were not within the jurisdiction of the court, and, of course, that they had been unjustly persecuted, they were liable to lie for several months, and whence they were dismissed totally without compensation. Instances occurred, in which defendants were brought from a distance to the Presidency, and when they declared their intention of pleading, that is, objecting to the jurisdiction of the court, the prosecution was dropped; but was again renewed; the defendant brought down to Calcutta, and again upon his offering to plead, the prosecution was dropped. The very act of being seized, was in India, the deepest disgrace, and so degraded a man of any rank that, under the Mahomedan government, it never was attempted but in cases of the utmost delinquency.*

* Mills, ii. 560-2.

In merely reading these cases of

The proud man's contumely, the oppressor's wrong,

it is difficult to repress the burning indignation of one's spirit. What shame, what disgrace, that under the laws of England, and in a country to which we owe so much wealth and power, such a system of reckless and desperate injustice should for a long series of years have been practising! But if it be difficult to read of it without curses and imprecations, what must it have been to bear? How must the wretched, hopeless, harassed, persecuted, and outraged people have called on Brahma for that tenth Avatar which should sweep their invincible, their iron-handed and iron-hearted oppressors, as a swarm of locusts from their fair land! Let any one imagine what must be the state of confusion when the zemindars, or higher collectors of the revenues were thus plagued in the sphere of their arduous duties, and called out of it, to the distant capital. When they were degraded in the eyes, and removed from the presence of the ryots, what must have been the natural consequence, but neglect and license on the part of the ryot, only too happy to obtain a little temporary ease? But the ryots themselves did not escape, as we have already seen. Such, however, continued this dismal state of things to the very end of the century. Lord Cornwallis complained in 1790, " that excepting the class of shroffs and banyans, who reside almost entirely in great towns, the inhabitants of these provinces were hastily advancing to a general state of poverty and wretchedness." Lord Cornwallis projected *his* plans, and in 1802, Sir Henry Strachey, in answer to interrogatories sent to the Indian judges, drew a gloomy picture of the result of all the schemes of finance and judicature that had been adopted. He represented that the zemindars, by the sale of their lands, in default of the payment of their stipulated revenue, were almost universally destroyed, or were reduced to the condition of the lowest ryots. That, in one year (1796) nearly one tenth of all the lands in Bengal, Bahar, and Orissa, had been advertised for sale. That in two years alone, of the trial of the English courts, the accumulated causes threatened to arrest the course of justice: in one single district of Burdwan more than thirty thousand suits were before the judge; and that no candidate for justice could expect it in the course of an ordinary life. " The great men, formerly," said Sir Henry, "were the Mussulman rulers, whose places we have taken, and the Hindoo zemindars. These two classes are now ruined and destroyed." He adds, "exaction of revenue is now, I presume, and, perhaps, always was, the most prevailing crime throughout the country; and I know not how it is that extortioners appear to us in any other light than that of the worst and most pernicious species of robbers." He tells us that the lands of the Mahrattas in the neighbourhood of his district, Midnapore, were more prosperous than ours, though they were without regular courts of justice, or police. "Where," says he, "no battles are fought, the ryots remain unmolested by military exactions, and the zemindars are seldom changed, the country was in high cultivation, and the population frequently superior to our own."

Such was the condition and treatment of the natives of Indostan, at the commencement of the present century. In another chapter, on our policy and conduct in this vast and important region—it remains only to take a rapid glance at the effect of these two centuries of despotism upon these subjected millions, and to inquire what we have since been doing towards a better state of things,—more auspicious to them, and honourable to ourselves.

CHAPTER XVIII.

THE ENGLISH IN INDIA, CONTINUED.

We are accustomed to govern India—a country which God never gave us, by means which God will never justify.

Lord Erskine—Speech on Stockdale's Trial.

WE have traced something of the misery which a long course of avarice and despotism has inflicted on the natives of India, but we have not taken into the account its moral effect upon them. Generation after generation of Englishmen flocked over to Indostan, to gather a harvest of wealth, and to return and enjoy it at home. Generation after generation of Indians arose to create this wealth for their temporary visitors, and to sink deeper and deeper themselves into poverty. Happy had it been for them, had poverty and physical wretchedness come alone. But the inevitable con-

comitant of slavery and destitution appeared with
them, and to every succeeding generation in a more
appalling form—demoralization, vast as their multitude
and dreadful as their condition.   They were not more
unhappy than they were degraded in spirit and debased in feeling.   Ages of virtual though not nominal
slavery, beneath Mahomedan and Christian masters,
had necessarily done their usual work on the Hindus.
They had long ceased to be the gentle, the pure--
minded, the merciful Hindus.   They had become
cruel, thievish, murderous, licentious, as well as
blindly superstitious.   They had seen no religious
purity, no moral integrity practised—how were they
to become pure and honest?   They had felt only
cruelty and injustice—how were they to be anything
but cruel and unjust?   They had seen from age to
age, from day to day, from hour to hour, every sacred
tie of blood or honour, every moral obligation, every
great and eternal principle of human action violated
around them—how were they to reverence such things?
How were they to regard them but as solemn and
unprofitable mockeries?   They were accordingly corrupted into a mean, lying, depraved, and perfidious
generation—could the abject tools of a money-scraping
race of conquerors be anything else?—was it probable?
was it possible?   Philosophers and poetical minds,
when such, now and then, reached India, were astonished to find, instead of those delicate and spiritual
children of Brahma, of whom they had read such
delightful accounts—a people so sordid, and in many
instances so savage and cruel. They had not calculated,
as they might have done, the certain consequences of
long years of slavery's most fatal inflictions.   What

an eternal debt of generous and Christian retribution do we owe India for all this! What, indeed, are the pangs we have occasioned, the poverty we have created, the evils of all kinds that we have perpetrated, to the moral degradation we have induced, and the gross darkness, gross superstition, the gross sensuality we have thus, in fact, fostered and perpetuated? Had we appeared in India as Christians instead of conquerors; as just merchants instead of subtle plotters, shunning the name of tyrants while we aimed at the most absolute tyranny; had we been as conspicuous for our diffusion of knowledge as for our keen, ceaseless, and insatiable gathering of coin; long ago that work would have been done which is but now beginning, and our power would have acquired the most profound stability in the affections and the knowledge of the people.

At the period of which I have been speaking—the end of the last and the opening of the present century, the character of the Hindus, as drawn by eye witnesses of the highest authority, was most deplorable. Even Sir William Jones, than whom there never lived a man more enthusiastic in his admiration of the Hindu literature and antiquities, and none more ready to see all that concerned this people in sunny hues—even he, when he had had time to observe their character, was compelled to express his surprise and disappointment. He speaks of their cruelties with abhorrence: in his charge to the grand jury at Calcutta, June 10th, 1787, he observed, " Perjury seems to be committed by the meanest, and encouraged by some of the better sort of the Hindus and Mussulmans with as little remorse as if it were a proof of ingenuity, or even of merit"—that he had " no doubt that affidavits of any imaginary fact might be purchased in the markets of Calcutta as readily as any other article—and that, could the most binding form of religious obligation be hit upon, there would be found few consciences to bind."

All the travellers and historians of the time, Orme, Buchanan, Forster, Forbes, Scott Waring, etc., unite in bearing testimony to their grossness, filth, and disregard of their words; their treachery, cowardice, and thievishness; their avarice, equal to that of the whites, and their cunning and duplicity more than European; their foul language and quarrelsome habits—all the features of a people depraved by hereditary oppression and moral neglect. Their horrid and barbarous superstitions, by which thousands of victims are destroyed every year, are now familiar to all Europe. Every particular of these evil lineaments of character were most strikingly attested by the Indian judges, in their answers to the circular of interrogatories put to them in 1801, already alluded to. They all coincided in describing the general moral character of the inhabitants as at the lowest pitch of infamy; that very few exceptions to that character were to be found; that there was no species of fraud or villany that the higher classes would not be guilty of; and that, in the lower classes, were to be added, murder, robbery, adultery, perjury, etc., on the slightest occasion. One of them, the magistrate of Juanpore, added, " I have observed, among the inhabitants of this country, some possessed of abilities qualified to rise to eminence in other countries, *but a moral, virtuous man, I have never met amongst them.*"

Mr. Grant described the Bengalese as depraved and dishonest to a degree to which Europe could furnish no parallel; that they were "cunning, servile, intriguing, false, and hypocritically obsequious; that they, however, indemnified themselves for their passiveness to their superiors by their tyranny, cruelty, and violence to those in their power." Amongst themselves he says, "discord, hatred, abuse, slanders, injuries, complaints, and litigations prevail to a surprising degree. No stranger can sit down among them without being struck with the temper of malevolent contention and animosity as a prominent feature in the character of the society. It is seen in every village: the inhabitants live amongst each other in a sort of repulsive state. Nay, it enters into almost every family: seldom is there a household without its internal divisions and lasting enmities, most commonly, too, on the score of interest. The women, too, partake of this spirit of discord. Held in slavish subjection by the men, they rise in furious passions against each other, which vent themselves in such loud, virulent, and indecent railings, as are hardly to be heard in any other part of the world. . . . . . Benevolence has been represented as a leading principle in the minds of the Hindus; but those who make this assertion know little of their character. Though a Hindu would shrink with horror from the idea of directly slaying a cow, which is a sacred animal amongst them, yet he who drives one in his cart, galled and excoriated as she is by the yoke, beats her unmercifully from hour to hour, without any care or consideration of the consequence." Mr. Fraser Tytler, Lord Teignmouth, Sir James Mackintosh, and others, only expand the dark features of this melancholy picture; we need not therefore dwell largely upon it. The French missionary, the Abbé Dubois, and Mr. Ward, the English one, bear a like testimony. The latter, on the subject of Hindu humanity, asks— " Are these men and women, too, who drag their dying relations to the banks of rivers, at all seasons, day and night, and expose them to the heat and cold in the last agonies of death, without remorse; who assist men to commit self-murder, encouraging them to swing with hooks in their backs, to pierce their tongues and sides—to cast themselves on naked knives or bury themselves alive—throw themselves in rivers, from precipices, and under the cars of their idols;— who murder their own children—burying them alive, throwing them to the alligators, or hanging them up alive in trees, for the ants and crows, before their own doors, or by sacrificing them to the Ganges;—who burn alive, amidst savage shouts, the heart-broken widow, by the hands of her own son, and with the corpse of a deceased father;—who every year butcher thousands of animals, at the call of superstition, covering themselves with blood, consigning their carcases to the dogs, and carrying their heads in triumph through the streets? are these the benignant Hindus."

It may be said that these cruelties are the natural growth of their superstitions. True; but, up to the period in question, who had endeavoured to correct, or who cared for their superstitions so that they paid their taxes? To this hour, or, at least, till but yesterday, many of these bloody superstitions have had the actual sanction of the British countenance! To this hour the dreadful indications of their cruel and treacherous character, apart from their superstitions, from time to time affright Europe. We have latterly heard much of the horrible deeds of the Thugs and Phasingars. Where such dreadful associations and habits are prevalent to the extent described, there must be a most monstrous corruption of morals, shock· ing neglect of the people, and consequent annihilation of everything like social security and civilization. In what, indeed, does the practice and temper of the Thugs differ from those of the Decoits, who abounded at the period in question? These were gangs of robbers who associated for their purposes, and practised by subtle subterfuge or open violence, as best suited the occasion. They went in troops, and made a common assault on houses and property, or dispersed themselves under various disguises, to inveigle their victims into their power. Mr. Dowdeswell, in a report to government, in 1809, says, "robbery, rape, and murder itself are not the worst figures in this horrid and disgusting picture. An expedient of common occurrence with the Decoits, merely to induce a confession of property supposed to be concealed, is to burn the proprietor with straws or torches until he discloses the property or perishes in the flames." He mentions one man who was convicted of having committed fifteen murders in nineteen days, and adds that, "volumes might be filled with the atrocities of the Decoits, every line of which would make the blood run cold with horror." He does, indeed, give some details of them of the most amazing and harrowing description.

Sir Henry Strachey in his Report already quoted, says, "the crime of decoity, in the district of Calcutta, has, I believe, greatly increased since the British administration of justice. The number of convicts confined at the six stations of this division (independent of Zillah twenty-four pergunnahs) is about 4000. Of them *probably nine-tenths are decoits.* Besides these, some hundreds of late years have been transported. The number of persons convicted of decoity, however great it may appear, is certainly small in proportion to those who are guilty of the crime. At Midnapore I find, by the reports of the police darogars, that in the year 1802, a period of peace and tranquillity, they sent intelligence of no less than ninety three robberies, most of them, as usual, committed by large gangs. With respect to fifty-one of these robberies, not a man was taken, and for the remaining forty-two, very few, frequently only one or two in each gang." Other judges describe the extent to which decoity existed, as being much vaster than was generally known, and calculated to excite the most general terror throughout the country.

This is an awful picture of a people approaching to one hundred millions, and of a great and splendid country, which has been for the most part in our hands for more than a century. It only remains now to inquire what has been done since the opening of the nineteenth century for the instruction and general amelioration of the condition of this vast multitude of human beings, and thereby for our own justification as a Christian nation. Warren Hastings said most truly, that throwing aside all pretences of any other kind that many were disposed to set up, the simple truth was that "by the sword India had been acquired, and by the sword it must be maintained." If the forcible conquest of a country be, therefore, a crime against the rights of nations and the principles of religion, what retribution can we make for our national offences, except by employing our power to make the subjected people happy and virtuous? But if we do not even hold conquest to be a crime, or war to be unchristian, where is the man that will not deem that we have assumed an awful responsibility on the plainest principles of the gospel, by taking into our hands the fate of so many millions of human creatures, thus degraded, thus ignorant and unhappy? It is impossible either to " do justice, to love mercy, or to walk humbly before God," without as zealously seeking the social and eternal benefit of so great a people, as we have sought, and still seek, our own advantage, in the possession of their wealth. Over this important subject I am unfortunately bound to pass, by my circumscribed limits, in a hasty manner. The subject would require a volume. It is with pleasure, however, that we can point to certain great features in the modern history of improvement in India. It is with pleasure that we can say that some of the most barbarous rites of the Hindu superstitions have been removed. That infanticide, and the burning of widows have been abolished by the British influence; and that though the horrible immolations of Juggernaut are not terminated, they are no longer so unblushingly sanctioned, and even encouraged by British interference. These are great steps in the right path. To Colonel Walker, and Mr. Duncan, the governor of Bombay, immortal thanks and honour are due, for first leading the way in this track of great reforms, by at once discouraging, dissuading from, and finally abolishing infanticide in Guzerat. One of the most beneficial acts of the

Marquis Wellesley's government, was to put this
horrible custom down in Saugur.   How little anything, however, but the extraction of revenue had
throughout all the course of our dominion in India
been regarded till the present century, the Christian
Researches of Mr. Buchanan made manifest.   The
publication of that book, coming as it did from a gentleman most friendly to our authorities there, was the
commencement of a new era in our Indian history.
It at once turned, by the strangeness of its details, the
eyes of all the religious world on our Indian territories, and excited a feeling which more than any other
cause has led to the changes which have hitherto
been effected.   At that period (1806), in making a
tour through the peninsula of Indostan, he discovered
that everything like attention to the moral or religious
condition of either natives or colonists was totally
neglected.   That all the atrocious superstitions of the
Hindus were not merely tolerated, but even sanctioned,
and some of them patronized by our government.
That though there were above twenty English regi-
ments in India at that time, *not one of them had a chaplain,* (p. 80).   That in Ceylon, where the Dutch had
once thirty-two Protestant churches, we had then but
two English clergymen in the whole island ! (p. 93).
That there were in it by computation 500,000 natives
professing Christianity; who, however, "had not one
complete copy of the Scriptures in the vernacular
tongue," and consequently, they were fast receding
into paganism, (p. 95).   That the very English were
more notorious for their infidelity than for anything
else, and by their presence did infinite evil to the
natives.   That, in that very year, when the governor

of Bombay announced to the supreme government at Calcutta, his determination to attempt to extirpate infanticide from Guzerat—a practice, be it remembered, which in that province alone *destroyed annually* 3000 *children !**—this cool commercial body warned him, not " even for the *speculative* success of that benevolent project, to hazard the *essential interests* of the state !" (p. 52). That all the horrors of burning widows were perpetrated to the amount of from seven hundred to *one thousand* of such diabolical scenes annually. That the disgusting and gory worship of Juggernaut was not merely practised, but was actually licensed and patronized by the English government. That very year it had imposed a tax on all pilgrims going to the temples in Orissa and Bengal, had appointed British officers, British gentlemen to superintend the management of this hideous worship and the receipt of its proceeds. That the internal rites of the temple consisted in one loathsome scene of prostitution, hired bands of women being kept for the purpose ; its outward rites the crushing of human victims under the car of the idol.

Thus the Indian government had, in fact, instead of discouraging such practices in the natives, taken up the trade of public murderers, and keepers of houses of ill fame, and that under the sacred name of religious tolerance ! A more awful state of things it is impossible to conceive; nor one which more forcibly demonstrates what the whole of this history proclaims, that there is no state of crime, corruption, or villany, which by being familiarized to them, and coming to regard

* It is said that infanticide, spite of the legal prohibition, is still privately perpetrated to a great extent in Cutch and Guzerat.

them as customary, educated men, and men of originally good hearts and pure consciences, will not eventually practise with composure, and even defend as right. What defences have we not heard in England of these very practices? It was not till recently that public opinion was able to put down the immolation of widows,* nor till this very moment that the Indian government has been shamed out of trading in murder and prostitution in the temples of Juggernaut. Thus, for more than thirty years has this infamous trade at Juggernaut been persisted in, from the startling exposure of it by Buchanan, and in the face of all the abhorrence and remonstrances of England—for more than a century and a half it has been tolerated. The plea on which it has been defended is that of delicacy towards the *opinions* of the natives. That delicacy thus delicately extended where money was to be made, has not in a single case been practised for a single instant where our interest prompted a different conduct. We have seized on the lands of the natives; on their revenues; degraded their persons by the lash, or put them to death without any scruple. But this plea has been so strongly rebutted by one well acquainted with India, in the Oriental Herald, that before quitting this subject it will be well to quote it here. "The assumption that our empire is an empire of opinion in India, and that it would be endangered by restraining the bloody and abominable rites of the natives, is as false as the inference is unwarranted. Our empire is *not* an empire of opinion, it is not even an empire of law: it has been acquired; it is still governed; and can only be retained, unless the whole system of its government is altered, by the direct in-

* Nominally, in 1829; but not actually till considerably later.

fluence of force.   No portion of the country has been
voluntarily ceded, from the love borne to us by the
original possessors.   We were first permitted to land
on the sea coast to sell our wares, as humble and solicitous traders, till by degrees, sometimes by force and
sometimes by fraud, we háve possessed ourselves of an
extent of territory containing nearly a hundred millions of human beings.   We have put down the
ancient sovereigns of the land, we have stripped the
nobles of all their power; and by continual drains on
the industry and resources of the people, we take from
them all their surplus and disposable wealth.   There
is not a single province of that country that we have
ever acquired but by the direct influence which our
strength and commanding influence could enforce, or
by the direct agency of warlike operations and superior skill in arms.   There is not a spot throughout the
whole of this vast region whereon we rule by any
other medium than that by which we first gained our
footing there—simple force.   There is not a district
in which the natives would not gladly see our places
as rulers supplied by men of their own nation, faith,
and manners, so that they might have a share in their
own affairs ; nor is there an individual, out of all the
millions subject to our rule in Asia, whose opinion is
ever asked as to the policy or impolicy of any law or
regulation about to be made by our government, however it may press on the interests of those subject by
its operation.   It is a delusion which can never be too
frequently exposed, to believe that our empire in India
is an empire of opinion, or to imagine that we have
any security for our possession of that country, except
the superiority of our means for maintaining the dominion of force."—vol. ii. p. 174.

CHAPTER XIX.

THE ENGLISH IN INDIA,—CONCLUDED.

THE preceding chapter is an awful subject of contemplation for a Christian nation. An empire over one hundred millions acquired by force, and held by force for the appropriation of their revenues! Even this dominion of force is a fragile tenure. We even now watch the approaches of the gigantic power of Russia towards these regions with jealousy and alarm; and it is evident that at once security to ourselves, and atonement to the natives, are only to be found in the amelioration of their condition: in educating and Christianizing them, and in amalgamising them with British interests and British blood as much as possible. The throwing open of these vast regions, by the abolition of the Company's charter of trade, to the enterprise and residence of our countrymen, now offers us ample means of moral retribution; and it is with peculiar interest that we now turn to every symptom of a better state of things.

A new impulse is given to both commerce and agriculture. The march of improvement in the cultivation and manufacture of various productions is begun. The growth of wheat is encouraged, and even large quantities of fine flour imported thence into England. The indigo trade has become amazing by the improvement in the manipulation of that article. Sugar, coffee, opium, cotton, spices, rice, every product of this rich and varied region, will all find a greater demand, and consequently a greater perfection from culture, under these circumstances. There is, in fact, no species of vegetable production which, in this glorious country, offering in one part or another the temperature of every known climate, may not be introduced. Such is the fertility of the land under good management, that the natives often now make 26*l*. per acre of their produce. The potato is becoming as much esteemed there as it has long been in Europe and America. Tea is likely to become one of its most important articles of native growth. Our missionaries of various denominations—episcopalians, catholics, baptists, methodists, moravians, etc., are zealously labouring to spread knowledge and Christianity; and there is nothing, according to the Christian brahmin, Rammohun Roy, which the Indian people so much desire as an English education. Let that be given, and the fetters of caste must be broken at once. The press, since the great struggle in which Mr. Buckingham was driven from India for attempting its freedom, has acquired a great degree of freedom. The natives are admitted to sit on petty juries; slavery is abolished; and last, and best, education is now extensively and zealously promoted. The Company was bound by the terms of its charter in 1813 to devote 10,000*l*. annually to educating natives in the English language and English knowledge, which,

though but a trifling sum compared with the vast
population, aided by various private schools, must have
produced very beneficial effects. Bishop Heber states
that on his arrival in Bengal he found that there were
fifty thousand scholars, chiefly under the care of Protestant missionaries. These are the means which must
eventually make British rule that blessing which it
ought to have been long ago. These are the means
by which we may atone, and more than atone, for all
our crimes and our selfishness in India. But let us
remember that we are—after the despotism of two centuries, after oceans of blood shed by us, and oceans of
wealth drained by us from India, and after that blind
and callous system of exaction and European exclusion
which has perpetuated all the ignorance and all the
atrocities of Hindu superstition, and laid the burthen
of them on our own shoulders—but at this moment on
the mere threshold of this better career. Let us remember that still, at this hour, Indostan is, in fact,
the IRELAND OF THE EAST! It is a country pouring
out wealth upon us, while it is swarming with a population of one hundred millions in the lowest state of
poverty and wretchedness. It swarms with robbers
and assassins of the most dreadful description: and it
is impossible that it should be otherwise. It is said to
be happy and contented under our rule; but such a
happiness as its boldest advocates occasionally give us a
glimpse of, may God soon remove from that oppressed
country. Indeed, such are the features of it, even as
drawn by its eulogists, as make us wonder that such
wretchedness should exist under English sway. Our
travellers describe the mass of the labouring people
as stunted in stature, especially the women; as half

famished, and with hardly a rag to their backs. Mr.
Tucker, himself a Director, and Deputy-Chairman of
the Court of Directors, asks, " Whether it be possible for them to believe that a government, which
seems disposed to appropriate a vast territory as *universal landlord,* and to collect, not *revenue,* but *rent,* can
have any other view than to extract from the people
the utmost portion which they can pay?" and adds,
that " if the deadly hand of the tax-gatherer perpetually hover over the land, and threaten to grasp that
which is not yet called into existence, its benumbing
influence must be fatal, and the fruits of the earth
will be stifled in the very germ."

Yet this is the constant system; and the poor
ryots who cultivate farms of from six to twenty-four
acres, but generally of the smaller kind, requiring
only one plough, which, with other implements and a
team of oxen, costs about 6*l.*, are compelled to farm not
such as they chose, but such as are allotted to them;
to pay from one-half to two-thirds of their gross produce. If they attempt to run away from it, they are
brought back and flogged, and forced to work. If
after all, they cannot pay their quota, Sir Thomas
Munro tells you, "*it must be assessed upon the rest.*"
That where a crop *even is less than the seed,* the peasantry *should always be made to pay the full* rent where
they can. And that all complaints on the part of the
ryot, " should be listened to with very great caution."
Is it any wonder that Indostan is, and always has
been full of robbers? Is this system not enough to
make men run off, and do anything but work thus
without hope? But it is not merely the work: look
at the task-masters set over them. " A very large

proportion of the talliars," says Sir Thomas Munro,
"are themselves thieves; all the kawilgars are themselves robbers exempting them; and though they
are now afraid to act openly, there is no doubt that
many of them still secretly follow their former practices. Many potails and curnums also harbour thieves;
so that no traveller can pass through the ceded districts without being robbed, who does not employ his
own servants or those of the village to watch at night;
and even this precaution is often ineffectual. Many
offenders are taken, but great numbers also escape, for
connivance must also be expected among the kawilgars and the talliars, who are themselves thieves;
and the inhabitants are often backward in giving information from the fear of *assassination*." Colonel
Stewart in 1825, asserted in his " Considerations on
the Policy of the Government of India," that "if we
look for absolute and bodily injury produced by our
misgovernment, he did not believe that all the cruelties practised *in the lifetime* of the worst tyrant that
ever sat upon a throne, even amounted to the quantity
of human suffering inflicted by the Decoits *in one year*
in Bengal." The prevalence of Thugs and Phasingars does not augur much improvement in this
respect yet; nor do recent travellers induce us to
believe that the picture of popular misery given us
about half a dozen years ago by the author of " Re-
flections on the Present state of British India," is yet
become untrue.

" Hitherto the poverty of the cultivating classes,
men who have both property and employment, has
been alone considered; but the extreme misery to
which the immense mass of the unemployed popula-

tion are reduced, would defy the most able pen adequately to describe, or the most fertile imagination to conceive. . . . . On many occasions of ceremony in families of wealthy individuals, it is customary to distribute alms to the poor; sometimes four annas, about three-pence, and rarely more than eight annas each. When such an occurrence is made known, the poor assemble in astonishing numbers, and the roads are covered with them from twenty to fifty miles in every direction. On their approaching the place of gift, no notice is taken of them, though half famished, and almost unable to stand, till towards the evening, when they are called into an inclosed space, and huddled together for the night, in such crowds, that notwithstanding their being in the open air, it is surprising how they escape suffocation. When the individual who makes the donation perceives that all the applicants are in the inclosure, (by which process he guards against the possibility of any poor wretch receiving his bounty twice), he begins to dispense his alms, either in the night, or on the following morning, by taking the poor people, one by one, from the place of their confinement, and driving them off as soon as they have received their pittance. The number of people thus accumulated, generally amounts to from twenty to fifty thousand; and from the distance they travel, and the hardships they endure for so inconsiderable a bounty, some idea may be formed of their destitute condition.

"In the interior of Bengal there is a class of inhabitants who live by catching fish in the ditches and rivulets; the men employing themselves during the whole day, and the women travelling to the nearest

city, often a distance of fifteen miles, to sell the produce. The rate at which these poor creatures perform their daily journey is almost incredible, and the
sum realized is so small as scarcely to afford them the
necessaries of life. In short, throughout the whole
of the provinces the crowds of poor wretches who are
destitute of the means of subsistence are beyond relief,
On passing through the country, they are seen to pick
the undigested grains of food from the dung of ele-
phants, horses, and camels; and if they can procure
a little salt, large parties of them sally into the fields
at night, and devour the green blades of corn or rice
the instant they are seen to shoot above the surface.
Such, indeed, is their wretchedness that they envy the
lot of the convicts working in chains upon the roads,
and have been known to incur the danger of criminal
prosecution, in order to secure themselves from starv-
ing by the allowance made to those who are condemned
to hard labour."

Such is the condition of these native millions, from
whose country our countrymen, flocking over there,
according to the celebrated simile of Burke, " like
birds of prey and of passage, to collect wealth, have
returned with most splendid fortunes to England."
What is the avowed slavery of some half million of
negroes in the West Indies, who have excited so much
interest amongst us, to the virtual slavery of these
hundred millions of Hindus in their own land? It is
declared that these poor creatures are happy under
our government,—but it should be recollected that so
it has been, and is, said of the negroes; and it should
be also recollected what Sir John Malcolm said, in
1824, in a debate at the India-house — himself a

governor and a laudator of our system, that " even
the instructed classes of natives have a hostile feeling
towards us, which was not likely to decrease from the
necessity they were under of concealing it. My attention," he said, " has been during the last five-and-
twenty years particularly directed to this dangerous
species of secret war carried on against our authority,
which is *always carried on* by numerous though un-
seen hands. The spirit is kept up by letters, by
exaggerated reports, and by pretended prophecies.
When the time appears favourable from the occurrence
of misfortune to our arms, from rebellion in our provinces, or from mutiny in our troops, circular letters
and proclamations are dispersed over the country with
a celerity that is incredible. *Such documents are read
with avidity.* Their contents are in most cases the
same. The English are depicted as *usurpers* of low
caste, and as tyrants, who have sought India only to
degrade them, to rob them of their wealth, and sub-
vert their usages and religion. The native soldiers are
always appealed to, and the advice to them is in all
instances I have met with, the same,—' your European
tyrants are few in number—*murder them !* ' "

How far are these evils diminished since the last
great political change in India—since the abolition of
the Company's charter, and they became, not the
commercial monopolists, but the governors of India?
Dr. Spry, of the Bengal Medical Staff, can answer
that in his " Modern India," published in 1837.
The worthy doctor describes himself as a short time
ago (1833) being on an expedition to reduce some
insurrectionary Coles in the provinces of Benares and
Dinapore. "Next morning," he says, " Feb. 9th,

we went out in three parties to burn and destroy villages! Good fun, burning villages!" The mode of expression would lead one to suppose that the doctor extremely enjoyed "the good fun of burning villages;" but the general spirit of his work being sensible and humane, we are bound to suppose that his expressions and his notes of admiration are ironical, and meant to indicate the abhorrence such acts deserves; for he immediately tells us that these Coles seemed very inoffensive sort of people, and laid down their arms in large numbers the moment they were invited to do so.

Dr. Spry tells us that the Anglo-Indian government, in 1836, had come to the admirable resolution to make the English language the vernacular tongue throughout Indostan. That would be, in effect, to make it entirely an English land—to leaven it rapidly, and for ever, with the spirit, the laws, the literature, and the religion of England. It is impossible to make the English language the vernacular tongue, without at the same time producing the most astonishing moral revolution which ever yet was witnessed on the earth. English ideas, English tastes, English literature and religion, must follow as a matter of course. It is curious, indeed, already to hear of the instructed natives of Indostan holding literary and philosophical meetings in English forms, debating questions of morals and polite letters, and adducing the opinions of Milton, Shakspeare, Newton, Locke, etc. Dr. Spry states that the Committee of Public Instruction are about to establish schools for educating the natives in English, at Patnah, Dacca, Hazeeribagh, Gohawati, and other places; and that the native

princes in Nepaul, Manipur, Rajpootanah, the Pun-
jaub, etc. were receiving instruction in English, and
desirous to promote it in their territories. This is
most encouraging; but Dr. Spry gives us other facts
of a less agreeable nature. From these we learn that
the ancient canker of India, excessive and unremitting
exaction, is at this moment eating into the very vitals
of the country as actively as ever. He says that "it
is in the territories of the independent native chiefs
and princes that great and useful works are found,
and maintained. In our territories, the canals, bridges,
reservoirs, wells, groves, temples, and caravansaries,
the works of our predecessors, from revenues expressly
appropriated to such undertakings, are going fast to
decay, together with the feelings which originated
them; and unless a new and more enlightened policy
shall be followed, of which the dawn may, perhaps, be
distinguished, will soon leave not a trace behind. A
persistance for a short time longer in our selfish administration will level the face of the country, as it has
levelled the ranks of society, and leave a plain surface
for wiser statesmen to act on.

"At present, the aspect of society presents no middle
class, and the aspect of the country is losing all those
great works of ornament and utility with which we
found it adorned. Great families are levelled, and
lost in the crowd; and great cities have dwindled into
farm villages. The work of destruction is still going
on; and unless we act on new principles will proceed
with desolating rapidity. How many thousand links
by which the affections of the people are united to
the soil, and to their government, are every year
broken and destroyed by our selfishness and ignorance;

and yet, if our views in the country extended beyond
the returns of a single harvest, beyond the march of a
single detachment, or the journey of a single day, we
could not be so blind to their utility and advantage."
He adds: "By our revenue management we have
shaken the entire confidence of the rural population,
who now no longer lay out their little capital in village improvement, lest our revenue officers, at the
expiration of their leases, should take advantage of
their labours, and impose an additional rent. . . . . .
With regard to Hindustan, those natives who are
unfriendly to us *might with justice declare our conduct
to be more allied to Vandalism than to civilization.* . . .
Burke's severe rebuke still holds good,—that if the
English were driven from India, they would leave
behind them no memorial worthy of a great and enlightened nation; no monument of art, science, or
beneficence; no vestige of their having occupied and
ruled over the country, except such traces as the
vulture and the tiger leave behind them."—pp. 10-18.
He tells us that a municipal tax was imposed under
pretence of improving and beautifying the towns, but
that the improvements very soon stopped, while the
tax is still industriously collected. In the appendix
to his first volume, we find detailed all the miseries of
the ryots as we have just reviewed them; and he tells
us that of this outraged class are *eleven-twelfths of the
population!* and quotes the following sentence from
"The Friend of India." "A proposal was some time
since made, or rather a wish expressed, to domesticate
the art of caricaturing in India. Here is a fine subject. . The artist should first draw the lean and emaciated ryot, scratching the earth at the tail of a plough

drawn by two half-starved, bare-ribbed bullocks. Upon his back he would place the more robust Seeputneedar, and upon his shoulders the Durputneedar; he, again, should sustain the well-fed Putneedar; and, seated upon his shoulders should be represented, to crown the scene, the big zemindar, that compound of milk, sugar, and clarified butter. . . .The poor ryot pays for all! He is drained by these middle-men; he is cheated by his banker out of twenty-four per cent. at least; and his condition is beyond description or imagination."

Dr. Spry attests the present continuance of those scenes of destitution and abject wretchedness which I have but a few pages back alluded to. He has seen the miserable creatures picking up the grains of corn from the soil of the roads. " I have seen," says he, " hundreds of famishing poor, traversing the jungles of Bundlecund, searching for wild berries to satisfy the cravings of hunger. Many, worn down by exhaustion or disease, die by the road-side, while mothers, to preserve their offspring from starvation, sell or give them to any rich man they can meet!" He himself, in 1834, was offered by such a mother her daughter of six years old for fourteen shillings!— vol. i. 297.

These are the scenes and transactions in our great Indian empire—that splendid empire which has poured out such floods of wealth into this country; in which such princely presents of diamonds and gold have been heaped on our adventurers; from the gleanings of which so many happy families in England* "live at

* Even so recently as 1827 we find some tolerably regal instances of regal gifts to our Indian representatives. Lord and Lady Amherst on a tour in the provinces arrived at Agra. Lady

home at ease," and in the enjoyment of every earthly luxury and refinement. For every palace built by returned Indian nabobs in England; for every investment by fortunate adventurers in India stock; for every cup of wine and delicious viand tasted by the families of Indian growth amongst us, how many of these Indians themselves are now picking berries in the wild jungles, sweltering at the thankless plough only to suffer fresh extortions, or snatching with the bony fingers of famine, the bloated grains from the manure of the high-ways of their native country!

I wonder whether the happy and fortunate—made happy and fortunate by the wealth of India, ever think of these things?—whether the idea ever comes across them in the luxurious carriage, or at the table crowded with the luxuries of all climates?—whether they

Amherst received a visit from the wife of Hindoo Row and her ladies. They proceeded to invest Lady Amherst with the presents sent for her by the Byza Bhye. They put on her a turban richly adorned with the most costly diamonds, a superb diamond necklace, ear-rings, anklets, bracelets, and amulets of the same, valued at 30,000*l.* sterling. A complete set of gold ornaments, and another of silver, was then presented. Miss Amherst was next presented with a pearl necklace, valued at 5,000*l.*, and other ornaments of equal beauty and costliness. Other ladies had splendid presents—the whole value of the gifts amounting to 50,000*l.* sterling!

In the evening came Lord Amherst's turn. On visiting the Row, his hat was carried out and brought back on a tray covered. The Row uncovered it, and placed it on his lordship's head, overlaid with the most splendid diamonds. His lordship was then invested with other jewels to the reputed amount of 20,000*l.* sterling. Presents followed to the members of his suite. Lady Amherst took this opportunity of retiring to the tents of the Hindu ladies, *where presents were again given;* and a bag of 1000 rupees to her ladyship's female servants, and 500 rupees to her interpretess.

Oriental Herald, vol. xiv. p. 444.

glance in a sudden imagination from the silken splendour of their own abodes, to the hot highways and
the pestilential jungles of India, and see those naked,
squalid, famishing, and neglected creatures, thronging
from vast distances to the rich man's dole, or feeding
on the more loathsome dole of the roads? It is impossible that a more strange antithesis can be pointed
out in human affairs. We turn from it with even a
convulsive joy, to grasp at the prospects of education
in that singular country. Let the people be educated,
and they will soon cease to permit oppression. Let
the English engage themselves in educating them, and
they will soon feel all the sympathies of nature awaken
in their hearts towards these unhappy natives. In the
meantime these are all the features of a country suffering under the evils of a long and grievous thraldom.
They are the growth of ages, and are not to be removed but by a zealous and unwearying course of
atoning justice. Spite of all flattering representations
to the contrary, the British public should keep its eye
fixed steadily on India, assuring itself that a debt of
vast retribution is there due from us; and that we
have only to meet the desire now anxiously manifested
by the natives for education, to enable us to expiate
towards the children all the wrongs and degradations
heaped for centuries on the fathers; and to fix our
name, our laws, our language and religion, as widely
and beneficently there as in the New World!

CHAPTER XX.

THE FRENCH IN THEIR COLONIES.

WE may dismiss the French in a few pages, merely because they are only so much like their neighbours. It would have been a glorious circumstance to have been able to present them as an exception; but while they have shown as little regard to the rights or feelings of the people whose lands they have invaded for the purpose of colonization, they seem to have been on the whole more commonplace in their cruelties. In Guiana they drove back the Indians as the Dutch and the Portuguese did in their adjoining settlements. In the West Indies, they exterminated or enslaved the natives very much as other Europeans did. They were as assiduous as any people in massacring the Charaibs, and they suffered perhaps more than any other nation from the Charaibs in return. Their historian, Du Tertre, describes them as returning from a slaughtering expedition in St. Christopher's "*bien joyeux;*" so that it would appear as though they executed the customary murders of the time, with their accustomed gaiety. In the Mauritius they found nobody to kill. In Madagascar, they alternately massacred and were massacred themselves, and finally driven out of of the country by the exasperated natives for their cruelties. If they made themselves masters of countries of equal importance with the Spaniards, Portuguese, English, or even the Dutch, they had not the art to make them so, for if we include Louisiana, Canada, Newfoundland, Nova Scotia, Cape Breton, Madagascar, Mauritius, Guiana, various West Indian islands and settlements on the Indian and African coasts, the amount of territory is vast. The value of it to them, however, at no time, was ever proportionate in the least degree to the extent; and no European nation has been so unfortunate in the loss of colonies. Their attempt to possess themselves of Florida was abortive, but it was attended by a circumstance which deserves recording.

The Spaniards hearing that some Frenchmen had made a settlement in Florida about 1566, a fleet sailed thither, and discovered them at Fort Carolina. They attacked them, massacred the majority, and hanged the rest upon a tree, with this inscription,—" *Not as Frenchmen, but as heretics.*" They were Huguenots. Dominic de Gourgues, a Gascon of the same faith, a skilful and intrepid seaman, an enemy to the Spaniards, from whom he had received personal injuries, passionately fond of his country, of hazardous expeditions, and of glory, sold his estate, built some ships, and with a select band of his own stamp, embarked for Florida. He found, attacked, and defeated the Spaniards. All that he could catch he hung upon trees, with this inscription,—" *Not as Spaniards, but as assassins ;*"—a sentence which, had it been executed with equal justice on all who deserved it in that day, would have half depopulated Europe; for almost every man who went abroad was an assassin; and the rest who stayed at home applauded, and therefore abetted. Having thus satisfied his indignant sense of justice, de Gourgues returned home, and the French abandoned the country.

The French seemed to take the firmest hold on Canada; but their powerful neighbours, the English, took even that from them, as they had done their Acadia (Nova Scotia), Hudson's Bay, Newfoundland, Cape Breton, and the Island of St. John.

In all these settlements, they treated the Indians just as creatures that might be spared or destroyed,— driven out or not, as it best suited themselves. Francis I. invaded the papal charter to Spain and Portugal of all the New World, with an expression very characteristic of him. *"What! shall the kings of Spain and Portugal quietly divide all America between them, without suffering me to take a share as their brother? I would fain see the article of Adam's will that bequeaths that vast inheritance to them!"* But he did not seem to suspect for a moment, that if Adam's will could be found, the most conspicuous clause in it would have been that the earth should be fairly divided amongst his children; and that one family should not covet the heritage of another, much less that Cain should be always murdering Abel. Accordingly, Samuel de Champlain, whose name has been given to Lake Champlain, had scarcely laid the foundations of Quebec, the future capital of Canada, than the subjects of Francis began to violate every clause which could possibly have been in Adam's will. Champlain found the Indians divided amongst themselves, and he adopted the policy since employed by the English in the East with so much greater success, not exactly that recommended by the apostle, to live in peace with all men, as far as in you lies, but to set your neighbours by the ears, so that you may take the advantage of their quarrels and disasters.

One of the greatest curses which befel the North American Indians on the invasion of the Europeans, was, that several of these *refined* and *Christian* nations came and took possession of neighbouring regions. Being indeed so refined and Christian, one might naturally have supposed that this would prove a happy circumstance for the savages. One would have supposed that thus surrounded on all sides, as it were, by the light of civilization and the virtue of Christianity, nothing could possibly prevent the savages from becoming civilized and Christian too. One would have supposed that such miserable, cruel, and dishonest savages, seeing whichever way they turned, nothing but images of peace, wisdom, integrity, self-denial, generosity, and domestic happiness, would have become speedily and heartily ashamed of themselves. That they would have been fairly overwhelmed with the flood of radiance covering those nations which had been for so many ages in the possession of Christianity. That they would have been penetrated through and through with the benevolence and goodness, the sublime graces, and winning sweetness of so favoured and regenerated a race! Nothing of the sort, however, took place. The savages looked about them, and saw people more powerful, indeed, but in spirit and practice ten times more savage than themselves. What a precious crew of hypocrites must they have

regarded these white invaders when they heard them
begin to talk of their superior virtue, and to call them
barbarians! There were the French in Canada,
Nova Scotia, and other settlements; there were the
Dutch in their Nova Belgia, and the English in Massachusets, all regarding each other with the most
deadly hatred, and all rampant to wrest, either from
the Indians, or from one another, the very ground
that each other stood upon.

The people brought with them from Europe,
crimes and abominations that the Indians never knew.
The Indians never fought for conquest, but to defend
their hunting grounds—lands which their ancestors
had inhabited for generations, and which they firmly
believed were given to them by the Great Spirit; but
these white invaders had a boundless and quenchless
thirst for every region that they could set their eyes
upon. They claimed it by pretences, of which the
simple Indians could neither make head nor tail—
they talked of popes and kings on the other side of
the water as having given them the Indians' countries,
and the Indians could not conceive what business
these kings and popes had with them. But the
whites had arguments which they *could not* withstand
—*gunpowder and rum!* They forced a footing in the
Indian countries, and then they gave them rum to
take away their brains, that they might take away
first their peltries, and then more land. There is
nothing in history more horrible than the conduct to
which the Dutch, French and English resorted in their
rivalries in the north-east of America. Each party
subdued the tribes of Indians in their own immediate neighbourhood, by force and fraud, and then em-

ployed them against the Indians who were in alliance with their rivals. Instead of mutually, as Christians should, inculcating upon them the beauty and the duty, and the advantages of peace, they instigated them, by every possible means, and by the most devilish arguments, to betray and exterminate one another, and not only one another, but to betray and exterminate, if possible, their white rivals. They made them furious with rum, and put fire-arms into their hands, and hounded them on one another with a demoniac glee. They took credit to themselves for inducing the Indians to *scalp* one another! They gave them a premium upon these horrible outrages, and we shall see that even the Puritans of New England gave at length so much as 1000*l.* for every Indian scalp that could be brought to them! They excited these poor Indians by the most diabolical means, and by taking advantage of their weak side, the proneness to vengeance, to acts of the most atrocious nature, and then they branded them, when it was convenient, as most fearful and bloody savages, and on that plea drove them out of their rightful possessions, or butchered them upon them.

I am not talking of imaginary horrors—I am speaking with all the soberness which the contemplation of such things will permit—of a deliberate system of policy pursued by the French, Dutch, and English, in these regions for a full century, and which eventually terminated in the destruction of the greater part of these Indian nations, and in the expulsion of the remainder. We shall see that even the English urged their allies—the Five Nations—continually to attack and murder the French and their Indian allies;

and in all their wars with the French in Canada, hired, or bribed, or compelled these savages to accompany them, and commit the very devastations for which they afterwards upbraided them, and which they made a plea for their extirpation. But of that anon; my present business is with the French; and though the facts which I have now to relate regard their conduct rather in our colonies than their own, yet they cannot be properly introduced anywhere else; and they could not have been introduced impartially here without these few preliminary observations.

The French were soon stripped of their other settlements in this quarter by the English. It was from Canada that they continued to annoy their rivals of New York and New England, till finally driven thence by the victory of Wolfe at Quebec; and it was principally on the northern side of the St. Lawrence that their territory lay. On that side, the great tribe of the Adirondacks, or, as they termed them, the Algonquins, lay, and became their allies; with tribes of inferior note. On the south side lay the great nation of the Iroquois, so termed by them; or "The Five Nations of United Indians," as they were called by the English. These were very warlike nations—the Mohawks, Oneidas, Onondagas, Cayugas, and Senekas—whose territories extended along the south-eastern side of the St. Lawrence, into the present States of Pennsylvania, New York, Connecticut, Massachusets, Maine, and New Hampshire—a country eighty leagues in length, and more than forty broad.

To drive out these nations, so as to deprive them of any share in the profitable fur trade which the Algonquins carried on for them, and to get possession of so fine a country, Champlain readily accompanied the Algonquins in an expedition of extermination against them. The Algonquins knew all the intricacies of the woods, and all the modes and stratagems of Indian warfare; and, aided by the arms and ammunition of the French, they would soon have accomplished Champlain's desire of exterminating the Iroquois, had not the Dutch, then the possessors of New York, furnished the Iroquois also with arms and ammunition, for it was not to their interest that these five nations, who brought their furs to them, should be reduced.

In 1664 the English dispossessed the Dutch of their Nova Belgia, and turned it into New York ; and began to trade actively with the Indian nations for their furs. The French, who had hoped to monopolise this trade, which they had found very profitable, by exterminating the Iroquois, and throwing the whole hunting business into the hands of tribes in their alliance, now saw the impolicy of having vainly attacked so powerful a race as that of the Iroquois, or Five Nations. They now used every means to reconcile them, and win them over. They sent Jesuit missionaries, who lived in the simplest manner amongst them, and with their powers of insinuation and persuasion laboured to give them favourable ideas of their nation. But the English were as zealous in their endeavours, and, as might naturally be expected, succeeded in engrossing all the fur trade with the Iroquois, who had received so many injuries from the French.*   Irritated by this circum-

* How clearly these shrewd Indians saw through the designs of their enemies, and how happily they could ridicule them, is shewn by

stance, the French again determined on the ferocious scheme of exterminating the Iroquois. Nursing this horrible resolve, they waited their opportunity, and put upon themselves a desperate restraint, till they should have collected a force in the colony equal to the entire annihilation of the Iroquois people. This time seemed to have arrived in 1687, when, under Denonville, they had a population of 11,249 persons, one third of whom were capable of bearing arms. Having a disposable force of near 4,000 people, they were secure in their own mind of the accomplishment of their object; but, to make assurance doubly sure,

the speech of Garangula, one of their chiefs, when M. de la Barre, the governor in 1684, was proposing one of these hollow alliances. All the time that de la Barre spoke, Garangula kept his eyes fixed on the end of his pipe. As soon as the governor had done, he rose up, and said most significantly, " Yonondio!" (the name they always gave to the governor of Canada), "you must have believed, when you left Quebec, that the sun had burnt up all the forests which render our country inaccessible to the French ; or that the lakes had so far overflowed their banks that they had surrounded our castles, and that we could not get out of them. Yes, Yonondio, surely you must have dreamt so, and the curiosity of seeing so great a wonder has brought you so far. Now you are undeceived, since I and the warriors here present, are come to assure you that the Senekas, Cayugas, Onon-dagas, Oneidas, and Mohawks, are yet alive! I thank you, in their name, for bringing back into their country the *Calumut* which your predecessor received from their hands. It was happy for you that you left under ground that murdering hatchet that has been so often dyed in the blood of the French. Hear, Yonondio! I do not sleep; I have my eyes open ; and the sun which enlightens me, shews me a great captain at the head of a company of soldiers, who speaks as if he were dreaming. *He* says that he came to the lake to smoke on the great *Calumut* with the Onondagas; but *Garangula* says that he sees to the contrary—it was to knock them on the head, if sickness had not weakened the arms of the French."

Colden's Hist. of the Five Nations, vol. i. p. 70.

they hit upon one of those schemes that have been so
much applauded through all Christian Europe, under
the name of "happy devices,"—"profound strokes of
policy,"—"chefs d'œuvres of statesmanship,"—that
is, in plain terms, plans of the most wretched deceit,
generally for the compassing of some piece of diabolical butchery or oppression. The "happy device,"
in this instance, was to profess a desire for peace and
alliance, in order to get the most able Indian chiefs into
their power before they struck the decisive blow. There
was a Jesuit missionary residing amongst the Iroquois
—the worthy Lamberville. This good man, like
his brethen in the South, whose glorious labours and
melancholy fate we have already traced, had won the
confidence of the Iroquois by his unaffected piety,
his constant kindness, and his skill in healing their
differences and their bodily ailments. They looked
upon him as a father and a friend. The French, on
their part, regarded this as a fortunate circumstance,—
not as one might have imagined, because it gave them
a powerful means of reconciliation and alliance with
this people, but because it gave them a means of
effecting their murderous scheme. They assured Lamberville that they were anxious to effect a *lasting peace*
with the Iroquois, for which purpose they begged him
to prevail on them to send their principal chiefs to meet
them in conference. He found no difficulty in doing
this, such was their faith in him. The chiefs appeared,
and were immediately clapped in irons, embarked at
Quebec, and sent to the galleys!

I suppose there are yet men calling themselves
Christians, and priding themselves on the depth of
their policy, that will exclaim—"Oh, capital!—what

a happy device !"   But who that has a head or a heart
worthy of a man will not mark with admiration the
conduct of the Iroquois on this occasion.   As soon as
the news of this abominable treachery reached the
nation, it rose as one man, to revenge the insult and
to prevent the success of that scheme which now became too apparent.   In the first place they sent for
Lamberville, who had been the instrument of their
betrayal, and—put him to death!   No, they did *not*
put him to death.   That was what the *Christians*
would have done, without any inquiry or any listening to his defence.   The *savage* Iroquois thus addressed him—" We are authorised by every motive
to treat you as an enemy; but we cannot resolve to
do it.   Your heart has had no share in the insult that
has been put upon us; and it would be unjust to
punish you for a crime you detest still more than ourselves.   But you must leave us.   Our rash young
men might consider you in the light of a traitor, who
delivered up the chiefs of our nation to shameful
slavery."   These savages, whom Europeans have
always termed Barbarians, gave the Missionary
guides, who conducted him to a place of safety, and
then flew to arms.*

The wretched Denonville and his politic people
soon found themselves in a situation which they richly
merited.   They had a numerous and warlike nation
thus driven to the highest pitch of irritation, surrounding them in the woods.   On the borders of the lakes,
or in the open country, the French could and did
carry devastation amongst the Iroquois; but on the
other hand the Indians, continually sallying from the
forests, laid waste the French settlements, destroyed

* Raynal.

the crops of the planters, and drove them from their fields. The French became heartily sick of the war they had thus wickedly raised, and were on the point of putting an end to it when one of their own Indian allies, a Huron, called by the English authors Adario, but by the French Le Rat, one of the bravest and most intelligent chiefs that ever ranged the wilds of America, prevented it by a stratagem as cunning, and more successful, than their own. He delivered an Iroquois prisoner with some story of an aggravated nature to the French commandant of the fort of Machillimakinac, who, not aware of Denonville being in treaty with the Iroquois, put him to death, and thus roused again all the ancient flame.

In this war, such were the barbarities of the French and their Indian allies, that they roused a spirit of revenge that soon brought the most cruel evils upon themselves. They laid waste the villages of the Five Nations with fire. Near Cadarakui Fort, they surprised and put to death the inhabitants of two villages who had settled there at their own invitation, and on their faith, but whom they now feared might act as spies against them. Many of these people were given up to a body of the Canadian Indians, called *Praying* or *Christian* Indians, to be tormented at the stake. In another village finding only two old men, they were cut to pieces, and put into the war kettle for the *Praying Indians* to feast on.* To revenge these unheard of abominations, the Five Nations carried a war of retaliation into Canada. They came suddenly in July of the next year, 1688, upon Montreal, 1200 strong, while Denonville and his lady were

* Colden, i. 81.

there; burnt and laid waste all the plantations round it, and made a terrible massacre of men, women, and children. Above a thousand French are said to have been killed on this occasion, and twenty-six taken, most of whom were burnt alive. In the autumn they returned, and carried fire and tomahawk through the island; and had they known how to take fortified places would have driven the French entirely out of Canada. As it was, they reduced them to the most frightful state of distress.

To such a pitch of fury did the French rise against the Five Nations through the sufferings which they received at their hands, that they now seemed to have lost the very natures of men. It is to the eternal disgrace of both French and English that they instigated and bribed the Indians to massacre and scalp their enemies—but it seems to be the peculiar infamy of the French to have imitated the Indians in their most barbarous customs, and have even prided themselves on displaying a higher refinement in cruelty than the savages themselves. The New Englanders, indeed, are distinctly stated by Douglass, to have handed over their Indian prisoners to be tormented by their Naraganset allies, but with the French this savage practice seems to have been frequent. I have just noticed a few instances of such inhuman conduct; but the old governor, Frontenac, stands pre-eminent above all his nation for such deeds. From 1691 to 1695, nothing was more common than for his Indian prisoners to be given up to his Indian allies to be tormented. One of the most horrible of these scenes on record was perpetrated under his own eye at Montreal in 1691. The intendant's lady, the Jesuits, and many influential people used all possible intreaties to save the prisoner from such a death, but in vain. He was given up to the *Christian* Indians of *Loretto*, and tormented in such a manner as none but a fiend could tolerate.* There was only one step beyond this, and that was for the French to enact the torturers themselves. That step was reached in 1695, at Machili-makinak Fort; and whoever has not strong nerves had better pass the following relation, which yet seems requisite to be given if we are to understand the full extent of the inflictions the American Indians have received from Europeans.

The successes of the Iroquois had driven the French to madness—and the prisoner was an Iroquois. " The prisoner being made fast to a stake, so as to have room to move round it, a *Frenchman* began the horrid tragedy by broiling the flesh of the prisoner's legs, from his toes to his knees, with the red-hot barrel of a gun. His example was followed by an *Utawawa*, and they relieved one another as they grew tired. The prisoner all this while continued his death-song, till they clapped a red-hot frying-pan on his buttocks, when he cried out ' Fire is strong, and too powerful.' Then all their Indians mocked him as wanting courage and resolution. ' You,' they said, ' a soldier and a captain, as you say, and afraid of fire: —you are not a man.' "

They continued their torments for two hours without ceasing. An *Utawawa*, being desirous to outdo the *French* in their refined cruelty, split a furrow from the prisoner's shoulder to his garter, and, filling it with gunpowder, set fire to it. This gave him exquisite

* Colden, i. 441.

pain, and raised excessive laughter in his tormentors. When they found his throat so much parched that he was no longer able to gratify their ears with his howling, they gave him water to enable him to continue their pleasure longer. But, at last, his strength failing, an *Utawawa* flayed off his scalp, and threw burning coals on his skull. Then they untied him, and bid him run for his life. He began to run, tumbling like a drunken man. They shut up the way to the east; and made him run westward, the way, as they think, to the country of miserable souls. He had still force left to throw stones, till they put an end to his misery by knocking him on the head with one. After this, every one cut a slice from his body, to conclude the tragedy with a feast.*

Such is the condition to which the practice of injustice and cruelty can reduce men calling themselves civilized. We need not pursue further the history of the French in Canada, which consists only in bickerings with the English and butchery of the Indians. Having, therefore, given this specimen of their treatment of the natives in their colonies, or in the vicinity of them, we will dismiss them with an incident illustrative of their policy, which occurred in Louisiana.

When the French settled themselves in that country, they found, amongst the neighbouring tribes, the Natchez the most conspicuous. Their country extended from the Mississippi to the Appalachian mountains. It had a delightful climate, and was a beautiful region, well watered, most agreeably enlivened with hills, fine woods, and rich open prairies. Numbers of the French flocked over into this delicious country, and it

* Colden's Hist. of " The Five Nations," i. 195.

was believed that it would form the centre of the great colony they hoped to found in that part of America. If the Natchez were such a people as Chateaubriand has pictured them, they must have been a noble race indeed. They were, like the Peruvians, worshippers of the sun, and had vast temples erected to their god. They received the French as the natives of most discovered countries have received the Europeans, with the utmost kindness. They even assisted them in forming their new plantations amongst them, and the most cordial and advantageous friendship appeared to have grown between the two nations. Such friendship, however, could not possibly exist between the common run of Europeans and Indians. The Europeans did not go so far from home for friendship; they went for dominion. Accordingly, the French soon threw off the mask of friendship, and treated their hosts as slaves. They · seized on whatever they pleased, dictated their will to the Natchez, as their masters, and drove them from their cultivated fields, and inhabited them themselves. The deceived and indignant people did all in their power to stop these aggressions. They reasoned, implored, and entreated, but in vain. Finding this utterly useless, they entered into a scheme to rid themselves of their oppressors, and engaged all the neighbouring nations to aid in the design. A secret and universal league was established amongst the Indian nations wherever the French had any settlements. They were all to be massacred on a certain day. To apprise all the different nations of the exact day, the Natchez sent to every one of them a little bundle of bits of wood, each containing the same number, and that number being the number

of the days that were to precede the day of general
doom. The Indians were instructed to burn in each
town one of these pieces of wood every day, and on
the day that they burnt the last they were simul-
taneously to fall on the French, and leave not one
alive. As usual, the success of the conspiracy was
defeated by the compassion of an individual. The
wife, or mother, of the great chief of the Natchez had
a son by a Frenchman, and from this son she learned
the secret of the plot. She warned the French commandant of the circumstance, but he treated her
warning with indifference. Finding, therefore, that
she could not succeed in putting the French on their
guard against a people they had now come to despise,
she resolved that, if she could not avert the fate of the
whole, she would at least afford a chance of safety to
a part. The bits of wood were deposited in the
temple of the sun, and her rank gave her access to the
temple. She abstracted a number of the bits of wood,
and thus precipitated the day of rising in that province.
The Natchez, on the burning of the last piece, fell on
the French, and, out of two hundred and twenty-two
French, massacred two hundred,—men, women, and
children. The remainder were women, whom they
retained as prisoners.

The Natchez, having accomplished this destruction,
were astonished to find that not one of their allies had
stirred; and the allies were equally astonished at the
rising of the Natchez, whilst they had yet several
pieces of wood remaining. The French, however, in
the other parts of the country, were saved; fresh reinforcements arrived from Europe, and the unfortunate
Natchez felt all the fury of their vengeance. Part

were put to the sword; great numbers were caught and sent to St. Domingo, as slaves; the rest fled for safety into the country of the Chickasaws. The Chickasaws were called upon to give them up; but they had more sense of honour and humanity than Europeans,—they indignantly refused; and, when the French marched into their territories, to compel them by force, bravely attacked and repelled them, with repeated loss. As in Canada, Madagascar, India, and other places, the French reaped no permanent advantage from their treachery and cruelties, as the other European nations did. Louisiana was eventually ceded, in 1762, to the Spaniards, just as the French families, from Nova Scotia, Canada, St. Vincent, Granada, and other colonies won by the English, were flocking into it as a place of refuge. They had all the odium and the crime of aboriginal oppression, and left the earth so basely obtained, to the enjoyment of others no better than themselves.

CHAPTER XXI.

THE ENGLISH IN AMERICA.

The man who finds an unknown country out,
By giving it a name, acquires, no doubt,
A gospel title, though the people there
The pious Christian thinks not worth his care.
Bar this pretence, and into air is hurled,
The claim of Europe to the *Western World*.

Churchill.

WE shall now have to deal entirely with our own nation, or with those principally derived from it. We shall now have to observe the conduct entirely of Protestants towards the aborigines of their settlements: and the Catholic may ask with triumphant scorn, " Where is the mighty difference between the ancient professors of our faith, and the professors of that faith which you proudly style the reformed ! You accuse the papal church of having corrupted and debased national morality in this respect,—in what does the morality of the Protestants differ ?" I am sorry to say in nothing. The Protestants have only too well imitated the conduct and clung to the doctrine of the Catholics as it regards the rights of humanity. It is to the disgrace of the papal church that it did not inculcate a more Christian morality; it is to the far deeper disgrace of Protestants, that, pretending to abandon the corruptions and cruelties of the papists, they did not abandon their wretched pretences for seizing upon the possessions of the weak and the unsuspecting. So far, however, from the behaviour of the Protestants forming a palliation for that of the Catholics, it becomes an aggravation of it; for it is but the ripened fruit of that tree of false and mischievous doctrine which they had planted. They had set the example, and boldly preached the right, and pleaded the divine sanction for invasion, oppression, and extermination—such example and exhortation are only too readily adopted—and the Protestant conduct was but the continuation of papal heresy. The

New Presbyter was but old Priest writ large.

While we see, then, to the present hour the perpetuated consequences of the long inculcation of papal delusions, we must, however, confess that for the Protestants there was, and is, less excuse than for the Catholic laity. They had given up the Bible into the hands of their priests, and as a matter of propriety received the faith which they held from their dictation: the Protestants professed that "the Bible and the Bible alone, was the religion of the Protestants." The Catholics having once persuaded themselves that the Pope was the infallible vicegerent of God on earth, might, in their blind zeal, honestly take all that he proclaimed to them as gospel truth; but the Protestants disavowed and renounced his authority and infallibility. They declared him to be the very anti-

Christ, and his church the great sorceress that made drunk the nations with the cup of her enchantments. What business then had they with the papal doctrine, that the heathen were given to the believers as a possession? The Pope declared that, as the representative of the Deity on earth, he claimed the world, and disposed of it as he pleased. But the Protestants protested against any such assumption, and appealed to the Bible; and where did they find any such doctrine in the Bible? Yet Elizabeth of England, granted charters to her subjects to take possession of all countries not yet seized on by Christian nations, with as much implicit authority as the Pope himself. It is curious to hear her proclaiming her intimate acquaintance with the Scripture, and yet so blindly and unceremoniously setting at defiance all its most sacred precepts. "I am supposed," said she, in her speech on proroguing parliament in 1585, "to have many studies, but most philosophical. I must yield this to be true, that I suppose few that are not professors, have read more; and I need not tell you that I am not so simple that I understand not, nor so forgetful that I remember not; and yet, amidst my many volumes, I hope God's book hath not been my seldomest lectures, in which we find that which by reason all ought to believe."

It had been well if she had made good her boasting by proving practically that she had understood, and had not forgotten the real doctrines of the Christian code. But Elizabeth, as well as her father, was, in every respect, except that of admitting the Pope's supremacy, as thorough a Catholic as the best of them; and we see her granting to Sir Humphrey

Gilbert, of Compton in Devonshire, in 1578, a charter as ample in its endowments as that which the king of Spain himself gave to Columbus, on the authority of the Pope's bull, and securing to herself exactly the same ratio of benefit: the Spanish commission was, in fact, her model. She conferred on Sir Humphrey all lands and countries that he might discover, that were not already taken possession of by some Christian prince. He was to hold them of England, with full power of willing them to his heirs for ever, or disposing of them in sale, on the simple condition of reserving one-fifth of all the gold and silver found to the crown. She afterwards gave a similar charter to Sir Walter Raleigh: and her successor, James I., still further imitated the Pope by dividing the continent of North America, under the name of North and South Virginia, between two trading companies, as the Pope had divided the world between Spain and Portugal.

It is really lamentable to see how utterly empty was the pretence of reformation in the government of England at that time. How utterly ignorant or regardless Protestant England was of the most sacred and unmistakeable truths of the New Testament, while it professed to model itself upon them. The worst principles of the papal church were clung to, because they favoured the selfishness of despotism. The rights of nations were as infamously and recklessly violated; and from that time to this, Protestant England and Protestant America continue to spurn every great principle of Christian justice in their treatment of native tribes: they have substituted power for conscience, gunpowder and brandy for truth and mercy, and expulsion from their lands and houses for charity, " that suffereth long and is kind."

The shameless impudence and hypocrisy by which nations calling themselves Christians have ever persisted, and still persist, in this sweeping and wholesale public robbery and violence, was happily ridiculed by Churchill.

> Cast by a tempest on a savage coast,
> Some roving buccaneer set up a post;
> A beam, in proper form, transversely laid,
> Of his Redeemer's cross the figure made,—
> Of that Redeemer, with whose laws his life,
> From first to last, had been one scene of strife;
> His royal master's name thereon engraved,
> *Without more process the whole race enslaved;*
> *Cut off that charter they from Nature drew,*
> *And made them slaves to men they never knew!*
> Search ancient histories, consult records,
> Under this title the *most Christian Lords,*
> Hold,—thanks to conscience—more than half the ball;—
> O'erthrow this title, they have none at all.

But the national cupidity that was proof to the caustic ridicule of Churchill, has been proof to the still more powerful assault of public execration, under the growth of Christian knowledge. The Bible is now in almost every man's hand; its burning and shining light blazes full on the grand precept, " Do as thou would'st be done by;" and are the tribes of India, or Africa, or America, or Oceanica, the better for it? Are they not still our slaves and our Gibeonites, and driven before our arms like the wild beasts of the desert? We need not therefore stay to express our abhorrence of Spanish cruelty, or describe at great length the deeds of own countrymen in any quarter of the globe,—it is enough to say that English and American treatment of the aborigines of their colonies is but Spanish cruelty repeated. With one or two beautiful exceptions, which we shall have the greatest pleasure in pointing out, no more regard has been paid to the rights or the feelings of the North American Indians by the English and their descendants, than was paid to the South Americans by the Spanish and Portuguese.

Every reader of history is aware of the melancholy and disastrous commencement of most of our American colonies. The great cause was that they were founded in injustice. Adventurers, with charters from the English monarch in their pockets, as the Spaniards and Portuguese had the Pope's bull in theirs, landed on the coast of America and claimed it for their own, reckoning the native inhabitants of no more account than the bears and fallow-deer of the woods. They had got a grant of the country from their own king; but whence had he got *his* grant? That is not quite so clear. The Pope's claim is intelligible enough: he was, in his own opinion, God's viceroy and steward, and disposed of his world in that character; but the Bible was the English monarch's law, and where did the Bible appoint Elizabeth or James God's steward? Where did it appoint either of them " a judge and a ruler over " the Indians? Truly Elizabeth, with all her vaunting, had read her Bible to little purpose, as we fear most monarchs and their ministers to the present hour have done. We must say of the greater part of North America, as Erskine said of India—" it is a country which God never gave us, and acquired by means that he will never justify."

The misery attending the first planting of our colonies in America was equal to the badness of our principles. The very first thing which the colonists in the majority of cases seem to have done, was to insult and maltreat the natives, thus making them their mortal enemies, and thus cutting off all chance of the succours they needed from the land, and the security essential to their very existence. For about a century, nothing but wretchedness, failure, famine, massacres by the Indians, were the news from the American colonies. The more northern ones, as Nova Scotia, Canada, and New York, we took from the French and the Dutch; the more southern, as Florida and Louisiana, were obtained at a later day from the Spaniards. We shall here therefore confine our brief notice chiefly to the manner of settling the central eastern states, particularly Virginia, New England, and Pennsylvania.

For eighty-two years from the granting of the charter by Elizabeth to Sir Humphrey Gilbert, to the abandonment of the country by Sir Walter Raleigh for his El Dorado visions, the colony of Virginia suffered nothing but miseries, and was become, at that period, a total failure. The first settlers were, like the Spaniards, all on fire in quest of gold. They got into squabbles with the Indians, and the remnant of them was only saved by Sir Francis Drake happening to touch there on his way home from a cruise in the West Indies. A second set of adventurers were massacred by the Indians, not without sufficient provocation; and a third perished by the same means, or by famine induced by their unprincipled and impolitic treatment of the natives. The first successful settlement which was formed was that of James-Town, on James River, in Chesapeak Bay, in 1607. But even here scarcely had they located themselves, when their abuse of the Indians involved them in a savage warfare with them. They took possession of their hunting-grounds without ceremony; and they cheated them in every possible way in their transactions with them, especially in the purchases of their furs. That they might on the easiest terms have lived amicably with the Indians, the history of the celebrated Captain John Smith of that time sufficiently testifies. He had been put out of his rank, and treated with every con-tumely by his fellow colonists, till they found them-selves on the verge of destruction from the enraged natives. They then meanly implored him to save them, and he soon effected their safety by that obvious policy which, if men were not blinded by their own wickedness, would universally best answer their pur-pose. He began to conciliate the offended tribes; to offer them presents and promises of kindness; and the consequence was, they soon flocked into the settlement again in the most friendly manner, and with plenty of provisions. But even Smith was not sufficiently aware of the power of friendship; he chose rather to attack some of the Indians than to treat with them, and the consequence was that he fell into their hands, and was condemned to die the death of torture.

But here again, the better nature of the Indians saved him : and that incident occurred which is one of the most romantic in American history. He was saved from execution at the last moment, by the Indian beauty Pocahontas, the daughter of the great Sachem Powhatan. This young Indian woman, who is celebrated by the colonists and writers of the time, as of a remarkably fine person, afterwards married a Mr. Rolfe, an English gentleman of the colony. She

was brought over by him to see England, and presented at court, where she was received in a distinguished manner by James and his queen. This
marriage, which makes a great figure in the early
history of the colony, was a most auspicious event
for it. It warmly disposed the Indians towards the
English. They were anxious that the colonists should
make other alliances with them of the same nature,
and which might have been attended with the happiest
consequences to both nations; but though some of the
best families of Virginia now boast of their descent
from this connexion, the rest of the colonists of the
period held aloof from Indian marriages as beneath
them. They looked on the Indians rather as creatures
to be driven to the woods—for, unlike the negroes, they
could not be compelled to become slaves—than to be
raised and civilized; and therefore, spite of the better
principles which the short government of that excellent man Lord Delaware had introduced, they were
soon again involved in hostilities with them. The
Indians felt deeply the insult of the refusal of alliance
through marriage with them; they felt the daily irritation of attempts to overreach them in their bargains,
and they saw the measures they were taking to seize
on their whole country. They saw that there was
to be no common bond of interest or sympathy between them; that there was to be a usurping and a
suffering party only; and they resolved to cut off the
grasping and haughty invaders at a blow. A wide
conspiracy was set on foot; and had it not been in
this case, as in many others, that the compassionate
feelings of one of the Indians partially revealed the
plot at the very moment of its execution, not an

Englishman would have been left alive. As it was, a dreadful massacre ensued; and more than a fourth of the colonists perished. The English, in their turn, fell on the Indians, and a bloody war of extermination followed. When the colonists could no longer reach them in the depths of their woods, they offered them a deceitful peace. The Indians, accustomed in their own wars to enter sincerely into their treaties of peace when inclined to bury the tomahawk—were duped by the more artful Europeans. They came forth from their woods, planted their corn, and re-sumed their peaceful hunting. Just as the harvest was ripe, the English rushed suddenly upon them, trampled down their crops, set fire to their wigwams, and chased them again to the woods with such slaughter, that some of the tribes were totally ex-terminated!

Such was the mode of settling Virginia. What trust or cordiality could there afterwards be between such parties? Accordingly we find, from time to time, in the history of this colony, fresh plots of the natives to rid themselves of the whites, and fresh ex-peditions of the whites to clear the country of what they termed the wily and perfidious Indians. These dreadful transactions, which continued for the most part while the English government continued in that country, gave occasion to that memorable speech of Logan, the chief of the Shawanees, to Lord Dunmore the governor: a speech which will remain while the English language shall remain, to perpetuate the memory of English atrocity, and Indian pathos.—" I now ask of every white man, whether he hath ever entered the cottage of Logan when hungry, and been refused food? Whether coming naked, and perishing with cold, and Logan has not clothed him? During the last war, so long and so bloody, Logan has remained quietly upon his mat, wishing to be the advocate of peace. Yes, such is my attachment to white men, that even those of my nation, when they pass by me, pointed at me, saying—'*Logan is the friend of white men!*' I had even thought of living among you; but that was before the injury I received from one of you. Last summer, Colonel Cressup massacred in cold blood, and without any provocation, all the relations of Logan. He spared neither his wife nor his children. *There is not now one drop of my blood in the veins of any living creature!* This is what has excited my revenge. I have sought it. I have killed several of your people, and my hatred is appeased. For my country I rejoice at the beams of peace; but imagine not that my joy is instigated by my fear. Logan knows not what fear is. He will never turn his back in order to save his life. *But alas! no one remains to mourn for Logan when he shall be no more!*"

The conduct of the English towards the natives in THE CAROLINAS may be summed up in a single passage of the Abbé Raynal : " Two wars were carried on against the natives of the most extravagant description. All the wandering or fixed nations between the ocean and Appalachian mountains, were attacked and massacred without any interest or motive. Those who escaped being put to the sword, either submitted or were dispersed." The remnant of the tribe of the Tuscaroras fled into the state of New York.

MARYLAND, in its early history, also exhibits its quota of Indian bloodshed; but much of this is chargable to the account of the colonists of Virginia. Lord Baltimore, who first colonised this province in the reign of Charles I., was a Catholic, who sought an asylum for his persecuted brethren of the same faith. Since the change of religion in England, the Catholics had experienced the bitterness of that persecution of which they, while in power, had been so liberal. This seems to have had an excellent effect upon some of them. Lord Baltimore and the colonists who went out with him, being most of them of good Catholic families, determined to allow liberty of conscience, and admitted people of all sorts. This gave great offence to their royalist neighbours in Virginia, who, not permitting any liberty of religious sentiment, found those whom they drove away by their severities flocking into Maryland, and being there well received, strengthening it at their expense. They therefore circulated all kinds of calumnies amongst the Indians against the Maryland Catholics, especially telling them that they were Spaniards—a name of horror to Indian ears. Alarmed by this representation, they fell on the colonists whom they had at first received with their usual kindness, laid waste their fields, massacred without mercy all that they could meet; and were not undeceived till after a long course of patient endurance and friendly representation.

The settlement of NEW ENGLAND presents some new features. It was not merely a settlement of English Protestants, but of the Protestants of Protestants—the Puritans. A class of persons having thus made two removes from Popery; having not only protested against the errors of Rome, but against those of the very church which had seceded from Rome, and professed to purify itself from its corruptions; having, moreover, suffered severely for their religious faith, might be supposed to have acquired far clearer views of the rights of humanity from their better acquaintance with the Bible, and might be expected to respect the persons and the property of the natives in whose lands they went to settle, more than any that went before them. They went as men who had been driven out of their own country, and from amongst their own kindred, for the maintenance of the dearest privileges and the most sacred claims of men; and they might be supposed to address the natives as they reached their coast in terms like these: " Ancient possessors of a free country, give us a place of refuge amongst you. You are termed savages, but you cannot be more savage than the people of our own land, who have inflicted dreadful cruelties and mutilations on us and our friends for the faith we have in God. We fly from savages who pretend to be civilized, but have learned no one principle of civilization, to savages who pretend to no civilization, but yet have, on a thousand occasions, received white men to their shores with benevolence and tears of joy. What the savages of Europe are, a hundred regions drenched in the blood of their native children can tell; that we deem you less savage than them, the very act of our coming to you testifies. Give us space amongst you, and let us live as brethren."

For a time, indeed, they acted as men who might be supposed thus to speak. The going out and landing in this new country of this band of religious adventurers, have been and continue to be celebrated as the setting forth and landing of " The Pilgrim

Fathers." It is in itself an interesting event: the pilgrimage of a little host of voluntary exiles, for the sake of their religion, from their native country, to establish a new country in the wilderness of the New World. It is more interesting from the fact, that their associates and descendants have grown into one of the most intelligent and powerful portions of the freest, and, perhaps, happiest nation on the globe. Their landing on the coast of Massachusets was effected under circumstances of peculiar hardship. It took place at a spot to which they gave the name of New Plymouth, on the 11th of November, 1620. The weather was extremely severe; and they were but badly prepared to contend with it. During the winter one half of their number perished through famine, and diseases brought on by their hardships. The natives, too, came down to oppose their settlement,* and it is difficult now to imagine how such religious people could reconcile to their consciences an entrance by force on the territories of a race on whom they had no claim. They had, indeed, purchased a tract of land of one of the chartered companies in England; but one is at a loss to conceive how any English company could sell a country in

* The natives of this coast had some years before been carried off in considerable numbers by a British kidnapper, one Captain Hunt, who sold them in the Mediterranean to the Spaniards as Moors of Barbary. The indignation of the Indians on the discovery of this base transaction and their warlike character, put a stop to this trade, which might otherwise have become as regular a department of commerce as the African slave-trade ; but it naturally threw the most formidable obstacles in the way of settling colonies here, and brought all the miseries of mutual outrage and revenge on both settlers and natives.—*Douglass's Summary of the First Planting of North America,* vol. i. p. 364.

another hemisphere already inhabited, and to which they had not the slightest title to show, except " the Bucanier's Post." As well might a company of Indians sell some of their countrymen a slice of territory on the coast of Kent; and just as good a title would the Indians have to land, if they could, in spite of our Kentish yeomen, and establish themselves on the spot. Moreover, these Pilgrim Fathers had wandered from their original destination, and had not purchased this land at all of anybody at that time. No doubt the Fathers *thought* that they had a right to settle in a wild country; and simply fell in with the customs and doctrines of the times. We might, however, have expected clearer notions of natural right from their acquaintance with the Bible; for we shall presently see that there were men of their own country, and in their own circumstances, that would not have been easy to have taken such possession in such a manner. We may safely believe that the Fathers did according to their knowledge; but the precedent is dangerous, and could not in these times be admitted: the Fathers did not, in fact, obtain any grant from the English till four years afterwards (1624). When they had once got a firm footing, Massasoit, the father of the famous Philip of Pokanoket, whom these same settlers pursued to the death with all his tribe, except such as they sold for slaves to Bermudas, granted them a certain extent of lands. Subsequently purchases from the Indians began to be considered more necessary to a good title.

Eight years afterwards another company of the same people, under John Endicott, formed a settlement in Massachusets Bay, and founded the town of Salem. In the following year a third company, of not less than three hundred in number, joined them. These in the course of time seeking fresh settlements, founded at different periods, Boston, Charlestown, Dorchester, Roxborough, and other towns; great numbers now, allured by the flourishing state of the colony, flocked over, and amongst them Harry Vane, the celebrated Sir Harry Vane of the revolutionary parliament, and Hugh Peters, the chaplain of Oliver Cromwell. Some difference of opinion amongst them occasioned a considerable body of them to settle in Providence and Rhode Island. These were under the guidance of their venerable pastor Roger Williams, a man who deserves to be remembered while Christianity continues to shed its blessings on mankind. Mr. Williams had penetrated through the mists of his age, to the light of divine truth, and had risen superior to the selfishness of his countrymen. He maintained the freedom of conscience, the right of private judgment, the freedom of religious opinion from the touch of the magistrate. The spirit of true Christianity had imbued his own spirit with its love. Above all—for it was the most novel doctrine, and as we have seen by the practice of the whole Christian world, the hardest to adopt—he maintained the sacred right of the natives to their own soil; and refused to settle upon it without their consent. *He and his followers purchased of the Indians the whole territory which they took possession of!* This is a fact which we cannot record without a feeling of intense delight, for it is the first instance of such a triumph of Christian knowledge and principle, over the corrupt morality of Europe. We nowhere read till now, through all this bloody and revolting history of European aggressions, of any single man treating with

the savage natives as with men who had the same in-
alienable rights as themselves.* It is the first bright
dawn of Christian day from the darkness of ages; the
first boundary mark put down between the possessions
of the unlettered savage, and the lawless desires of the
schooled but uncivilized European; the first recogni-
tion of that law of property in the possessors of the
soil of every country of the earth, until the complete
establishment of which, blood must flow, the weak
must be trodden down by the strong, and civilization
and Christianity must pause in their course. Honour
to Roger Williams and his flock in Narraganset Bay!
The Puritan settlements still continued to spread.
Connecticut, and New Hampshire, and Maine were
planted by different bodies from Massachusets Bay;
and the Indians, who found that the whites diffused
themselves farther and farther over their territories,
and soon ceased to purchase as Roger Williams had
done, or even to ask permission; began to remon-
strate. Remonstrances however produced little effect.
The Indians saw that if they did not make a stand
against these encroachments they must soon be driven
out of their ancestral lands, and exterminated by those
tribes on which they must be forced. They resolved
therefore to exterminate the invaders that would hear
no reason. The Pequods, who lay near the colony of
Connecticut, called upon the Narragansets in 1637,
to join them in their scheme. The Narragansets revealed it to the English, and both parties were speedily

---

* Purchases were, indeed, made by others; but it was seize first, and
bargain afterwards, when the soil was already defended by muskets,
and the only question with the natives was, " Shall we take a trifle for
our lands, or be knocked on the head for them?"

in arms against each other. The different colonies of
New England had entered into an association for common defence. The people of Connecticut called on
those of Massachusets Bay for help, which was ac-
corded; but before its arrival the soldiers of Connecticut, who seemed on all occasions eager to shed Indian
blood, had attacked the Pequods where they had posted
themselves, in a sort of rude camp in a swamp, defended with stakes and boughs of trees. The Pequods
were supposed to be a thousand strong, besides having all their women and children with them; but their
simple fortification was soon forced, and set fire to;
and men, women, children perished in the flames, or
were cut down on rushing out, or seized and bound.
The Massachusets forces soon after joined them, and
then the Indians were hunted from place to place with
unrelenting fury. They determined to treat them,
not as brave men fighting for their invaded territories,
for their families and posterity, but as wild beasts.
They massacred some in cold blood, others they handed
over to the Narragansets to be tortured to death; and
great numbers were sold into Bermudas as slaves. In
less than three months, the great and ancient tribe of
the Pequods had ceased to exist. What did Roger.
Williams say to this butchery by a Christian people?
But the spirit of resentment against the Indians grew
to such a pitch in those states that nothing but the
language of Cotton Mather, (the historian of New
England,) can express it. He calls them devils incarnate, and declares that unless he had "a pen made of a
porcupine's quill and dipped in aquafortis he could not
describe all their cruelties." Could they be possibly
greater than those of the Puritan settlers, who were at

once the aggressors, and bore the name of Christian? So deadly, indeed, became the vengeance of these colonists, that they granted a public reward to any one who should kill an Indian. The Assembly, says Douglass, in 1703, voted 40*l.* premium for each Indian scalp or captive. In the former war the premium was 12*l.* In 1706, he says, "about this time premiums for Indian scalps and captives were advanced by act of Assembly; viz: per piece to impressed men 10*l.*, to volunteers in pay 20*l.*, to volunteers serving without pay 50*l.*, with the benefit of the captives and plunder. Col. Hilton, with 220 men, ranges the eastern frontiers, and kills many Indians. In 1722 the premium for scalps was 100*l.* In 1744 it had risen to 400*l.* old tenor; for the years 1745, 6, and 7, it stood at the enormous sum of 1000*l.* per head to volunteers, scalp or captive (!) and 400*l.* per head to impressed men, wages and subsistence money to be deducted.* In 1744 the Cape-Sables, and St. John's Indians being at war with the colonies, Massachusets-Bay declared them rebels; forbad the Pasamaquody, Penobscot, Noridgwoag, Pigwocket, and all other Indians west of St. John's to hold any communication with them, and offered for their scalps,—males 12 years old, and upwards, 100*l.* new tenor; for such, as captives, 105*l.* For *women and children* 50*l.*, scalps!—55*l.*, captives! The Assembly soon after, hearing that the Penobscot and Noridgwoag Indians had joined the French, extended premiums for scalps and captives to all places west of Nova Scotia, and advanced them to 250*l.* new tenor, to volunteers; and 100*l.* new tenor to troops in pay.†

In 1722, a Captain Harman, with 200 men, sur-

* Douglass' Summary, i. 556-65. † Ibid. i. 321.

prised the Indians at Noridgwoag, and brought off twenty-six scalps, *and that of Father Ralle*, a French Jesuit.* The savage atrocities here committed by the New Englanders were frightful. They massacred men, women, and children; pillaged the village, robbed and set fire to the church, and mangled the corpse of Father Ralle most brutally.† For these twenty-six scalps, at the then premium, the good people of Massachusets paid 2600*l.* A Captain Lovel, also, seems to have been an active scalper. " He collected," says Raynal, "a band of settlers as ferocious as himself, and set out to hunt savages. One day he discovered ten of them quietly sleeping round a large fire. He murdered them, carried their scalps to Boston, and secured the promised reward, of course 1000*l.* ! Who could suppose that the land of the Pilgrim Fathers, the land of the noble Roger Williams, could have become polluted with horrors like these !"

And why were the Indians now so sharply pursued —why such sums given as tempted these Harmans and Lovels? Why the scalp of Father Ralle to be stripped away from him?—Because Father Ralle had proclaimed a very certain, but very disagreeable truth. He preached to the Indians, " That their lands were given to them and their children unalienably and for ever, according to the Christian sacred oracles." What is so inconvenient as to preach Bible truth in countries flagrant with injustice? The Indians began to murmur; gave the English formal warning to leave the lands within a set time, and as they did not move, began to drive off their cattle. This was declared rebellion, the soldiery were set on them, and 100*l.* a head proclaimed for their scalps.

* Douglass' Summary, i. 199.   † Drake's Book of the Indians.

This is called Governor Dummer's war; but the most celebrated war was that of Philip of Pokanoket, which occurred between this war and that of the destruction of the Pequods. The cause of Philip's war, which broke out in 1675, and lasted upwards of a year, was exactly that of this subsequent one, and indeed of every war of New England with the Indians— the dissatisfaction of the Indians with the usurpation of the whites. The New England people, religious people though they were, seem to have been more irritable, more jealous, more regardless of the rights of the Indians, and more quick and deadly in their vengeance on any shew of spirit in the natives, than any other of the North American colonies. The monstrous, and were it not for the testimony of unimpeachable history, incredible sums offered for scalps by these states, testify to the malignant spirit of revenge which animated them. Even towards the Narragansets, their firmest and most constant friends, who lived amongst them, they shewed an irritability and a savage relentlessness that are to us amazing. On the faintest murmur of any dissatisfaction of this tribe on account of their lands, or of any other tribe making overtures of alliance to it, they were up in arms, and ready to exterminate it. So early as 1642, they charged Miantinomo, the great sachem of the Narragansets, with conspiring to raise the Indians against them. The people of Connecticut immediately proposed, without further proof or examination, to fall on the Indians and kill them. This bloody haste was, however, withstood by Massachusets.* They summoned Miantinomo before the court. He came, and

* Hutchinson—Gov. Winthrop's Journal.

it is impossible not to admire his sedate and dignified bearing there. He demanded that his accusers should be brought face to face, and that if they could prove him guilty of conspiracy against the colony, he was ready to suffer death; but if they could not, they should suffer the same punishment. "His behaviour," says Hutchinson, "was grave, and he gave his answers with great deliberation and seeming ingenuity. *He would never speak but in the presence* of two of *his counsellors*, that they might be witnesses of everything which passed. (No doubt he had seen enough of 'that pen and ink work,' of which the Indians so often complained). Two days were spent in treaty. He denied all that he was charged with, and pretended that the reports to his disadvantage were raised by Uncas, the sachem of the Mohegins, or some of his people. He was willing to renew his former engagements; that if any of the Indians, even the Niantics, who, he said, were as his own flesh and blood, should do any wrong to the English, so as neither he nor they could satisfy without blood, he would deliver them up, and leave them to mercy. *The people of Connecticut put little confidence in him, and could hardly be kept from falling upon him,* but were at last prevailed upon by the Massachusets to desist for the present."*

Poor Miantinomo did not long escape. Two years afterwards, in a war with his enemy, Uncas, he was taken prisoner, and the colonists were only too glad to have an opportunity of getting rid of a man of mind and influence, who felt their aggressions and feared for his race—they outdid the savage captor in their resentment against him. Instead of interceding

* Hutchinson's Massachusets Bay, p. 113.

on his behalf and recommending mercy, by which they might, at once, have set a Christian example, and have made a fast friend, they procured his death. Uncas, with a generosity worthy of the highest character, instead of killing his captive, as he was entitled by the rules of Indian war, delivered him into the hands of the New-Englanders, and the New-Englanders again returned him to Uncas, desiring him to kill him, but without the usual tortures. It is wonderful that they did not purchase his scalp, or that they excused the torture; but a number of the English inhabitants went out and gratified themselves with witnessing his death.*

It was not to be marvelled at that such general treatment, and such a crowning deed exasperated the Narragansets to a dangerous degree. They nourished a rooted revenge, which shewed itself on the breaking out of Philip of Pokanoket's war. They engaged to bring to his aid 4000 Indians.

Philip was one of the noblest specimens of the North American Indian. He was of a fine and active person; accomplished in all exercises of his nation, in war and hunting. He had that quick sense of injuries, and that sense of the honour and rights of his people which characterise the patriot; qualities which, though in the most cultivated and enlightened mind they may hurry their possessor on occasionally to sharp and vindictive acts, are the very essentials of that lofty and noble disposition without which no great deed is ever done. Had Philip contended for his country against its invaders on anything like equal terms, he would have been its saviour,—the naked Indians

* Hutchinson, p. 138.

against the powers and resources of the English! It was hopeless,—he could only become the Caractacus, or the Cassibelaunus of his nation.

Philip has been painted by his enemies as a dreadful, perfidious, and cruel wretch;—but had Philip been the survivor how would he have painted them? With their shameless encroachments, their destruction of Indians, their blood-money, and their scalps, purchased at 1000*l.* each! Philip had the deepest causes of resentment. His father, Massasoit, had received the strangers and sold them land. They speedily compelled him to sign a deed, in which by " that pen and ink work" which the Indians did not understand, but which they soon learned to know worked them the most cruel wrongs, they had made him to acknowledge himself and his subjects the subjects of King James. Philip denied that his father had any idea of the meaning of such a treaty,—any idea of surrendering to the English more than the land he sold them; or if he had done so, that he had any right to give away the liberties of his nation and posterity; the government amongst the Indians not being hereditary, but elective. Philip, however, was compelled to retract and renounce such doctrines in another public document. But the moment he became at liberty, he held himself, and very justly, free from the stipulations of a compulsory deed.

But these were not all Philip's grievances. His only and elder brother, Wamsutta, or Alexander, for the entertainment of similar patriotic sentiments, had been seized in his own house by ten armed men sent by Governor Winslow, and carried before him as a caitiff, though he was at that time the powerful sachem of the Narragansets, his father being dead. The outrage and insult had such an effect upon the highspirited youth, that they threw him into a fever, which speedily proved fatal.*

They were these and the like injuries that drove Philip to concert that union of the Indians which, in 1675, alarmed New England. We need not follow the particulars of the war. It was hastened by a premature disclosure; and Philip has been always taxed as a murderer for putting to death John Sausaman, a renegade Indian who betrayed the plot to the English. The man was a confessed and undoubted traitor, and his death was exactly what the English would have inflicted, and was justified, not merely by the summary proceeding in such cases of the Indians, but by the laws of *civilized war*, if such an odd contradiction of terms may pass. Philip, after a stout resistance, and after performing prodigies of valour, was chased from swamp to swamp, and at length shot by another traitor Indian, who cut off his hand and head, and brought them to the English. His head was exposed on a gibbet at Plymouth for twenty years; his hand, known by a particular scar, was exhibited in savage triumph, and his mangled body refused burial. His only son, a mere boy, was sold into slavery.

It was during this war that the settlers lived in such a state of continual alarm from the Indians, and such adventures and passages of thrilling interest took place, as will for ever furnish topics of conversation in that country. It was then that the congregation was alarmed while in church at Hadley, in Massachusets,

* Hutchinson's Hist. of Massachusets Bay. Also Douglass, Hubbard, Gorge, and other historians of the time.

on a fast-day by the Indians, and were compelled to leave their devotions to defend themselves, when they were surprised by seeing a grave and commanding personage, whom they had not before noticed, assume the command, lead them to victory, and as suddenly again disappear. This person was afterwards found to be Goffe, one of the English regicide judges, then hiding in that neighbourhood. These facts Mr. Cooper has made good use of in his story of " The Borderers."

But the facts of more importance to our history are, that in this war 3000 Indians were said to be destroyed. The Narragansets alone, were reduced from 2000 to about 100 men. After the peace was restored 400 Indians were ordered to assemble at Major Walker's, at Catchecho, 200 of whom were culled as most notorious, some of them put to death, and the rest sent abroad and sold as slaves. Yet all these severities and disasters to the Indians did not extinguish their desire to resist the aggressions of the whites. On all sides, the Tarrateens, the Penobscots, the Five Nations, and various other tribes, continued to harass them; filling them with perpetual fears, and inflicting awful cruelties and devastations on the solitary borderers. These were the necessary fruits of that rancorous spirit with which the harshness and injustice of the settlers had inspired them. Randolph, writing to William Penn from New England in 1688, says — " This barbarous people, the Indians, were now evilly treated by this government, who made it their business to encroach upon their lands, and by degrees to drive them out of all. That was the grounds and the beginning of the last war." And that was the ground of all the wars waged in the country against this unhappy people.

CHAPTER XXII.

THE ENGLISH IN AMERICA — SETTLEMENT OF PENNSYLVANIA.

But it may be said, it is one thing to sit at home in our study and write of Christian principles, and another to go out into new settlements amongst wild tribes, and maintain them; that it is easy to condemn the conduct of others, but might not be so easy to govern our own temper, when assailed on all sides with signal dangers, and irritated with cruelties; that the Indians would not listen to persuasion; that they were faithless, vindictive beyond measure, and fonder of blood than of peace; that there was no possible mode of dealing with them but driving them out, or exterminating them.—Arise, William Penn, and give answer! These are the very things that in his day he heard on all hands. On all hands he was pointed to arms, by which the colonies were defended: he was told that nothing but force could secure the colonists against the red men: he was told that there was no faith in them, and therefore no faith could be kept with them. He believed in the power of Christianity, and therefore he did not believe these assertions. He believed the Indians to be men, and that they were, therefore, accessible to the language and motives of humanity. He believed in the omnipotence of justice and good faith, and disbelieved all the sophistry by which wars and violence are maintained by an interested generation. He resolved to try the experiment of kindness and peace : it was a grand and a momentous trial : it was no other than to put the truth of Christianity to the test, and to learn whether the World's philosophy or that of the Bible were the best. It was attempted to alarm him by all kinds of bloody bugbears : he was ridiculed as an enthusiast, but he calmly cast himself on his conviction of the literal truth of the Gospel, and the result was the most splendid triumph in history. He demonstrated, in the face of the world, and all its arguments and all its practice, that peace may be maintained when men will it; and that there is no need, and therefore no excuse, for the bloodshed and the violence that are perpetually marking the expanding boundaries of what is oddly enough termed civilization.

William Penn received a grant of the province to which he gave the name of Pennsylvania, as payment for money owing to his father, Admiral Penn, from the government. He accepted this grant, because it secured him against any other claimant from Europe. It gave him a title in the eyes of the Christian world ; but he did not believe that it gave him any other title. He knew in his conscience that the country was already in the occupation of tribes of Indians, who inherited it from their ancestors by a term of possession, which probably was unequalled by anything

which the inhabitants of Europe had to shew for their
territories.   I cannot better state Penn's proceedings
on this occasion than in the words of the Edinburgh
Review, when noticing Clarkson's Life of this Christian statesman.

" The country assigned to him by the royal charter
was yet full of its original inhabitants; and the principles of William Penn did not allow him to look
upon that gift as a warrant to dispossess the first inhabitants of the land.   He had accordingly appointed his
commissioners the preceding year to treat with them
for the fair purchase of part of their lands, and for
their joint possession of the remainder; and the terms
of the settlement being now nearly agreed upon, he
proceeded very soon after his arrival to conclude the
settlement, and solemnly to pledge his faith, and to
ratify and confirm the treaty, in right both of the Indians and the planters.   For this purpose a grand
convocation of the tribes had been appointed near the
spot where Philadelphia now stands; and it was agreed
that he and the presiding Sachems should meet and
exchange faith under the spreading branches of a prodigious elm-tree that grew on the banks of the river.
On the day appointed, accordingly, an innumerable
company of the Indians assembled in that neighbour-·
hood, and were seen, with their dark faces and bran-
dished arms, moving in vast swarms in the depth of
the woods that then overshaded that now cultivated
region.   On the other hand, William Penn, with a
moderate attendance of friends, advanced to meet
them.   He came, of course, unarmed—in his usual
plain dress—without banners, or mace, or guard, or
carriages, and only distinguished from his companions

by wearing a blue sash of silk network (which, it seems, is still preserved by Mr. Kett, of Seething Hall, near Norwich), and by having in his hand a roll of parchment, on which was engrossed the confirmation of the treaty of purchase and amity. As soon as he drew near the spot where the Sachems were assembled, the whole multitude of the Indians threw down their weapons, and seated themselves on the ground in groups, each under his own chieftain, and the presiding chief intimated to William Penn that the natives were ready to hear him.

"Having been thus called upon he began:—' The Great Spirit,' he said, ' who made him and them, who ruled the heaven and the earth, and who knew the innermost thoughts of man, knew that he and his friends had a hearty desire to live in peace and friendship with them, and to serve them to the uttermost of their power. It was not their custom to use hostile weapons against their fellow-creatures, for which reason they had come unarmed. Their object was not to do injury, and thus provoke the Great Spirit, but to do good. They were then met on the broad pathway of goodfaith and goodwill, so that no advantage was to be taken on either side, but all was to be openness, brotherhood, and love.' After these and other words, he unrolled the parchment, and, by means of the same intrepreter, conveyed to them, article by article, the conditions of the purchase, and the words of the compact then made for their eternal union. Among other things, they were not to be molested, even in the territory they had alienated, for it was to be common to them and the English. They were to have the same liberty to do all things therein relating to the improvement of their grounds and providing sustenance for their families, which the English had. If disputes should arise between the two, they should be settled by twelve persons, half of whom should be English, and half Indians. He then paid them for the land, and made them many presents besides from the merchandise which had been open before them. Having done this, he laid the roll of parchment on the ground, observing again that the ground should be common to both people. He then added that he would not do as the Marylanders did, that is, call them children, or brothers only : for often parents were apt to whip their children too severely, and brothers sometimes would differ; neither would he compare the friendship between him and them to a chain, for the rain might sometimes rust it, or a tree might fall and break it; but he should consider them as the same flesh and blood as the Christians, and the same as if one man's body was to be divided into two parts. He then took up the parchment, and presented it to the Sachem who wore the horn in the chaplet, and desired him and the other Sachems to preserve it carefully for three generations, that their children might know what had passed between them, just as if he himself had remained with them to repeat it.

" The Indians in return, made long and stately harangues, of which, however, no more seems to have been remembered, but that ' they pledged themselves to live in love with William Penn and his children as long as the sun and moon shall endure.' Thus ended this famous treaty, of which Voltaire has remarked with so much truth and severity, ' That it was the only one ever concluded which was not ratified by an oath, and the only one that never was broken.'

" Such indeed was the spirit in which the negotiation was entered into, and the corresponding settlement concluded, that for the space of more than
seventy years, and so long indeed as the Quakers retained the chief power in the government, the peace
and amity were never violated; and a large and most
striking, though solitary, example afforded of the
facility with which they who are really sincere and
friendly in their own views, may live in harmony with
those who are supposed to be peculiarly fierce and
faithless. We cannot bring ourselves to wish that
there were nothing but Quakers in the world, because
we fear it would be insupportably dull; but when we
consider what tremendous evils daily arise from the
petulance and profligacy, and ambition and irritability
of sovereigns and ministers, we cannot help thinking
it would be the most efficacious of all reforms to choose
all those ruling personages out of that plain, pacific,
and sober-minded sect."

There is no doubt that Penn may be declared the
most perfect Christian statesman that ever lived. He
had the sagacity to see that men, to be made trust-
worthy, need only to be treated as men;—that the
doctrines of the New Testament were to be taken
literally and fully; and he had the courage and
honesty, in the face of all the world's practice and
maxims, to confide in Christian truth. It fully justified him. What are the cunning and the so-called
profound policy of the most subtle statesmen to this?
This confidence, at which the statesmen of our own
day would laugh as folly and simplicity, proved to be
a reach of wisdom for beyond their narrow vision.
But it is to be feared that the selfishness of govern-

ments is as much concerned as their short-sightedness in the clumsy and ruinous manner in which affairs between nations are managed; for what would become of armies and navies, places and pensions, if honest treatment should take place of the blow first and the word after, and of all that false logic by which aggression is made to appear necessary?

The results of this treaty were most extraordinary. While the Friends retained the government of Pennsylvania it was governed without an army, and was never assailed by a single enemy. The Indians retained their firm attachment to them; and, more than a century afterwards, and after the government of the state had long been resumed by England, and its old martial system introduced there, when civil war broke out between the colonies and the mother country, and the Indians were instigated by the mother to use the tomahawk and the scalping-knife against the children, using,—according to her own language, which so roused the indignation of Lord Chatham,—"every means which God and Nature had put into her power," to destroy or subdue them,—these Indians, who laid waste the settlements of the colonists with fire, and drenched them in blood, remembered the treaty with the *sons of Onas*, AND KEPT IT INVIOLATE! They had no scruple to make war on the other colonists, for they had not been scrupulous in their treatment of them, and they had many an old score to clear off; but they had always found the Friends the same,—their friends and the friends of peace,—and they reverenced in them the sacred principles of faith and amity. Month after month the Friends saw the destruction of their neighbours' houses and lands; yet they lived in peace in the midst of this desolation. They heard at night the shrieks of the victims of the red men's wrath, and they saw in the morning where slaughter had reached neighbouring hearths, and where the bloody scalp had been torn away; but their houses remained untouched. Every evening the Indians came from their hidden lairs in the woods, and lifted the latches of their doors, to see if they remained in full reliance on their faith, and then they passed on. Where a house was secured with lock or bolt, they knew that suspicion had entered, and they grew suspicious too. But, through all that bloody and disgraceful war, only two Friends were killed by the Indians; and it was under these circumstances :—A young man, a tanner, had gone from the village where he lived to his tan-yard, at some distance, through all this period of outrage. He went and came daily, without any arms, with his usual air of confidence, and therefore in full security. The Indians from the thickets beheld him, but they never molested him. Unfortunately, one day he went as usual to his business, but carried a gun on his arm. He had not proceeded far into the country when a shot from the bush laid him dead. When the Indians afterwards learned that he was merely carrying the gun to kill birds that were injuring his corn, " Foolish young man," they said ; " we saw him carrying arms, and we inferred that he had changed his principles."

The other case was that of a woman. She had lived in a village which had been laid waste, and most of the inhabitants killed, by the Indians. The soldiers, from a fort not far off, came, and repeatedly entreated her to go into the fort, before she experienced the same fate as her neighbours.   For a long time she refused, but at length fear entered her mind, and she went with them.   In the fort, however, she became wretched.   She considered that she had abandoned the principles of peace by putting herself under the protection of arms.   She felt that she had cast a slander on the hitherto inviolate faith of the Indians, which might bring most disastrous consequences on other Friends who yet lived in the open country on the faith of the Indian integrity.   She therefore determined to go out again, and return to her own house.   She went forth, but had scarcely reached the first thicket when she was shot by the Indians, who now looked upon her as an enemy, or at least as a spy.

These are the only exceptions to the perfect security of Friends through all the Indian devastations in America; for wherever there were Friends, any tribe of Indians felt bound to recognize the sons of Father Onas : they would have been ashamed to injure an unarmed man, who was unarmed because he preserved peace as the command of the Great Spirit.   It was during this war that the very treaty made with Penn was shewn by the Indians to some British officers, being preserved by them with the most sacred care, as a monument of a transaction without a parallel, and equally honourable to themselves as to the Friends.

What a noble testimony is this to the divine nature and perfect adaptation of Christianity to all human purposes; and yet when has it been imitated? and how little is heard of it !   From that day to the present both Americans and English have gone on outraging and expelling the natives from their lands;

and it was but the other day that the English officers
at the Cape were astonished that a similar conduct
towards the Caffres produced a similar result. How
lost are the most splendid deeds of the Christian philosopher on the ordinary statesman! But the Friends
are a peaceable people, and "doing good they blush to
find it fame." If they would make more noise in the
world, and din their good deeds in its ears, they
would be never the worse citizens. The landing of
the Pilgrim Fathers in America is annually celebrated
in New England with great ceremony and eclat. It
has been everywhere extolled by those holding similar religious views, and has been eulogised in poetry
and prose. The landing of the Friends in Pennsylvania was a landing of the Pilgrim Fathers not less
important: they went there under similar circumstances: they fled from persecution at home—a bit-
terer and more savage persecution even than befel
the Puritans—to seek a home in the wilderness.
They equalled the good Roger Williams in their justice to the Indians—they bought their lands of them—
and they far exceeded him and his followers in their
conception of the power of Christianity, and their
practical demonstration of it. They are the only
people in the history of the world that have gone into
the midst of a fierce and armed race, and a race irritated with rigour too, without arms;* established a

* Missionaries, especially the Jesuits, and the English in the South
Sea Islands, form the only exceptions, and these partially. The Jesuits, though they did not commonly bear arms, taught the use of
them, and led, in fact, the most effective troops to battle in Paraguay.
The South Sea missionaries form the strongest exceptions: they are,
indeed, but guests, and not the governors; but their conduct is admirable, and we may believe will not alter with power.

state on the simple basis of justice, and to the last hour of their government maintained it triumphantly on the same. Their conduct to the Indians never altered for the worse; Pennsylvania, while under their administration, never became, as New England, a slaughter-house of the Indians. The world cannot charge them with the extinction of a single tribe—no, nor with that of a single man !

It is delightful to close this chapter of American settlements with so glorious a spectacle of Christian virtue ;—would to God that it were but more imitated !*

* Mr. Bannister, in an excellent little work (British Colonization and the Coloured Tribes), just published, and which ought to be read by every one for its right-mindedness and sound and most important views, has regretted that William Penn did not take a guarantee from the British crown, in his charter, for the protection of the Indians from other states, and from his own successors. It is to be regretted ; nor is it meant here to assert that the provisions of his government were as complete as they were pure in principle. Embarrassments of various kinds prevented him from perfecting what he had so nobly begun ; yet the feeling with which his political system is regarded, must be that of the following passage :—

" Virtue had never perhaps inspired a legislation better calculated to promote the felicity of mankind. The opinions, the sentiments, and the morals, corrected whatever might be defective in it. Accordingly the prosperity of Pennsylvania was very rapid. This republic, without either wars, conquests, struggles, or any of those revolutions which attract the eyes of the vulgar, soon excited the admiration of the whole universe. Its neighbours, notwithstanding their savage state, were softened by the sweetness of its manners ; and distant nations, notwithstanding their corruption, paid homage to its virtues. All delighted to see those heroic days of antiquity realized, which European manners and laws had long taught every one to consider as entirely fabulous."—*Raynal,* vol. vii. p. 292.

CHAPTER XXIII.

THE ENGLISH IN AMERICA TILL THE REVOLT OF THE COLONIES.

In Carolina's palmy bowers,
Amid Kentucky's wastes of flowers,
Where even the way-side hedge displays
Its jasmines and magnolias;
O'er the monarda's vast expanse
Of scarlet, where the bee-birds glance
Their flickering wings, and breasts that gleam
Like living fires;—that dart and scream—
A million little knights that run
Warring for wild-flowers in the sun;—
His eye might rove through earth and sky,
His soul was in the days gone by.

WE may pass rapidly over this space. The colonial principles of action were established regarding the Indians, and they went on destroying and demoralizing them till the reduction of Canada by the English. That removed one great source of Indian destruction; for while there was such an enemy to repulse, the Indians were perpetually called upon and urged forward in the business of slaughter and scalping. It was the same, indeed, on every frontier where there was an enemy, French or Spanish. We have the

history of Adair, who was a resident in the south-
western states for above forty years. This gentleman,
who has given us a very minute account of the manners, customs, and opinions of the Choctaws, Cherokees, and Chickasaws, amongst whom he chiefly
resided in the Carolinas, and who is firmly convinced
that they are descended from the Ten Tribes of Israel,
and, moreover, gives us many proofs of the excel-
lence of their nature—yet, most inconsistently, is loud
in praise of the French policy of setting the different
Indian nations by the ears ; and condemnation of anything like conciliation and forbearance.   Speaking of
some such attempts in 1736, he says—" Our rivals,
the French, never neglect so favourable an opportunity of securing and promoting their interests. We
have known more than one instance wherein *their
wisdom* has not only found out proper means to dis-
concert the most dangerous plans of disaffected savages,
*but likewise to foment, and artfully to encourage, great
animosities between the heads of ambitious rival families,
till they fixed them in an implacable hatred against each
other, and all of their respective tribes.*" *

That he was in earnest in his admiration of such a
policy, he goes on to relate to us, with the greatest
naiveté and in the most circumstantial manner, how he
recommended to the Governor of South Carolina to
employ the Choctaws to scalp and extirpate the French
traders in Louisiana, who, no doubt, interfered with
his own gains.   He lets us know that he got such
a commission; and informs us particularly of the
presents and flatteries with which he plied a great
Choctaw chief, called Red Shoes, to set him on this

* Adair's History of the American Indians, p. 249.

work; in which he was successful. " I supplied each of them with arms, ammunition, and presents in plenty; gave them a French scalping-knife, which had been used against us, and even vermilion, to be used in the flourishing way, with the dangerous French snakes, when they killed and scalped them. . . . . . They soon went to work—they killed the strolling French pedlars — turned out against the Mississippi Indians and Mobillians, and the flame raged very high. A Choctaw woman gave a French pedlar warning: he mounted his horse, but Red Shoes ran him down in about fifteen minutes, and had scalped him before the rest came up. . . . Soon after a great number of Red Shoes' women came to me with the French scalps and other trophies of war." . . . " In the next spring, 1747," he tells us " a large body of Muskohges and Chickasaws embarked on the Mississippi, and went down it to attack the French settlements. Here they burned a large village, and their leader being wounded, they in revenge killed all their prisoners; and overspread the French settlements in their fury like a dreadful whirlwind, destroying all before them, to the astonishment and terror even of those that were far remote from the skirts of the direful storm." This candid writer tells us that the French Louisianians were now in a lamentable state—but, says he, " they had no reason to complain; we were only retaliating innocent blood which *they* had caused to be shed by *their* red mercenaries!" He laments that some treacherous traders put a stop to his scheme, or they would soon have driven all the French out of Alabama.*

* Adair, p. 314—321.

Who were the savages? and how did the English expect the Indians, under such a course of tuition, to become civilized? This was the state of things in the south. In the north, not a war broke out between England and France, but the same scenes were acting between the English American settlements and Canada. In 1692 we find Captain Ingoldsby haranguing the chiefs of the Five Nations at Albany, and exhorting them to " keep the enemy in perpetual alarm by the incursions of parties into their country." And the Indian orator shrewdly replying—"Brother Corlear (their name for the governor of New York) is it not to secure your frontiers? Why, then, not one word of your people that are to join us? We will carry the war into the heart of the enemy's country —but, brother Corlear, how comes it that none of our brethren, fastened in the same chain with us, offer their hand in this general war? Pray, Corlear, how come Maryland, Delaware River, and New England to be disengaged? Do they draw their arms out of the chain? or has the great king commanded that the few subjects he has in this place should make war against the French alone?"*

It was not always, however, that the Indians had to complain that the English urged them into slaughter of the French and did not accompany them. The object of England in America now became that of wresting Canada entirely from France. For this purpose, knowing how essential it was to the success of this enterprise that they should not only have the Indians well affected, so as to prevent any incursions of the French Indians into their own states while the

* Colden, i. 148.

British forces were all concentrated on Canada, and still more how absolutely necessary to have a large body of Indians to pioneer the way for them through the woods, without which their army would be sure to be cut off by the French Indians—great endeavours were now made to conclude treaties of peace and mutual aid with all the great tribes in the British American colonies. Such treaties had long existed with the Five Nations, now called the Six Nations, by the addition of the remainder of the Tuscarora Indians who had escaped from our exterminating arms in North Carolina, and fled to the Five Nations; and also with the Delaware and Susquehanna Indians. Conferences were held with the chiefs of these tribes and British Commissioners from Pennsylvania, Maryland, New York and Virginia, and, ostensibly, a better spirit was manifested towards the Indian people. The most celebrated of these conferences were held at Philadelphia in 1742; at Lancaster in Pennsylvania in 1744; and at Albany, in the state of New York, in 1746. The details of the conferences develope many curious characteristics both of the white and the red men. Canassateego, an Onondaga chief, was the principal speaker for the Indians on all these occasions, and it would be difficult to point to the man in any country, however civilized and learned, who has conducted national negotiations with more ability, eloquence, and sounder perception of actual existing circumstances, amid all the sophistry employed on such occasions by European diplomatists—

That lead to bewilder, and dazzle to blind.—*Beattie.*

It had been originally agreed that a certain sum should be given to the Indians, or rather its value in goods, to compensate them for their trouble and time in coming to these conferences; that their expenses should be paid during their stay; and that all their kettles, guns, and hatchets should be mended for them; and the speakers took good care to remind the colonists of these claims, and to have them duly discharged. As it may be interesting to many to see what sort of goods were given on these occasions, we may take the following as a specimen, which were delivered to them at the conference of 1742, in part payment for the cession of some territory.

500 pounds of powder.	60 kettles.
600 pounds of lead.	100 tobacco tongs.
45 guns.	100 scissars.
60 Stroud matchcoats.	500 awl blades.
100 blankets.	120 combs.
100 Duffil matchcoats.	2000 needles.
200 yards half-thick.	1000 flints.
100 shirts.	24 looking-glasses.
40 hats.	2 pounds of vermilion.
40 pairs shoes and buckles.	100 tin pots.
40 pairs stockings.	1000 tobacco pipes.
100 hatchets.	200 pounds of tobacco.
500 knives.	24 dozen of gartering.
100 hoes.	25 gallons of rum.

In another list we find no less than *four dozens of jew's harps.* Canassateego, on the delivery of the above goods, made a speech which lets us into the real notions and feelings of the Indians on what was going on in that day. "We received from the proprietor," said he, "yesterday, some goods in consideration of our release of the lands on the west side of Susquehanna. It is true, we have the full quantity according to agreement; but, if the proprietor had been here in person, we think, in regard to our numbers and poverty, he would have made an addition to them. If the goods were only to be divided amongst the Indians present, a single person would have but a small portion; but if you consider what numbers are left behind equally entitled with us to a share, there will be extremely little. We therefore desire, if you have the keys of the proprietor's chest, you will open it and take out a little more for us.

" We know our lands are now become more valuable. *The white people think we don't know their value; but we are sensible that the land is everlasting, and the few goods we receive for it, are soon worn out and gone.* For the future we will sell no lands but when Brother Onas is in the country; and we will know beforehand the quantity of goods we are to receive. Besides, we are not well used with respect to the lands still unsold by us. Your people daily settle on our lands, and spoil our hunting. We must insist on your removing them, as you know they have no right to settle to the north of the Kittochtinny Hills."

As it was necessary to conciliate them, more goods were given and justice promised. On the other hand, the English complaining of the Delawares having sold some land without authority from the Six Nations, on whom they were dependent, Canassateego pronounced a very severe reprimand to the Delawares, and ordered them to do so no more.

At the conference of 1744, the Indians gave one of those shrewd turns for their own advantage to the boastings of the whites, which shew the peculiar humour that existed in the midst of their educational gravity. The governor of Maryland vaunting of a great sea-fight in which the English had beaten the

French; Canassateego immediately observed: "In that great fight you must have taken a great quantity of rum, the Indians will therefore thank you for a glass. It was handed round to them in *very small* glasses, called by the governor *French glasses.* The Indians drank it, and at the breaking up of the council that day, Canassateego said, "Having had the pleasure of drinking a *French glass* of the great quantity of rum taken, the Indians would now, before separating be glad to drink an English glass, to make us rejoice with you in the victory." It was impossible to waive so ingenious a demand, and a *large glass,* to indicate the superiority of English liberality, was now handed round.

In this conference, the Indians again complained of the daily encroachments upon them, and of the inadequate price given for the lands they sold. The Governor of Maryland boldly told them that the land was in fact acquired by the English by conquest, and that they had besides a claim of possession of 100 years. To this injudicious speech the Indians replied with indignation, "What is one hundred years in comparison of the time since *our claim* began?—since we came out of this ground? For we must tell you that long before one hundred years *our ancestors came out of this very ground,* and their children have remained here ever since. *You* came out of the ground in a country that lies beyond the seas; *there* you may have a just claim; but *here* you must allow us to be your elder brethren, and the lands to belong to us long before you knew anything of them." They then reminded them of the manner in which they had received them into the country. In figurative language they observed, "When the Dutch came here, above a hundred years ago, we were so well pleased with them that we tied their ship to the bushes on the shore; and afterwards liking them better the longer they stayed with us, and thinking the bushes too slender, we removed the rope and tied it to the trees; and as the trees were liable to be blown down, or to decay of themselves, we, from the affection that we bore them, again removed the rope, and tied it to a strong and high rock (here the interpreter said they mean the Oneido country); and not content with this, for its further security, we removed the rope to the big mountain (here the interpreter said, they mean the Onondaga country), and there we tied it very fast, and rolled wampum about it, and to make it still more secure, we stood upon the wampum, and sat down upon it to defend it, and to prevent any hurt coming to it, and did our best endeavours that it might remain for ever. During all this time the Dutch acknowledged our right to the lands, and solicited us from time to time, to grant them parts of our country. When the English governor came to Albany, and we were told the Dutch and English were become one people, the governor looked at the rope which tied the ship to the big mountain, and seeing that it was only of wampum and liable to rot, break, and perish in a course of years, he gave us a silver chain, which he told us would be much stronger, and would last for ever.

"We had then," said they pathetically, "room enough and plenty of deer, which was easily caught; and though we had not knives, hatchets, or guns, we had knives of stone, and hatchets of stone, and bows and arrows, which answered our purpose as well as the English ones do now, for we are now straitened; we are often in want of deer; we have to go far to seek it, and are besides liable to many other inconveniences, and particularly from *that pen-and-ink work that is going on at the table!*" pointing to the secretary. "You know," they continued, "when the white people came here they were poor—they have got our lands, and now *they* are become rich, and *we* are poor. *What little we get for the land soon goes away, but the land lasts for ever!*"

It was necessary to soothe them—the governor had raised a spirit which told him startling truths. It shewed that the Indians were not blind to the miserable fee for which they were compelled to sell their country. "Your great king," said they, "might send you over to conquer the Indians; but it looks to us that God did not send you—if he had, he would not have placed the sea where he has, to keep you and us asunder." The governor addressed them in flattering terms, and added, "We have a chest of new goods, and the key is in our pockets. You are our brethren: the Great King is our common Father, and we will live with you as children ought to do—in peace and love."

The Indians were strenuously exhorted to use all means to bring the western natives into the league. At the Conference of 1746, held at Albany, it became sufficiently evident for what object all this conciliation and these endeavours to extend their alliance amongst the Indians were used. A great and decisive attack upon Canada was planning: and it is really awful to read the language addressed to the assembled Indians, to inflame them with the spirit of the most malignant

hatred and revenge against the French. Mr. Cad-
wallader Colden, one of His Majesty's Council and
Surveyor-general of New York, and the historian of
the Five Nations, on whose own authority these
facts are stated, addressed the Indians, owing to the
Governor's illness, in the speech prepared for the
occasion. He called upon them to remember all the
French had done to them ; what they did at Onondaga;
how they invaded the Senekas; what mischiefs they
did to the Mohawks ; how many of their countrymen
suffered at the fire at Montreal; how they had sent
priests amongst them to lull them to sleep, when they
intended to knock them on the head. " I hear," then
added he, " they are attempting to do the same now.
I need not remind you what revenge your fathers
took for these injuries, when they put all the isle of
Montreal, and a great part of Canada, to fire and
sword. Can you think the French forget this? No !
they are watching secretly to destroy you. But if
your fathers could now rise out of their graves, how
would their hearts leap with joy to see this day, when
so glorious an opportunity is put into your hands to
revenge all the injuries of your country, etc. etc." He
called on them to accompany the English, to win
glory, and promised them great reward.

But these horrible fire-brands of speech,— these
truly " burning words" were not all the means used.
English gentlemen were sent amongst the tribes to
arouse them by every conceivable means. The celebrated Mr. William Johnson of Mohawk, who had
dreamed himself into a vast estate in that country,*

* Mr. Johnson, who was originally a trader amongst the Mohawks,
indulged them in all their whims. They were continually dreaming

and who afterwards, as Sir William Johnson, was so
distinguished as the leader of the Indians at the fall
of Quebec, and the conquest of Canada, now went
amongst the Mohawks, dressed like a Mohawk chief.
He feasted them at his castle on the Mohawk river;
he gave them dances in their own country style, and
danced with them; and led the Mohawk band to this
very conference.

This enterprise came to nothing; but for the successful one of 1759 the same stimulants were applied,
and the natives, to the very Twightwees and Chickasaws, brought into the league, either to march against
the French, or to secure quiet in the states during the
time of the invasion of Canada.   And what was their
reward?   Scarcely was Canada reduced, and the
services of the Indians no longer needed, when they
found themselves as much encroached upon and insulted as ever.   Some of the bloodiest and most desolating wars which they ever waged against the English
settlements, took place between our conquest of Canada and our war against the American colonies themselves.   It was the long course of injuries and insults

that he had given them this, that, and the other thing; and no greater
insult can, according to their opinions, be offered to any man
than to call in question the spiritual authenticity of his dream.   At
length the chief *dreamed* that Mr. Johnson had given him his uniform
of scarlet and gold.   Mr. Johnson immediately made him a present
of it: but the next time he met him, he told him that *he* had now
begun to dream, and that he had dreamed that the Mohawks had
given him certain lands, describing one of the finest tracts in the
country, and of great extent.   The Indians were struck with consternation.   They said: "He surely had not dreamed that, had he?"
He replied that he certainly had.   They therefore held a council, and
came to inform him that they had confirmed his dream; but begged
that he would not dream any more.   He had no further occasion.

which the Indians had suffered from the settlers that made them so ready to take up the tomahawk and scalping-knife at the call, and induced by the blood-money, of the mother-country against her American children. The employment and instigation of the Indians to tomahawk the settlers brings down British treatment of the Indians to the very last moment of our power in that country. What were our notions of such enormities may be inferred from their being called in the British Parliament *"means which God and nature have put into our hands,"*—and from Lord Cornwallis, our general then employed against the Americans, expressing, in 1780, his *"satisfaction* that the Indians had pursued and *scalped* many of the enemy!"

This was our conduct towards the Indians to the last hour of our dominion in their country. We drove them out of their lands, or cheated them out of them by making them drunk. We robbed them of their furs in the same manner; and on all occasions we inflamed their passions against their own enemies and ours. We made them ten times more cruel, perfidious, and depravedly savage than we found them, and then upbraided them as irreclaimable and merciless, and thereon founded our convenient plea that they must be destroyed, or driven onward as perishing shadows before the sun of civilization.

Before quitting the English in America, we need only, to complete our view of their treatment of the natives, to include in it a glance at that treatment in those colonies which we yet retain there; and that is furnished by the following Parliamentary Report, (1837.)

NEWFOUNDLAND.

To take a review of our colonies, beginning with Newfoundland. There, as in other parts of North America, it seems to have been, for a length of time, accounted a " meritorious act " to kill an Indian.*

On our first visit to that country, the natives were seen in every part of the coast.   We occupied the stations where they used to hunt and fish, thus reducing them to want, while we took no trouble to indemnify them, so that, doubtless, many of them perished by famine ; we also treated them with hostility and cruelty, and "many were slain by our own people, as well as by the Micmac Indians," who were allowed to harass them.   They must, however, have been recently very numerous, since, in one place, Captain Buchan found they had " run up fences to the extent of 30 miles," with a variety of ramifications, for the purpose of conducting the deer down to the water, a work which would have required the labour of a multitude of hands.

It does not appear that any measures were taken to open a communication with them before the year 1810, when, by order of Sir. J. Duckworth, an attempt was made by Captain Buchan, which proved ineffectual.   At that time he conceived that their numbers around their chief place of resort, the Great Lake, were reduced to 400 or 500. Under our treatment they continued rapidly to diminish; and it appears probable that the last of the tribe left at large, a man and a woman, were shot by two Englishmen in 1823.   Three women had been taken prisoners shortly before, and they died in captivity.   In the colony of Newfoundland, it may therefore be stated that we have exterminated the natives.†

---

* Cotton Mather records that, amongst the early settlers, it was considered a " religious act to kill Indians."

A similar sentiment prevailed amongst the Dutch boors in South Africa, with regard to the natives of the country.   Mr. Barrow writes, " A farmer thinks he cannot proclaim a more meritorious action than the murder of one of these people.   A boor from Graaf Reinet, being asked in the secretary's office, a few days before we left town, if the savages were numerous or troublesome on the road, replied, ' he had only shot four,' with as much composure and indifference as if he had been speaking of four partridges.   I myself have heard one of the humane colonists boast of having destroyed, with his own hands, near 300 of these unfortunate wretches."

† See Evidence given by Capt. Buchan.

CANADIAN INDIANS.

The general account of our intercourse with the North American Indians, as distinct from missionary efforts, may be given in the words of a converted Chippeway chief, in a letter to Lord Goderich : " We were once very numerous, and owned all Upper Canada, and lived by hunting and fishing; ·but the white men who came to trade with us taught our fathers to drink the fire-waters, which has made our people poor and sick, and has killed many tribes, till we have become very small."*

It is a curious fact, noticed in the evidence, that, some years ago, the Indians practised agriculture, and were able to bring corn to our settlements, then suffering from famine ; but we, by driving them back and introducing the fur trade, have rendered them so completely a wandering people, that they have very much lost any disposition which they might once have felt to settle. All writers on the Indian race have spoken of them, in their native barbarism, as a noble people; but those who live among civilised men, upon reservations in our own territory, are now represented as " reduced to a state which resembles that of gipsies in this country." Those who live in villages among the whites " are a very degraded race, and look more like dram-drinkers than people it would be possible to get to do any work."

To enter, however, into a few more particulars.—The Indians of New Brunswick are described by Sir H. Douglass, in 1825, as " dwindled in numbers," and in a " wretched condition."

Those of Nova Scotia, the Micmacs (by Sir J. Kempt), as disinclined to settle, and in the habit of bartering their furs, " unhappily, for rum."†

General Darling's statement as to the Indians of the Canadas, drawn up in 1828, speaks of the interposition of the government being urgently called for in behalf of the helpless individuals whose landed possessions, where they have any assigned to them, are daily plundered by their designing and more enlightened white brethren.‡

Of the Algonquins and Nipissings, General Darling writes, " Their situation is becoming alarming, by the rapid settlement and improvement of the lands on the banks of the Ottawa, on which they were placed by the government in the year 1763, and which tract they have naturally considered as their own. The result of the present state of

---

* Papers, Abor. Tribes, 1834, p. 135.

† Ibid. 147. ‡ Ibid. 22.

things is obvious, and such as can scarcely fail in time to be attended with bloodshed and murder; for, driven from their own resources, they will naturally trespass on those of other tribes, who are equally jealous of the intrusion of their red brethren as of white men. Complaints on this head are increasing daily, while the threats and admonitions of the officers of the department have been insufficient to control the unruly spirit of the savage, who, driven by the calls of hunger and the feelings of nature towards his offspring, will not be scrupulous in invading the rights of his brethren, as a means of alleviating his misery, when he finds the example in the conduct of his white father's children practised, as he conceives, towards himself." *

The general also speaks of the "degeneracy" of the Iroquois, and of the degraded condition of most of the other tribes, with the exception of those only who had received Christian instruction. Later testimony is to the same effect. The Rev. J. Beecham, secretary to the Wesleyan Missionary Society, says he has conversed with the Chippeway chief above referred to, on the condition of the Indians on the boundary of Upper Canada. That he stated most unequivocally that previously to the introduction of Christianity they were rapidly wasting away; and he believed that if it had not been for the introduction of Christianity they would speedily have become extinct. As the causes of this waste of Indian life, he mentions the decrease of the game, the habit of intoxication, and the European diseases. The small-pox had made great ravages. He adds, "The information which I have derived from this chief has been confirmed by our missionaries stationed in Upper Canada, and who are now employed among the Indian tribes on the borders of that province. My inquiries have led me to believe, that where Christianity has not been introduced among the aboriginal inhabitants of Upper Canada, they are melting away before the advance of the white population. This remark applies to the Six Nations, as they are called, on the Great River; the Mohawks, Oneidas, Onondagas, Senacas, Cayugas, and Tuscaroras, as well as to all the other tribes on the borders of the province." Of the ulterior tribes, the account given by Mr. King, who accompanied Captain Back in his late Arctic expedition, is deplorable: he gives it as his opinion, that the Northern Indians have decreased greatly, and decidedly from contact with the Europeans."

Thus, the Cree Indians, once a powerful tribe, " have now degenerated into a few families, congregated about the European establish-

* Papers, Abor. Tribes, p. 24.

ments, while some few still retain their ancient rights, and have become partly allies of a tribe of Indians that were once their slaves." He supposes their numbers to have been reduced within thirty or forty years from 8,000 or 10,000, to 200, or at most 300, and has no doubt of the remnant being extirpated in a short time, if no measures are taken to improve their morals and to cultivate habits of civilization. It should be observed that this tribe had access to posts not comprehended within the Hudson's Bay Company's prohibition, as to the introduction of spirituous liquors, and that they miserably show the effects of the privilege.

The Copper Indians also, through ill-management, intemperance, and vice, are said to have decreased within the last five years to one-half the number of what they were.

The early quarrels between the Hudson's Bay and the North West Companies, in which the Indians were induced to take a bloody part, furnished them with a ruinous example of the savageness of Christians.*

SOUTH AMERICA.

In South America, British Guiana occupies a large extent of country between the rivers Orinoco and Amazons, giving access to numbers of tribes of aborigines who wander over the vast regions of the interior. The Indian population within the colony of Demerára and Essequibo, is derived from four nations, the Caribs, Arawacks, Warrows, and Accaways.

It is acknowledged that they have been diminishing ever since the British came into possession of the colony. In 1831 they were computed at 5096 ; and it is stated "it is the opinion of old inhabitants of the colony, and those most competent to judge, that a considerable diminution has taken place in the aggregate number of the Indians of late years, and that the dimunition, although gradual, has become more sensibly apparent within the last eight or ten years." The diminution is attributed, in some degree, to the increased use of rum amongst them.†

There are in the colony six gentlemen bearing the title of " Protectors of Indians," whose office it is to superintend the tribes ; and

* See Papers relating to Red River Settlement, 1815, 1819 : especially Mr. Coltman's Report, pp. 115, 125.

† Letter from Jas. Hackett, Esq., Civil Commissioner, to Sir B. D'Urban. Papers, Abor. Tribes, 1834, pp. 194, 198.

under them are placed post-holders, a principal part of whose business it is to keep the negroes from resorting to the Indians, and also to attend the distribution of the presents which are given to the latter by the British government; of which, as was noticed with reprehension by Lord Goderich, rum formed a part.

It does not appear* that anything has been done by government for their moral or religious improvement, excepting the grant in 1831, by Sir B. D'Urban, of a piece of land at Point Bartica, where a small establishment was then founded by the Church Missionary Society. The Moravian Mission on the Courantin was given up in 1817; and it does not appear that any other Protestant Society has attended to these Indians.

In 1831, Lord Goderich writes,† " I have not heard of any effort to convert the Indians of British Guiana to Christianity, or to impart to them the arts of social life."

It should be observed that no injunctions to communicate either are given in the instructions for the "Protectors of Indians," or in those for the post-holders; and two of the articles of the latter, (Art. 14 and Art. 15,) tend directly to sanction and encourage immorality. All reports agree in stating that these tribes have been almost wholly neglected, are retrograding, and are without provision for their moral or civil advancement; and with due allowance for the extenuating remarks on the poor account to which they turned their lands, when they had them, and the gifts (baneful gifts some of them) which have been distributed, and on the advantage of living under British laws, we must still concur in the sentiment of Lord Goderich, as expressed in the same letter, upon a reference as to sentence of death passed upon a native Indian for the murder of another. " It is a serious consideration that we have subjected these tribes to the penalties of a code of which they unavoidably live in profound ignorance; they have not even that conjectural knowledge of its provisions which would be suggested by the precepts of religion, if they had even received the most elementary instruction in the Christian faith. They are brought into acquaintance with civilised life not to partake its blessings, but only to feel the severity of its penal sanctions.

" A debt is due to the aboriginal inhabitants of British Guiana of a very different kind from that which the inhabitants of Christendom may, in a certain sense, be said to owe in general to other barbarous tribes. The whole territory which has been occupied by

---

* Papers, Abor. Tribes, pp. 183, 193.   † Papers, p. 182.

Europeans, on the northern shores of the South American Continent, has been acquired by no other right than that of superior power ; and I fear that the natives whom we have dispossessed, have to this day received no compensation for the loss of the lands on which they formerly subsisted. However urgent is the duty of economy in every branch of the public service, it is impossible to withhold from the natives of the country the inestimable benefit which they would derive from appropriating to their religious and moral instruction some moderate part of that income which results from the culture of the soil to which they or their fathers had an indisputable title.*

CARIBS.

Of the Caribs, the native inhabitants of the West Indies, we need not speak, as of them little more remains than the tradition that they once existed.

---

* Papers, Abór. Tribes, pp. 181, 182.

CHAPTER XXIV.

TREATMENT OF THE INDIANS BY THE UNITED STATES.

" We were born on this spot; our fathers lie buried in it.   Shall
we say to the bones of our fathers—' Arise and come with us into a
foreign land ? ' "— *Speech of a Canadian Indian to the French invaders.*

It was to be hoped that that great republic, the
United States of North America, having given so
splendid an example of resistance to the injustice of
despotism, and of the achievement of freedom in a
struggle against a mighty nation, calculated to call
forth all the generous enthusiasm of brave men,
would have given a practical demonstration of true
liberty to the whole world: that they would have
shewn that it was possible for a republic to exist,
which was wise and noble enough to be entirely free:
that the sarcasm of Milton should not at least be
thrown at them—

License they mean when they cry liberty !

The world, however, was doomed to suffer another disappointment in this instance, and the enemies of freedom to enjoy another triumph. The Americans left that highest place in human legislation, the adoption of the divine precept of doing as they would be done by, as the basis of their constitution, still unoccupied. We had the mortification of seeing the old selfishness which had disgraced every ancient republic, and had furnished such destructive arguments to the foes of mankind, again unblushingly displayed. The Americans proclaimed themselves not noble, not generous, not high-minded enough to give that freedom to others which they had declared, by word and by deed, of the same price as life to themselves. They once more mixed up the old crumbling composition of iron and clay, slavery and freedom, and moulded them into an image of civil polity, which must inevitably fall asunder. They published a new libel on man— in the very moment of his most heroic and magnanimous enthusiasm—shewing him as mean and sordid. While he raised his hand to protest to admiring and huzzaing millions, that there was no value in life without liberty, the manacles prepared for the negroes protruded themselves from his pocket, his impassioned action at once took the air of theatrical rant, and the multitudes who were about to admire, laughed out, or groaned, as they were more or less virtuous. The pompous phrases of " Divine liberty! Glorious liberty! Liberty the birthright of every man that breathes!" became the most bitter and humbling mockery, and gave way to the merry sneer of Matthews—" What! d'ye call it liberty when a man may not larrup his own nigger?"

A more natural tone was assumed as regarded the
Indians. They were declared to be free and independent nations; not citizens of the United States,
but the original proprietors of the soil, and therefore
as purely irresponsible to the laws of the United
States as any neighbouring nations. They were
treated with, as such, on every occasion; their territories and right of self-government were acknowledged by such treaties. " There is an abundance of
authorities," says Mr. Stuart, in his ' Three Years in
North America,' " in opposition to the pretext, that
the Indians are not now entitled to live under their
own laws and constitutions; but it would be sufficient
to refer to the treaties entered into, year after year,
between the United States and them as separate
nations."

" There are two or three authorities, independent
of state papers, which most unambiguously prove
that it was never supposed that the state governments
should have a right to impose their constitution or
code of laws upon any of the Indian nations. Thus
Mr. Jefferson, in an address to the Cherokees, says—
" I wish sincerely you may succeed in your laudable
endeavours to save the remnant of your nation by
adopting industrious occupations. In this you may
always rely on the counsel and assistance of the
United States." In the same way the American ne-
gotiators at Ghent, among whom were the most emi-
nent American statesmen, Mr. John Quincy Adams
and Mr. Henry Clay, in their note addressed to the
British Commissioners, dated September 9, 1814, use
the following language: — " The Indians residing
within the United States are so far independent that

they live under their own customs, and not under the laws .of the United States." Chancellor Kent, of New York state (the Lord Coke or Lord Stair of the United States), has expressly laid it down, that " it would seem idle to contend that the Indians were citizens or subjects of the United States, and not alien and sovereign tribes;" and the Supreme Court of the United States have expressly declared, that " the person who purchases land from the Indians within their territory incorporates himself with them; and, so far as respects the property purchased, holds his title under their protection, *subject to their laws:* if they annul the grant, we know of no tribunal which can revise and set aside the proceeding." Mr. Clay's language is quite decided:—" The Indians residing within the United States are so far independent that they live under their own customs, and not under the laws of the United States; that their rights, where they inhabit or hunt, are secured to them by boundaries defined in amicable treaties between the United States and themselves." Mr. Wirt, the late Attorney-General of the United States, a man of great legal authority, has stated it to be his opinion, " that the territory of the Cherokees is not within the jurisdiction of the State of Georgia, but within the sole and exclusive jurisdiction of the Cherokee nation; and that, consequently, the State of Georgia has no right to extend her laws over that territory." General Washington in 1790, in a speech to one of the tribes of Indians, not only recognizes the same national independence, but adds many solemn assurances on behalf of the United States. " The general government only has the power to treat with the Indian nations, and any treaty formed and held without its authority will not be binding.

"Here, then, is the security for the remainder of your lands. No state nor person can purchase your lands, unless by some public treaty held under the authority of the United States. *The general government will never consent to your being defrauded, but it will protect you in all your just rights.*

"But your great object seems to be the security of your remaining lands, and I have, therefore, upon this point, meant to be sufficiently strong and clear . . . . That, in future, you cannot be defrauded of your lands. That you possess the right to sell, and the right of refusing to sell your lands. . . . That, therefore, the sale of your lands in future will depend entirely upon yourselves. But that, when you find it for your interest to sell any part of your lands, the United States must be present, by their agent, and will be your security that you shall not be defrauded in the bargain you make. . . . . The United States will be true and faithful to their engagements."

These are plain and just declarations; and, had they been faithfully maintained, would have conferred great honour on the United States. How they have been maintained, all the world knows. The American republicans have followed faithfully, not their own declarations, but the maxims and the practices of their English progenitors. The Indians have been declared savage and irreclaimable. They have been described as inveterately attached to hunting and a roving life, as a stumbling-block in the path of civilization. As perfectly incapable of settling down to the pursuits of agriculture, social arts, and domestic habits. It has been declared necessary, on these grounds, to push them out of the settled territories, and every means has been used to compel them to abandon the lands of their ancestors, and to seek a fresh country in the wilds beyond the Mississippi. Even so respectable an author as Malte Brun has, in Europe, advanced a doctrine in defence of this sweeping system of Indian expatriation. " Even admitting that the use of ardent spirits has deteriorated their habits and thinned their numbers, we cannot suppose that the Indian population was ever more than twice as dense as at present, or that it exceeded one person for each square mile of surface. Now, in highly civilized countries, like France and England, the population is at the rate of 150 or 200 persons to the square mile. It may safely be affirmed, therefore, that the same extent of land from which one Indian family derives a precarious and wretched subsistence, would support 150 families of civilized men, in plenty and comfort. But most of the Indian tribes raise melons, beans, and maize; and were we to take the case of a people who lived entirely by hunting, the disproportion would be still greater. *If God created the earth for the sustenance of mankind, this single consideration decides the question* as to the sacredness of the Indians' title to the lands which they roam over, but do not, in any reasonable sense, occupy."— v. 224.

A more abominable doctrine surely never was broached. It breathes the genuine spirit of the old Spaniard; and, if acted upon, would produce an everlasting confusion. Every nation which is more densely populated than another, may, on this principle, say to that less densely peopled state, you are not as thickly planted as God intended you to be; you amount only to 150 persons to the square mile, we are 200 to the same space; therefore, please to walk out, and give place to us, who are your superiors, and who more justly fulfil God's intentions by the law of density. The Chinese might fairly lay claim to Europe on that ground; and our own swarming poor to every large park and thinly peopled district that they happened to see.

"This single consideration," indeed, is a very good reason why the Indians should be advised to leave off a desultory life, and take to agriculture and the arts; or it is a very sufficient reason why the Europeans should ask leave to live amongst them, and thus more fully occupy the country, in what the French geographer calls a reasonable sense. And it remained for M. Malte Brun to show that they have ever refused to do either the one or the other. They have, on all occasions when the Europeans have gone amongst them, "in a reasonable sense," received them with kindness, and even joy. They have been willing to listen to their instructions, and ready to sell them their lands to live upon. But it has been the "unreasonableness" of the whites that has everywhere soon turned the hearts, and made deaf the ears, of the natives. We have seen the lawless violence with which the early settlers seized on the Indians' territories, the lawless violence and cruelty with which they rewarded them evil for good, and pursued them to death, or instigated them to the commission of all bloody and desperate deeds. These are the causes why the Indians have remained uncivilized wanderers; why they have refused to listen to the precepts of

Christianity; and why they roam over, rather than occupy, those lands on which they have been suffered to remain. From the days of Elliot, Mayhew, Brainard, and their zealous compeers, there have never wanted missionaries to endeavour to civilize and christianize; but they have found, for the most part, their efforts utterly defeated by the wicked and unprincipled acts, the wicked and unprincipled character of the Europeans. When the missionaries have preached to the shrewd Indians the genuine doctrines of Christianity, they have immediately been struck with the total discrepancy between these doctrines and the lives and practices of their European professors. "If these are the principles of your religion," they have continually said, "go and preach them to your countrymen. If they have any efficacy in them, let us see it shewn upon them. Make them good, just, and full of this love you speak of. Let them regard the rights and property of Indians. You have also a people amongst you that you have torn from their own country, and hold in slavery. Go home and give them freedom; do as your book says, —as you would be done by. When you have done that, come again, and we will listen to you."

This is the language which the missionaries have had everywhere in the American forests to contend with.* When they have made by their truly kind and

---

* Mr. Mayhew in his journal, writes, that the Indians told him, that they could not observe the benefit of Christianity, because the English cheated them of their lands and goods; and that the use of books made them more cunning in cheating. In his Indian itineraries, he desired of Ninicroft, sachem of the Narragansets, leave to preach to his people. Ninicroft bid him go and make the English good first,

christian spirit and lives some impression, the spirit
and lives of their countrymen have again destroyed
their labours. The fire-waters, gin, rum, and brandy,
have been introduced to intoxicate, and in intoxication
to swindle the Indians out of their furs and lands.
Numbers of claims to lands have been grounded on
drunken bargains, which in their soberness the Indians
would not recognize; and the consequences have been
bloodshed and forcible expulsion. Before these causes
the Indians have steadily melted away, or retired
westwards before the advancing tide of white emigra-
tion. Malte Brun would have us believe that in the
United States there never were many more than
twice the present number. Let any one look at the
list of the different tribes, and their numbers in 1822,
quoted by himself from Dr. Morse, and then look at
the numbers of all the tribes which inhabited the old
States at the period of their settlement.

In New England - - - - -	2,247
New York - - - - - -	5,184
Ohio - - - - - - -	2,407
Michigan and N. W. territories - - -	28,380
Illinois and Indiana - - - - -	17,006
Southern States east of Mississippi - -	65,122
West of Mississippi and north of Missouri -	33,150
Between Missouri and Red River - -	101,070
Between Red River and Rio del Norte -	45,370
West of Rocky Mountains - - -	171,200
	471,136

and desired Mr. Mayhew not to hinder him in his concerns. Some
Indians at Albany being asked to go into a meeting-house, declined,
saying, "the English went into those places to study how to cheat
poor Indians in the price of beaver, for they had often observed that
when they came back from those places they offered less money than
before they went in."

The slightest glance at this table shews instantly the fact, that where the white settlers have been the longest there the Indians have wofully decreased. The farther you go into the Western wilderness the greater the Indian population. Where are the populous tribes that once camped in the woods of New York, New England, and Pennsylvania? In those states there were twenty years ago about 8000 Indians; since then, a rapid diminution has taken place. In the middle of the seventeenth century, and after several of the tribes were exterminated, and after all had suffered severely, there could not be less, according to the historians of the times, than forty or fifty thousand Indians within the same limits. The traveller occasionally meets with a feeble remnant of these once numerous and powerful tribes, lingering amid the now usurped lands of their country, in the old settled states; but they have lost their ancient spirit and dignity, and more resemble troops of gipsies than the noble savages their ancestors were. A few of the Tuscaroras live near Lewistown, and are agriculturists: and the last of the Narragansets, the tribe of Miantinomo, are to be found at Charlestown, in Rhode Island, under the notice of the Boston missionaries. Fragments of the Six Nations yet linger in the State of New York. A few Oneidas live near the lake of that name, now christianized and habituated to the manners of the country. Some of the Senecas and Cornplanters remain about Buffalo, on the Niagara, and at the head-waters of the Alleghany river. Amongst these Senecas, lived till 1830, the famous orator Red-Jacket; one of the most extraordinary men which this singular race has produced.

The effect of his eloquence may be imagined from
the following passage, to be found in "Buckingham's
Miscellanies selected from the Public Journals."

"More than thirty years (this was written about
1822) have rolled away since a treaty was held on
the beautiful acclivity that overlooks the Canandai-
gua Lake. Two days had passed away in negotiation
with the Indians for the cession of their lands. The
contract was supposed to be nearly completed, when
Red-Jacket arose. With the grace and dignity of a
Roman senator he drew his blanket around him, and
with a piercing eye surveyed the multitude. All was
hushed. Nothing interposed to break the silence,
save the gentle rustling of the tree-tops under whose
shade they were gathered. After a long and solemn,
but not unmeaning pause, he commenced his speech
in a low voice and sententious style. Rising gradually
with the subject, he depicted the primitive simplicity
and happiness of his nation, and the wrongs they had
sustained from the usurpations of white men, with
such a bold but faithful pencil, that every auditor was
soon roused to vengeance, or melted into tears. The
effect was inexpressible. But ere the emotions of
admiration and sympathy had subsided, the white
men became alarmed. They were in the heart of an
Indian country, surrounded by ten times their number,
who were inflamed by the remembrance of their injuries, and excited to indignation by the eloquence of
a favourite chief. Appalled and terrified, the white
men cast a cheerless gaze upon the hordes around
them. A nod from one of the chiefs might be the
onset of destruction, but at this portentous moment
Farmers-brother interposed."

In the year 1805 a council was held at Buffalo, by the chiefs and warriors of the Senecas, at the request of Mr. Cram from Massachusets. The missionary first made a speech, in which he told the Indians that he was sent by the Missionary Society of Boston, to instruct them "how to worship the Great Spirit," and not to get away their lands and money; that there was but one true religion, and they were living in darkness, etc. After consultation, Red-Jacket returned, on behalf of the Indians, the following speech, which is deservedly famous, and not only displays the strong intellect of the race, but how vain it was to expect to christianize them, without clear and patient reasoning, and in the face of the crimes and corruptions of the whites.

"*Friend and brother*, it was the will of the Great Spirit that we should meet together this day. He orders all things, and he has given us a fine day for our council. He has taken his garment from before the sun, and caused it to shine with brightness upon us. Our eyes are opened that we see clearly; our ears are unstopped that we have been able to hear distinctly the words that you have spoken. For all these favours we thank the Great Spirit and him only.

"*Brother*, this council-fire was kindled by you. It was at your request that we came together at this time. We have listened with great attention to what you have said; you requested us to speak our minds freely: this gives us great joy, for we now consider that we stand upright before you, and can speak whatever we think. All have heard your voice, and all speak to you as one man; our minds are agreed.

"*Brother*, you say you want an answer to your

talk before you leave this place. It is right you
should have one, as you are at a great distance from
home, and we do not wish to detain you; but we will
first look back a little, and tell you what our fathers
have told us, and what we have heard from the white
people.

" *Brother, listen to what we say.*   There was a time
when our forefathers owned this great island.   Their
seats extended from the rising to the setting sun.
The Great Spirit had made it for the use of Indians.
He had created the buffalo, the deer, and other animals for food.   He made the beaver and the bear, and
their skins served us for clothing.   He had scattered
them over the country, and taught us how to take them.
He had caused the earth to produce corn for bread.
All this he had done for his red children, because he
loved them.   If we had any disputes about hunting-
grounds, they were generally settled without the shed-
ding of much blood; but an evil day came upon us:
your forefathers crossed the great waters, and landed
on this island.   Their numbers were small; they found
friends, and not enemies; they told us they had fled
from their own country for fear of wicked men, and
came here to enjoy their religion.   They asked for a
a small seat.   We took pity on them, granted their
request, and they sate down among us.   We gave
them corn and meat, they gave us poison* in return.
The white people had now found out our country,
tidings were carried back, and more came amongst us;
yet we did not fear them, we took them to be friends:
they called us brothers, we believed them, and gave
them a larger seat.   At length their numbers had

* Spirituous liquors.

greatly increased, they wanted more land, — they wanted our country! Our eyes were opened, and our minds became uneasy. Wars took place; *Indians were hired to fight against Indians,* and many of our people were destroyed. They also brought strong liquors among us; it was strong and powerful, and has slain thousands.

"*Brother,* our seats were once large, and yours were very small. You have now become a great people, and we have scarcely a place left to spread our blankets. You have got our country, but are not satisfied;—*you want to force your religion upon us.*

"*Brother, continue to listen.* You say that you are sent to instruct us how to worship the Great Spirit agreeably to his mind, and if we do not take hold of the religion which you white people teach, we shall be unhappy hereafter. You say that you are right, and we are lost; how do you know this? We understand that your religion is written in a book; if it was intended for us as well as you, why has not the Great Spirit given it to us, and not only to us, why did he not give to our forefathers the knowledge of that book, with the means of understanding it rightly? We only know what you tell us about it; how shall we know when to believe, being so often deceived by the white people?

"*Brother,* you say there is but one way to worship and serve the Great Spirit. If there is but one religion, why do you white people differ so much about it? why not all agree, as you can all read the book?

"*Brother,* we do not understand these things. We are told that your religion was given to your forefathers, and has been handed down from father to son.

We also have a religion which was given to our forefathers, and has been handed down to us their children.
We worship that way. *It teaches us to be thankful for
all the favours we receive ; to love each other, and to be
united ;—we never quarrel about religion.*

" *Brother,* the Great Spirit has made us all; but
he has made a great difference between his white and
red children. He has given us a different complexion,
and different customs. To you he has given the arts;
to these he has not opened our eyes. We know these
things to be true. Since he has made so great a difference between us in other things, why may we not
conclude that he has given us a different religion
according to our understanding? The Great Spirit
does right: he knows what is best for his children :
we are satisfied.

" *Brother,* we do not wish to destroy your religion,
or take it from you; we only want to enjoy our own.

" *Brother,* you say you have not come to get our
land or our money, but to enlighten our minds. I will
now tell you that I have been at your meetings, and
saw you collecting money from the meeting. I
cannot tell what this money was intended for, but
suppose it was your minister; and, if we should con-
form to your way of thinking, perhaps you may want
some from us.

" *Brother,* we are told that you have been preaching
to the white people in this place. These people are
our neighbours; we are acquainted with them : we
will wait a little while, and see what effect your
preaching has upon them. If we find it does them
good, makes them honest and less disposed to cheat
Indians, we will then consider again what you have
said.

"*Brother,* you have now heard our answer to your talk; and this is all we have to say at present. As we are going to part, we will come and take you by the hand, and hope the Great Spirit will protect you on your journey, and return you safe to your friends."

The Missionary, hastily rising from his seat, refused to shake hands with them, saying "there was no fellowship between the religion of God and the works of the devil." The Indians smiled and retired in a peaceable manner.* Which of these parties best knew the real nature of religion? At all events the missionary was awfully deficient in the spirit of his own, and in the art of winning men to embrace it.

* Winterbottom's America.

CHAPTER XXV.

TREATMENT OF THE INDIANS BY THE UNITED STATES,—CONTINUED.

THE Friends have for many years had schools for the education of the children in different States, and persons employed to engage the Indians in agriculture and manual arts, but they, as well as the missionaries, complain that their efforts have been rendered abortive by the continual removals of the red people by the government.

Scarcely was the war over, and American independence proclaimed, when a great strife began betwixt the Republicans and the Indians, for the Indian lands —a strife which extended from the Canadian lakes to the gulph of Florida, and has continued more or less to this moment. Under the British government, the boundaries of the American states had never been well defined. The Americans appointed commissioners to determine them, and appear to have resolved that all Indian claims within the boundaries of the St. Lawrence, the great chain of lakes, and the Mississippi, should be extinguished. They certainly embraced a compact and most magnificent expanse of territory. It was true that the Indians, the ancient and rightful possessors of the soil, had yet large tracts within these lines of demarcation; but, then, what was the power of the Indians to that of the United States? They *could* be compelled to evacuate their lands, and it was resolved that they *should*. It is totally beyond the limits of my work to follow out the progress of this most unequal and iniquitous strife; whoever wishes to see it fully and very fairly portrayed may do so in a work by an American—"Drake's Book of the North American Indians." I can here only simply state, that a more painful and interesting struggle never went on between the overwhelming numbers of the white men, armed with all the powers of science, but unrestrained by the genuine sentiments of religion, and the sons of the forest in their native simplicity. The Americans tell us that this apparently hard and arbitrary measure will eventually prove the most merciful. That the Indians cannot live by the side of white men; they are always quarrelling with and murdering them; and that is but too true; and the Indians in strains of the most indignant and pathetic eloquence, tell us the reason why. It is because the white invaders are eternally encroaching on their bounds, destroying their deer and their fish, and murdering the Indians too without ceremony. It is this recklessness of law and conscience, and the ever-rolling tide of white population westward, which raised up Tecumsch, and his companions, to combine the northern tribes in resistance. Brant assured the American commissioners, that unless they made the Ohio and the Muskingum their boundaries, there could be no peace with the Indians. These are the causes that called forth Black-Hauk from the Ouisconsin, with the Winnebagoes, the Sacs, and Foxes; that roused the Little-Turtle, with his Miamies, and many other chiefs and tribes, to inflict bloody retribution on their oppressors, but finally to be compelled themselves only the sooner to yield up their native lands. These are the causes that, operating to the most southern point of the United States, armed the great nations of the Seninoles, the Creeks, the Choctaws, Chickasaws, and Cherokees; and have made famous the exterminating campaigns of General Jackson, the bloody spots of Fort Mimms, Autossee, Tippecanoe, Talladega, Horse-shoe-bend, and other places of wholesale carnage. At Horse-shoe-bend, General Jackson says—" determined to exterminate them, I detached General Coffee with the mounted and nearly the whole of the Indian force, early in the morning (March 27, 1814), to cross the river about two miles below their encampment, and to surround the Bend, so that none of them should escape by crossing the river."

"At this place," says Drake, " the disconsolate tribes of the South had made a last great stand; and had a tolerably fortified camp. It was said they were 1000 strong." They were attacked on all sides; the fighting was kept up five hours; *five hundred and fifty-seven* were left dead on the peninsula, and a great number killed by the horsemen, in crossing the river. *It is believed that not more than twenty escaped!* "We continued," says the *brave General Jackson*, "to destroy many of them who had concealed themselves under the banks of the river, until we were prevented by the night!"

And what had these unfortunate tribes done, that they should be exterminated? Simply this:—When the United States remodelled the southern states, reducing the Carolinas and Georgia, and creating the new states of Alabama, Tenessee, and Mississippi, they stipulated, in behalf of Georgia, to extinguish all the Indian titles to lands in that State, "as soon as it could be done on peaceable terms." Georgia, impatient to seize on these lands, immediately employed all means to effect this object. When the Indians, in national council, would not sell their lands, they prevailed on a half-breed chief, M'Intosh, and a few others, of no character, to sell them; and, on this mock title, proceeded to expel the Indians. The Indians resisted; an alarm of rebellion was sounded through the States, and General Jackson sent to put it down. The Indians, as in all other quarters, were compelled to give way before the irresistible American power. We cannot go at length into this bloody history of oppression; but the character of the whole may be seen in that of a part.

But the most singular feature of the treatment of the Indians by the Americans is, that while they assign their irreclaimable nature as the necessary cause of their expelling or desiring to expel them from all the states east of the Mississippi, their most strenuous and most recent efforts have been directed against those numerous tribes, that were not only extensive but rapidly advancing in civilization. So far from refusing to adopt settled, orderly habits, the Choctaws, Chickasaws, Creeks, and Cherokees, were fast conforming both to the religion and the habits of the Americans. The Creeks were numbered in 1814 at 20,000. The Choctaws had some years ago 4041 warriors, and could not therefore be estimated at less than four times that number in total population, or 16,000. In 1810, the Cherokees consisted of 12,400 persons; in 1824 they had increased to 15,000. The Chickasaws reckoned some years ago 1000 warriors, making the tribe probably 4000.

The Creeks had twenty years ago cultivated lands, flocks, cattle, gardens, and different kinds of domestic manufactures. They were betaking themselves to manual trades and farming. "The Choctaws," Mr. Stuart says, "have both schools and churches. A few books have been published in the Choctaw language. In one part of their territory, where the population amounted to 5627 persons, there were above 11,000 cattle, about 4000 horses, 22,000 hogs, 530 spinning-wheels, 360 ploughs, etc." The missionaries speak in the highest terms of their steadiness and sobriety; and one of their chiefs had actually offered himself as a candidate for Congress. All these tribes are described as rapidly progressing in education and civilization, but the Cherokees present a character which cannot be contemplated without the liveliest admiration. These were the tribes amongst whom Adair spent so many years, about the middle of the last century, and whose customs and ideas as delineated by him, exhibited them as such fine material for cultivation. Since then the missionaries, and especially the Moravians, have been labouring with the most signal success. A school was opened in this tribe by them in 1804, in which vast numbers of Cherokee children have been educated. Such, indeed, have been the effects of cultivation on this fine people, that they have assumed all the habits and pursuits of civilized life. Their progress may be noted by observing the amount of their possessions in 1810, and again, fourteen years afterwards, in 1824. In the former year they had 3 schools, in the latter 18; in the former year 13 grist-mills, in the latter 36; in the former year 3 saw-mills, in the latter 13; in the former year 467 looms, in the latter 762; in the former year 1,600 spinning-wheels, in the latter 2,486; in the former year 30 wagons, in the latter 172; in the former year 500 ploughs, in the latter 2,923; in the former year 6,100 horses, in the latter 7,683; in the former year 19,500 head of cattle, in the latter 22,531; in the former year 19,600 swine, in the latter 46,732; in the former year 1,037 sheep, in the latter 2,546, and 430 goats; in the former year 49 smiths, in the latter 62 smiths' shops. Here is a steady and prosperous increase; testifying to no ordinary existence of industry, prudence, and good management amongst them, and bearing every promise of their becoming a most valuable portion of the community. They have, Mr. Stuart tells us, several public roads, fences, and turnpikes. The soil produces maize, cotton, tobacco, wheat, oats, indigo, sweet and Irish potatoes. The natives carry on a considerable trade with the adjoining states, and some of them export cotton to New Orleans. Apple and peach orchards are common, and gardens well cultivated. Butter and cheese are the produce of their dairies. There are many houses of public entertainment kept by the natives. Numerous and flourishing villages are seen in every section of the country. Cotton and woollen cloths and blankets are everywhere. Almost every family in the nation produces cotton for its own consumption. Nearly all the nation are native Cherokees.

" A printing-press has been established for several years; and a newspaper, written partly in English, and partly in Cherokee, has been successfully carried on. This paper, called the Cherokee Phœnix, is written entirely by a Cherokee, a young man under thirty. It had been surmised that he was assisted by a white man, on which he put the following notice in the paper :—" No white has anything to do with the management of our paper. No other person, whether white or red, besides the ostensible editor, has written, from the commencement of the Phœnix, half a column of matter which has appeared under the editorial head."*

The starting of this Indian newspaper by an Indian, is one of the most interesting facts in the history of civilization. In this language nothing had been written or printed. It had no written alphabet. This young Indian, already instructed by the missionaries in English literature, is inspired with a desire to open the world of knowledge to his countrymen in their vernacular tongue. There is no written character, no types. Those words familiar to all native ears, have no corresponding representation to the eye. These are gigantic difficulties to the young Indian, and as the Christian would call him, *savage* aspirant and patriot. But he determines to conquer them all. He travels into the eastern states. He invents letters which shall best express the sounds of his native tongue; he has types cut, and commences a newspaper. There is nothing like it in the history of

* Stuart's Three Years in North America, ii. 177.

nations in their first awakening from the long fixedness of wild life. This mighty engine, the press, once put in motion by native genius in the western wilderness, books are printed suitable to the nascent intelligence of the country. The Gospel of St. Matthew is translated into Cherokee, and printed at the native press. Hymns are also translated and printed. Christianity makes rapid strides. The pupils in the schools advance with admirable rapidity. There is a new and wonderful spirit abroad. Not only do the Indians throng to the churches to listen to the truths of life and immortality, but Indians themselves become diligent ministers, and open places of worship in the more remote and wild parts of the country. Even temperance societies are formed. Political principles develope themselves far in philosophical advance of our proud and learned England. The constitution of the native state contains admirable stamina; trial by jury prevails; and universal suffrage — a right, to this moment distrustfully withheld from the English people, is there freely granted, and judiciously exercised; every male citizen of eighteen years old having a vote in all public elections.

The whole growth and being, however, of this young Indian civilization is one of the most delightful and animating subjects of contemplation that ever came before the eye of the lover of his race. Here were these Indian savages, who had been two hundred years termed irreclaimable; whom it had been the custom only to use as the demons of carnage, as creatures fit only to carry the tomahawk and the bloody scalping-knife through Cherry-Valley, Gnadenhuetten, or Wyoming; and whom, that work done, it was declared, must be cast out from the face of civilized man, as the reproach of the past and the incubus of the future,—here were they gloriously vindicating themselves from those calumnies and wrongs, and assuming in the social system a most beautiful and novel position. It was a spectacle on which one would have thought the United States would hang with a proud delight, and point to as one of the most noble features of their vast and noble country. What did they do? They chose rather to give the lie to all their assertions, that they drove out the Indians because they were irreclaimable and un-amalgamable, and to shew to the world that they expelled them solely and simply because they scorned that one spot of the copper hue of the aborigines should mar the whiteness of their population. They compel us to exclaim with the indignant Abbé Raynal, "And are these the men whom both French and English have been conspiring to extirpate for a century past?" and suggest to us his identical answer,— "But perhaps they would be ashamed to live amongst such models of heroism and magnanimity!"

However, everything which irritation, contempt, political chicanery, and political power can effect, have been long zealously at work to drive these fine Nations out of their delightful country, and beyond the Mississippi; the boundary which American cupidity at present sets between itself and Indian extirpation. Spite of all those solemn declarations, by the venerable Washington and other great statesmen already quoted; spite of the most grave treaties, and especially one of July 2d, 1791, which says, "The United States solemnly guarantee to the Cherokee nation all their lands not hereby ceded," by a juggle betwixt the State of Georgia and Congress, the Cherokees have been virtually dispossessed of their country. From the period of the American independence to 1802, there had been a continual pressure on the Cherokees for their lands, and they had been induced by one means or another to cede to the States more than *two hundred millions* of acres. How reluctantly may be imagined, by the decided stand made by them in 1819, when they peremptorily protested that they would not sell another foot. That they needed all they had, for that they were becoming more and more agricultural, and progressing in civilization. One would have thought this not only a sufficient but a most satisfactory plea to a great nation by its people; but no, Georgia ceded to Congress territories for the formation of two new states, Alabama and Mississippi, and Georgia in part of payment receives the much desired lands of the Cherokees. Georgia, therefore, assumes the avowed language of despotism, and decrees by its senate, in the very face of the clear recognitions of Indian independence already quoted, *that the right of discovery and conquest was the title of the Europeans; that every foot of land in the United States was held by that title; that the right of the Indians was merely temporary; that they were tenants at will, removable at any moment, either by negotiation or force.* "It may be contended," says the Report of 1827, "with much plausibility, that there is in these claims more of force than of justice; *but they are claims which have been recognized and admitted by the whole civilized world*, AND IT IS UNQUESTIONABLY TRUE, THAT, UNDER SUCH CIRCUMSTANCES, FORCE *becomes* RIGHT !"*

* Stuart, ii. 173.

This language once adopted there needed no further argument about right or justice. Georgia took its stand upon Rob Roy's law,

> That he shall take who has the power,
> And he shall keep who can;

and it forthwith proceeded to act upon it. It decreed in 1828, that the territories of the Cherokees should be divided amongst the different counties of Georgia; that after June 1st, 1830, the Cherokees should become the subjects of Georgia; that all Cherokee laws should be abolished, and all Cherokees should be cut off from any benefit of the laws of the State—that is, that no Indian, *or descendent of one*, should be capable to act as a witness, or to be a party in any suit against a white man. The Cherokees refusing to abandon their hereditary soil without violence, an act was passed prohibiting any white man from residing in the Cherokee country without a permit from the governor, and on the authority of this, soldiers were marched into it, and *the missionaries carried off* on a Sunday. An attempt was made to crush that interesting newspaper press, by forcing away every white man assisting in the office. Forcible possession was taken of the Indian gold mines by Georgian laws, and the penal statutes exercised against the Indians who did not recognize their authority. The Cherokees, on these outrages, vehemently appealed to Congress. They said—"how far we have contributed to keep bright the chain of friendship which binds us to these United States, is within the reach of your knowledge; it is ours to maintain it, until, perhaps, the plaintive voice of an Indian from the south shall no more be heard within your walls of legislation. Our nation and our people may cease to exist, before another revolving year reassembles this august assembly of great men. We implore that our people may not be denounced as savages, unfit for the good neighbourhood guaranteed to them by treaty. We cannot better express the rights of our nation, than they are developed on the face of the document we herewith submit; and the desires of our nation, than to pray a faithful fulfilment of the promises made by its illustrious author through his secretary. Between the compulsive measures of Georgia and our destruction, we ask the interposition of your authority, and remembrance of the bond of perpetual peace pledged for our safety—the safety of the last fragments of some mighty nations, that have grazed for a while upon your civilization and prosperity, but which are now tottering on the brink of angry billows, whose waters have covered in oblivion other nations that were once happy, but are now no more.

" The schools where our children learn to read the Word of God; the churches where our people now sing to his praise, and where they are taught ' that of one blood he created all the nations of the earth;' the fields they have cleared, and the orchards they have planted; the houses they have built,—are dear to the Cherokees; and there they expect to live and to die, on the lands inherited from their fathers, as the firm friends of the people of these United States."

This is the very language which the simple people of all the new regions whither Europeans have penetrated, have been passionately and imploringly addressing for three hundred years, but in vain. We seem again to hear the supplicating voice of the people of

the Seven Reductions of Paraguay, addressed to the
expelling Spaniards and Portuguese. In each case it
was alike unavailing. The Congress returned them
a cool answer, advising the Cherokees to go over the
Mississippi, where "the soil should be theirs while
the trees grow, or the streams run." But they had
heard that language before, and they knew its value.
The State of Georgia had avowed the doctrine of
conquest, which silences all contracts and annuls all
promises. It is to the honour of the Supreme Court
of the United States that, on appeal to it, *it* annulled
the proceedings of Georgia, and recognised the rightful possession of the country by the Cherokees. But
what power shall restrain all those engines of irritation
and oppression, which white men know how to employ
against coloured ones, when they want their persons
or their lands. Nothing will be able to prevent the
final expatriation of these southern tribes: they must
pass the Mississippi till the white population is swelled
sufficiently to require them to cross the Missouri;
there will then remain but two barriers between them
and annihilation—the rocky mountains and the Pacific
Ocean. Whenever we hear now of those tribes, it is
of some fresh act of aggression against them—some
fresh expulsion of a portion of them—and of melancholy Indians moving off towards the western wilds.

Such is the condition to which the British and their
descendants have reduced the aboriginal inhabitants
of the vast regions of North America,—the finest race
of men that we have ever designated by the name
of savage.

> What term we savage? The untutored heart
> Of Nature's child is but a slumbering fire;
> Prompt at a breath, or passing touch to start
> Into quick flame, as quickly to retire;

Ready alike its pleasance to impart,
  Or scorch the hand which rudely wakes its ire :
Demon or child, as impulse may impel,
Warm in its love, but in its vengeance fell.

And these Columbian warriors to their strand
  Had welcomed Europe's sons, and rued it sore :—
Men with smooth tongues, but rudely armed hand;
  Fabling of peace, when meditating gore;
Who their foul deeds to veil, ceased not to brand
  The Indian name on every Christian shore.
What wonder, on such heads, their fury's flame
Burst, till its terrors gloomed their fairer fame?

For they were not a brutish race, unknowing
  Evil from good; their fervid souls embraced
With virtue's proudest homage, to o'erflowing,
  The mind's inviolate majesty.   The past
To them was not a darkness; but was glowing
  With splendour which all time had not o'ercast;
Streaming unbroken from creation's birth,
When God communed and walked with men on earth.

Stupid idolatry had never dimmed
  The Almighty image in their lucid thought.
To Him alone their zealous praise was hymned ;
  And hoar Tradition from her treasury brought
Glimpses of far-off times, in which were limned,
  His awful glory ;—and their prophets taught
Precepts sublime,—a solemn ritual given,
In clouds and thunder, to their sires from heaven.*

And in the boundless solitude which fills,
  Even as a mighty heart, their wild domains ;
In caves and glens of the unpeopled hills ;
  And the deep shadow that for ever reigns
Spirit-like, in their woods ; where, roaring, spills
  The giant cataract to the astounded plains,—
Nature, in her sublimest moods, had given
Not man's weak lore,—but a quick flash from heaven.

---

* See Adair's History of the American Indians.

Roaming in their free lives, by lake and stream;
  Beneath the splendour of their gorgeous sky;
Encamping, while shot down night's starry gleam,
  In piny glades, where their forefathers lie;
Voices would come, and breathing whispers seem
  To rouse within, the life which may not die;
Begetting valorous deeds, and thoughts intense,
And a wild gush of burning eloquence.

Such appeared to me ten years ago, when writing these stanzas, the character of the North American Indians; such it appears to me now. What an eternal disgrace to both British and Americans if this race of " mighty hunters before the Lord" shall, at the very moment when they shew themselves ready to lay down the bow and throw all the energies of their high temperament into civilized life, still be repelled and driven into the waste, or to annihilation. Their names and deeds and peculiar character are already become part of the literature of America; they will hereafter present to the imagination of posterity, one of the most singular and interesting features of history. Their government, the only known government of pure intellect; their grave councils; their singular eloquence; their stern fortitude; their wild figures in the war-dance; their " fleet foot" in the ancient forest; and all those customs, and quick keen thoughts which belong to them, and them alone, will for ever come before the poetic mind of every civilized people. Shall they remain, to look back to the days in which the very strength of their intellects and feelings made them repel the form of civilization, while they triumph in the universal diffusion of knowledge and Christian hope? or shall it continue to be said,

The vast, the ebbless, the engulphing tide
  Of the white population still rolls on !
And quailed has their romantic heart of pride,—
  The kingly spirit of the woods is gone.
Farther and farther do they wend to hide
  Their wasting strength ; to mourn their glory flown ;
And sigh to think how soon shall crowds pursue
Down the lone stream where glides the still canoe.

CHAPTER XXVI.

THE ENGLISH IN SOUTH AFRICA.

HAVING now quitted North America, let us sail southward. There we may direct our course east or west, we may pass Cape Horn, or the Cape of Good Hope, and enter the Pacific or the Indian Ocean, secure that on whatever shore we may touch, whether on continent or island, we shall find the Europeans oppressing the natives on their own soil, or having exterminated them, occupying their place. We shall find our own countrymen more than all others widely diffused and actively employed in the work of expulsion, moral corruption, and destruction of the aboriginal tribes. We talk of the atrocities of the Spaniards, of the deeds of Cortez and Pizarro, as though they were things of an ancient date, things gone by, things of the dark old days; and seem never for a moment to suspect that these dark old days were not a whit more

shocking than our own, or that our countrymen, protestant Englishmen of 1838, can be compared for a
moment to the Red-Cross Knights of Mexican and
Peruvian butcheries. If they cannot be compared, I
blush to say that it is because our infamy and crimes
are even more wholesale and inhuman than theirs.
Do the good people of England, who "sit at home at
ease," who build so many churches and chapels, and
flock to them in such numbers,—who spend about
170,000*l.* annually on Bibles, and more than half a
million annually in missions and other modes of civilizing and christianizing the heathen, and therefore
naturally flatter themselves that they are rapidly
bringing all the world to the true faith; do they or
can they know that at this very moment, wherever
their Bibles go, and wherever their missionaries are
labouring, their own government and their own countrymen are as industriously labouring also, to scatter
the most awful corruption of morals and principles
amongst the simple natives of all, to us, new countries?
that they are introducing diseases more pestilent than
the plague, more loathsome than the charnel-house
itself, and more deadly than the simoom of the tropical
deserts, that levels all before it? Do they know,
that even where their missionaries, like the prophets
of old, have gone before the armies of God, putting
the terrors of heathenism to flight, making a safe path
through the heart of the most dreadful deserts; dividing the very waters, and levelling the old mountains
of separation and of difficulty—

By Faith supported and by Freedom led,
A fruitful field amid the desert making,
And dwell secure where kings and priests were quaking,
And taught the waste to yield them wine and bread.—*Pringle.*

Do they know, that when these holy and victorious men have thus conquered all the difficulties they calculated upon, and seen, by God's blessing, the savage reclaimed, the idolater convinced, the wilderness turned into a garden, and arts, commerce, and refined life rising around them, a more terrible enemy has appeared in the shape of European, and chiefly English corruption? That out of that England—whence they had carried such beneficent gifts, such magnificent powers of good—have come pouring swarms of lawless vagabonds worse than the Spaniards, and worse than the Buccaneers of old, and have threatened all their works with destruction? Do they know that in South Africa, where Smidt, Vanderkemp, Philip, Read, Kay and others, have done such wonders, and raised the Hottentot, once pronounced the lowest of the human species, and the Caffre, not long since styled the most savage, into the most faithful Christians and most respectable men; and in those beautiful islands that Ellis and Williams have described in such paradisiacal colours, that roving crews of white men are carrying everywhere the most horrible demoralization, that every shape of European crime is by them exhibited to the astonished people—murder, debauchery, the most lawless violence in person and property; and that the liquid fire which, from many a gin-shop in our own great towns, burns out the industry, the providence, the moral sense, and the life of thousands of our own people, is there poured abroad by these monsters with the same fatal effect? Whoever does not know this, is ignorant of one of the most fearful and gigantic evils which beset the course of human improvement, and render abortive a vast amount of the funds so liberally supplied, and the labours so nobly undergone, in the cause of Christianity. Whoever does not know this, should moreover refer to the Parliamentary Report of 1837, on the Aboriginal Tribes.

The limits which I have devoted to a brief history of the treatment of these tribes by the European nations have been heavily pressed upon by the immense mass of our crimes and cruelties, and I must now necessarily make a hasty march across the scenes here alluded to; but enough will be seen to arouse astonishment, and indicate the necessity of counter-agencies of the most impulsive kind.

The Dutch have been applauded by various historians for the justice and mildness which they manifested towards the natives of their Cape colony. This may have been the case at their first entrance in 1652, and until they had purchased a certain quantity of land for their new settlement with a few bottles of brandy and some toys. It was their commercial policy, in the language of the old school of traders, to " first creep and then go." It was in the same assumed mildness that they insinuated themselves into the spice islands of India. Nothing, however, is more certain than that in about a century they had possessed themselves of all the Hottentot territories, and reduced the Hottentots themselves to a state of the most abject servitude. The Parliamentary Report just alluded to, describes the first governor, Van Riebeck, in the very first year of the settlement, looking over the mud-walls of his fortress on " the cattle of the natives, and wondering at the ways of Providence that could bestow such very fine gifts on heathens." It also presents us with two very characteristic extracts from his journal at this moment.

" December 13th, 1652.—To-day the Hottentots came with thousands of cattle and sheep close to our fort, so that their cattle nearly mixed with ours. We feel vexed to see so many fine head of cattle, and not to be able to buy to any considerable extent. If it had been indeed allowed, we had opportunity to-day to deprive them of 10,000 head, which, however, if we obtain orders to that effect, can be done at any time, and even more conveniently, because they will have greater confidence in us. With 150 men, 10,000 or 11,000 head of black cattle might be obtained without danger of losing one man; and many savages might be taken without resistance, in order to be sent as slaves to India, as they still always come to us unarmed.

" December 18.—To-day the Hottentots came again with thousands of cattle close to the fort. If no further trade is to be expected with them, what would it matter much to take at once 6,000 or 8,000 beasts from them? There is opportunity enough for it, as they are not strong in number, and very timid; and since not more than two or three men often graze a thousand cattle close to our cannon, who might be easily cut off, and as we perceive they place very great confidence in us, we allure them still with show of friendship to make them the more confident. It is vexatious to see so much cattle, so necessary for the refreshment of the Honourable Company's ships, of which it is not every day that any can be obtained by friendly trade."

It is sufficiently clear that no nice scruples of conscience withheld Governor Van Riebeck from laying hand on 10 or 11,000 cattle, or blowing a few of the keepers away with his cannons.

The system of oppression, adds the Report, thus began, never slackened till the Hottentot nation were cut off, and the small remnant left were reduced to abject bondage. From all the accounts we have seen respecting the Hottentot population, it could not have been less than 200,000, but at present they are said to be only 32,000 in number.

In 1702 the Governor and Council stated their inability to restrain the plunderings and outrages of the colonists upon the natives, on the plea that such an act would implicate and ruin half the colony ; and in 1798, Barrow, in his Travels in Southern Africa, thus describes their condition :—" Some of their villages might have been expected to remain in this remote and not very populous part of the colony. Not one, however, was to be found. There is not, in fact, in the whole district of Graaff Reynet, a single horde of independent Hottentots, and perhaps not a score of individuals who are not actually in the service of the Dutch. These weak people—the most helpless, and, in their present condition, perhaps the most wretched of the human race,—duped out of their possessions, their country, and their liberty, have entailed upon their miserable offspring a state of existence to which that of slavery might bear the comparison of happiness. It is a condition, however, not likely to continue to a very remote posterity. Their numbers, of late years, have been rapidly on the decline. It has generally been observed, that where Europeans have colonized, the less civilized nations have always dwindled away, and at length totally disappeared. . . . There is scarcely an instance of cruelty said to have been committed against the slaves in the West Indian islands, that could not find a parallel from the Dutch farmers towards the Hottentots in their service. Beating and cutting with thongs of the sea-cow (hippopotamus), or rhinoceros, are only gentle punishments; though those sort of whips, which they call *sjambocs*, are most horrid instruments, being tough, pliant, and heavy almost as lead. Firing small shot into the legs and thighs of a Hottentot is a punishment not unknown to some of the monsters who inhabit the neighbourhood of Camtoos. By a resolution of the old government, a boor was allowed to claim as his property, till the age of twenty-five, all the children of the Hottentots to whom he had given in their infancy a morsel of meat. At the expiration of this period, the odds are two to one that the slave is not emancipated; but should he be fortunate enough to escape at this period, the best part of his life has been spent in a profitless servitude, and he is turned adrift without any thing he can call his own, except the sheep-skin on his back."

These poor people were fed on the flesh of old ewes, or any animal that the boor expected to die of age; or, in default of that, a few quaggas or such game were killed for them. They were tied to a wagon-wheel and flogged dreadfully for slight offences; and when a master wanted to get rid of one, he was sometimes sent on an errand, followed on the road, and shot.* The cruelties, in fact, practised on the Hottentots by the Dutch boors were too shocking to be related. Maiming, murder, pursuing them like wild beasts, and shooting at them in the most wanton manner, were amongst them. Mr. Pringle stated that he had in his possession a journal of such

* Pringle's African Sketches, p. 380.

deeds, kept by a resident at so late a period as from 1806 to 1811, which consisted of forty-four pages of such crimes and cruelties, which were too horrible to describe. Such as we found them when the Cape finally became our possession, such they remained till 1828, when Dr. Philip published his " Researches in South Africa," which laying open this scene of barbarities, Mr. Fowell Buxton gave notice of a motion on the subject in Parliament. Sir George Murray, then Colonial Secretary, however, most honourably acceded to Mr. Buxton's proposition before such motion was submitted, and an Order in Council was accordingly issued, directing that the Hottentots should be admitted to all the rights, and placed on the same footing as the rest of his Majesty's free subjects in the colony. This transaction is highly honourable to the English government, and the result has been such as to shew the wisdom of such liberal measures. But before proceeding to notice the effect of this change upon the Hottentots, let us select as a specimen of the treatment they were subject to, even under our rule, the destruction of the last independent Hottentot kraal, as related by Pringle.

" Among the principal leaders of the Hottentot insurgents in their wars with the boors, were three brothers of the name of Stuurman. The manly bearing of Klaas, one of these brothers, is commemorated by Mr. Barrow, who was with the English General Vandeleur, near Algoa Bay, when this Hottentot chief came, with a large body of his countrymen, to claim the protection of the British." " We had little doubt," says Mr. Barrow, " that the greater number of the Hottentot men who were assembled at the bay, after receiving favourable accounts from their comrades of the treatment they experienced in the British service, would enter as volunteers into this corps; but what was to be done with the old people, the women andchildren? Klaas Stuurman found no difficulty in making provision for them. ' Restore,' said he, ' the country of which our fathers have been despoiled by the Dutch, and we have nothing more to ask.' I endeavoured to convince him," continues Mr. Barrow, " how little advantage they were likely to obtain from the possession of a country, without any other property, or the means of deriving a subsistence from it. But he had the better of the argument. ' We lived very contentedly,' said he, ' before these Dutch plunderers molested us; and why should we not do so again if left to ourselves? Has not the *Groot Baas* (the Great Master) given plenty of grass-roots, and berries, and grashoppers for our use? and, till the Dutch destroyed them, abundance of wild animals to hunt? and will they not turn and multiply when these destroyers are gone?'"

How uniform is the language of the uncivilized man wherever he has been driven from his ancient habits by the white invaders,—trust in the goodness of Providence, and regret for the plenty which he knew before they came. These words of Klaas Stuurman are almost the same as those of the American Indian Canassateego to the English at Lancaster in 1744.

But we are breaking our narrative. Klaas was killed in a buffalo hunt, and his brother David became the chief of the kraal. " The existence of this independent kraal gave great offence to the neighbouring boors. The most malignant calumnies were propagated against David Stuurman. The kraal was watched most jealously, and every possible occasion embraced of preferring complaints against the people, with a view of getting them rooted out, and reduced to the same state of servitude as the rest of their nation. For seven years no opportunity presented itself; but in 1810, when the colony was once more under the government of England, David Stuurman became outlawed in the following manner:—

" Two Hottentots belonging to this kraal, had engaged themselves for a certain period in the service of a neighbouring boor; who, when the term of their agreement expired, refused them permission to depart —a practice at that time very common, and much connived at by the local functionaries. The Hottentots, upon this, went off without permission, and returned to their village. The boor followed them thither, and demanded them back; but their chief, Stuurman, refused to surrender them. Stuurman was, in consequence, summoned by the landdrost Cuyler, to appear before him; but, apprehensive probably for his personal safety, he refused or delayed compliance. His arrest and the destruction of his kraal were determined upon. But as he was known to be a resolute man, and much beloved by his countrymen, it was considered hazardous to seize him by open force, and the following stratagem was resorted to:—

" A boor, named Cornelius Routenbach, a heemraad (one of the landdrost's council), had by some means gained Stuurman's confidence, and this man engaged to entrap him. On a certain day, accordingly, he sent an express to his friend Stuurman, stating that the Caffres had carried off a number of his

cattle, and requested him to hasten with the most
trusty of his followers to aid him in pursuit of the
robbers. The Hottentot chief and his party instantly
equipped themselves and set out. When they reached
Routenbach's residence, Stuurman was welcomed with
every demonstration of cordiality, and, with four of
his principal followers, was invited into the house. On
a signal given, the door was shut, and at the same
moment the landdrost (Major Cuyler), the field-com-
mandant Stoltz, and a crowd of boors, rushed upon
them from an inner apartment, and made them all
prisoners. The rest of the Hottentot party, who had
remained outside, perceiving that their captain and
comrade had been betrayed, immediately dispersed
themselves. The majority, returning to their kraal,
were, together with their families, distributed by the
landdrost into servitude to the neighbouring boors.
Some fled into Caffreland; and a few were, at the
earnest request of Dr. Vanderkemp, permitted to join
the missionary institution at Bethelsdorp. The chief
and his brother Boschman, with two other leaders of
the kraal, were sent off prisoners to Cape Town,
where, after undergoing their trial before the court of
justice, upon an accusation of resistance to the civil
authorities of the district, they were condemned to
work in irons for life, and sent to Robber Island to
be confined among other colonial convicts.

" Stuurman's kraal was eventually broken up, the
landdrost Cuyler *asked and obtained*, as a grant for
for himself (Naboth's vineyard again!), the lands the
Hottentots had occupied. *Moreover this functionary
kept in his own service, without any legal agreement*, some
of the children of the Stuurmans, until after the arrival
of the Commissioners of Inquiry in 1823.

" Stuurman and two of his comrades, after remaining some years prisoners in Robben Island, contrived
to escape, and effected their retreat through the whole
extent of the colony into Caffreland, a distance of
more than six hundred miles!   Impatient, however,
to return to his family, Stuurman, in the year 1816,
sent out a messenger to the missionary, Mr. Read,
from whom he had formerly experienced kindness,
entreating him to endeavour to procure permission for
him to return in peace.   Mr. Read, as he himself informed me, made application on his behalf to the landdrost Cuyler,—but without avail.   That magistrate
recommended that he should remain where he was.
Three years afterwards, the unhappy exile ventured
to return into the colony without permission.   But he
was not long in being discovered and apprehended,
and once more sent a prisoner to Cape Town, where
he was kept in close confinement till the year 1823,
when he was finally transported as a convict to New
South Wales.   What became of Boschman, the third
brother, I never learned.   Such was the fate of the
last Hottentot chief who attempted to stand up for the
rights of his country."

Mr. Pringle adds, that this statement, having been
published by him in England in 1826, the benevolent
General Bourke, then Lieutenant-Governor at the
Cape, wrote to the Governor of New South Wales,
and obtained some alleviation of the hardships of his
lot for Stuurman; that, in 1829, the children of
Stuurman, through the aid of Mr. Bannister, presented
a memorial to Sir Lowry Cole, then governor at the
Cape, for their father's recall, but in vain; but that, in
1831, General Bourke, being himself Governor of

New South Wales, obtained an order for his liberation ; but, ere it arrived, 'the last chief of the Hottentots' had been released by death."

Such was the treatment of the Hottentots under the Dutch and under the English; such were the barbarities and ruthless oppressions exercised on them till the passing of the 50th Ordinance by Acting-Governor Bourke in 1828, and its confirmation by the Order in Council in 1829, for their liberation. This act, so honourable to the British government, became equally honourable to the Hottentots, by their conduct on their freedom, and presents another most important proof that political justice is political wisdom. After the clamour of the interested had subsided, and after a vain attempt to reverse this ordinance, a grand experiment in legislation was made. A tract of country was granted to the Hottentots; they were placed on the frontiers with arms in their hands, to defend themselves, if necessary, from the Caffres ; and they were told that they must now show whether they were capable of maintaining themselves as a people, in peace, civil order, and independence. Most nobly did they vindicate their national character from all the calumnies of indolence and imbecility that had been cast upon them,—most amply justify the confidence reposed in them! "The spot selected," says Pringle, "for the experiment, was a tract of wild country, from which the Caffre chief, Makomo, had been expelled a short time before. It is a sort of irregular basin, surrounded on all sides by lofty and majestic mountains, from the numerous kloofs of which six or seven fine streams are poured down the subsidiary dells into the central valley. These rivulets, bearing the euphonic Caffre names of Camalu, Zebenzi, Umtóka, Mankazána, Umtúava, and Quonci, unite to form the Kat River, which finds its way through the mountain barrier by a stupendous *poort*, or pass, a little above Fort Beaufort.   Within this mountain-basin, which from its great command of the means of irrigation is peculiarly well adapted for a dense population, it was resolved to fix the Hottentot settlement."

It was in the middle of the winter when the settlement was located.   Numbers flocked in from all quarters; some possessing a few cattle, but far the greater numbers possessing nothing but their hands to work with.   They asked Captain Stockenstrom, their great friend, the lieutenant-governor of the frontier, and at whose suggestion this experiment was made, what they were to do, and how they were to subsist. He told them, "if they were not able to cultivate the ground with their fingers, they need not have come there."   Government, even under such rigorous circumstances, gave them no aid whatever except the gift of fire-arms, and some very small portion of seed-corn to the most destitute, to keep them from thieving. Yet, even thus tried, the Hottentots, who had been termed the fag-end of mankind, did not quail or despair.   In the words of Mr. Fairbairn, the friend of Pringle, "The Hottentot, escaped from bonds, stood erect on his new territory; and the feeling of being restored to the level of humanity and the simple rights of nature, softened and enlarged his heart, and diffused vigour through every limb!"   They dug up roots and wild bulbs for food, and persisted without a murmur, labouring surprisingly, with the most wretched implements, and those who had cattle assisting those who

had nothing, to the utmost of their ability. All
winter the Caffres, from whom this location had been
unjustly wrested by the English, attacked them with
a fury only exceeded by their hope of now regaining
their territory from mere Hottentots, thus newly
armed, and in so wretched a condition. But, though
harassed night and day, and never, for a moment,
safe in their sleep, they not only repelled the as-
sailants, but continued to cultivate their grounds with
prodigious energy. They had to form dams across
the river, as stated by Mr. Read, before the Parliamentary committee, and water-courses, sometimes to
the depth of ten, twelve, and fourteen feet, and that
sometimes through solid rocks, and with very sorry
pickaxes, iron crows, and spades; and few of them.
These works, says Mr. Read, have excited the admiration of visitors, as well as the roads, which they had
to cut to a considerable height on the sides of the
mountains.

At first, from the doubts of colonists as to the propriety of entrusting fire-arms, and so much self-government to these newly liberated men, it was proposed
that a certain portion of the Dutch and English should
be mixed with them. The Hottentots, who felt this
want of confidence keenly, begged and prayed that
they might be trusted for two years; and Captain
Stockenstrom said to them, " Then show to the world
that you can work as well as others, and that without
the whip." Such indeed was their diligence, that the
very next summer they had abundance of vegetables,
and a plentiful harvest. In the second year they not
only supported themselves, but disposed of 30,000 lbs.
of barley for the troops, besides carrying other pro-

duce to market at Graham's Town. Their enemies the Caffres made peace with them, and those of their own race flocked in so rapidly that they were soon 4,000 in number, seven hundred of whom were armed with muskets. The settlement was left without any magistrate, or officers, except the native field-cornets, and heads of parties appointed by Captain Stockenstrom, yet they continued perfectly orderly. Nay, they were not satisfied without possessing the means of both religious and other instruction. Within a few months after their establishment, they sent for Mr. Read, the missionary, and Mr. Thompson was also appointed Dutch minister amongst them. They established temperance societies, and schools. Mr. Read says, that during the four years and a half that he was there, they had established seven schools for the larger children, and one school of industry, besides five infant schools. And Captain Stockenstrom, writing to Mr. Pringle in 1833, says, " So eager are they for instruction, that when better teachers cannot be obtained, if they find any person that can merely spell, they get him to teach the rest the little he knows. They travel considerable distances to attend divine service regularly, and their spiritual guides speak with delight of the fruits of their labours. " Nowhere have temperance societies been half so much encouraged as among this people, formerly so prone to intemperance; and they have of their own account petitioned the government that their grants of land may contain a prohibition against the establishment of canteens, or brandy-houses. They have repulsed the Caffres on every side on which they have been attacked, and are now upon the best terms with that people. They pay every tax

like the rest of the inhabitants. They have cost the
government nothing except a little ammunition for their
defence, about fifty bushels of maize, and a similar
quantity of oats for seed-corn, and the annual stipend
for their minister. *They have rendered the Kat river by
far the safest part of the frontier; and the same plan
followed up on a more extensive scale would soon enable
government to withdraw the troops altogether.*" In 1834,
Captain Bradford found that they had subscribed
499*l.* to build a new church, and had also proposed to
lay the foundation of another.   In 1833 they paid in
taxes 2,300 rix-dollars, and their settlement was in a
most flourishing condition.   Dr. Philip, before the
Parliamentary Committee of 1837, stated that their
schools were in admirable order; their infant schools
quite equal to anything to be seen in England; and
the Committee closed its evidence on this remarkable
settlement with this striking opinion: "*Had it, indeed,
depended on the Hottentots, we believe the frontier would
have been spared the outrages from which they as well as
others have suffered.*"

Of two things in this very interesting relation, we
hardly know which is the most surprising—the avidity
with which a people long held in the basest thraldom
grasp at knowledge and civil life, or the blind selfishness of Englishmen, who, in the face of such splendid
scenes as these, persist in oppression and violence.
How easy does it seem to do good! How beautiful
are the results of justice and liberality! How glorious
and how profitable too, beyond all use of whips, and
chains, and muskets, are treating our fellow men with
gentleness and kindness—and yet after this came the
Caffre commandoes and the Caffre war!

Of the same, or a kindred race with the Hottentots, are the Bosjesmen, or Bushmen, and the Griquas; their treatment, except that they could not be made slaves of, has been the same. The same injustice, the same lawlessness, the same hostile irritation, have been practised towards them by the Dutch and English as towards the Hottentots. The bushmen, in fact, were Hottentots, who, disdaining slavery and resenting the usurpations of the Europeans on their lands, took arms, endeavoured to repel their aggressors, and finding that impracticable, fled to the woods and the mountains; others, from time to time escaping from intolerable thraldom, joined them. These bushmen carried on a predatory warfare from their fastnesses with the oppressors of their race, and were in return hunted as wild beasts. Commandoes, a sort of military battu, were set on foot against them. Every one knows what a battu for game is. The inhabitants of a district assemble at the command of an officer, civil or military, to clear the country of wild beasts. They take in a vast circle, beating up the bushes and thickets, while they gradually contract the circle, till the whole multitude find themselves inclosing a small area filled with the whole bestial population of the neighbourhood, on which they make a simultaneous attack, and slaughter them in one promiscuous mass. A commando is a very similar thing, except that in it not only the bestial population of the country, but the human too, are slaughtered by the inhuman. These commandoes, though they have only acquired at the Cape a modern notoriety, have been used from the first day of discovery. They were common in the Spanish and Portuguese colonies, and under the same name, as may be seen in almost any of the Spanish and Portuguese historians of the West Indies and South America.

The manner in which these commandoes were conducted at the Cape was described, before the Parliamentary Committee of 1837,* to be a joint assemblage of burghers and military force for the purpose of enforcing restitution of cattle. Sir Lowry Cole authorized in 1833 any field-cornet, or deputy field-cornet, to whom a boor may complain, to send a party of soldiers on the track and recover the cattle. These persons are often of the most indifferent class of society. It is the interest of these men, as much as that of the boors, to make inroads into the country of the Griquas, Bushmen, or Caffres, and sweep off droves of cattle. These people can call on everybody to aid and assist, and away goes the troop. The moment the Caffres perceive these licensed marauders approaching their kraal, they collect their cattle as fast as they can, and drive them off towards the woods. The English pursue—they surround them if possible—they fall on them; the Caffres, or whoever they are, defend their property—their only subsistence, indeed; then ensues bloodshed and devastation. The cattle are driven off; the calves left behind to perish; the women and children, the whole tribe, are thrown into a state of absolute famine. Besides these " joint assemblages of burghers and military force," there are parties entirely military sent on the same errand ; and to such a pitch of vengeance have the parties arrived that whole districts have been laid in flames and reduced to utter deserts. Such has been our system—

* See pp. 38—42 of Ball's edit.

the system of us humane and virtuous English, till
1837! To these dreadful and wicked expeditions
there was no end, and but little cessation, for the
boors were continually going over the boundaries into
the countries of Bushmen, Caffres, or Guiquas, just
as they pleased. They went over with vast herds and
eat them up. "In 1834 there were said to be," says
the Report, "about 1,500 boors on the other side of
the Orange River, and for the most part in the Griqua
country. Of these there were 700 boors for several
months during that year in the district of Philipolis
alone, with at least 700,000 sheep, cattle, and horses.
Besides destroying the pastures of the people, in
many instances their corn-fields were destroyed by
them, and in some instances they took possession of
their houses. It was contended that the evil could
not be remedied; that the state of the country was
such that the boors could not be stopped; and yet an
enormous body of military was kept up on the frontiers at a ruinous expense to this country. The last
Caffre war, brought on entirely by this system of
aggression, by these commandoes, and the reprisals
generated by them, cost this country 500,000l., and
put a stop to trade and the sale of produce to the
value of 300,000l. more!" Yet the success of a different policy was before the colony, in the case of the
Kat River Hottentots, and that so splendid a one,
that the Report says, had it been attended to and followed out, all these outrages might have been spared.

Such are commandoes.—So far as they related to
the Bushmen, the following facts are sufficiently indicative. In 1774 an order was issued for the extirpation of the Bushmen, and three commandoes were

sent to execute it. In 1795, the Earl of Macartney, by proclamation, authorized the landdrosts and magistrates to take the field against the Bushmen, in such expeditions; and Mr. Maynier gave in evidence, that in consequence, when he was landdrost of Graaf Reynet, parties of from 200 to 300 boors were sent out, who killed many hundreds of Bushmen, *chiefly women and children*, the men escaping; and the children too young to carry off for slaves had their brains knocked out against the rocks.* Col. Collins, in his tour to the north-eastern boundary in 1809, says one man told him that within a period of six years parties under his orders had killed or taken 3,200 of these unfortunate creatures; and another, that the actions in which he had been engaged had destroyed 2,700. That the total extinction of the Bushmen race was confidently hoped for, but sufficient force for the purpose could not be raised. But Dr. Philips' evidence, presented in a memorial to government in 1834, may well conclude these horrible details of the deeds of our countrymen and colonists.

"A few years ago, we had 1,800 Boschmen belonging to two missionary institutions, among that people in the country between the Snewbergen and the Orange River, a country comprehending 42,000 square miles; and had we been able to treble the number of our missionary stations over that district, we might have had 5,000 of that people under instruction. In 1832 I spent seventeen days in that country, travelling over it in different directions. I then found the country occupied by the boors, and the Boschmen population had disappeared, with the exception of

* Report, 1837, p. 32, 33.

those that had been brought up from infancy in the
service of the boors. In the whole of my journey,
during the seventeen days I was in the country, I met
with two men and one woman only of the free inhabitants, who had escaped the effects of the commando
system, and they were travelling by night, and concealing themselves by day, to escape being shot like
wild beasts. Their tale was a lamentable one: their
children had been taken from them by the boors, and
they were wandering about in this manner from place
to place, in the hope of finding out where they were,
and of getting a sight of them."

I have glanced at the treatment of the Griquas in
the last page but one. Those people were the offspring of colonists by Hottentot women, who finding
themselves treated as an inferior race by their kinsmen
of European blood, and prevented from acquiring property in land, or any fixed property, fled from con-
tumely and oppression to the native tribes.

Amongst the vast mass of colonial crime, that of the
treatment of the half-breed race by their European
fathers constitutes no small portion. Everywhere this
unfortunate race has been treated alike; in every
quarter of the globe, and by every European people.
In Spanish America it was the civil disqualification
and social degradation of this race that brought on the
revolution, and the loss of those vast regions to the
mother country. In our East Indies, what thousands
upon thousands of coloured children their white fathers
have coolly abandoned; and while they have themselves returned to England with enormous fortunes,
and to establish new families to enjoy them, have left
there their coloured offspring to a situation the most

painful and degrading—a position of perpetual contempt and political degradation. In our West Indies how many thousands of their own children have been sold by their white fathers, in the slave-market, or been made to swelter under the lash on their own plantations. Here, in South Africa, this class of descendents were driven from civilization to the woods and the savages, and a miserable and savage race they became. It was not till 1800 that any attempts were made to reclaim them, and then it was no parental or kindred feeling on the part of the colonists that urged it; it was attempted by the missionaries, who, as in every distant scene of our crimes, have stepped in between us and the just vengeance of heaven, between us and the political punishment of our own absurd and wicked policy, between us and the miserable natives. Mr. Anderson, their first missionary, found them "a herd of wandering and naked savages, subsisting by plunder and the chase. Their bodies were daubed with red paint, their heads loaded with grease and shining powder, with no covering but the filthy caross over their shoulders. Without knowledge, without morals, or any traces of civilization, they were wholly abandoned to witchcraft, drunkenness, licentiousness, and all the consequences which arise from the unchecked growth of such vices. With his fellow-labourer, Mr. Kramer, Mr. Anderson wandered about with them five years and a half, exposed to all the dangers and privations inseparable from such a state of society, before they could induce them to locate where they are now settled."

With one exception, they had not one thread of European clothing amongst them. They were in the habit of plundering one another, and saw no manner of evil in this, or any of their actions. Violent deaths were common. Their usual manner of living was truly disgusting, and they were void of shame. They were at the most violent enmity with the Bushmen, and treated them on all occasions where they could, with the utmost barbarity. So might these people, wretched victims of European vice and contempt of all laws, human or divine, have remained, had not the missionaries, by incredible labours and patience, won their good will. They have now reduced them to settled and agricultural life; brought them to live in the most perfect harmony with the Bushmen; and in 1819 such was their altered condition that a fair was established at Beaufort for the mutual benefit of them and the colonists, at which business was done to the amount of 27,000 rix dollars; and on the goods sold to the Griquas, the colonists realized a profit of from 200 to 500 per cent!

Let our profound statesmen, who go on from generation to generation fighting and maintaining armies, and issuing commandoes, look at this, and see how infinitely simple men, with but one principle of action to guide them—Christianity—outdo them in their own profession. They are your missionaries, after all the boast and pride of statesmanship, who have ever yet hit upon the only true and sound policy even in a worldly point of view;* who, when the profound statesmen have turned men into miserable and exasperated savages, are obliged to go and again turn them from savages to men,—who, when these wise

* William Penn is the only exception, and he was a preacher and in some degree a missionary.

scatesmen have spent their country's money by millions and shed blood by oceans, and find troubles and frontier wars, and frightful and fire-blackened deserts only growing around—go, and by a smile and a shake of the hand, restore peace, replace these deserts by gardens and green fields, and hamlets of cheerful people; and instead of involving you in debt, find you a market with 200 to 500 per cent. profit!

" It was apparent," says Captain Stockenstrom, " to every man, that if it had not been for the influence which the missionaries had gained over the Griquas we should have had the whole nation down upon us." What a humiliation to the pride of political science, to the pride of so many *soi-disant* statesmen, that with so many ages of experience to refer to, and with such stupendous powers as European statesmen have now in their hands, a few simple preachers should still have to shew them the real philosophy of government, and to rescue them from the blundering and ruinous positions in which they have continually placed themselves with uneducated nations! " If these Griquas had come down upon us," continues Captain Stockenstrom, " we had no force to arrest them; and I have been informed, that since I left the colony, the government has been able to enter into a sort of treaty with the chief Waterboer, of a most beneficial nature to the Corannas and Griquas themselves, as well as to the safety of the northern frontier."

If noble statesmen wish to hear the true secret of good and prosperous government, they have only to listen to this chief, " who boasts," to use the words of the Parliamentary Report, " no higher ancestry than that of the Hottentot and the Bushman."—" I feel that

I am bound to govern my people by Christian principles. The world knows by experience, and I know in my small way, and I know also from my Bible, that the government which is not founded on the principles of the Bible must come to nothing. When governments lose sight of the principles of the Bible, partiality, injustice, oppression and cruelty prevail, and then suspicion, want of confidence, jealousy, hatred, revolt, and destruction succeed. Therefore I hope it will ever be my study, that the Bible should form the foundation of every principle of my government; then I and my people will have a standard to which we can appeal, which is clear, and comprehensive, and satisfactory, and by which we shall all be tried, and have our condition determined in the day of judgment. The relation in which I stand to my people as their chief, as their leader, binds me, by all that is sacred and dear, to seek their welfare and promote their happiness; and by what means shall I be able to do this? This I shall best be able to do by alluding to the principles of the Bible. Would governors and governments act upon the simple principle by which we are bound to act as individuals, that is, to do as we would be done by, all would be well. I hope, by the principles of the gospel, the morals of my people will continue to improve; and it shall be my endeavour, in humble dependence on the Divine blessing, that those principles shall lose none of their force by my example. Sound education I know will civilize them, make them wise, useful, powerful, and secure amongst their neighbours; and the better they are educated, the more clearly will they see that the principles of the Bible are the best principles for the government of individuals, of families, of tribes, and of nations."

Not only governors but philosophers may listen to this African chief with advantage. Some splendid reputations have been made in Europe by merely taking up some one great principle of the Christian code and vaunting it as a wonderful discovery. A thousand such principles are scattered through the Bible, and the greatest philosophers of all, as well as the profoundest statesmen, are they who are contented to look for them there, and in simple sincerity to adopt them.

CHAPTER XXVII.

THE ENGLISH IN SOUTH AFRICA,—CONTINUED.

THE details of our barbarisms toward the Hottentots, Bushmen, and Griquas, in the last chapter, are surely enough at this late period of the world to make the wise blush and the humane weep, yet what are they compared to our atrocities towards the Caffres? These are, as described by Pringle, a remarkably fine race of people. "They a are tall, athletic, and handsome race of men, with features often approaching to the European, or Asiatic model, and, excepting their woolly hair, exhibiting few of the peculiarities of the negro race. Their colour is a clear dark brown. Their address is frank, cheerful, and manly. Their government is patriarchal, and the privileges of rank are carefully maintained by the chieftains. Their principal wealth and means of subsistence consist in their numerous herds of cattle. The females also cultivate pretty extensively maize, millet, water-melons, and a few other esculents; but they are decidedly a nation of *herdsmen*—war, hunting, barter, and agriculture being only occasional occupations.

" In their customs and traditions there seem to be indications of their having sprung, at some remote period, from a people of much higher civilization than is now exhibited by any of the tribes of Southern Africa; whilst the rite of circumcision, universally practised among them without any vestige of Islamism, and several other traditionary customs greatly resembling the Levitical rules of purification, would seem to indicate some former connexion with a people of Arabian, Hebrew, or perhaps, Abyssinian lineage. Nothing like a regular system of idolatry exists among them; but we find some traces of belief of a Supreme Being, as well as of inferior spirits, and sundry superstitious usages that look like the shattered wrecks of ancient religious institutions."*

One of the first of this race, whom this amiable and excellent man encountered in South Africa, was at Bethelsdorp, the missionary settlement, and under the following circumstances :—" A Caffre woman, accompanied by a little girl of eight or ten years of age, and having an infant strapped on her back above her mantle of tanned bullock's hide. . She was in the custody of a black constable, who stated that she was one of a number of female Caffres who had been made prisoners

* African Sketches, p. 414.

by order of the Commandant on the frontier for crossing the line of demarcation without permission, and
that they were now to be *given out in servitude* among
the white inhabitants of this district. While the constable was delivering his message, the Caffre woman
looked at him and us with keen and intelligent glances,
and though she very imperfectly understood his language, she appeared fully to comprehend its import.
When he had finished she stepped forward, drew her
figure up to its full height, extended her right arm,
and commenced a speech in her native language, the
Amakosa dialect. Though I did not understand a
single word that she uttered, I have seldom been more
struck with surprise and admiration. The language,
to which she appeared to give full and forcible intona-
tion, was highly musical and sonorous; her gestures
were natural, graceful, and impressive, and her dark
eyes and handsome bronze countenance were full of
eloquent expression. Sometimes she pointed back to
her own country, and then to her children. Sometimes she raised her tones aloud, and shook her
clenched hand, as if she denounced our injustice, and
threatened us with the vengeance of her tribe. Then,
again, she would melt into tears, as if imploring cle-
mency, and mourning for her helpless little ones.
Some of the villagers who gathered round, being
whole or half Caffres, interpreted her speech to the
missionary, but he could do nothing to alter her destination, and could only return kind words to console
her. For my part, I was not a little struck by the
scene, and could not help beginning to suspect that
my European countrymen, who thus made captives of
harmless women and children, were, in reality, greater

barbarians than the savage natives of Caffraria." He
had soon only too ample proofs of the correctness of
his surmise. This fine race of people, who strikingly
resemble the North American Indians in their character, their eloquence, their peculiar customs and traditions of Asiatic origin, have exactly resembled them
in their fate. They have been driven out of their
lands by the Europeans, and massacred by thousands
when they have resented the invasion.

The Hottentots were exterminated, or reduced to
thraldom, and the European colonists then came in
contact with the Caffres, who were numerous and
warlike, resisted aggression with greater effect, but
still found themselves unable with their light assagais
to contend with fire-arms, and were perpetually driven
backwards with shocking carnage, and with circumstances of violent oppression which it is impossible to
read of without the strongest indignation. Up to 1778
the Camtoos River had been considered the limit of
the colony on that side; but at that period the Dutch
governor, Van Plattenburgh, says Pringle, "in the
course of an extensive tour into the interior, finding
great numbers of colonists occupying tracts beyond
the frontier, instead of recalling them within the legal
limits, he extended the boundary (according to the
ordinary practice of Cape governors before and since),
adding, by a stroke of his pen, about 30,000 square
miles to the colonial territory." The Great Fish River
now became the boundary; which Lord Macartney in
1798, claiming all that Van Plattenburgh had so summarily claimed, confirmed.

It is singular how uniform are the policy and the
modes of seizing upon native possessions by Euro-

peans. In America we have seen how continually, when the bulk of the people, or the legitimate chiefs, would not cede territory, the whites made a mock purchase from somebody who had no right whatever to sell, and on that title proceeded to drive out the real owners. In this case, Plattenburgh, to give a colour of justice to his claim, sent out Colonel Gordon in search of Caffres as far as the Keiskamma, who conducted a *few* to the governor, who consented that the Great Fish River *should* be the boundary. The real chief, Jalumba, it appears, however, had not been consulted; but the colonists the next year *reminded* him of the recent treaty with his tribe, and requested him to evacuate that territory. Jalumba refused—a commando was assembled—the *intruders*, in colonial phrase, but the real and actual owners, were expelled: Jalumba's own son Dlodlo was killed, and 5,200 head of cattle driven off. This was certainly a wholesale beginning of plunder and bloodshed; but, says the same author, "this was not the worst—Jalumba and his clan were destroyed by a most infamous act of treachery and murder; the details of which may be found in Thompson and Kay."

It was on such a title as this, that Lord Macartney claimed this tract of country for the English in 1797, the Cape having been conquered by us. It does not appear, however, that any very vigorous measures were employed for expelling the natives from this region till 1811, when it was resolved to drive them out of it, and a large military and burgher force under Col. Graham was sent out for that purpose. The expulsion was effected with the most savage rigour. This *clearing* took up about a year. In the course

of it Landdrost Stokenstrom lost his life by the
Caffres, and T'Congo, the father of the chiefs Pato,
Kamo, and T'Congo, was butchered by a party of
boors while he lay on his mat dying of a mortal disease.
The Caffres begged to be allowed to wait to cut their
crops of maize and millet, nearly ripe, arguing that.
the loss of them would subject them to a whole year
of famine;—not a day was allowed them.   They were
driven out with sword and musket.   Men and women,
wherever found, were promiscuously shot, though
they offered no resistance.   "Women," says Lieutenant Hart, whose journal of these transactions is
quoted by Pringle, "were killed *unintentionally*, because the boors could not distinguish them from men
among the bushes, and so, to make sure work, they
shot *all* they could reach."   They were very anxious
to seize Islambi, a chief who had actively opposed
them, for they had been, like Plattenburgh, treating
with *one* chief, Gaika, for cession of claims which he
frankly told them belonged to *several* quite independent of him.   On this subject, occurs this entry in
Mr. Hart's journal:—" Sunday, Jan. 12, 1812.   At
noon, Commandant Stollz went out with two companies to look for Slambi (Islambi), but saw nothing of
him.   *They met only with a few Caffres, men·and
women, most of whom they shot.*   About sunset, five
Caffres were seen at a distance, one of whom came
to the camp with a message from Slambi's son, requesting permission to wait till the harvest was over,
and that then he (if his father would not), would go
over the Great Fish River quietly.   This messenger
would not give any information respecting Slambi,
but said he did not know where he was.   However,

*after having been put in irons, and fastened to a wheel
with a riem* (leathern thong) *about his neck,* he said,
that if the commando went with him, before daylight
he would bring them upon 200 Caffres, all asleep."
Having thus treated a messenger from a free chief,
and attempted to compel him to betray his master,
away went this commando on the agreeable errand of
surprising and murdering 200 innocent people in their
sleep. But the messenger was made of much better
stuff than the English. He led them about on a wild-
goose chase for three days, when finding nothing they
returned, and brought him back too.

Parties of troops were employed for several weeks
in burning down the huts and hamlets of the natives,
and destroying their fields of maize, by trampling
them down with large herds of cattle, and at length
the Caffres were forced over the Great Fish River, to
the number of 30,000 souls, leaving behind them a
large portion of their cattle, captured by the troops;
many of their comrades and females, shot in the
thickets, and not a few of the old and diseased, whom
they were unable to carry along with them, to perish
of hunger, or become a prey to the hyenas.

" The results of this war of 1811 were," says the
Parliamentary Report of 1837, " first, a succession of
new wars, not less expensive, and more sanguinary
than the former; second, the loss of thousands of good
labourers to the colonists (and this testimony as to
the actual service done by Caffre labourers, comprises
the strong opinion of Major Dundas, when landdrost
in 1827, as to their good dispositions, and that of
Colonel Wade to the same effect); and thirdly, the
checking of civilization and trade with the interior for
a period of twelve years.

The gain was some hundreds of thousands of acres of land, which might have been bought from the natives for comparatively a trifle.

In 1817, those negotiations which had been entered into with Gaika, as if he were the sole and paramount king of Caffreland, were renewed by the governor, Lord Charles Somerset. Other chiefs were present, particularly Islambi, but no notice was taken of them; it was resolved, that Gaika was the paramount chief, and that he should be selected as the champion of the frontiers against his countrymen. Accordingly, we hear, as was to be expected, that the very next year a formidable confederacy was entered into amongst the native chiefs against this Gaika. In the league against him, and for the protection of their country, were his own uncles, Islambi and Jaluhsa, Habanna, Makanna, young Kongo, chief of the Gunuquebi, and Hintza, the principal chief of the Amakosa, to whom in rank Gaika was only secondary. To support their adopted puppet, Col. Brereton was ordered to march into Caffreland. The inhabitants were attacked in their hamlets, plundered of their cattle, and slaughtered or driven into the woods; 23,000 cattle carried off, 9000 of which were given to Gaika to reimburse him for his losses.

Retaliation was the consequence. The Caffres soon poured into the colony in numerous bodies eager for revenge. The frontier districts were overrun; several military posts were seized; parties of British troops and patroles cut off; the boors were driven from the Zureveld, and Enon plundered and burnt.

This and the other efforts of the outraged Caffres, which were now made to avenge their injuries and.

check the despoiling course of the English, were organized under the influence and counsel of Makanna, a prophet who assumed the sacred character to combine and rouse his countrymen to overturn their oppressors: for not knowing the vast resources of the English, he fondly deemed that if they could vanquish those at the Cape they should be freed from their power; " and then," said he, " we will sit down and eat honey !"

In this, as in so many other particulars, the Caffres resemble the American Indians. Scarcely a confederacy amongst those which have appeared for the purpose of resisting the aggressions on the Indians but have been inspired and led on by prophets, as the brother of Tecumseh, amongst the Shawanees; the son of Black-Hauk, Wabokieshiek, amongst the Sacs; Monohoe, and others, amongst the Creeks who fell at the bloody battle of Horse-shoe-bend.

Makanna had by his talents and pretences raised himself from the common herd to the rank of a chief, and soon gained complete ascendency over all the chiefs except Gaika, to whom he was opposed as the ally of the English. He went amongst the missionaries and acquired so much knowledge of Christianity as served him to build a certain motley creed upon, by which he mystified and awed the common people. After Col. Brereton's devastations he roused up his countrymen to a simultaneous attack upon Graham's Town. He and Dushani, the son of Islambi, mustered their exasperated hosts to the number of nine or ten thousand in the forests of the Great Fish River, and one morning at the break of day these infuriated troops were seen rushing down from the mountains near Graham's Town to assault it. A bloody conflict ensued: the Caffres, inflamed by their wrongs and the eloquence of Makanna, fought desperately; but they were mown down by the European artillery, fourteen hundred of their warriors were left on the field, and the rest fled to the hills and woods. The whole burgher militia of the colony were called out to pursue them, and to ravage their country in all directions. It was resolved to take ample vengeance on them: their lands were laid waste—their corn trampled down under the feet of the cavalry, their villages burnt to the ground—and themselves chased into the bush, where they were bombarded with grape-shot and congreve-rockets. Men, women, and children, were massacred in one indiscriminate slaughter. A high price was set upon the heads of the chiefs, especially on that of Makanna, and menaces added, that if they were not brought in, nothing should prevent the total destruction of their country. Not a soul was found timid or traitorous enough to betray their chiefs; but to the surprise of the English, Makanna himself, to save the remainder of his nation, walked quietly into the English camp and presented himself before the commander. "The war," said he, " British chiefs, is an unjust one; for you are striving to extirpate a people whom you forced to take up arms. When our fathers, and the fathers of the Boors first settled in the Zureveld, they dwelt together in peace. Their flocks grazed on the same hills; their herdsmen smoked together out of the same pipes; they were brothers, until the herds of the Amakosa increased so as to make the hearts of the boors sore. What these covetous men could not get from our fathers for old buttons, they took by force. Our fathers were

MEN; they loved their cattle; their wives and children lived upon milk; they fought for their property. They began to hate the colonists, who coveted their all, and aimed at their destruction.

"Now their kraals and our fathers' kraals were separate. The boors made commandoes on our fathers. Our fathers drove them out of the Zureveld. We dwelt there because we had conquered it. There we married wives, and there our children were born. The white men hated us, but they could not drive us away. When there was war, we plundered you. When there was peace, some of our bad people stole; but our chiefs forbade it. Your treacherous friend, Gaika, always had peace with you, yet, when his people stole he shared in the plunder. Have your patroles ever, in time of peace, found cattle, runaway slaves, or deserters in the kraals of *our* chiefs? Have they ever gone into Gaika's country without finding such cattle, such slaves, such deserters in Gaika's kraals? But he was your friend; and you wished to possess the Zureveld. You came at last like locusts.* We stood; we could do no more. You said, 'Go over the Fish River—that is all we want.' We yielded, and came here. We lived in peace. Some bad people stole, perhaps; but the nation was quiet—the chiefs were quiet. Gaika stole—his chiefs stole—his people stole. You sent him copper; you sent him beads; you sent him horses—on which he rode to steal more. *To us you sent only commandoes!*

"We quarrelled with Gaika about grass—no business of yours. You sent a commando.† You took our

---

* Col. Graham's Campaign in 1811-12.
† Col. Brereton's Expedition in 1818.

last cow. You left only a few calves, which died for want, along with our children. You gave half the spoil to Gaika—half you kept yourselves. Without milk — our corn destroyed, we saw our wives and children perish—we saw that we must ourselves perish. We fought for our lives—we failed—and you are here. Your troops cover the plains and swarm in the thickets, where they cannot distinguish the men from the women, and shoot all.*

" You want us to submit to Gaika. That man's face is fair to you, but his heart is false; leave him to himself, and *we* shall not call on you for help. Set Makanna at liberty; and Islambi, Dushani, Kongo, and the rest, will come to make peace with you at any time you fix. But if you will make war, you may indeed kill the last man of us; but Gaika shall not rule over the followers of those who think him a woman."†

It is said that this energetic address, containing so many awful truths, affected some of those who heard it even to tears. But what followed? The Caffres were still sternly commanded to deliver up their other chiefs; treachery is said to have been used to compass it, but in vain; so the English made a desert of the whole country, and carried off 30,000 head of cattle.‡ Makanna was sent to Cape-Town, and thence transported to Robben Island, a spot appropriated to felons and malefactors doomed to work in irons. Here, in an attempt with some few followers to effect his escape, he was drowned by the upsetting of the boat, and died cheering his unfortunate companions till the billows swept him from a rock to which he clung.§

* Thompson, ii. 347.   ‡ Captain Stockenstrom.
† Ibid. and Kay, 266.   § Pringle's African Sketches.

The English had hitherto gratified their avarice and bad passions with their usual freedom in their colonies, on those who had no further connexion with them than happening to possess goodly herds under their eye; but now they turned their hand upon their *friend* and ally, Gaika. Having devoured, by his aid, his countrymen, they were ready now to devour him. Gaika was called upon to give up a large portion of Caffre land, that is, from the Fish River to the Keisi and Chumi rivers—a tract which added about 2,000 square miles to our own boundaries. This he yielded most reluctantly, and only on condition that the basin of the Chumi, a beautiful piece of country, should not be included, and that all his territory should be considered neutral ground. Gaika himself narrowly escaped being seized by the English in 1822—for what cause does not appear,—but it does appear that he only effected his escape in the mantle of his wife; and that in 1823 a large force, according to the evidence of Capt. Aichison, in which he was employed, surprised the kraals of his son Macomo, and took from them 7,000 beasts. Well might Gaika say—"When I look at the large tract of fine country that has been taken from me, I am compelled to say that *though protected, I am rather oppressed by my protectors.*" *

This Macomo, the son of Gaika, seems to be a fine fellow. Desirous of cultivating peace and the friend-ship of the English; desirous of his people receiving the benefits of civilization and the Christian religion; yet, notwithstanding this, and notwithstanding the alliance which had subsisted between the English and his father, his treatment at the hands of the Cape

* Thompson, ii. 348.

government has always been of the most harsh and
arbitrary kind.   He has been driven with his people
from one location to another, and the most serious
devastation committed on his property.   Pringle's
words regarding him are—"He has uniformly protected the missionaries and traders; has readily
punished any of his people who committed depre-
dations on the colonists, and on many occasions has
given four or five-fold compensation for stolen cattle
driven through his territory by undiscovered thieves
from other clans.   Notwithstanding all this, however,
and much more stated on his behalf in the Cape
papers, colonial oppression continues to trample down
this chief with a steady, firm, relentless foot."   The
same writer gives the following instance of the sort of
treatment which was received from the authorities by
this meritorious chief.

" On the 7th of October last (1833), Macomo was
invited by Mr. Read to attend the anniversary meeting of an auxiliary missionary society at Philipton,
Kat River.   The chief went to the military officer
commanding the nearest frontier post, and asked permission to attend, but was peremptorily refused.   He
ventured, nevertheless, to come by another way, with
his ordinary retinue, but altogether unarmed, and
delivered in his native tongue a most eloquent speech
at the meeting, in which he seconded a motion, proposed by the Rev. Mr. Thompson, the established
clergyman, for promoting the conversion of the Caffres.   Alluding to the great number of traders residing
in Caffreland, contrasted with the rude prohibition
given to his attending this Christian assembly, he
said, in the forcible idiom of his country—' There are

no Englishmen at Kat River; there are no Englishmen at Graham's Town; they are all in my country,
with their wives and children, in perfect safety, while
I stand before you as a rogue and a vagabond, having
been obliged to come by stealth.'* Then, addressing
his own followers, he said—'Ye sons of Kahabi, I
have brought you here to behold what the Word of
God hath wrought. These Hottentots were but yesterday as much despised and oppressed as to-day are
we—the Caffres: but see what the Great Word has
done for them! They were dead—they are now alive;
they are men once more. Go and tell my people what
you have seen and heard; for such things as you have
seen and heard, I hope ere long to witness in my own
land. God is great, who has said it, and will surely
bring it to pass!' In the midst of this exhilarating
scene—the African chief recommending to his followers the adoption of that GREAT WORD which brings
with it at once both spiritual and social regeneration—
they were interrupted by the sudden appearance of a
troop of dragoons, despatched from the military post
to arrest Macomo for having crossed the frontier line
without permission. This was effected in the most
brutal and insulting manner possible, and not without
considerable hazard to the chieftain's life, from the
ruffian-like conduct of a drunken sergeant, although
not the slightest resistance was attempted."†

It should be borne in mind by the reader that this
Kat River settlement, where Macomo was attending

---

* There were about 200 traders from the colony residing in Caffreland, many of them with their wives and children, at the moment
Macomo was thus treated!

† African Sketches, 467.

the meeting, is the same from which he had been expelled in 1829, and in which the Hottentots were
located, and, as I have already related, were making
such remarkable progress. Macomo had therefore
not only repassed the boundary line over which he
had been driven, and the repassing of which the
government would naturally regard with great jealousy, knowing well what injury they had done him,
and which the sight of his old country must forcibly
revive in his mind, knowing also that they were
at this moment planning fresh outrages against him.
This meeting took place in October, 1833, and therefore, at that very time, an order was signed by the
governor for his removal from the lands he was then
occupying; for the Parliamentary Report informs us
that Sir Lowry Cole, before leaving the colony for
Europe, on the 10th of August, 1833, signed an order
for removing the chief Tyalie from the Muncassana
beyond the boundaries; and in November of that year
Captain Aichison was ordered to remove Macomo,
Botman, and Tyalie, beyond the boundary; that is,
beyond the Keiskamma, which he says he did. Capt.
Aichison stated in evidence before the Select Committee, that he could assign no cause for this removal,
and he never heard any cause assigned. But this was
not the worst. These poor people, thus driven out
in November, when all their corn was green, and that
and the crops of their gardens and their pumpkins
thus lost, were suffered to return in February, 1834,
and again, in October of that year, driven out a
second time! Colonel Wade stated in evidence, that
at the time of their second removal, 21st of October,
1834, " they had rebuilt their huts, established their

cattle kraals, and commenced the cultivation of their gardens." He stated that, together with Colonel Somerset, he made a visit to Macomo and Botman's kraal, across the Keiskamma, and that Macomo rode back with them, when they had recrossed the river and reached the Omkobina, a tributary of the Chumie. " These valleys were swarming with Caffres, as was the whole country in our front as far as the Gaga; the people were all in motion, carrying off their effects, and driving away their cattle towards the drifts of the river, and to my utter amazement the whole country around and before us was in a blaze. Presently we came up with a strong patrol of the mounted rifle corps, which had, it appeared, come out from Fort Beaufort that morning; the soldiers were busily employed in burning the huts and driving the Caffres towards the frontier."

Another witness said, " the second time of my leaving Caffreland was in October, last year, in company with a gentleman who was to return towards Hantam. We passed through the country of the Gaga at ten o'clock at night; the Caffres were enjoying themselves after their custom, with their shouting, feasting, and midnight dances; they allowed us to pass on unmolested. Some time after I received a letter from the gentleman who was my travelling companion on that night, written just before the breaking out of the Caffre war: in it he says, 'you recollect how joyful the Caffres were, when we crossed the Gaga; but on my return a dense smoke filled all the vales, and the Caffres were seen lurking here and there behind the mimosa; a patrol, commanded by an officer, was driving them beyond the colonial boundary. (This piece

of country has very lately been claimed by the colony.)
I saw one man near me, and I told my guide to call
him to me: the poor fellow said, ' No, I cannot come
nearer; that white man looks too much like a soldier;"
and all our persuasions could not induce him to advance near us. ' Look,' said he, pointing to the as-
cending columns of smoke, ' what the white men are
doing.' Their huts and folds were all burned."

Such was the treatment of the Caffres up to the end
of 1834, notwithstanding the most forcible and pathetic
appeals to their English tyrants. Dr. Philip stated
that, speaking with these chiefs at this time, he said to
Macomo, that he had reason to believe that the governor, when he came to the frontier, would listen to
all his grievances, and treat him with justice and generosity. " These promises," he replied, " we have had
for the last fifteen years;" and pointing to the huts
then burning, he added, " things are becoming worse:
these huts were set on fire last night, and we were told
that to-morrow the patrol is to scour the whole district, and drive every Caffre from the west side of the
Chumie and Keiskamma at the point of the bayonet."
And Dr. Philip having stated rather strongly the necessity the chiefs would be under of preventing all
stealing from the colony as the condition of any peaceable relations the governor might enter into with them,
Botman made the following reply: " The governor
cannot be so unreasonable as to make our existence as
a nation depend upon a circumstance which is beyond
the reach of human power. Is it in the power of any
governor to prevent his people stealing from each
other ? Have you not within the colony magistrates,
policemen, prisons, whipping-posts, and gibbets ? and

do you not perceive that in spite of all these means to make your people honest, that your prisons continue full, and that you have constant employment for your magistrates, policemen, and hangmen, without being able to keep down your colonial thieves and cheats? A thief is a wolf; he belongs to no society, and yet is the pest and bane of all societies. You have your thieves, and we have thieves among us; but we cannot as chiefs, extirpate the thieves of Caffreland, more than we can extirpate the wolves, or you can extirpate the thieves of the colony. There is however this difference between us: we discountenance thieves in Caffreland, and prevent, as far as possible, our people stealing from the colony; but you countenance the robbery of your people upon the Caffres, by the sanction you give to the injustice of the patrol system. Our people have stolen your cattle, but you have, by the manner by which you have refunded your loss, punished the innocent; and after having taken our country from us, without even a shadow of justice, and shut us up to starvation, you threaten us with destruction for the thefts of those to whom you left no choice but to steal or die by famine."

What force and justice of reasoning in these abused Caffres! what force and injustice of action in the English! Who could have believed that from the moment of our becoming masters of the Cape colony such dreadful and wicked scenes as these could be going on, up to 1834, by Englishmen. But the end was not yet come; other, and still more abominable deeds were to be perpetrated. Another war broke out, and the people of England asked, why? Dr. Philip, before the Parliamentary Committee, said,—

" The encroachments of the colonists upon the Caffres, when they came in contact with them on the banks of the Gamtoos river; their expulsion from the Rumfield, now Albany, in 1811; the commandoes of Colonel Brereton, in 1818; our conduct to Gaika, our ally, in 1819, in depriving him of the country between the Fish and Keiskamma Rivers; the injury inflicted upon Macomo and Gaika, by the ejectment of Macomo and his people, with many of the people of Gaika, from the Kat River, in 1829; the manner in which the Caffres were expelled from the west bank of the Chumie and Keiskamma, in 1833, and, subsequently, again (after having been allowed to return) in 1834; and the working of the commando system, down to December, 1834,—were sufficient in themselves to account for the Caffre war, if the Caffres are allowed to be human beings, and to possess passions like our own."

To all this series of insults and inflictions were soon added fresh ones.

" On the 2nd December, of this very year," continued Dr. Philip, " Ensign Sparkes went to one of the Chief Eno's kraals, for the purpose of getting some horses, supposed to have been stolen. Not finding them there, he proceeded to take by force a large quantity of cattle as an indemnity. This proceeding roused the dormant anger of the Caffres; they surrounded his party, and manifested an intention of attacking it. They did not, however, venture upon a general engagement, though one of them, more daring, and perhaps a greater loser than the rest, wounded Ensign Sparkes in the arm with an assagai, or spear, whilst the soldiers under his com-

mand were busily employed in driving the cattle out
of the bush. Macomo no sooner heard of this affair,
than he gave up of his own property, to the colony,
400 head of cattle, and went himself frequently to
visit the young man who had been wounded, expressing great sorrow at what had occurred. This conduct
was highly praiseworthy, as it was evidently for the
sake of preventing any misunderstanding, but more
especially so, because the deed had been committed,
not by one of his people, but by a Caffre belonging
to Eno's tribe. On the 18th of the same month, a
patrol under Lieut. Sutton seized a number of cattle
at one of Tyalie's kraals, for some horses alleged to
have been stolen, but not found there. On this
occasion the Caffres seem to have determined to resist
to the last. An affray took place, in which they were
so far successful as to retake the cattle. Two of
them were, however, shot dead, and two dangerously
wounded, one of whom was Tyalie's own brother (not,
however, Macomo), who had two slugs in his head.
An individual residing in the neutral territory, refer-
ring to this affair, thus expressed his opinion : ' The
system carried on, and that to the last moment, is the
cause the Caffres could not bear it any longer. The
very immediate cause was the wounding of Gaika's
son, at which the blood of every Caffre boiled.' "

According to the evidence of John Tzatzoe, " every
Caffre who saw Xo-Xo's wound, went back to his hut,
took his assagai and shield, and set out to fight, and
said, ' It is better that we die than be treated thus.' "

The war being thus wantonly and disgracefully
provoked by the English, Sir Benjamin D'Urban,
the governor, marched into the territory of the Caffre

king Hintza, and summoned him to his presence. The king, alarmed, and naturally expecting some fresh act of mischief, fled, driving off his cattle to a place of security. He was threatened with immediate procla- mation of war if he did not return; and to convince him that there would be no dallying, Colonel Smith immediately marched his troops into the mountain districts where Hintza had taken refuge, was very near seizing him by surprise, and carried off 10,000 head of cattle. Hintza, now, on sufficient security being given, came to the camp, where the various charges were advanced against him, and the following modest conditions of peace proposed,—that he should surrender 50,000 head of cattle, 1,000 horses, and emancipate all his Fingoe slaves. There was no alter- native but agreeing to these terms; but unfortunately for him, the Fingoe slaves, now considering themselves put under the patronage of the governor, and knowing how fond the English are of Caffre cattle, carried off 15,000 head belonging to the people. The people flew to arms—and Hintza was made responsible. The governor declared to him that if he did not put a stop to the fighting in three hours, and order the deli- very of the 50,000 head of cattle, he would hang him, his son Creili, and his counsellor and brother Bookoo, on the tree under which they were sitting.* Poor Hintza issued his orders—the fighting ceased, but the cattle did not arrive. He therefore proposed to go, under a sufficient guard, to enforce the delivery himself. The proposal was accepted, and he set out with Col. Smith and a body of cavalry. Col. Smith

* Dr. Murray's Letter in the South African Advertizer, Feb. 20, 1836.

assured him on commencing their march, that if he attempted to escape he should certainly shoot him. We shall soon see how well he kept his word. They found the people had driven the cattle to the mountains, and Hintza sent one of his counsellors to command them to stop. On the same day they came to a place where the cattle-track divided, and they followed that path, at the advice of Hintza, which led up an abrupt and wooded hill to the right, over the precipitous banks of the Kebaka river. What followed we give in the language of Col. Smith :—

" It had been observed that this day Hintza rode a remarkably fine horse, and that he led him up every ascent; the path up this abrupt and wooded hill above described is by a narrow cattle-track, occasionally passing . through a cleft of the rock. I was riding alone at the head of the column, and having directed the cavalry to lead their horses, I was some three or four horses' length in front of every one, having previously observed Hintza and his remaining two followers leading their horses behind me, the corps of Guides close to them; when nearing the top, I heard a cry of ' Hintza,' and in a moment he dashed past me through the bushes, but was obliged, from the trees, to descend again into the path. I cried out, 'Hintza, stop !' I drew a pistol, and presenting it at him, cried out, ' Hintza,' and I also reprimanded his guard, who instantly came up; he stopped and smiled, and I was ashamed of my suspicion. Upon nearing the top of this steep ascent, the country was perfectly open, and a considerable tongue of land running parallel with the rugged bed of the Kebaka, upon a gradual descent of about two miles, to a turn of the river,

where were several Caffre huts. I was looking back
to observe the march of the troops, when I heard a
cry of ' Look, Colonel!' I saw Hintza had set off
at full speed, and was 30 yards a-head of every one;
I spurred my horse with violence, and coming close
up with him, called to him; he urged his horse the
more, which could beat mine; I drew a pistol, it
snapped; I drew another, it also snapped; I then was
sometime galloping after him, when I spurred my
horse alongside of him, and struck him on the head
with the butt-end of a pistol; he redoubled his efforts
to escape, and his horse was three lengths a-head of
mine. I had dropped one pistol, I threw the other
after him, and struck him again on the head. Having
thus raced about a mile, we were within half a mile of
the Caffre huts; I found my horse was closing with
him ; I had no means whatever of assailing him, while
he was provided with his assagais; I therefore resolved
to attempt to pull him off his horse, and I seized
the athletic chief by the throat, and twisting my
hand in his karop, I dragged him from his seat, and
hurled him to the earth; he instantly sprang on his
legs, and sent an assagai at me, running off towards
the rugged bed of the Kebaka. My horse was most
unruly, and I could not pull him up till I reached the
Caffre huts. This unhorsing the chief, and his waiting to throw an assagai at me, brought Mr. George
Southey of the corps of Guides up; and, at about 200
yards' distance, he twice called to Hintza, in Caffre,
to stop, or he would shoot him. He ran on ; Mr.
Southey fired, and only slightly struck him in the leg,
again calling to him to stop, without effect; he fired,
and shot him through the back; he fell headlong

forwards, but springing up and running forwards, closely pursued by my aide-de-camp, Lieutenant Balfour, he precipitated himself down a kloof into the Kebaka, and posting himself in a narrow niche of the rock, defied any attempt to secure him; when, still refusing to surrender, and raising an assagai, Mr. George Southey fired, and shot him through the head. Thus terminated the career of the chief Hintza, whose treachery, perfidy, and want of faith, made him worthy of the nation of atrocious and indomitable savages over whom he was the acknowledged chieftain. One of his followers escaped, the other was shot from an eminence. About half a mile off I observed the villain Mutini and Hintza's servant looking on."

Such is the relation of the destroyer of Hintza, and surely a more brutal and disgusting detail never came from the chief actor of such a scene. England has already testified its opinion both of this act and of this war; and "this nation of atrocious and indomitable savages," both before and since this transaction, have given such evidences of sensibility to the law of kindness as leave no doubt where the "treachery, perfidy, and want of faith," really lay. At the very time this affair was perpetrated, two British officers had gone with proposals from the governor to the Caffre camp. While they remained there they were treated most respectfully and honourably by these "irreclaimable savages," and dismissed unhurt when the intelligence arrived of Hintza's having been made prisoner. What a contrast does this form to our own conduct!

The war was continued after the event of the death of Hintza, until the Caffres had received what the governor considered to be "sufficient" punishment;

this consisted in the slaughter of 4,000 of their warriors, including many principal men. "There have been taken from them also," says a despatch, "besides the conquest and alienation of their country, about 60,000 head of cattle, almost all their goats; their habitations everywhere destroyed, and their gardens and corn-fields laid waste."*

The cost of this war to the British nation, is estimated at 241,884*l.* besides putting a stop to the trade with the colony amounting to 30,000*l.* per annum, though yet in its infancy. If any one wishes to know how absurd it is to talk of the Caffres as "atrocious and indomitable savages," he has only to look into the Parliamentary Report, so often referred to in this chapter, in order to blush for our own barbarism, and to execrate the wickedness which could, by these reckless commandoes and exterminating wars, crush or impede that rising civilization, and that growing Christianity, which shew themselves so beautifully in this much abused country. It is the wickedness of Englishmen that has alone stood in the way of the rapid refinement of the Caffre, as it has stood in the way of knowledge and prosperity in all our colonies.

"Whenever," says John Tzatzoe, a Caffre chief, who had, before the war at his own place, a missionary and a church attended by 300 people, "the missionaries attempt to preach to the Caffres, or whenever I myself preach or speak to my countrymen, they say, ' Why do not the missionaries first go and preach to the people on the other side; why do not they preach to their own countrymen, and convert them first?'"

But the very atrocity of this last war roused the

* Report on the Aboriginal Tribes, 1837. Ball's edit. p. 115.

spirit of the British nation, awakened parliamentary investigation; the Caffre territory is restored by order of government; a new and more rational system of policy is adopted, and it is to be hoped will be steadily persevered in.

CHAPTER XXVIII.

THE ENGLISH IN NEW HOLLAND AND THE ISLANDS OF THE PACIFIC.

IN this chapter we shall take a concluding view of our countrymen amongst the aborigines of the countries they have visited or settled in; and in doing this it will not be requisite to go back at all into the past. To trace the manner in which they possessed themselves of these regions, or in which they have from that period to the present extended their power, and driven back the natives, would be only treading over for the tenth time the scenes of arbitrary assumption and recklessness of right, which must be, now, but too familiar to my readers. We will, therefore, merely look at the present state of English conduct in those remote regions; and, for this purpose, the materials lie but too plentifully before us. With the exception of the missionary labours, the presence of the Europeans in these far regions is a fearful curse. The two great prominent features of their character there, are violence and debauchery. If they had gone thither only to seize the lands of the natives, as they have done everywhere else, it might have excited no surprise; for who, after perusing this volume, should wonder that the Europeans are selfish: if they had totally exterminated the aborigines with the sword and the musket, it might even then have passed in the ordinary estimate of their crimes, and there might have been hope that they might raise some more imposing, if not more virtuous, fabric of society than that which they had destroyed; but here, the danger is that they will demolish a rising civilization of a beautiful and peculiar character, by their pestilent profligacy. That dreadful and unrighteous system, which Columbus himself introduced in the very first moment of discovery, and which I have more than once pointed to, in the course of this volume, as a very favourite scheme of the Europeans, and especially the English, the convict system—the penal colony system —the throwing off the putrid matter of our corrupt social state on some simple and unsuspecting country, to inoculate it with the rankness of our worst moral diseases, without relieving ourselves at all sensibly by the unprincipled deed, has here shewn itself in all its hideousness. New South Wales and Van Dieman's Land have been sufficient to curse and demoralize all this portion of the world. They have not only exhibited the spectacle of European depravity in the most frightful forms within themselves, but the contagion of their evil and malignity has been blown across the ocean, and sped from island to island with destructive power.

In these colonies, no idea of any right of the natives to the soil, or any consideration of their claims, comforts, or improvements, seem to have been entertained. Colonies were settled, and lands appropriated, just as they were needed; and if the natives did not like it, they were shot at. The Parliamentary Inquiry of 1836, elicited by Sir Willliam Molesworth, drew forth such a picture of colonial infamy as must have astonished even the most apathetic; and the Report of 1837 only confirms the horrible truth of the statements then made.

It says: " These people, unoffending as they were towards us, have, as might have been expected, suffered in an aggravated degree from the planting amongst them of our penal settlements. In the formation of these settlements it does not appear that the territorial rights of the natives were considered, and very little care has since been taken to protect them from the violence or the contamination of the dregs of our countrymen.

" The effects have consequently been dreadful beyond example, both in the diminution of their numbers and in their demoralization."

Mr. Bannister, late attorney-general for that colony, says in his recent work, " British Colonization and the Coloured Tribes,"—" In regard to New South Wales, some disclosures were made by the secretary of the Church Missionary Society, Mr. Coates, and by others, that are likely to do good in the pending inquiries concerning transportation; and if that punishment is to be continued, it would be merciful to destroy all the natives by military massacre, as a judge of the colony once coolly proposed for a particular district, rather than let them be exposed to the lingering death they now undergo. *But half the truth was not told as to New South Wales.* Military massacres have been probably more common there than elsewhere; in 1826, Governor Darling ordered such massacres—and in consequence, one black native, at least, was shot at a stake in cool blood. The attorney-general of the colony* remonstrated against illegal orders of this kind, and was told that the secretary of state's instructions authorized them."

Lord Glenelg, however, adopted in his despatch to Sir James Stirling in 1835 a very different language, in consequence of an affair on the Murray River. The natives on this river, "in the summer of the year 1834, murdered a British soldier, having in the course of the previous five years killed three other persons. In the month of October, 1834, Sir James Stirling, the governor, proceeded with a party of horse to the Murray River, in search of the tribe in question. On coming up with them, it appears that the British horse charged this tribe without any parley, and killed fifteen of them, not, as it seems, confining their vengeance to the actual murderers. After the rout, the women who had been taken prisoners were dismissed, having been informed, " that the punishment had been inflicted because of the misconduct of the tribe; that the white men never forget to punish murder; that on this occasion the women and children had been spared; but if any other persons should be killed by them, not one would be allowed to remain on this side of the mountains."

That is, these white men, " who never forget to

* Mr. Bannister.

punish murder," would, if another person was killed by
the natives, commit a wholesale murder, and drive the
natives out of one other portion of their country. Lord
Glenelg, however, observed that it would be necessary that inquiry should be made whether some act of
harshness or injustice had not originally provoked the
enmity of the natives, before such massacres could be
justified. His language is not only just, but very descriptive of the cause of these attacks from the natives.

" It is impossible to regard such conflicts without
regret and anxiety, when we recollect how fatal, in
too many instances, our colonial settlements have
proved to the natives of the places where they have
been formed; and this too by a series of conflicts in
every one of which it has been asserted, and apparently with justice, that the immediate aggression
has not been on our side. The real causes of these
hostilities are to be found in a course of petty encroachments and acts of injustice committed by the
new settlers, at first submitted to by the natives, and
not sufficiently checked in the outset by the leaders of
the colonists. Hence has been generated in the minds
of the injured party a deadly spirit of hatred and vengeance, which breaks out at length into deeds of atrocity, which, in their turn, make retaliation a necessary
part of self-defence."*

It is some satisfaction that the recent inquiries have
led to the appointment of a protector of the Aborigines,
but who shall protect them from the multitudinous
evils which beset them on all sides from their intercourse with the whites—men expelled by the laws from
their own country for their profligacy, or men corrupted

* Despatch to Sir James Stirling, 23d July, 1835.

by contact with the plague of their presence? Grand individual massacres, and cases of lawless aggression, such as occasioned the abandonment of the colony at Raffles' Bay, on the northern coast of Australia, where for the trifling offence of the theft of an axe, the sentinels were ordered to fire on the natives whenever they approached, and who yet were found by Captain Barker, the officer in command when the order for the abandonment of the place arrived, to be " a mild and merciful race of people;" such great cases of violence may be prevented, or reduced in number, but what ubiquitous protector is to stand between the natives and the stock-keepers (convicts in the employ of farmers in the outskirts of the colony), of the cedar-cutters, the bush-rangers, and free settlers in the remote and thinly cultivated districts?—a race of the most demoralized and fearful wretches on the face of the earth, and who will shoot a native with the same indifference as they shoot a kangaroo. Who shall protect them from the diseases and the liquid fire which these penal colonies have introduced amongst them? These are the destroying agencies that have compelled our government to commit one great and flagrant act of injustice to remedy another—actually to pursue, run down, and capture, as you would so many deer in a park, or as the Gauchos of the South American Pampas do wild cattle with their lassos, the whole native population of Van Dieman's land; and carry them out of their own country, to Flinder's Island? Yes, to save these wretched people from the annihilation which our moral corruption and destitution of all Christian principle were fast bringing upon them, we have seized and expelled them all from their native land. What a strange alternative, between destruction by our violence and our vices, and the commission of an act which in any other part or age of the world would be regarded as the most wicked and execrable. We have actually turned out the inhabitants of Van Dieman's Land, because we saw that it was "a goodly heritage," and have comfortably sate down in it ourselves; and the best justification that we can set up is, that if we did not pass one general sentence of transportation upon them, we must burn them up with our liquid fire, poison them with the diseases with which our vices and gluttony have covered us, thick as the quills on a porcupine, or knock them down with our bullets, or the axes of our wood-cutters! What an indescribable and monstrous crime must it be in the eye of the English to possess a beautiful and fertile island,—that the possessors shall be transported as convicts to make way for the convicts from this kingdom who have been pronounced by our laws too infamous to live here any longer! To such a pass are we come, that the Jezebel spirit of our lawless cupidity does not merely tell us that it will give us a vineyard, but whatever country or people we lust after.

We have then, totally cleared Van Dieman's Land of what Colonel Arthur himself, an agent of this sweeping expulsion of a whole nation, calls "a noble-minded race,"* and have reduced the natives of New Holland, so far as we have come in contact with them, to misery.

This is the evidence given by Bishop Broughton:—" They do not so much retire as decay; wherever Europeans meet with them, they appear to

* Despatch to Lord Goderich, 6th April, 1833.

wear out, and gradually to decay : they diminish in numbers ; they appear actually to vanish from the face of the earth. I am led to apprehend that within a very limited period, a few years," adds the Bishop, " those who are most in contact with Europeans will be utterly extinct—I will not say exterminated—but they will be extinct."

As to their moral condition, the bishop says of the natives around Sidney—" They are in a state which I consider one of extreme degradation and ignorance; they are, in fact, in a situation much inferior to what I suppose them to have been before they had any communication with Europe." And again, in his charge, " It is an awful, it is even an appalling consideration, that, after an intercourse of nearly half a century with a Christian people, these hapless human beings continue to this day in their original benighted and degraded state. I may even proceed farther, so far as to express my fears that our settlement in their country has even deteriorated a condition of existence, than which, before our interference, nothing more miserable could easily be conceived. While, as the contagion of European intercourse has extended itself among them, they gradually lose the better properties of their own character, they appear in exchange to acquire none but the most objectionable and degrading of ours."

The natives about Sidney and Paramatta are represented as in a state of wretchedness still more deplorable than those resident in the interior.

" Those in the vicinity of Sidney are so completely changed, they scarcely have the same pursuits now ; they go about the streets begging their bread, and begging for clothing and rum. From the diseases introduced among them, the tribes in immediate connexion with those large towns almost became extinct; not more than two or three remained, when I was last in New South Wales, of tribes which formerly consisted of 200 or 300."

Dr. Lang, the minister of the Scotch church, writes, " From the prevalence of infanticide, from intemperance, and from European diseases, their number is evidently and rapidly diminishing in all the older settlements of the colony, and in the neighbourhood of Sidney especially, they present merely the shadow of what were once numerous tribes." Yet even now " he thinks their number within the limits of the colony of New South Wales cannot be less than 10,000—an indication of what must once have been the population, and what the destruction. It is only," Dr. Lang observes, " through the influence of Christianity, brought to bear upon the natives by the zealous exertions of devoted missionaries, that the progress of extinction can be checked."

Enormous as are these evils, it would be well if they stopped here; but the moral corruption of our penal colonies overflows, and is blown by the winds, like the miasma of the plague, to other shores, and threatens with destruction one of the fairest scenes of human regeneration and human happiness to which we can turn on this huge globe of cruelty for hope and consolation. Where is the mind that has not dwelt in its young enthusiasm on the summer beauty of the Islands of the Pacific? That has not, from the day that Captain Cook first fell in with them, wandered in imagination with our voyagers and missionaries through their fairy scenes—been wafted in some magic bark over those blue and bright seas—been hailed to the sunny shore by hundreds of simple and rejoicing people—been led into the hut overhung with glorious tropical flowers, or seated beneath the palm, and feasted on the pine and the bread-fruit? These are the things which make part of the poetry of our memory and our youth. There is not a man of the slightest claims to the higher and better qualities of our nature to whom the existence of these oceanic regions of beauty has not been a subject of delightful thought, and a source of genial inspiration. Here in fancy—

> The white man landed!—need the rest be told?
> The New World stretched its dusk hand to the old;
> Each was to each a marvel, and the tie
> Of wonder warmed to better sympathy.
> Kind was the welcome of the sun-born sires,
> And kinder still their daughters' gentler fires.
> Their union grew: the children of the storm
> Found beauty linked with many a dusky form;
> While these in turn admired the paler glow,
> Which seem'd so white in climes that knew no snow.
> The chase, the race, the liberty to roam
> The soil where every cottage shewed a home;
> The sea-spread net, the lightly launched canoe,
> Which stemmed the studded Archipelago,
> O'er whose blue bosom rose the starry isles;
> The healthy slumber caused by sportive toils;
> The palm, the loftiest dryad of the woods,
> Within whose bosom infant Bacchus broods,
> While eagles scarce build higher than the crest
> Which shadows o'er the vineyard in her breast;
> The cava feast, the yam, the cocoa's root,
> Which bears at once the cup, and milk, and fruit;
> The bread-tree, which, without the ploughshare, yields
> The unreaped harvest of unfurrowed fields,

And bakes its unadulterated loaves
Without a furnace in unpurchased groves,
And flings off famine from its fertile breast,
A priceless market for the gathering guest :—
These, with the solitudes of seas and woods,
The airy joys of social solitudes :—

The Island—Lord Byron.

These were the dreams of many a young dreamer—
and yet they were the realities of the Indian seas.
But even there, regeneration was needed to make this
ocean-paradise perfect. Superstition and evil passions
marred the enjoyment of the natives. Mr. William
Ellis, the able secretary of the London Missionary
Society, and author of Polynesian Researches, says—
" They were accustomed to practise infanticide, probably more extensively than any other nation; they
offered human sacrifices in greater numbers than I
have read of their having been offered by any other
nation; they were accustomed to wars of the most
savage and exterminating kind. They were lazy too,
for they found all their wants supplied by nature.
' The fruit ripens,' said they, ' and the pigs get fat
while we are asleep, and that is all we want; why,
therefore, should we work ? ' The missionaries have
presented them with that which alone they needed to
insure their happiness,— Christianity; and the consequence has been, that within the last twenty years
they have conveyed a cargo of idols to the depôt
of the Missionary Society in London; they have
become factors to furnish our vessels with provisions,
and merchants to deal with us in the agricultural
growth of their own country. Their language has
been reduced to writing, and they have gained the
knowledge of letters. They have, many of them,

emerged from the tyranny of the will of their chiefs into the protection of a written law, abounding with liberal and enlightened principles, and 200,000 of them are reported to have embraced Christianity."

The most beautiful thing is, that when they embraced Christianity, they embraced it in its fulness and simplicity. They had no ancient sophisms and political interests, like Europe, to induce them to accept Christianity by halves, admitting just as much as suited their selfishness, and explaining away, or shutting their eyes resolutely to the rest; they, therefore, furnished a most striking practical proof of the manner in which Christianity would be understood by the simple-hearted and the honest, and in doing this they pronounced the severest censures upon the barbarous and unchristian condition of proud Europe. " When," says Mr. Ellis, " Christianity was adopted by the people, human sacrifices, infant murder, and *war, entirely ceased.*" Mr. Ellis and Mr. Williams agree that *they also immediately gave freedom to all their slaves. They never considered the two things compatible.*

According to the evidence of Mr. Williams, the Tahitian and Society Islands are christianized; the Austral Island group, about 350 miles south of Tahiti; the Harvey Islands, about 700 miles west of Tahiti; the Vavou Islands, and the Hapai and the Sandwich Islands, where the American missionaries are labouring, and are 3,000 miles north of Tahiti, and the inhabitants also of the eastern Archipelago, about 500 or 600 miles east of Tahiti.

The population of these Islands, including the Sandwich Islands, are about 200,000. The Navigators' Islands, Tongatabu, and the Marquesas, are partially under the influence of the gospel, where missionary labours have just been commenced. They are supposed to contain from 100,000 to 150,000 people.

Wherever Christianity has been embraced by them, the inhabitants have become actively industrious, and, to use the words of Mr. Williams, are "very apt indeed" at learning European trades. Mr. Ellis's statement is:—"There are now carpenters who hire themselves out to captains of ships to work at repairs of vessels, etc., for which they receive regular wages; and there are blacksmiths that hire themselves out to captains of ships, for the purpose of preparing iron-work required in building or repairing ships. The natives have been taught not only to construct boats, but to build vessels, and there are, perhaps, twenty (there have been as many as forty) small vessels, of from forty to eighty or ninety tons burthen, built by the natives, navigated sometimes by Europeans, and manned by natives, all the fruit of the natives' own skill and industry. They have been taught to build neat and comfortable houses, and to cultivate the soil. *They have new wants;* a number of articles of clothing and commerce are necessary to their comfort, and they cultivate the soil to supply them. At one island, where I was once fifteen months without seeing a single European excepting our own families, there were, I think, twenty-eight ships put in for provisions last year, and all obtained the supplies they wanted. Besides cultivating potatoes and yams, and raising stock, fowls and pigs, the cultivation, the spinning and the weaving of the cotton has been introduced by missionary artizans; and there are some of the chiefs, and a number of the people, especially in one of the islands,

who are now decently clothed in garments made after
the European fashion, produced from cotton grown in
their own gardens, spun by their own children, and
woven in the islands.   One of the chiefs of the island
of Rarotonga, as stated by the missionaries, never
wears any other dress than that woven in the island.
They have been taught also to cultivate the sugar-
cane, which is indigenous, and to make sugar, and
some of them have large plantations, employing at
times forty men.   They supply the ships with this
useful article, and, at some of the islands, between
fifty and sixty vessels touch in a single year.   The
natives of the islands send a considerable quantity
away; I understand that one station sent as much as
forty tons away last year.   In November last a vessel
of ninety tons burthen, built in the islands, was sent
to the colony of New South Wales laden with Tahitian-
grown sugar.   Besides the sugar they have been taught
to cultivate, they prepare arrow-root, and they sent
to England in one year, as I was informed by merchants in London, more than had been imported into
this country for nearly twenty previous years.   Cattle
also have been introduced and preserved, chiefly by
the missionaries ; pigs, dogs, and rats were the only
animals they had before, but the missionaries have
introduced cattle among them.   While they continued
heathen, they disregarded, nay, destroyed some of
those first landed among them ; but since that time
they have highly prized them, and by their attention
to them they are now so numerous as to enable the
natives to supply ships with fresh beef at the rate of
threepence a pound.   The islanders have also been
instructed by the missionaries in the manufacture of

cocoa-nut oil, of which large quantities are exported. They have been taught to cultivate tobacco, and this would have been a valuable article of commerce had not the duty in New South Wales been so high as to exclude that grown in the islands from the market. The above are some of the proofs that Christianity prepares the way for, and necessarily leads to, the civilization of those by whom it is adopted. There are now in operation among a people who, when the missionaries arrived, were destitute of a written language, seventy-eight *schools, which contain between* 12,000 *and* 13,000 *scholars.* The Tahitians have also a simple, explicit, and wholesome *code of laws,* as the result of their imbibing the principles of Christianity. This code of laws is printed and circulated among them, understood by all, and acknowledged by all as the supreme rule of action for all classes in their civil and social relations. The laws have been productive of great benefits."

Here again they have far outstripped us in England. When shall we have a code of laws, so simple and compact, that it may be "printed and circulated amongst us, and understood by all?" The benefits resulting from this intelligible and popular code, Mr. Ellis tells us, have been great. No doubt of it. The benefits of such a code in England would be incalculable; but when will the lawyers, or our enlightened Parliament let us have it? The whole scene of the reformation, and the happiness introduced by Christianity into the South-Sea Islands, is, however, most delightful. Such a scene never was exhibited to the world since its foundation. Mr. Williams' recent work, descriptive of these islands and the missionary labours there, is fascinating as Robinson Crusoe himself, and infinitely more important in its relations. If ever the idea of the age of gold was realized, it is here; or rather,

Where none contest the fields, the woods, the streams;—
The goldless ages, where gold disturbs no dreams.

Besides the benefits accruing from this improved state to the natives, great are the benefits that accrue from it to the Europeans. The benefit of commerce, from their use of European articles, is and must be considerable. They furnish, too, articles of commerce in no small quantities. Instead of European crews now, in case of wreck on their coasts, being murdered and devoured, they are rescued from the waves at the risk of the lives of the people themselves, and received, as the evidence and works of Ellis and Williams testify, in most remarkable instances, with the greatest hospitality.

But all this springing civilization — this young Christianity, — this scene of beauty and peace, are endangered. The founders of a new and happier state, the pioneers and artificers of civilization, stand aghast at the ruin that threatens their labours,—that threatens the welfare,—nay, the very existence of the simple islanders amongst whom they have wrought such miracles of love and order. And whence arises this danger? whence comes this threatened ruin? Is some race of merciless savages about to burst in upon these interesting people, and destroy them? Yes, the same "irreclaimable and indomitable savages," that have ravaged and oppressed every nation which they have conquered, " from China to Peru." The same savages that laid waste the West Indies; that mas-

sacred the South Americans; that have chased the
North Americans to the "far west;" that shot the
Caffres for their cattle; that have covered the coasts
of Africa with the blood and fires and rancorous
malice of the slave-wars; that have exterminated
millions of Hindus by famine, and hold a hundred
millions of them, at this moment, in the most abject
condition of poverty and oppression; the same savages
that are at this moment also carrying the Hill Coolies
from the East—as if they had not a scene of enormities
there wide enough for their capacity of cruelty—to
sacrifice them in the West, on the graves of millions
of murdered negroes; the same savages are come
hither also. The savages of Europe, the most heart-
less and merciless race that ever inhabited the earth
—a race, for the range and continuance of its atrocities, without a parallel in this world, and, it may
be safely believed, in any other, are busy in the South
Sea Islands. A roving clan of sailors and runaway
convicts have revived once more the crimes and character of the old bucaniers. They go from island to
island, diffusing gin, debauchery, loathsome diseases,
and murder, as freely as if they were the greatest
blessings that Europe had to bestow. They are the
restless and triumphant apostles of misery and destruction; and such are their achievements, that it is
declared that, unless our government interpose some
check to their progress, they will as completely annihilate the islanders, as the Charibs were annihilated in
the West Indies. When Captain Cook was at the
Sandwich Islands, he estimated the inhabitants at
400,000. In 1823, Mr. Williams made a calculation,
and found them about 150,000. Mr. Daniel Wheeler,

a member of the Society of Friends, who has just returned from those regions, states that they now are
reduced to 110,000; a diminution of 40,000 in fifteen
years. Captain Cook estimated the population of
Tahiti at 200,000: when the missionaries arrived
there, there were not above 8,000.

What a shocking business is this, that when Christianity has been professed in Europe for this 1800
years, it is from Europe that the most dreadful corruption of morals, and the most dismal defiance of
every sound principle come. If Christianity, despised and counterfeited by its ancient professors, flies
to some remote corner of the globe, and there unfolds
to simple admiring eyes her blessings and her charms,
out, from Europe, rush hordes of lawless savages, to
chase her thence, and level to the dust the dwellings
and the very being of her votaries. Shall this be!
Will no burning blush rise to European cheeks at this
reflection? But let us hear what was said on this
subject before the British Parliament.

"It will be hard, we think, to find compensation, not
only to Australia, but to New Zealand, and to the innumerable islands of the South Seas, for the murders,
the misery, the contamination which we have brought
upon them. Our runaway convicts are the pests
of savage as well as of civilized society; so are our
runaway sailors; and the crews of our whaling vessels,
and of the traders from New South Wales, too frequently act in the most reckless and immoral manner
when at a distance from the restraints of justice: in
proof of this we need only refer to the evidence of
the missionaries.

"It is stated that there have been not less than 150

or 200 runaways at once on the island of New Zealand, counteracting all that was done for the moral improvement of the people, and teaching them every vice.

" 'I beg leave to add,' remarks Mr. Ellis, ' the desirableness of preventing, by every practicable means, the introduction of ardent spirits among the inhabitants of the countries we may visit or colonize. There is nothing more injurious to the South Sea islanders than seamen who have absconded from ships, setting up huts for the retail of ardent spirits, called grog-shops, which are the resort of the indolent and vicious of the crews of the vessels, and in which, under the influence of intoxication, scenes of immorality, and even murder, have been exhibited, almost beyond what the natives witnessed among themselves while they were heathen. The demoralization and impediments to the civilization and prosperity of the people that have resulted from the activity of foreign traders in ardent spirits, have been painful in the extreme. In one year it is estimated that the sum of 12,000 dollars was expended, in Taheité alone, chiefly by the natives, for ardent spirits.'

" The lawless conduct of the crews of vessels must necessarily have an injurious effect on our trade, and on that ground alone demands investigation. In the month of April, 1834, Mr. Busby states there were twenty-nine vessels at one time in the Bay of Islands; and that seldom a day passed without some complaint being made to him of the most outrageous conduct on the part of their crews, which he had not the means of repressing, since these reckless seamen totally disregarded the usages of their own country, and the unsupported authority of the British resident.

" The Rev. J. Williams, missionary in the Society Islands, states, ' that it is the common sailors, and the lowest order of them, the very vilest of the whole, who will leave their ship and go to live amongst the savages, and take with them all their low habits and all their vices.' The captains of merchant vessels are apt to connive at the absconding of such worthless sailors, and the atrocities perpetrated by them are excessive; they do incalculable mischief by circulating reports injurious to the interests of trade. On an island between the Navigator's and the Friendly group, he heard there were on one occasion a hundred sailors who had run away from shipping. Mr. Williams gives an account of a gang of convicts who stole a small vessel from New South Wales, and came to Raiatia, one of the Sandwich Islands, where he resided, representing themselves as shipwrecked mariners. Mr. Williams suspected them, and told them he should inform the governor, Sir T. Brisbane, of their arrival, on which they went away to an island twenty miles off, and were received with every kindness in the house of the chief. They took an opportunity of stealing a boat belonging to the missionary of the station, and made off again. The natives immediately pursued, and desired them to return their missionary's boat. Instead of replying, they discharged a blunderbus that was loaded with cooper's rivets, which blew the head of one man to pieces; they then killed two more, and a fourth received the contents of a blunderbus in his hand, fell from exhaustion amongst his mutilated companions, and was left as dead. This man, and a boy who had saved himself by diving, returned to their island. ' The natives were very respectable persons; and had it not been that we were established in the estimation of the people, our lives would have been sacrificed. The convicts then went in the boat down to the Navigator's Islands, and there entered with savage ferocity into the wars of the savages. One of these men was the most savage monster that ever I heard of: he boasted of having killed 300 natives with his own hands.'

"And in June 1833, Mr. Thomas, Wesleyan missionary at the Friendly Islands, still speaks of the mischief done by ill-disposed captains of whalers, who, he says, ' send the refuse of their crews on shore to annoy us;' and proceeds to state, 'the conduct of many of these masters of South-Sea whalers is most abominable; they think no more of the life of an heathen than of a dog. And their cruel and wanton behaviour at the different islands in those seas has a powerful tendency to lead the natives to hate the sight of a white man.' Mr. Williams mentions one of these captains, who with his people had shot twenty natives, at one of the islands, for no offence; and 'another master of a whaler, from Sidney, made his boast, last Christmas, at Tonga, that he had killed about twenty black fellows, —for so he called the natives of the Samoa, or Navigator's Islands—for some very trifling offence; and not satisfied with that, he designed to disguise his vessel, and pay them another visit, and get about a hundred more of them.' ' Our hearts,' continues Mr. Thomas, ' almost bleed for the poor Samoa people; they are a very mild, inoffensive race, very easy of access; and as they are near to us, we have a great hope of their embracing the truth, viz. that the whole group will do so; for you will learn from

Mr. Williams' letter, that a part of them have already turned to God.   But the conduct of our English savages has a tone of barbarity and cruelty in it which was never heard of or practised by them.' "

But these are not all the exploits of these white savages. Those who have seen in shop-windows in London, dried heads of New Zealanders, may here learn how they come there, and to whom the phrenologists and *curiosi* are indebted.

" Till lately the tattooed heads of New Zealanders were sold at Sidney as objects of curiosity; and Mr. Yate says he has known people give property to a chief for the purpose of getting them to kill their slaves, that they might have some heads to take to New South Wales.

" This degrading traffic was prohibited by General Darling, the governor, upon the following occasion : In a representation made to Governor Darling, the Rev. Mr. Marsden states, that the captain of an English vessel being, as he conceived, insulted by some native women, set one tribe upon another to avenge his quarrel, and supplied them with arms and ammunition to fight.

" In the prosecution of the war thus excited, a party of forty-one Bay of Islanders made an expedition against some tribes of the South. Forty of the former were cut off; and a few weeks after the slaughter, a Captain Jack went and purchased thirteen chiefs' heads, and, bringing them back to the Bay of Islands, emptied them out of a sack in the presence of their relations.   The New Zealanders were, very properly, so much enraged that they told this captain they should take possession of the ship, and put the laws of their country into execution. When he found that they were in earnest, he cut his cable and left the harbour, and afterwards had a narrow escape from them at Taurunga. He afterwards reached Sidney, and it came to the knowledge of the governor, that he brought there ten of these heads for sale, on which discovery the practice was declared unlawful. Mr. Yate mentions an instance of a captain going 300 miles from the Bay of Islands to East Cape, enticing twenty-five young men, sons of chiefs, on board his vessel, and delivering them to the Bay of Islanders, with whom they were at war, merely to gain the favour of the latter, and to obtain supplies for his vessel. The youths were afterwards redeemed from slavery by the missionaries, and restored to their friends. Mr. Yate once took from the hand of a New-Zealand chief a packet of corrosive sublimate, which a captain had given to the savage in order to enable him to poison his enemies."

Such is the general system. The atrocious character of particular cases would be beyond credence, after all that has now been shewn of the nature of Europeans, were they not attested by the fullest and most unexceptionable authority. The following case was communicated by the Rev. S. Marsden, to Governor-general Darling, and was also afterwards reported to the governor in person by two New Zealand chiefs. Governor Darling forwarded the account of it to Lord Goderich, together with the depositions of two seamen of the brig *Elizabeth*, and those of J. B. Montefiore, Esq., and A. Kennis, Esq. merchants of Sidney, who had embarked on board the *Elizabeth* on its return to Entry Island, and had there learned the

particulars of the case, had seen the captive chief sent
ashore, and had been informed that he was sacrificed.

"In December 1830, a Captain Stewart, of the brig
Elizabeth, a British vessel, on promise of ten tons of
flax, took above 100 New Zealanders concealed in his
vessel, down from Kappetee Entry Island, in Cook's
Strait, to Takou, or Bank's Peninsula, on the Middle
Island, to a tribe with whom they were at war. He
then invited and enticed on board the chief of Takou,
with his brother and two daughters: 'When they
came on board, the captain took hold of the chief's
hand in a friendly manner, and conducted him and
his two daughters into the cabin; shewed him the
muskets, how they were arranged round the sides of
the cabin. When all was prepared for securing the
chief, the cabin-door was locked, and the chief was
laid hold on, and his hands were tied fast; at the same
time a hook, with a cord to it, was struck through the
skin of his throat under the side of his jaw, and the
line fastened to some part of the cabin: in this state
of torture he was kept for some days, until the vessel
arrived at Kappetee. One of his children clung fast
to her father, and cried aloud. The sailors dragged
her from her father, and threw her from him; her
head struck against some hard substance, which killed
her on the spot.' The brother, or nephew, Ahu (one
of the narrators), 'who had been ordered to the fore-
castle, came as far as the capstan and peeped through
into the cabin, and saw the chief in the state above
mentioned.' They also got the chief's wife and two
sisters on board, with 100 baskets of flax. All the
men and women who came in the chief's canoe were
killed. 'Several more canoes came off also with flax,

and the people were all killed by the natives of Kappetee, who had been concealed on board for the purpose,
and the sailors who were on deck, who fired upon
them with their muskets.' The natives of Kappetee
were then sent on shore with some sailors, with orders
to kill all the inhabitants they could find; and it was
reported that those parties who went on shore murdered many of the natives; none escaped but those
who fled into the woods. The chief, his wife and two
sisters were killed when the vessel arrived at Kappetee,
and other circumstances yet more revolting are added."

We will now close this black recital of crimes by
one more case, in which the natives are represented
as the aggressors, though alone upon the evidence of
the accused party, and particularly on that of Captain
Guard, of whom Mr. Marshall of the *Alligator*, stated
that, "'in the estimation of the officers of the *Alligator*, the general sentiment was one of dislike and disgust at his conduct on board, and his conduct on
shore.' He has himself heard him say, that a musket-
ball for every New Zealander was the best mode of
civilizing the country.

" In April, 1834, the barque *Harriet*, J. Guard,
master, was wrecked at Cape Egmont, on the coast
of New Zealand. The natives came down to plunder,
but refrained from other violence for about ten days,
in which interval two of Guard's men deserted to the
savages. They then got into a fray with the sailors,
and killed twelve of them : on the part of the New
Zealanders twenty or thirty were shot. The savages
got possession of Mrs. Guard and her two children.
Mr. Guard and the remainder were suffered to retreat,
but surrendered themselves to another tribe whom

they met, and who finally allowed the captain to
depart, on his promising to return, and to bring back
with him a ransom in powder; and they retained
nine seamen as hostages. Three native chiefs accompanied Guard to Sidney. Captain Guard had been
trading with the New Zealanders from the year 1823,
and it was reported that his dealings with them had,
in some instances, been marked with cruelty. On
Mr. Guard's representation to the government at
Sidney, the *Alligator* frigate, Captain Lambert, and
the schooner *Isabella*, with a company of the 50th
regiment, were sent to New Zealand for the recovery
of Mrs. Guard and the other captives, with instructions, if practicable, to obtain the restoration of the
captives by amicable means. On arriving at the
coast near Cape Egmont, Captain Lambert steered
for a fortified village or pah, called the Nummo, where
Mrs. Guard was known to be detained. He sent
two interpreters on shore, who made promises of payment (though against Captain Lambert's order) to
the natives, and held out also a prospect of trade in
whalebone, on the condition that the women and
children should be restored. The interpreter could
not, from stress of weather, be received on board for
some days. The vessel proceeded to the tribe which
held the men in captivity, and they were at once
given up on the landing of the chiefs whom Captain
Lambert had brought back from Sidney. Captain
Lambert returned to the tribe at the Nummo, with
whom he had communicated through the interpreter,
and sent many messages to endeavour to persuade
them to give up the woman and one child (the other
was held by a third tribe), but without offering

ransom. On the 28th September, the military were landed, and two unarmed and unattended natives advanced along the sands. One announced himself as the chief who retained the woman and child, and rubbed noses with Guard in token of amity, expressing his readiness to give them up on the receipt of the promised 'payment.' 'In reply,' as Mr. Marshall, assistant-surgeon of the *Alligator*, who witnessed the scene, states, 'he was instantly seized upon as a prisoner of war' (by order of Captain Johnson, commanding the detachment), 'dragged into the whaleboat, and despatched on board the *Alligator*, in custody of John Guard and his sailors. On his brief passage to the boat insult followed insult; one fellow twisting his ear by means of a small swivel which hung from it, and another pulling his long hair with spiteful violence; a third pricking him with the point of a bayonet. Thrown to the bottom of the boat, she was shoved off before he recovered himself, which he had no sooner succeeded in doing than he jumped overboard, and attempted to swim on shore, to prevent which he was repeatedly fired upon from the boat; but not until he had been shot in the calf of the leg was he again made a prisoner of. Having been a second time secured, he was lashed to a thwart, and stabbed and struck so repeatedly, that, on reaching the *Alligator*, he was only able to gain the deck by a strong effort, and there, after staggering a few paces aft, fainted, and fell down at the foot of the capstan in a gore of blood. When I dressed his wounds, on a subsequent occasion, I found ten inflicted by the point and edge of the bayonet over his head and face, one in his left breast, which it was at first feared would prove, what it was evidently intended to have proved, a mortal thrust, and another in the leg.'

"Captain Lambert, who did not himself see the seizure, admits that the chief was unarmed when he came down to the shore, and that he 'certainly was severely wounded: he had a ball through the calf of his leg, and he had been struck violently on the head.'

"Captain Johnson proceeded to the pah or fortified village, found it deserted, and burnt it the next morning. On the 30th September, Mrs. Guard and one child were given up, and the wounded chief thereupon was very properly sent on shore, without waiting for the delivery of the other child; but 'in the evening of the same day,' Captain Lambert states, 'I again sent Lieutenant Thomas to ask for the child, whose patience and firmness during the whole of the negotiations, notwithstanding the insults that were offered to him, merit the greatest praise. He shortly after returned on board, having been fired at from one of the pahs while waiting outside the surf. Such treachery could not be borne, and I immediately commenced firing at them from the ship; a reef of rocks, which extend some distance from the shore, I regret, prevented my getting as near them as I could have wished. Several shots fell into the pahs, and also destroyed their canoes.'*

"October 8. After some fruitless negotiation, all the soldiers and several seamen were landed, making a party of 112 men, and were stationed on two terraces of the cliff, one above the other, with a six-pounder carronade, while the interpreter and sailors were left below to wait for the boy. The New Zea-

---

* Parl. Papers, 1835. No. 585. p. 7.

landers approached at first with distrust; but at length a fine tall man came forward, and assured Mr. Marshall that the child should be immediately forthcoming, and also forbade our fighting, alleging that his ' tribe had no wish to fight at all.' Soon afterwards the boy was brought down on the shoulders of a chief, who expressed to Lieutenant M'Murdo his desire to go on board for the purpose of receiving a ransom:—

" On being told that none would be given, he turned away, when one of the sailors seized hold of the child, and discovered it was fastened with a strap or cord; to use his own expression, he had recourse to cutting away, and the child fell upon the beach. Another seaman, thinking the chief would make his escape, levelled his firelock, and shot him dead. The troops hearing the report of the musket, and thinking it was fired by the natives, immediately opened a fire from the top of the cliff upon them, who made a precipitate retreat to the pahs. The child being now in our possession, I made a signal to the ships for the boats, intending to reimbark the troops; but the weather becoming thick, and a shift of wind obliging the vessels to stand out to sea, and, at the same time, finding myself attacked by the natives, who were concealed in the high flax, I found my only alternative was to advance on the pahs. I therefore ordered Lieutenant Gunton with thirty men to the front, in skirmishing order, for the purpose of driving the natives from the high flax from which they were firing: this was done, and, as I have reason to think, with considerable loss on the part of the natives.'*

* Captain Johnson's report to the Governor of New South Wales. Parl. Papers, 1835. No. 583, p. 10.

" The body of the chief is said to have been mutilated, and the head cut off by a soldier, and kicked about.
It was identified by means of a brooch, which Mrs.
Guard said belonged to the chief, who had adopted
and protected her son. It is scarcely necessary to
add, that this wanton act met with the reprobation it
deserved from Captain Lambert and his officers.

" Captain Lambert states, that he should think there
were between twenty and thirty of the natives wounded
(and this, be it observed, after the child was recovered), but it was not ascertained. 'The English
went straight forward to attack the pahs, and they
had no communication with the natives after.' The
troops immediately took possession of the two villages;
and on quitting them, three days afterwards, burnt
them to the ground.' "

The language of Lord Goderich, on reviewing some
of these cases, must be that of every honourable man.

" ' It is impossible to read, without shame and indignation, the details which these documents disclose.
The unfortunate natives of New Zealand, unless some
decisive measures of prevention be adopted, will, I
fear, be shortly added to the number of those barbarous
tribes who, in different parts of the globe, have fallen
a sacrifice to their intercourse with civilized men, who
bear and disgrace the name of Christians. . . . I cannot contemplate the too probable results without the
deepest anxiety. There can be no more sacred duty
than that of using every possible method to rescue the
natives of those extensive islands from the further
evils which impend over them, and to deliver our own
country from the disgrace and crime of having either
occasioned or tolerated such enormities.' "

CHAPTER XXIX.

CONCLUSION.

Two gods divide them all—pleasure and gain :
For these they live, they sacrifice to these,
And in their service wage perpetual war
With conscience and with thee.   Lust in their hearts,
And mischief in their hands, they roam the earth
To prey upon each other; stubborn, fierce,
High-minded, pouring out their own disgrace.
Thy prophets speak of such; and, noting down
The features of the last degenerate times,
Exhibit every lineament of these.
Come then, and added to thy many crowns,
Receive one yet, as radiant as the rest,
Due to thy last and most effectual work,
Thy word fulfilled, the conquest of a world.

Cowper—The Task.

WE have now followed the Europeans to every region of the globe, and seen them planting colonies, and peopling new lands, and everywhere we have found them the same—a lawless and domineering race, seizing on the earth as if they were the first-born of creation, and having a presumptive right to murder and dispossess all other people. For more than three centuries we have glanced back at them in their course, and everywhere they have had the word of God in their mouth, and the deeds of darkness in

their hands.   In the first dawn of discovery, forth
they went singing the Te Deum, and declaring that
they went to plant the cross amongst the heathen.
As we have already observed, however, it turned out
to be the cross of one of the two thieves, and a bitter
cross of crucifixion it has proved to the natives where
they have received it.   It has stood the perpetual
sign of plunder and extermination.   The Spaniards
were reckless in their carnage of the Indians, and all
succeeding generations have expressed their horror of
the Spaniards.   The Dutch were cruel, and everybody abominated their cruelty.   One would have
thought that the world was grown merciful.   Behold
North America at this moment, with its disinherited
Indians !   See Hindustan, that great and swarming
region of usurpations and exactions !   Look at the
Cape, and ask the Caffres whether the English are
tender-hearted and just: ask the same question in
New Holland: ask it of the natives of Van Dieman's
Land,—men, transported from the island of their
fathers.   Ask the New Zealanders whether the warriors whose tattooed heads stare us in the face in our
museums, were not delicately treated by us.   Go,
indeed, into any one spot, of any quarter of the
world, and ask—no you need not ask, you shall hear
of our aggressions from every people that know us.
The words of Red-Jacket will find an echo in the
hearts of tens of millions of sorrowful and expatriated
and enthralled beings, who will exclaim, "you want
more land!—you want our country !"   It is needless
to tell those who have read this history that there is,
and can be, nothing else like it in the whole record of
mortal crimes.   Many are the evils that are done

under the sun; but there is and can be no evil like that monstrous and earth-encompassing evil, which the Europeans have committed against the Aborigines of every country in which they have settled. And in what country have they not settled? It is often said as a very pretty speech—that the sun never sets on the dominions of our youthful Queen; but who dares to tell us the far more horrible truth, that it never sets on the scenes of our injustice and oppressions! When we have taken a solemn review of the astounding transactions recorded in this volume, and then add to them the crimes against humanity committed in the slave-trade and slavery, the account of our enormities is complete; and there is no sum of wickedness and bloodshed—however vast, however monstrous, however enduring it may be—which can be pointed out, from the first hour of creation, to be compared for a moment with it.

The slave-trade, which one of our best informed philanthropists asserts is going on at this moment to the amount of 170,000 negroes a year, is indeed the dreadful climax of our crimes against humanity. It was not enough that the lands of all newly discovered regions were seized on by fraud or violence; it was not enough that their rightful inhabitants were murdered or enslaved; that the odious vices of people styling themselves the followers of the purest of beings should be poured like a pestilence into these new countries. It was not enough that millions on millions of peaceful beings were exterminated by fire, by sword, by heavy burdens, by base violence, by deleterious mines and unaccustomed severities—by dogs, by man-hunters, and by grief and despair—there yet

wanted one crowning crime to place the deeds of
Europeans beyond all rivalry in the cause of evil,—and
that unapproachable abomination was found in the
slave-trade.   They had seized on almost all other
countries, but they could not seize on the torrid regions
of Africa.   They could not seize the land, but they
could seize the people.   They could not destroy them
in their own sultry clime, fatal to the white men, they
therefore determined to immolate them on the graves
of the already perished Americans. To shed blood upon
blood, to pile bones upon bones, and curses upon curses.
What an idea is that!—the Europeans standing with
the lash of slavery in their hands on the bones of exterminated millions in one hemisphere, watching with
remorseless eyes their victims dragged from another
hemisphere—tilling, not with their sweat, but with
their heart's blood, the soil which is, in fact, the dust
of murdered generations of victims.   To think that
for three centuries this work of despair and death has
been going on—for three centuries!—while Europe
has been priding itself on the growth of knowledge
and the possession of the Christian faith; while
mercy, and goodness, and brotherly love, have been
preached from pulpits, and wafted towards heaven in
prayers!   That from Africa to America, across the
great Atlantic, the ships of outrage and agony have
been passing over, freighted with human beings denied
all human rights. The mysteries of God's endurance,
and of European audacity and hyrocrisy are equally
marvellous.   Why, the very track across the deep
seems to me blackened by this abominable traffic;—
there must be the dye of blood in the very ocean.
One might surely trace these monsters by the smell of

death, from their kidnapping haunts to the very sugar-mills of the west, where canes and human flesh are ground together. The ghosts of murdered millions, were enough, one thinks, to lead the way without chart or compass ! The very bed of the ocean must be paved with bones ! and the accursed trade is still going on ! We are still strutting about in the 'borrowed plumes of Christianity, and daring to call God our father, though we are become the tormentors of the human race from China to Peru, and from one pole to the other !*

The whole history of European colonization is of a piece. It is with grief and indignation, that passing before my own mind the successive conquests and colonies of the Europeans amongst the native tribes of newly-discovered countries, I look in vain for a single instance of a nation styling itself Christian and civilized, acting towards a nation which it is pleased to term barbarous with Christian honesty and common feeling. The only opportunity which the aboriginal tribes have had of seeing Christianity in its real form and nature, has been from William Penn and the missionaries. But both Penn and the missionaries have in every instance found their efforts neutralized, and their hopes of permanent good to their fellow-creatures blasted, by the profligacy and the unprincipled rapacity of the Europeans as a race. Never was there a race at once so egotistical and so terrible ! With the most happy complacency regarding them-

---

* Everything connected with this trade is astonishing. Queen Elizabeth eagerly embarked in it in 1563, and sent the notorious John Hawkins, knighted by her for this and similar deeds, out to Sierra Leone for a human cargo, with four vessels, three of which, as if it were the most pious of expeditions, bore the names of Jesus ! Solomon ! and John the Baptist !—See *Hakluyt's Voyages.*

selves as civilized and pious, while acting the savage
on the broadest scale, and spurning every principle of
natural or revealed religion. But where the missionaries have been permitted to act for any length of
time on the aboriginal tribes, what happy results have
followed. The savage has become mild; he has con-
formed to the order and decorum of domestic life; he
has shewn that all the virtues and affections which
God has implanted in the human soul are not extinct
in him; that they wanted but the warmth of sympathy
and knowledge to call them forth; he has become an
effective member of the community, and his productions have taken their value in the general market.
From the Jesuits in Paraguay to the missionaries in
the South Seas, this has been the case. The idiocy
of the man who killed his goose that he might get the
golden eggs, was wisdom compared to the folly of
the European nations, in outraging and destroying
the Indian races, instead of civilizing them. Let any
one look at the immediate effect amongst the South
Sea Islanders, the Hottentots, or the Caffres, of civilization creating a demand for our manufactures, and
of bringing the productions of their respective countries into the market, and then from these few and
isolated instances reflect what would have been now
the consequence of the civilization of North and South
America, of a great portion of South Africa, of the
Indian Islands, of the good treatment and encouragement of the millions of Hindustan. Let him imagine,
if he can, the immense consumption of our manufac-
tured goods through all these vast and populous countries, and the wonderful variety of their natural productions which they would have sent us in exchange.

There is no more doubt than of the diurnal motion of the earth, that by the mere exercise of common honesty on the part of the whites, the greater part of all these countries would now be civilized, and a tide of wealth poured into Europe, such as the strongest imagination can scarcely grasp; and that, too, purchased, not with the blood and tears of the miserable, but by the moral elevation and happiness of countless tribes. The waste of human life and human energies has been immense, but not more immense than the waste of the thousand natural productions of a thousand different shores and climates. The arrow-root, the cocoa-nut oil, the medicinal oils and drugs of the southern isles; the beautiful flax of New Zealand; sugar and coffee, spices and tea, from millions of acres where they might have been raised in abundance— woods and gums, fruits and gems and ivories, have been left unproduced or wasted in the deserts, because the wonderful and energetic race of Europe chose to be as lawless as they were enterprising, and to be the destroyers rather than the benefactors of mankind. For more than three centuries, and down to the very last hour, as this volume testifies, has this system, stupid as it was wicked, been going on. Thank God, the dawn of a new era appears at last !

The wrongs of the Hottentots and Caffres, brought to the public attention by Dr. Philip and Pringle,* have led to Parliamentary inquiry; that inquiry has

---

* This excellent man was a martyr to his advocacy of the claims of the Caffres. Powerful appeals on behalf of his widow, left in painful circumstances, have been made by Mr. Leitch Ritchie, in his " Life of Pringle," and by Mr. Bannister, in his " Colonization and the Coloured Tribes," which, if they are not effective, will reflect but little credit upon the government, or the philanthropic public.

led to others;—the condition of the natives of the
South Seas, and finally of all the aboriginal tribes in
our colonies, has been brought under review. The
existence of a mass of evils and injuries, so enormous
as to fill any healthy mind with horror and amazement,
has been brought to light; and it is impossible that
such facts, once made familiar to the British public,
can ever be lost sight of again. Some expiation has
already been made to a portion of our victims. Part
of the lands of the Caffres has been returned, a
milder and more rational system of treatment has been
adopted towards them. Protectors of the Aborigines
have in one or two instances been appointed. New
and more just principles of colonization have been
proposed, and in a degree adopted. In the proposed
Association for colonizing New Zealand, and in the
South Australian settlement* already made, these
better notions are conspicuous. But these symptoms
of a more honourable conduct toward the Aborigines,
are, with respect to the evils we have done, and the
evils that exist, but as the light of the single morning
star before the sun has risen. Many are the injuries
and oppressions of our fellow-creatures which the
philanthropic have to contend against; but there is no
evil, and no oppression, that is a hundredth part so
gigantic as this. There is no case in which we owe
such a mighty sum of expiation : all other wrongs are
but the wrongs of a small section of humanity compared with the whole. The wrongs of the Negro are
great, and demand all the sympathy and active attention
which they receive ; but the numbers of the negroes

---

* See a Lecture on this settlement, with letters from the settlers,
by Henry Watson, of Chichester.

in slavery are but as a drop in the bucket compared to the numbers of the aborigines who are perishing beneath our iron and unchristian policy. The cause of the aborigines is the cause of three-fourths of the population of the globe. The evil done to them is the great and universal evil of the age, and is the deepest disgrace of Christendom. It is, therefore, with pleasure that I have seen the "ABORIGINES' PROTECTION SOCIETY" raise its head amongst the many noble societies for the redress of the wrongs and the elevation of humanity that adorn this country. Such a society must become one of the most active and powerful agents of universal justice: it must be that or nothing, for the evil which it has to put down is tyrannous and strong beyond all others. It cannot fail without the deepest disgrace to the nation—for the honour of the nation, its Christian zeal, and its commercial interests, are all bound up with it. Where are we to look for a guarantee for the removal of the foulest stain on humanity and the Christian name? Our government may be well disposed to adopt juster measures; but governments are not yet formed on those principles, and with those views, that will warrant us to depend upon them.

There is no power but the spirit of Christianity living in the heart of the British public, which can secure justice to the millions that are crying for it from every region of the earth. It is that which must stand as the perpetual watch and guardian of humanity; and never yet has it failed. The noblest spectacle in the world is that constellation of institutions which have sprung out of this spirit of Christianity in the nation, and which are continually labouring to redress wrongs and diffuse knowledge and happiness wherever the human family extends.   The ages of dreadful in-flictions, and the present condition of the native tribes in our vast possessions, once known, it were a libel on the honour and faith of the nation to doubt for a mo-ment that a new era of colonization and intercourse with unlettered nations has commenced; and I close this volume of the unexampled crimes and marvellous impolicy of Europe, with the firm persuasion—

That heavenward all things tend.   For all were once
Perfect, and all must be at length restored.
So God has greatly purposed; who would else
In his dishonoured works himself endure
Dishonour, and be wronged without redress.
Haste, then, and wheel away a shattered world
Ye slow revolving seasons!   We would see—
A sight to which our eyes are strangers yet—
A world that does not hate and dread His laws,
And suffer for its crime; would learn how fair
The creature is that God pronounces good,
How pleasant in itself what pleases Him.—*Cowper.*